Beyond Schoolmarms and Madams

D1616440

Beyond Schoolmarms and Madams

MONTANA WOMEN'S STORIES

Edited by Martha Kohl

Montana Historical Society Press

Helena

Front cover photo: During World War I, many women joined the workforce both for the economic opportunity and out of a sense of patriotism. The War Department cataloged this photo of two women working on the Great Northern Railway near Great Falls, c. 1918. National Archives, Records of War Department, General and Special Staffs 165-WW-595-D-14

Frontispiece: Butte native Irene Wold (on the left, with her friend Helen in Tlemcen, Algeria, in 1944) titled this photograph "Combat Kids." Wold joined the U.S. Army Nurse Corps in 1941 and served in both Algeria and France. MHS Photo Archives PAc 2008-34A1p17b

Page vi photo: World War I opened new opportunities for the daughters of railroad workers in Livingston. Italian immigrant Natalina Indendi and coworker Hazel Cole—pictured here in crisp new overalls—were among the women hired to wipe down engines, grease wheels, and operate the roundhouse turntables. As union members, they received equal pay for their work. Courtesy the Whithorn Collection, Yellowstone Gateway Museum, 2006.044.8833

Cover and book design by Diane Gleba Hall
Printed in the United States

Copyright © 2016 by the Montana Historical Society Press, 225 N. Roberts Street, P.O. Box 201201, Helena, Montana 59620-1201. All rights reserved.

Distributed by National Book Network, 4501 Forbes Boulevard, Suite 200, Lanham, MD 20706, (800) 462-6420, http://www.nbnbooks.com/

16 17 18 19 20 21 22 23 24   10 9 8 7 6 5 4 3 2 1

LIBRARY OF CONGRESS CATALOGING-IN-PUBLICATION DATA
Beyond schoolmarms and madams : Montana women's stories / edited by Martha Kohl. — First edition.

pgs.   cm

Includes bibliographical references and index.

ISBN 978-1-940527-83-3 (pbk. : alk. paper)

1. Women—Montana—Biography. 2. Women—Montana—History. 3. Montana—Biography. I. Kohl, Martha, editor. II. Title: Montana women's stories.

CT3262.M9B49 2015
920.72—dc23
2015032145

For my mother, Seena Kohl, whose groundbreaking work on women's roles and commitment to feminism informed my own

Contents

Introduction

INEVITABLY, social history places us at the crowded crossroads of public and private life. It demands that we celebrate individual agency while recognizing the larger forces—cultural, economic, political, geographic, ideological, and technological—that shape the lives of ordinary people. From this vantage point, the Montana Historical Society spent 2014 examining the stories of Montana women as part of a yearlong Women's History Matters project.

The occasion for the project was the centennial of women's suffrage in Montana. On November 3, 1914, Montana men voted 53 to 47 percent in favor of equal suffrage. That year, Montana (and Nevada, which also passed a suffrage amendment in 1914) joined nine other western states in extending voting rights to non-Native women. (Indian women would have to wait until passage of the 1924 Indian Citizenship Act to gain access to the ballot.) Two years later, Montanans elected Jeannette Rankin to the U.S. House of Representatives—the first woman elevated to that body—along with Maggie Smith Hathaway and Emma Ingalls to the Montana House and May Trumper to the post of superintendent of public instruction. Women's suffrage mattered.

As important as suffrage and the suffrage movement was, however, we knew from the start that we wanted to use the centennial as a springboard to tell a broader, more inclusive story. An informal survey of Montanans validated that choice. At workshops and presentations, I started to ask teachers, librarians, museum professionals, and others to name ten women in Montana history. Almost everyone surveyed stalled out after three: Congresswoman Rankin, frontier photographer Evelyn Cameron, and Lewis and Clark Expedition member Sacagawea. But when encouraged to think more broadly, stories poured out—about great-grandmothers who homesteaded near Malta, widowed mothers who eked out a living in Butte, and aunts who served in the WAVES during World War II. In other words, Montanans knew about fascinating women—they just didn't consider them historical. We hope this project changes that.

The decision to expand history beyond the famous required hard choices, and the first step in this project was choosing which topics, and women, to feature. For guidance, we turned to an advisory committee comprised of university-based academic historians, museum-based public historians, and community-based independent historians. Benjamin Clark (then executive director, MonDak Heritage Center, Sidney), Anya Jabour (professor of history, University of Montana–Missoula), Elizabeth Jameson (Imperial Oil and Lincoln McKay Chair, Department of History, University of Calgary), Mary Murphy (professor of history, Montana State University–Bozeman), Diane Sands (community historian, Missoula), and Karen Stevenson (community historian, Miles City) graciously agreed to serve and provided valuable advice.

At a meeting in February 2013, the committee noted that there was no one Montana story. They wanted features that reflected the state's diversity: eastern and western; urban, rural, and small town; Indian, white, African American, Asian, and Hispanic; married, widowed, and single; young and old; immigrant and native-born; religious and nonreligious; rich and poor. The committee also recommended that essays focus as much on ordinary women as on trailblazers, as much on the twentieth century as the nineteenth, and more on themes than on individuals. In short, the committee insisted that we place women's individual stories within the larger context of their times to examine the impact of culture, class, geography, life-cycle, and ideology on Montana women.

Together we generated an ambitious list of topics: women's work (paid and unpaid), religion and spirituality, reproduction and motherhood, control over fertility, childhood, coming of age, discrimination, activism, education, women's rights and the law (including enforcement), cultural preservation, politics, arts, health and health care, sexuality, family life, and the remarkable role of women's organizations in shaping community life. After soliciting suggestions from professional and community historians, tribal culture committees, and tribal college faculty, we also developed an impressive list of individuals whose lives intersected with one or more of these larger topics and for whom sources existed.

Montana Historical Society staff members Ellen Baumler (interpretive historian), Kayla Blackman (project intern), Jodie Foley (state archivist), Rowena Harrington (assistant registrar), Kate Hampton (community preservation coordinator), Molly Holz (director of publications), Kirby Lambert (director of outreach and interpretation), and Delores Morrow (photograph archives manager) helped with the daunting task of narrowing the list of almost 250 ideas down to one of just over 100. Project authors—especially Annie Hanshew and Laura Ferguson (whose knowledge of Montana Indian history proved particularly invaluable)—further refined the list.

First published on the Women's History Matters blog and now collected in this anthology, the resulting essays were even better than we had dared to hope. Readers will find Montana's most famous women—Pretty Shield, Jeannette Rankin, Mary Fields, Ella Knowles Haskell, Nannie Alderson, Elouise Cobell—and meet a host of new characters: activists, athletes, businesswomen, educators, health care providers, mothers, pilots, politicians, and veterans. Most essays tie the stories of individual women and women's organizations to larger historical issues and themes. Each essay tells a story that passed what we called the "so what?" test. And they all illuminate the many ways that gender shaped women's experiences and opportunities throughout the Treasure State's history.

That history, and these essays, span several hundred years—from early nineteenth-century indigenous women warriors to twenty-first-century Blackfeet banker Elouise Cobell. They span geography—from the western Montana women who worked for the U.S. Forest Service to Miles City doctor Sadie Lindeberg. And they span ideology—from the members of the Montana Federation of Colored Women's Clubs, who led the fight for laws banning segregation in public accommodations—to the Women of the Ku Klux Klan.

Although the project was originally designed to popularize existing research, many authors went beyond that initial mandate, conducting original research to tell hitherto untold stories. Thus, this anthology deepens and broadens our understanding of what it has meant to be female in Montana across the centuries while making this important history accessible to all readers, historians and nonhistorians alike.

• • •

MANY AUTHORS contributed to the project. Annie Hanshew, Laura Ferguson, and Ellen Baumler wrote the lion's share of the essays—and this book is a credit to their hard work. Marcella Sherfy Walter, Mary Murphy, Kayla Blackman, Kirby Lambert, Martha Kohl, Jodie Foley, Anya Jabour, Ken Robison, Jennifer Hill, Kate Hampton, and Natalie Scheidler also contributed entries that grew out of specific research interests.

Many others helped behind the scenes. Kayla Blackman accomplished most of the photo research and deserves much credit for the illustrations, along with Montana Historical Society Press photo editor Glenda Bradshaw. Thanks go also to my coworkers at the Montana Historical Society (especially the photo archives staff—Delores Morrow, Becca Kohl, Matthew Peek, Natalie Waterman, Tom Ferris, and Melissa Watlington—and museum registrar Rowena Harrington); colleagues around the state—at University of Montana's K. Ross Toole Archives and Special Collections, Montana State University's Merrill G. Burlingame Archives and Special Collections, and Fort Benton's Joel F. Overholser Historical Research Center—as well as the newspapers, photographers, and families who shared images from their own collections. Diane Gleba Hall created a beautiful book built on a foundation laid by editors Ursula Smith, Molly Holz, Christy Eckerle, and Ann Seifert. Marc Lewis—a Massachusetts teacher who serendipitously attended a workshop organized by the Montana Historical Society in the summer of 2015—provided the title. Other colleagues and friends offered invaluable support and will forgive me for not including their names here.

MARTHA KOHL
Helena, Montana, 2016

Beyond
Schoolmarms
and Madams

Nineteenth-Century Indigenous Women Warriors

Laura Ferguson

AMONG the indigenous peoples of Montana, being a warrior was not an exclusively male occupation. Women commonly dominated the realms of housekeeping, food preparation, and child-rearing. They influenced leadership, articulated their political concerns, and exercised a great deal of control over economic, domestic, and intertribal matters. A few women, however, gave up their traditional domestic role altogether and became "career warriors."

People who knew these female warriors personally—tribal members, traders, missionaries, and military officers—provide details about their lives in oral histories, expedition journals, and drawings. The women's military skill and bravery caught non-Indians off guard since they were unaccustomed to women participating in combat. The women's male enemies were perhaps even more taken aback, sometimes fearing these women warriors possessed special, even supernatural abilities.

One especially fearless warrior was Kaúxuma Núpika, a Kootenai woman who was also a cultural intermediary and prophet. In 1808, young Kaúxuma Núpika married a Frenchman working for the explorer David Thompson. She was so rowdy that Thompson exiled her from his camp. She divorced her husband, claimed to have been changed into a man, and then took a succession of wives.

Dressing as a man, Kaúxuma Núpika traveled from tribe to tribe throughout the Northwest, predicting epidemics, the invasion by Europeans, and the destruction of tribal villages by a great force that would "bury them under the ground." In 1811, she promised to deliver a letter from Spokane House to Fort Estakatadene on the Fraser River. For reasons unknown, she and her wife went hundreds of miles out of their way, ending up at

Port Astoria, Oregon, where she drew an accurate map of the inland territory between the coast range and the Rocky Mountains for David Stuart, Thompson's rival.

Upon her return, Kaúxuma Núpika took up arms for the Salish, who knew her as Ingace Onton, but also worked as an intermediary between tribes, as she spoke at least four indigenous languages. In a battle with the Blackfeet, she was stabbed several times in the chest, but, witnesses claimed, the wounds closed up almost immediately, leading her enemies to believe she had supernatural protection. In 1837, Kaúxuma Núpika saved a Salish band by tricking the Blackfeet, who greatly outnumbered their Salish enemies. The Blackfeet then ambushed Kaúxuma Núpika and, fearing she would not die otherwise, cut out her heart and chopped it into pieces. That same year, a smallpox epidemic decimated tribes across the Northwest, perhaps as she had foreseen.

Kwilqs was a Šínmsčín, a Pend d'Oreille woman who led the life of a warrior rather than marrying. Her name means "Red Shirt" in reference to a British uniform coat she wore. Among the Salish and Pend d'Oreille peoples, Kwilqs was known as a nurturing, brave, and fearless woman. She also excelled at riding and combat.

Jesuit missionaries Fathers Pierre-Jean De Smet and Nicholas Point, who came to the Northwest in 1841, described Kwilqs's military feats in their journals. Point witnessed Kwilqs in action when the Pend d'Oreilles encountered their Blackfeet enemies in 1842. By his account, "Her bravery surprised the warriors, who were humiliated and indignant because it was a woman who had led the charge. . . . The Blackfeet immediately shot four shots almost at point-blank range, yet not a single Pend d'Oreille went down."

De Smet described Kwilqs in a battle against the Crows in 1846, confidently gathering fallen arrows from the middle of a battle so as to rearm the Pend d'Oreille troops. He wrote, "The famous Kuilix . . . accompanied by a few braves and armed with an axe, gave chase to a whole squadron of Crows. When they got back to camp, she said to her companions, 'I thought those big talkers were men, but I was wrong. Truly, they are not worth pursuing.'" Kwilqs survived into old age, greatly respected for her military courage.

One of Kwilqs's contemporaries was the outstanding Crow warrior Woman Chief. Born in 1806 into the White Clay (Gros Ventre) tribe, Woman Chief's childhood name was Pine Leaf. A Crow man kidnapped young Pine Leaf to replace his recently killed son and raised her to have a warrior's skills. In time, she proved her military abilities; in her first battle, she killed two Blackfeet men and captured a large herd of horses. She

This fanciful drawing of Pine Leaf/Woman Chief accompanied James Beckwourth's memoir, published in 1856. *The Life and Adventures of James P. Beckwourth* (New York, 1856), 203

continued to gain honors as a warrior and military strategist, earning the Crow name Bíawacheeitchish, Woman Chief.

Upon meeting this famous warrior, an American trader wrote, "She looked neither savage nor warlike. . . . She sat with her hands in her lap, folded, as when one prays. She is about 45 years old; appears modest and good natured." Woman Chief took four wives and was considered a war chief for over twenty years. She was killed by White Clay warriors in 1854 while on a peace mission to her natal tribe.

Kaúxuma Núpika, Kwilqs, and Woman Chief are only three of the indigenous women warriors who raided and fought alongside male warriors of their tribes during an era of rapid change. In more recent times, American Indian women have readily joined the U.S. military, volunteering in every major campaign since World War II.

"Becoming Better Citizens of Our Adopted Country": Montana's Ethnic Women's Groups

Marcella Sherfy Walter

"THANKSGIVING DAY is over and we have Women's Meeting Sale at Elling Rogenes and it is quite enjoyable when there are so many Norwegians together," Rakel Herein wrote in her daybook in 1917. Two years later, a March entry reads simply, "Have had Women's Meeting. . . . Yes it was extremely delightful." Herein arrived in Carbon County in 1899 as a twenty-year-old immigrant from Norway and married a local Norwegian immigrant sheep farmer within the year. Translated years after her 1943 death, Herein's scattered, terse daybook documents the birth and growth of five children and a lonely, despairing life. This context makes her descriptions of Red Lodge's St. Olaf Lutheran Church women's group—"delightful" and "enjoyable"— that much more telling. Herein yearned for the companionship and support of women who understood how hard it was to immigrate to a foreign, male-dominated western landscape. She found that companionship and support within the Women's Meeting.

Herein's Women's Meeting was one of hundreds of late nineteenth- and early twentieth-century Montana women's groups. Montana women gathered whenever they could under a wide range of banners: to pursue education, art, community improvement, children's activities, homemaking, health, their families' occupational interests, and church growth and

Cornish women in Anaconda came together to form the Daughters of St. George, shown here picnicking at Gregson Springs, July 30, 1925. MHS Photo Archives 941-933

stability. Typically, these women's groups supported the status quo, celebrating their members' primary roles as mothers, wives, and daughters; yet for the women themselves, they were lifelines leading out of their homes and into a larger world.

The state's ethnic women's organizations played the additional roles of providing companionship in a strange new land, preserving and adapting ethnic traditions, and helping women become engaged citizens in their adopted home. Such groups formed wherever substantial ethnic communities grew. Most ethnically based churches—like St. Olaf's in Red Lodge—had their women's group, altar guild, or aid society. In Butte and Anaconda's dense ethnic neighborhoods, Irish women could find companionship in the Daughters of Erin; German women in the Sisters of the Sons of Hermann; Scotch women in the Daughters of Scotia; women from Lebanon in the Lebanese Peace Society; Croatian and Slovenian women in the St. Anne's Society; and British women in the Daughters of St. George.

No matter the project at hand, ethnic groups first provided women friendship and the opportunity to commiserate, in their first language, about the difficulties of immigration, child-rearing, illness, and isolation. "Female troubles," for instance, could be talked over more comfortably among immigrant peers than with an English-speaking male doctor.

Although male ethnic groups often supported geopolitical causes reflecting conflict in their homeland—Irish independence, for example—immigrant women pursued fewer such issues, choosing to look ahead and build their new lives rather than dwell on Old Country issues. Emblematically, "Becoming better citizens of our adopted country" was a stated aspiration of Solheim Lodge No. 20, organized by the Butte Daughters of Norway in 1913.

Ethnic women's groups tackled projects that touched their hearts, responded to the reality of their husbands' dangerous work, and improved their new lives and communities. Their activities focused on caring for widows, orphans, and sick children; raising money for funeral payments and rituals; sponsoring other immigrants; and almost always supporting their churches. Thus, female ethnic groups sponsored plays, bake sales, raffles, card parties, fairs, and dances to support the construction and maintenance of church buildings, social halls, and parochial schools and to raise funds for ministers' salaries and children's groups. For example, in 1888, Anaconda's Catholic women—largely Irish—served lunch and suppers four days in a row at the Catholic Church Fair to pay for church repairs, a new iron fence, and the priest's residence.

Many women's group fund-raisers involved selling traditional foods and celebrating specific ethnic occasions so that the events doubled as community-building rituals and reminders of home. In Great Falls, the Greek women's group, the Daughters of Penelope, held pastry fund-raisers, while Anaconda's Norwegian women hosted lutefisk suppers to support Our Savior's Lutheran Church. In Butte, the Kolo, or Serbian Circle, held "Old World Cuisine" dinners with a menu that included salata, lamb, klobase, sarma, cicvara, vegetables, povitica, baklava, priganica, and apple or cheese strudel.

Ethnic women's groups consistently served in the shadow of their male counterparts. Although the Butte Serbian women understood that their sarma and povitica fund-raisers provided most of the funds to build a new Serbian Orthodox Church, church fathers did not always publicly recognize their fundamental role. Even so, ethnic women's groups often supported their male counterpart organizations. Lebanese women remembered cooking and serving poker-playing men at the Lebanese Hall on Butte's Galena Street.

As immigrant families and their children melted into their new language and lives, many women's ethnic organizations faded and died. Some, like the Butte Serbian Sisters and the Daughters of Norway, still survive; others merged with men's lodges. Now such groups focus on ethnic meals and celebrations, reminding themselves and their communities of the rich traditions they contributed to their adopted homes. "We enjoy the history of our heritage and celebrate the courage of our families and relatives who came to live in Butte," Ellen Regan remembered as a twenty-two-year member of the Daughters of Norway. Although no longer fundamental to the emotional and social needs of Montana newcomers, these evolving organizations still honor both ethnic identity and community service.

The Métis Girlhood of Cecilia LaRance

Laura Ferguson

CECILIA LARANCE was born in 1915 in a cabin on the South Fork of the Teton River. Her grandparents were among the Métis families who had settled along the Rocky Mountains between Heart Butte and Augusta in the late 1800s. Growing up in the distinct culture formed by the fusion of French, Scottish, Chippewa, and Cree heritages, Cecilia belonged to the last generation of children to experience the self-sufficiency and "old ways" of this Métis community.

The French Canadian LaRance family settled along the Rocky Mountain Front in the 1870s. Cecilia's grandmother, Marguerite LaRance, was the first person buried at the Métis cemetery nestled in the trees along the South Fork. Cecilia's father, James LaRance, was born at St. Peter's Mission west of Fort Benton. When James was left with three small children after his first wife's death, he married soft-spoken and hardworking Mabel Fellers, whose family had fled to Montana after the failed Northwest Rebellion of 1885.

The couple raised their family on a squatter's homestead on Willow Creek, furnishing their single-room cabin with a woodstove, a large table, and apple-box benches. James's rocker sat near Mabel's sewing machine by the window. The cabin lacked electricity and indoor plumbing, and the LaRances bathed in a galvanized tub behind two chairs draped with a sheet for privacy. Cecilia and her sisters shared a bed, their brothers slept on a foldout sofa, and the baby's hammock hung over the parents' bed. When guests visited, they slept in the only space left: under the table. "We didn't have room enough to keep a moth's suitcase in that house," Cecilia remembered.

Like other Métis families, the LaRances were self-sufficient. James LaRance was a trapper and woodcutter, supplying nearby communities with posts and poles that he traded for flour. Mabel sewed the family's clothes. Each child had two outfits—one for school, one for everyday wear. Mabel showed Cecilia how to make soap by mixing rendered fat with homemade lye and pouring it into a shallow wooden box to set. She also taught Cecilia how to can vegetables—grown in plots along Willow Creek—and how to store root vegetables and cabbages in a cellar for their winter supply.

Shown here around age fifteen, Cecilia LaRance Wiseman grew up on the Rocky Mountain Front in a self-sufficient Métis community. Courtesy Al Wiseman

The family kept a cow, a pig, and chickens. Gathering the eggs from their free-roaming chickens made Cecilia nervous because snakes also lived among the bushes where the chickens nested. Her other chores included cleaning the chimneys of the kerosene lamps, scrubbing the wood floors, and helping wash the laundry by hand. Each evening, Cecilia and her siblings stocked the wood boxes and filled the water buckets from the creek.

In summer, Cecilia picked serviceberries, strawberries, rose hips, and gooseberries, which she and her mother made into jams. She helped her grandmother pound buffalo berries and chokecherries into flat dried fruit that would keep through the winter, sometimes mixing the mashed berries with dried meat to make pemmican.

For supper, the LaRances ate venison or "le rababou" (rabbit stew) with "lugalet" (bannock, a traditional Scottish flatbread), but Cecilia recalled that their lunches were often nothing more than lard on bread. One of her fondest childhood memories was the smell of newly made sourdough bread wrapped in a clean dishcloth and stored in the beer-crate-turned-breadbox.

Cecilia and her siblings found ways to earn money for things that had to be purchased. In the 1920s, Montana was attempting to eradicate coyotes and prairie dogs. The children drowned them in their holes and brought in the tails for bounty. The summer when she was twelve, Cecilia cooked full-time at a nearby ranch. She also herded a neighbor's sheep and gathered wool that had caught in fences. On a rare trip to town, she could sell the sacks of wool for a little spending money.

Town was too far away for the Métis families to seek medical care, so in this, too, they were self-reliant. They mixed pine pitch with cottonwood buds, which contain an aspirin-like compound, to make an analgesic salve and used skunk grease (the boiled fat from skunks) to treat chest colds. Cecilia's Chippewa-Cree grandmother gathered medicinal plants and tied each bundle of dried wild herbs with a different color of string according to its use.

Their relative isolation also kept most Métis families, who were Catholic, from attending church, although they maintained their religious traditions. Families gathered at one another's homes to celebrate holidays, particularly New Year's Day, when celebrations lasted a week or more, or "until the fiddlers got tired out."

Cecilia attended Bellview School, but, to her regret, left school at fourteen. Her mother had attended Fort Shaw Indian boarding school and then Chemawa Indian High School in Salem, Oregon, but Cecilia's father was only educated through third grade. He insisted that his daughters needed no more than an eighth-grade education, and in 1931 Cecilia was married at sixteen to a man nearly twice her age who she had met at a Bellview dance.

The Métis families left their rural cabins in the 1930s, looking for work in nearby towns. The LaRances were one of the last families to leave, moving to Augusta in 1943 after losing their homestead to the Gleason ranch because they had never filed papers on it. By then, Cecilia LaRance Wiseman had a family of her own and was working in town, but she missed her childhood in the country when "we'd spend our days just walking in the hills and sitting down and watching what was going on across the way. We were happy."

Montana's Whiskey Women: Female Bootleggers during Prohibition

Annie Hanshew

IN NOVEMBER 1916, Montana voters approved a referendum for the statewide prohibition of alcohol. Montana's influential and well-organized branch of the Woman's Christian Temperance Union had led the effort to ban the manufacture and sale of liquor. The passage of the new law, which went into effect at the end of 1918, reflected the growing influence of female reform in Montana. Not all Montana women supported temperance, however, and, ironically, for some women, the ban on liquor created new and lucrative—albeit illegal—economic opportunities.

Although Montanans were pioneers in the prohibition movement, the law itself did little to curb drinking. Historian Michael Malone pointed out that the "enforcement of the law in wide open and fun-loving Montana proved nearly impossible." Moreover, the state's remoteness and abundant supply of wheat created ideal conditions for a thriving bootlegging economy. Although we now imagine bootlegging as a masculine activity dominated by gun-toting gangsters, in fact, many women were quick to cash in on the illegal liquor trade. Women around the state manufactured moonshine and operated "home speaks" and roadhouses to supplement the family income. Because it could be done at home in the kitchen, making "hooch" was an especially attractive industry for working-class women hoping to supplement their family incomes and for widows who could not easily work outside the home.

Given the strength of drinking culture in Butte, it is perhaps unsurprising that female bootleggers thrived in that "wide open" mining town.

Made of copper, rope, and wood, this ca. 1920 bootlegger's still is in the Montana Historical Society's collection. MHS Museum 1987.43.01 a-c, gift of Anna and George Zellick

When Butte voters opposed the Prohibition referendum in 1916, one dry advocate explicitly criticized the city's women who, she scolded, wouldn't vote for Prohibition "because you want to have beer on your own tables in your own homes."

Butte's female bootleggers included such diverse practitioners as Nora Gallagher, a widow who brewed in her kitchen so she could purchase Easter outfits for her five children, and eighty-year-old Lavinia Gilman, who was caught running a three-hundred-gallon still. Because many bootlegging operations were family affairs, children often participated as well. Helen McGonagle Moriarity recalled her role in her mother's liquor trade, which was cleverly paired with her existing laundry business. Moriarity's mother, Mary Ann, washed for miners living in a boarding house. As a teenager, Helen delivered booze hidden among the clean clothes for "fifty cents a pint and two dollars a gallon."

A woman did not have to live in one of Montana's urban areas to benefit from the underground liquor trade that Prohibition created. Female home-steaders, both married and single, supplemented their farm incomes with bootlegging. Bertie "Birdie" Brown, an African American woman from Missouri who homesteaded in eastern Fergus County, made home brew that locals described as the "best in the country." Tragically, Brown died from burns she received when her still exploded in 1933.

Perhaps the most fantastic story of a homesteading bootlegger is that of Josephine Doody, a former dance-hall girl who brewed moonshine at her remote cabin on the southern edge of Glacier National Park. According to the legend, Doody's future husband, Dan, a ranger at the park, had met and fallen in love with Josephine after seeing her at a dance hall in the railroad town of McCarthyville. Wishing to rid her of her opium habit, Dan tied Josephine to his mule, took her to his homestead, and locked her up to break her addiction. After Dan died in 1919, Doody remained at the homestead and became famous for her moonshine.

Researching Doody's life, author John Fraley found that the men working on James Hill's Great Northern Railway became her best patrons: "[T]he train would stop at Doody siding, and each toot of the whistle would mean one gallon of moonshine. Josephine delivered it across the Middle Fork of the Flathead River in a small boat." Doody died of pneumonia in 1936, and since then her legend has only grown. In 2009, a group of history buffs erected a headstone for her unmarked grave in Conrad. It reads, "Josephine Doody, October 16, 1853, January 16, 1936. The Bootleg Lady of Glacier Park."

The Twenty-first Amendment to the U.S. Constitution, ratified on December 5, 1933, repealed the Eighteenth Amendment and ended national Prohibition. Ironically, many of the same women who had first supported the "Great Experiment" now pushed for legalizing the sale of liquor because of the perceived increase in crime and public vice that accompanied Prohibition. For those women who had benefitted from bootlegging, the end of Prohibition spelled the end of a valuable economic opportunity. The resumption of legal channels for the manufacture and procurement of liquor meant less demand for their homemade hooch.

Faith Inspired Early Health Care

Ellen Baumler

CATHOLIC SISTERS and Protestant deaconesses established and refined health care in Montana. These dedicated women brought better medical care to the sick and played important roles in the evolution of nursing in the state.

The first five Sisters of Charity of Leavenworth (Kansas) came by stagecoach to Helena in 1869. Within a year, they established St. John's Hospital, the first Catholic hospital in the territory. These sisters were Montana's first trained nurses.

The sisters began canvassing Montana's remote camps on horseback, begging funds to establish a hospital in Deer Lodge. St. Joseph's saw its first patients in 1873 and went on to serve Deer Lodge for ninety years. Among other acts of service, the sisters tended the wounded after the Battle of the Big Hole in 1877. They cared for casualties among both soldiers and Nez Perce at the battlefield before returning to Deer Lodge with their patients under terrible conditions; once at the hospital, the sisters found maggots infesting the combatants' wounds.

Three more sisters traveled from Leavenworth in 1875 to Virginia City to open St. Mary's Hospital. One of them, Sister Irene McGrath, was a young novice, barely eighteen. By 1879, the mining camp had dwindled and patients were few. The sisters were never meant to be ornamental, and so they moved on.

Butte, with its filthy streets, foul air, and teeming underbelly desperately needed a hospital. Veteran Sister Mary Xavier McLaughlin stood at mine entrances begging funds. Six months and eight thousand dollars later, sisters built St. James Hospital in 1881. Their negotiated arrangements with the mining companies to provide employee health care came long before the concept of health maintenance organizations (HMOs). When Sister Mary Xavier died suddenly in 1884, the miners' reverence for the nuns became obvious. They sat up all night with the remains of "Sister Beggar," underscoring her spiritual and temporal impact.

Next, at the urging of Marcus Daly, the sisters opened St. Ann's Hospital in Anaconda in 1889. In another arrangement with the sisters, Daly's copper mining company required a small monthly subscription to the hospital fund from each employee, which allowed several additions to the building over the next decade.

In 1906, when Montana law required pharmacists to pass state board examinations, Sister Mary Gertrude Barrett of Butte's St. James Hospital became the first woman to pass this exam and become a registered pharmacist.

Billings was the sisters' final Montana frontier. St. Vincent's Hospital accepted its first patients in 1898. In 1916, when infantile paralysis afflicted at least 125 children in Billings, Mother Irene McGrath—the former novice at Virginia City—established the state's first children's ward.

The sisters' dedication to care for the sick extended to nurses' training. The first class at St. James School of Nursing in Butte graduated in 1909. St. John's in Helena and St. Vincent's in Billings also established training schools. When nurses' training later shifted from hospitals to academic institutions, these hospitals collaborated in a pre-clinical training program at Carroll College in Helena. The course prepared students for hospital

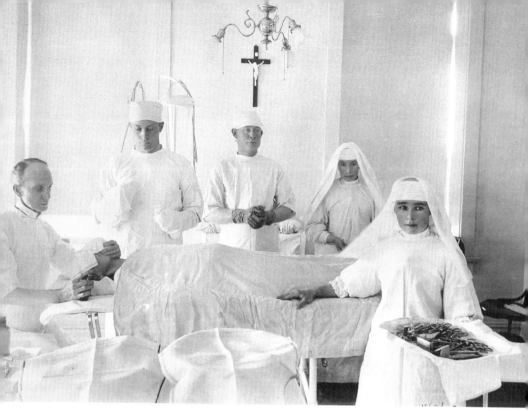

Beginning with the arrival of the Sisters of Charity of Leavenworth in 1869, religious women played a vital role in providing health care for Montanans. Here, Sister Camille (near instrument stand) and Sister St. Charles assist doctors (left to right) Thomas H. Pleasants, Fred Attix, and Joseph Brice with a 1909 surgery at St. Joseph's Hospital in Lewistown. MHS Photo Archives 949-002

training from 1943 to 1970. By 1967, more than a thousand nurses had graduated from St. James, and 60 percent of all the nurses in southwestern Montana had trained there.

The modern Sisters of Charity of Leavenworth Health System (SCLHS) incorporated in 1972; today, it includes eleven hospitals and four clinics for the poor and underserved in Colorado, California, Kansas, and Montana. In Montana, the SCLHS now includes St. James in Butte, St. Vincent's in Billings, and Holy Rosary Healthcare in Miles City, purchased from the Presentation Sisters in 1997.

As Montana evolved from a remote wilderness, medical services also evolved. The Montana Deaconess Hospital in Great Falls is equally important to the socio-religious and medical history of Montana.

The Deaconess Movement rose from within Methodist and other Protestant denominations. Its aim was to train women as social service and medical missionaries and to provide a Protestant alternative to Roman Catholic institutions. By the end of the nineteenth century, the Chicago Training School sent its graduates forth "to break down barriers of class, race, and gender through their services as teachers, nurses, and advocates of social reform."

Augusta Ariss, a deaconess and an 1897 graduate of the Chicago Training School, came to the fledgling Great Falls Deaconess Hospital as its first superintendent in 1902. She stayed for thirty-three years. In 1913, Ariss helped establish the State Board of Nursing; under her influence, nurses, not doctors, administered the board.

Under Ariss's leadership, the Deaconess Hospital in Great Falls ushered in a national trend to professionalize nurses' training programs. Deaconess hospitals opened in Butte, Sidney, Havre, and Billings; Deaconess teaching hospitals were located in Glasgow and Bozeman. The Great Falls facility served as the mother institution in Montana, supplying graduates to staff the state's other Deaconess institutions.

In 1937, Great Falls Deaconess Hospital's nursing school affiliated with Montana State College at Bozeman, fulfilling Augusta Ariss's longtime goal. Eventually, the Great Falls Deaconess Hospital evolved into the not-for-profit Benefis Health System of today.

In retrospect, the two groups of dedicated women—Catholic sisters and Protestant deaconesses—complemented each other well. Catholic sisters helped lay the earliest foundation upon which Montana's medical services rest. Protestant deaconesses helped professionalize and strengthen those services. Inspired and empowered by their faith, these Catholic and Protestant religious left a profound legacy that lives on in Montana's modern health care.

The Lifelong Quest of Frieda Fligelman and Belle Fligelman Winestine

Laura Ferguson

FRIEDA AND BELLE FLIGELMAN were born in Helena in 1890 and 1891, respectively. Their parents taught them the value of education, the importance of civic engagement, and the necessity of being reasonable. In the Fligelmans' Jewish household, "God was the idea of goodness," and being reasonable was inextricably linked to being a good person. On that premise, the Fligelman sisters became dedicated global citizens, actively participating in important twentieth-century social movements as part of their lifelong commitment "to do something *good* for the world."

That quest began in 1907 when Frieda persuaded her father to send her, and later Belle, to college rather than finishing school. Articulate, bright, and principled, both sisters excelled at the University of Wisconsin, coming of age during the Progressive Era's struggles for political, economic, and social equality. After graduating in 1910, Frieda joined the activists marching for women's suffrage in New York. Back on campus, Belle was elected president of the Women's Student Government Association and, as an editor for the student newspaper, championed progressive causes. During her senior year, she lobbied the Wisconsin legislature in favor of granting women the vote.

In 1914, Belle returned to Helena to write for the *Independent* and to promote women's suffrage. Stumping on street corners and traveling unchaperoned across Montana, Belle startled her audiences—and her parents—with her bold, "unladylike" determination to fight for her ideals. After covering Jeannette Rankin's political campaign for the newspaper, Belle helped elect Rankin to Congress in 1916 and then went to Washington,

D.C., as the congresswoman's secretary. Over the next two years, Belle observed that male leaders seldom addressed the needs of women and children. These needs—such as equal rights, equal pay, and peace—became her lifelong cause.

Meanwhile, Frieda enrolled in graduate school at Columbia University, where she studied under pioneering anthropologist Franz Boas. She earned a fellowship to study abroad for

Although Frieda Fligelman traveled widely while conducting research in sociolinguistics, she continually struggled to be taken seriously as a scholar. Here, she poses on a camel (left). MHS Photo Archives PAc 85-31

several years and focused her research on disproving the theories of racial hierarchies posited by Boas's rival, Lucien Lévy-Bruhl. Frieda, who was fluent in several languages, conducted a comprehensive study of the West African language Fulani, organizing it into categories of social significance in order to demonstrate that Fulani society, as exhibited in language, was as complex and sophisticated as any European society. When Frieda presented her research to the new chair of sociology at Columbia, he refused to acknowledge her work as legitimate sociology and denied Frieda her doctoral degree.

The dismissal of her research (arguably because she was a woman charting new academic territory) deprived Frieda of the opportunity to teach and to conduct research at the university level. Although European institutions published several of Frieda's scholarly works, she was unable to achieve her dream of working among her intellectual peers to advance innovative investigations into the sociological problems of her era.

Navigating a largely unfulfilling professional life during the 1930s and 1940s, Frieda also agonized over never having found a lifelong companion. She channeled these disappointments into writing, composing over thirteen hundred poems and transforming her heartache into hope:

> She had made of her loneliness
> So great an art
> That now its hurt became a melody
> And she was lost in wonder . . .

Forever a champion for the downtrodden, Frieda persevered. She returned to Helena in 1948 and established a one-woman think tank, the Institute for Social Logic. Using "social logic" to evaluate the preconceptions underlying public policies, Frieda challenged policies that were constructed on unsubstantiated claims rather than facts and that, therefore, perpetuated prejudices and oppression. She lectured widely on issues of racial discrimination and the need for reason in politics, seeking to inspire her listeners to fight for substantive social and political changes. Often regarded as a woman ahead of her times, Frieda said in 1977, "I never considered myself a revolutionary." Rather, she felt she had "a moral obligation to be reasonable."

Eventually, Frieda's genius was acknowledged. In 1967, the American Association for the Advancement of Science named her a fellow, and the World Congress of Sociology dedicated a collection of academic essays, *Language of Sociology*, to Frieda in 1974, recognizing her dissertation

Wearing the same dress she wore when she addressed the Wisconsin legislature on women's suffrage, Belle Fligelman poses in front of Belle Chabourne Hall at the University of Wisconsin.
MHS Photo Archives PAc 85-31

research as groundbreaking work in the emerging field of sociolinguistics. She died in Helena in 1978.

Belle, who had again returned to Helena with her husband Norman Wine-stine in 1920 to raise their three children, continued to support women's rights and humanitarian causes. She steadfastly lobbied the legislature on issues such as equal rights, child welfare, and education until her death in 1985.

The vital importance of women's issues—which Belle defined broadly as the essential concerns of humanity—and her belief that women possessed a greater capacity for reason than did men prompted her to advocate for more women in positions of public office and political leadership. "The world needs a lot of straightening out," Belle said.

Both Fligelman sisters applied their ideals toward bettering their world. As lifelong leaders in the League of Women Voters and the American Association of University Women, Frieda and Belle helped expand women's educational and political opportunities while encouraging people to understand world affairs—such as oppression, economics, war, and peace—as essentially feminist issues. During World War II, they raised funds to sponsor Jewish refugees fleeing Nazi Germany. They later opposed both the Korean and Vietnam wars. After witnessing the failed military attempts to achieve lasting peace over the course of the twentieth century, Belle said in 1976 that diplomacy—not military action—was the only way to achieve long-term solutions. She added, "Reason is what we need!"

Rose Gordon: Daughter of a Slave and Small-Town Activist

Jodie Foley & Marcella Sherfy Walter

ROSE GORDON was born in 1883 in White Sulphur Springs to a former slave and a black Scottish-born immigrant. Her commitment to service makes her life notable, while the grace and advocacy she showed in navigating the racist currents common to small-town Montana sheds light on the African American experience.

Rose's father, John, came to Montana Territory by steamboat in 1881 to cook on the mining frontier; her mother, Mary, followed a year later. The family purchased a home in White Sulphur Springs, where John worked as a chef for the town's primary hotel. At the time the family settled there, Meagher County was home to some forty-six hundred people, including thirty African Americans.

In the 1890s, John Gordon was killed in a train accident, leaving Mary Gordon to support five children by cooking, doing laundry, and providing nursing care for area families. Despite the long hours she gave to helping her mother, Rose graduated from high school as valedictorian. Her graduation oration, "The Progress of the Negro Race," ended with praise for the African American educator Booker T. Washington, and Rose's life thereafter gave testimony to Washington's emphasis on self-improvement, self-reliance, education, and nonconfrontational relationships with white people.

Rose Gordon aspired to be a doctor, but lacking the funds, she began nurse's training in Helena. She soon returned home to assist her mother financially. She found employment as a domestic and as a hotel clerk in nearby Lewistown. In 1913, she tried a second time to pursue higher education, this time studying physiotherapy in Spokane, Washington, but as before, family responsibilities drew her home. Thereafter, Gordon continued to seek medical training whenever and wherever she could, though she spent most of her time making a living and assisting family members, including her brother, well-known opera singer Taylor Gordon, after he returned to White Sulphur Springs.

Gordon and her mother ran a restaurant and variety store in town until her mother's death in 1924. She continued the business through the hardest years of the Depression. From 1935 through the 1940s, she also worked as a seamstress for the Works Progress Administration and owned and ran a café.

Second to medicine, Gordon's passion was writing. In the 1930s, she began her memoir, "Gone Are the Days," in which she juxtaposed descriptions of her parents' lives and her own with lively biographical portrayals of early Montana characters. For fifteen years, she unsuccessfully sought a publisher.

From the mid-1940s until her death in 1968, Gordon nursed elderly community residents in their homes, cared for newborns and their mothers, and provided multiple physical therapy treatments each week—often coordinating her work with area physicians. She offered patients diet, exercise, and general medical and homeopathic advice and remained current in naturopathic equipment and thinking. In 1949, she received a diploma from the College of Swedish Massage in Chicago. When White Sulphur Springs acquired a bustling sawmill in the 1950s, Gordon treated workers referred and paid for by the state's Industrial Accident Board.

Gordon also assumed the mantle of community historian, writing letters to the weekly *Meagher County News* on the deaths of many longtime residents. Each letter began, "I write to pay tribute to . . ." and in them, Gordon recalled the individual's specific contributions to the community.

Businesswoman and writer Rose Gordon poses with her brother, Taylor, in front of her White Sulphur Springs home in May 1960. MHS Photo Archives 951-717

By 1967, the *Meagher County News* was regularly publishing two columns by Gordon: "Centennial Notes" and "Rose Gordon's Recollections." In them, she presented significant portions of her still-unpublished autobiography.

Gordon belonged to the Meagher County Historical Association, the Montana Historical Society, the local hospital guild, the Grace Episcopal Church, and the Montana Federation of Colored Women's Clubs. Yet despite her active role in the community, her attempt to participate in local politics was soundly rebuffed. In 1951, she ran for mayor, ignoring an anonymous letter that threatened the resignation of all other city council members and employees should she be elected. After losing to the incumbent, 207 votes to 58, she wrote to the newspaper reminding the community that as a local business owner she was entitled to file for office and that white and "colored" soldiers were both currently dying in Korea for, among other things, better race relations.

This was not Gordon's only public statement on race relations. On May 9, 1968, following the Rev. Martin Luther King Jr.'s assassination, Gordon wrote a letter to the *Meagher County News* titled "The Battle of Pigment." In it, she acknowledged the racism she had faced in her lifetime, the debt owed to black soldiers who were "baptized into full citizenship by their bloodshed," and her view that life was too short to focus on those who could not accept people of a different color. It was an eloquent summation of her life experience and her personal approach to racism.

Gordon died six months later. Montana senator Mike Mansfield joined hundreds in sending Taylor, her one surviving brother, letters and cards of condolence. Community leaders served as pallbearers at her funeral. The editor of the *Meagher County News* wrote a poem about the woman who had paid tribute to so many others. He also gave a full page to remembrances from community members, who described Gordon's unselfishness, compassion, wit, and curiosity; her talent for making and keeping friends; her great chicken dinners; and the courage with which she confronted racism.

The Women's Protective Union

Mary Murphy

IN WHAT must have been an unusual sight on a June evening in 1890, thirty-three women walked into the Butte Miners' Union hall. They were waitresses, dressmakers, milliners, and saleswomen, and they had gathered to organize a protective association for Butte's women workers. As the

Butte Daily Miner reported the following day, "The ladies of Butte—God bless them!—are not going to be behind their brothers in demanding their rights." From its inception, the Butte Women's Protective Union (WPU) labored to improve the conditions of women's work and to extend a network of support and friendship to Butte's working women.

Most working women in Butte engaged in "commercialized domesticity." Miners, carpenters, blacksmiths, pipefitters, and men who worked in scores of other occupations dominated the mining city. Until well into the twentieth century, the majority of them were single. They needed to be fed, clothed, nursed, entertained, and generally looked after by women who performed domestic tasks for wages. Working men ate in cafés and boarding houses, slept in rooming houses, sent their laundry out, and spent their evenings in saloons, dance halls, and theaters. Except for the saloons, these were all places where women worked. Women's work made men's work possible.

Most working men in Butte were members of labor unions. In fact, the extensive nature of union membership had earned Butte the nickname "the Gibraltar of Unionism." The Women's Protective Union offered female workers a similar kind of organization and solidarity. The WPU eventually encompassed all female restaurant workers and a variety of hotel and motel maids, public building janitresses, hospital maids, girls who sold candy and popcorn in movie theaters, carhops at drive-ins, cocktail waitresses, and women employed at the local tamale factory. Best known of the early union's members were the "bucket girls" who worked in boarding houses and cafés, each day packing thousands of lunch buckets for three shifts of hard-rock miners. The WPU reached its peak membership of 1,149 in 1955.

The Women's Protective Union had a rich history of association with labor movements across the western United States. In 1903, it affiliated with the American Labor Union (ALU), an organization chiefly representing western miners. The WPU submitted to the ALU the proposal that female organizations be taxed at one-half the rate of male unions owing to the lesser wages paid to women. In 1905, after entertaining a variety of speakers from the nascent Industrial Workers of the World, the WPU voted to join that radical labor group. On July 9, 1909, the WPU received a charter from the Hotel and Restaurant Employees International Union but still retained its distinctive local name. For the following sixty-four years, the union remained an exclusively female organization.

Val Webster began working as a dishwasher when she was sixteen years old. A year later, she became a waitress and then a cook. Right from the

The WPU represented women who worked in service industries, including wait-resses, cooks, maids, elevator girls, and janitors. By the 1940s, the union had won eight-hour shifts and the right to overtime pay, sick leave, and paid vacations for its members. Above, a WPU member is shown working the candy counter at the Rialto Theater. Photograph Collection, BSBA, PH088 W.P.U./H.E.R.E.

beginning, she was a member of the WPU and eventually served for six-teen years as the union's business agent. As did many members, Val found not only job protection but friendship within the union. She remembered loving to attend union meetings and listening to the business agent and secretary talk about how they negotiated with and admonished bosses who sought to take advantage of members. After the meetings, she and friends would go out for ice cream.

The WPU was extremely successful in protecting its members. By 1945, women worked eight-hour shifts, six days a week. They had overtime pay, sick leave, and paid vacation. Few service workers in America enjoyed such ben-efits. However, like many labor associations that emerged in the nineteenth and early twentieth centuries, the WPU had a wider agenda than increasing wages and protecting job rules. It held classes in job skills for its members as well as classes in personal hygiene, child-care, and citizenship. Throughout its history, the WPU supported progressive political and economic causes: national health insurance, unemployment insurance, and a national retire-ment system. It also helped raise money for local improvements, like the municipal swimming pool, and, of course, supported fellow trade union members when they were organizing and striking.

In turn, the WPU expected and received support from male unions. In 1949, when the WPU went on strike for higher wages, Blanche Averett Copenhaver, the picket captain, recalled, "Everybody honored the picket lines. Teamsters wouldn't deliver. Building trades wouldn't do any work." The women got support from the bartenders, cooks, and waiters. Eventually the WPU wrested a raise for its members.

One of the most significant successes of the WPU occurred in the 1970s when members were able to unionize the workers of fast-food franchises that had moved into Butte, franchises that were not unionized elsewhere in the state.

In 1973, the female-only Women's Protective Union disappeared. The international union instructed the WPU to merge with the Cooks and Waiters Union, Local 22. After some resistance, the WPU complied, and the two unions formed the Culinary and Miscellaneous Workers Union, Local 457.

The Women's Protective Union demonstrated that working women in a town steeped in male privilege could hold their own. Women honed their speaking and organizing skills in union meetings, classes, and social gatherings. They came to respect one another's capabilities and skills. Their solidarity earned them the respect of other union members across the working terrain of Butte. The WPU showed in myriad ways what organized women can accomplish.

"You Have to Take What They Send You Now Days": Montana Women's Service in World War II

Annie Hanshew

WOMEN have worked for the American military in every major conflict, but until World War II they were largely classified as "civilians" and denied the benefits extended to men in uniform. The creation of the Women's Auxiliary Army Corps (later renamed the Women's Army Corps) in 1942 represented the first step toward official recognition of women's military service. Other branches of the military quickly followed suit, and, like their national counterparts, Montana women took advantage of new opportunities to serve in the armed forces.

Mary Jo Hopwood, who was born in Colorado but eventually settled in Darby, Montana, served for three years in the Navy's Women Accepted for Volunteer Emergency Service (WAVES). A combination of civic duty and desire for adventure motivated her to enlist: "[I]t was right after Pearl Harbor, and everybody was patriotic," she said. "[A]nd my brother was in the Navy, and I was just kinda restless. . . . It was adventure mostly." Although Hopwood worked in payroll, a common occupation for civilian women by the 1940s, she encountered doubts about her fitness to serve. "When we went in," she recalled, "[the] commander said, 'Well, I'm not used to having women around the office,' but he said, 'You have to take what they send you now days.'" Ultimately, that commander changed his mind, as did many other servicemen: "[T]hey didn't think much of all these women," Hopwood remembered. "But before we got out, they accepted us."

While Hopwood worked in the relatively safe world of Navy payroll, other servicewomen performed more traditionally masculine jobs. Juanita Cooke served in the U.S. Army Air Force as a member of the Women's Air Force Service Pilots (WASPS). Prior to the war, Cooke lived in California, where she worked as a cashier at a restaurant to earn money for flying lessons. She received her commercial pilot's license just before she joined the Air Force in 1943. During her service, Cooke transported planes, and frequently her flights took her to the air base in Great Falls.

Montanan Minnie Spotted Wolf broke the barriers of both race and gender when she enlisted in the Marine Corps Women's Reserve in July 1943. A member of the Blackfeet tribe, Spotted Wolf grew up on a ranch near Heart Butte. Her daughter later remembered Spotted Wolf as "real outdoorsy. . . . She was really good at breaking horses, and folks said she could outride guys into her early fifties." Spotted Wolf's ranch training served her well as a heavy-equipment operator for the Marines, and her unique background drew significant attention during the war. Headlines like "Minnie, Pride of the Marines, Is Bronc-Busting Indian Queen" dotted papers around the country.

Women who joined the armed forces had to prove that they could work in a masculine environment; they also had to demonstrate that they did not need special protection from their male coworkers. Historian Leisa Meyer argues that "a cultural inability to reconcile the categories of 'woman' and 'soldier'" led to "public fears of the consequences of establishing a women's army." In order to build acceptance for their newly formed female corps, the Army and Navy worked hard to safeguard the reputations of their female members. Mary Jo Hopwood recalled, "They thought we needed [to be] protected! . . . We were women, and they just figured you needed protecting from all the sailors that were around, so they put these restrictions on you."

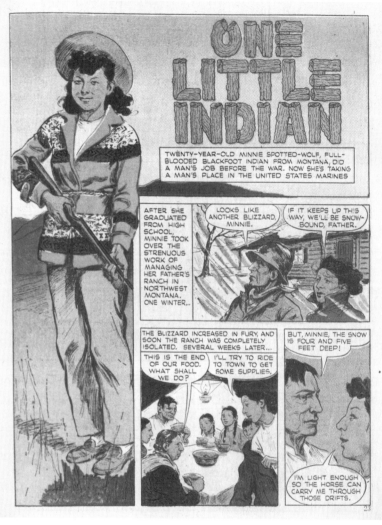

Minnie Spotted Wolf, of Heart Butte, is credited as the first American Indian woman to enlist in the Marines. According to her daughter, she joined the service despite being told by a recruiter that "the war was really not for women." Her status as a twentieth-century Blackfeet woman warrior, fighting on behalf of the U.S. government, was irresistible as propaganda. Courtesy Ruth Ferris

Hopwood believed that, like men's skepticism about women's ability to perform, this sense of paternalism faded over the course of the war: "[T]hey found that it wasn't necessary, that we really could control ourselves and take care of our own destinies. . . . But it was, just really, it was new to them. It was a new thing."

Although women gained the respect of their male comrades during their service, after the war their contributions were frequently downplayed. The lack of support for female soldiers disappointed Montana-born Grace Porter Miller, who served in the Women's Army Corps: "These women who served their country well came home without honors or recognition. Women veterans have been shortchanged all the way." Specifically, Miller pointed to the lack of medical care for World War II female veterans and the reluctance of male GIs to acknowledge female service members. For example, when Miller tried to join the Harlem Veterans of Foreign Wars, she was told that she would have to join the ladies auxiliary instead. "But I *was* a bona fide veteran!" she protested.

While the formal inclusion of women in the armed forces during World War II represented a large step forward, conservative gender expectations still dominated Montana after the war. Clearly, society had not fully reconciled the categories of "woman" and "soldier." Miller mused, "I have often tried to understand these responses. Perhaps men find it impossible to include women in their memories of the service: Girls aren't supposed to fight; women aren't supposed to be soldiers. Perhaps men think that acknowledgment that women served in the armed forces overseas during wartime would somehow detract from their own achievements as males. . . . [But] I have seldom argued. . . . I was too busy rebuilding my own life to bother about such things."

Ella Knowles: Portia of the People

Ellen Baumler

AMONG the formidable obstacles that prevented Ella Knowles from practicing law in Montana was the law itself—a statute prohibited women from this occupation. However, after much debate, upon statehood in 1889 Montana lawmakers amended the statute, allowing Knowles to take the bar exam. To their amazement, she passed with ease. In fact, Wilbur Fisk Sanders, one of the three examiners, remarked that "she beat all I have ever examined." Thus, Ella Knowles became the first woman licensed to practice law in Montana and the state's first female notary public, before going on to accomplish other "firsts."

Ella Knowles was born in 1860 in Northwood Ridge, New Hampshire. She completed teaching courses at the Plymouth State Normal School and taught in local schools for four years. She then attended Bates College in

Sometimes known as the "Portia of the People," Ella Knowles Haskell was a woman of many Montana firsts, including becoming Montana's first female attorney in 1889. Noted for her oratory skills, Haskell was also active in Populist politics and the women's suffrage campaign.
MHS Photo Archives 942-591

Lewiston, Maine, which at that time was one of very few coeducational colleges in the country. Honored in oratory and composition, she graduated from Bates in 1884, one of the first women to do so.

Knowles began to read law in New Hampshire, but, under doctor's orders, moved to Helena, Montana Territory, in 1888 to seek a healthier climate. She served as principal of Helena's West Side School for awhile but, to the dismay of her friends, gave up job security to resume legal studies under Helena attorney Joseph W. Kinsley. Through her gift of oratory, Knowles successfully lobbied the 1889 Montana territorial legislature to allow women to practice law, even though that same legislature rejected women's suffrage.

Although some fifty women nationwide had been licensed to practice law by 1890, the idea of a woman in the legal profession was still a novelty. Passing the bar was only half the battle. Knowles also had to recruit clients if she were to practice with her mentor, Joseph Kinsley. So, like most young men starting out in the profession, Knowles solicited all the Main Street merchants, trying to convince them to hire her as a bill collector.

No one would give her a chance. One merchant, tired of her hectoring, told her to knock on the doors of several of his wealthy customers. These women had borrowed umbrellas on rainy days and not returned them as promised. Knowles managed to return all the umbrellas, but the merchant refused to pay her for her services. He feared that Knowles had offended some of his best customers. When she opened the question to other customers in the shop, they backed her up, and the merchant paid her two quarters, her first fee. She kept those quarters for the rest of her life, and the merchant himself became a steady client.

Ella Knowles was an advocate of women's rights. Sometimes known as the "Portia of the People," she worked tirelessly for women's suffrage and converted many men to the cause. She was also a staunch member of the Populist Party, a third party that represented the anti-elitist views popular in the 1890s. In 1892, Knowles ran on the Populist ticket for attorney general of Montana, the second woman in the United States to run for that office. She covered three thousand miles in a rigorous campaign, losing the election by only a few votes—likely, in part, because women could not vote.

Henri Haskell, Knowles's Republican opponent in the race, was so impressed with her that he appointed her assistant attorney general after he was elected. Ella and Henri were married in 1895. Now Ella Haskell, she continued to practice law. In 1896, she became the first Montana woman elected as a delegate to a national political convention, attending the Populist Party convention in St. Louis.

In 1902, when Henri decided to move to Glendive, Knowles, always sure of her own direction, chose not to follow and divorced him. Taking back her maiden name, she moved to Butte, where she owned mining property, and became an expert in mining litigation. She negotiated several successful mining deals and reputedly once earned a ten-thousand-dollar fee, the largest ever paid to a woman attorney at the time. During her career, she argued and won cases before both the U.S. Circuit Court and U.S. Supreme Court.

Ella Knowles was a woman of many Montana firsts who worked hard in a highly unusual career for a woman of her time. Although she was independent and always outspoken, she won great respect because she was also charming, feminine, eloquent, and dignified. In 1911, at age fifty, alone in her Butte apartment, Knowles died from complications of a throat infection.

In the spring of 1997, Ella Knowles was inducted into the Gallery of Outstanding Montanans in the Capitol Rotunda in Helena. Her native New Hampshire also remembers her as one of the foremost pioneer attorneys of the Northwest, a woman ahead of her time.

Discrimination: The Case of Mrs. Wo Hop

Annie Hanshew

CHINESE IMMIGRANTS played an important role in the economic development of the West, including Montana. The 1860s mining boom and the subsequent railroad development in the region drew a diverse mix of people, including many Chinese. In spite of their role in building Montana,

BUTTE, Montana, October 22nd, 1892.

We, the undersigned, residents of Butte City, Silver Bow
County, Montana, do hereby certify and declare: that we are well
acquainted with MR WO HOP, a chinaman, resident of Butte City,
Montana, and ___Mrs. Wo Hop___ his __wife__ , whose photograph is
hereto attached and made a part of this certificate, to-wit:

That the said Wo Hop is one of the firm of "Wo Hop & Company"
chinese merchants, doing business in general merchandising and
chinese goods, in Butte City, Montana; and that we believe the said
Mrs. Wo Hop is the Wife of the said Wo Hop; that the said
Wo Hop habitually makes his living as a merchant as aforesaid, and
is not a day laborer, nor does he earn his living or any part thereof, as a laborer; and that from his said merchandising business
said Wo Hop supports and maintains the said ___Mrs. Wo Hop___
and his family.

WITNESS our hands and seals this 22nd day of October, 1892.

+ N a m e +
Business or official position.
+ N a m e +
Business or Official Position.

Although little is known about Mrs. Wo Hop—even her first name is lost to history
—the pass she carried reveals something of the world in which she lived. BSBA

Chinese pioneers faced intense discrimination, and their stories are often lost to history. The pass issued to Mrs. Wo Hop of Butte, shown on page 31, is one of the few pieces of evidence we have about her life. It illustrates the precarious position of the Chinese, and especially Chinese women, in late nineteenth-century Montana.

While American businesses had welcomed—and even recruited—Chinese workers in the mid-nineteenth century, by the 1880s native-born Americans on the West Coast increasingly blamed the Chinese for unemployment and lower wages. Pressure to end economic competition, paired with the idea that the Chinese were racially inferior by nature, culminated in the passage of the Chinese Exclusion Act in 1882. The act prohibited Chinese laborers from immigrating to the United States, and it was the first immigration law in American history to exclude a group based on nationality. The law allowed for the admission of certain upper-class individuals like merchants and teachers, but it was extremely difficult for these non-laborers to prove their status. Thus, until its repeal in 1943, the Chinese Exclusion Act effectively ended Chinese immigration.

Mrs. Hop, whose husband was a merchant in Butte, carried papers to prove that she was in America legally. As a Chinese woman, Mrs. Hop was in an especially dangerous position. The bulk of early Chinese immigrants to the United States were men, and Chinese women and families were seen as anomalies. The stereotype among native-born Americans was that Chinese women were brought to America as prostitutes. The Page Law of 1875 had imposed stiff penalties on the importation of Chinese prostitutes, and the enforcement of the law reflected a strong cultural assumption that women who immigrated from China were coming for illicit purposes. On the one hand, Americans valued the sanctity of marriage and put a premium on the unity of families. On the other hand, the stereotype of the Chinese prostitute still colored their assumptions. As a result, Chinese women faced the constant threat of deportation unless they could prove their marital status.

A close reading of Mrs. Wo Hop's papers reveals her tenuous legal position. They emphasize her status as a married, and thus reputable, woman whose husband "supports and maintains" her—thus allaying fears that she would become a burden to the state. They also point out that her husband "habitually makes his living as a merchant, and is not a day laborer." By the legal standards of the Chinese Exclusion Act, these characteristics made both husband and wife "desirable" Chinese, but the fact that Mrs. Wo Hop needed to carry these papers on her person shows how uncertain life in America could be for Chinese women.

Work Fit for "Two Fisted" Rangers:
Women in the U.S. Forest Service

Annie Hanshew

BECAUSE MONTANA contains vast tracks of public lands, the U.S. Forest Service played an important role in the state in the twentieth century. Known for its rough-and-tumble rangers and daring smokejumpers, the Forest Service is seemingly synonymous with the rugged style of masculinity associated with the American West. Even Smokey Bear, with his bulky muscles and stern face, seems like a man's man.

Nevertheless, women have worked for the Forest Service since its creation in 1905. Throughout the twentieth century, women's labor was indispensable to the Forest Service, even as women consistently struggled against the agency's masculine reputation and the belief that they were unsuited for forestry work. It was not until the 1970s and 1980s—when they moved into traditionally masculine fields like firefighting and law enforcement—that women were able to gain positions of leadership in the agency.

In the early twentieth century, women were generally limited to clerical positions within the Forest Service, and in some cases, even these "feminine" jobs were off-limits to them. Albert Cousins, an early forestry professional, recalled that some foresters preferred to hire men even for office work, "the idea being that a woman clerk would not handle the 'rough' work required in the administration of a forest, such as assembling and shipping fire tools, rustling fire fighters, etc. Such work properly was for a 'two fisted' ranger."

Despite this attitude, women long served as clerical "typewriters"; in the 1910s, female Forest Service employees also began to hold technical drawing and data collection and analysis positions. However, the agency rarely allowed women to work in the field. One important exception was female fire lookouts, although these women were supposed to call a male smoke chaser to fight any fires they spotted.

Rangers' wives were a second important exception. Wives performed clerical work, cooked and cleaned for forestry staff and firefighters, and sometimes even fought fires themselves, all without compensation. Their work was a boon for ranger districts that had neither sufficient staff nor funds.

One such wife was Harriet Evelth of Monarch, Montana. According to historian James G. Lewis, she "purportedly left her three small children behind during the Big Blowup of 1910 and rode twenty miles on horseback from Monarch to Neihart to take charge of a hundred men fighting a fire, not knowing whether the fire would jump the ravine and claim her home and family." This daring act earned Evelth the nickname "The Paul Revere of the Belts."

During World War II, labor shortages forced the Forest Service to allow more women into fieldwork. Women worked as fire patrols, cooks on the fireline, and truck drivers. They even logged and scaled lumber. But this shift was only temporary. After the war, returning GIs replaced women in these jobs, and the Forest Service resumed its practice of discouraging women from applying for fieldwork positions. A 1950s employment leaflet explained, "The field work of the Forest Service is strictly a man's job because of the arduous nature of the work and the work environment." Encouraged by the growing women's rights movement of the 1960s, however, women began to challenge this position.

On July 6, 1971, an article in the *New York Times* announced, "Women have invaded another traditionally all-male stronghold—the domain of the professional forest-fire fighter." The *Times* noted that, at the behest of twenty-one-year-old Janet Michell (whom the article described as a "petite 115-pounder from Boston, Mass."), the Forest Service had formed an all-female fire crew in Lolo, Montana. The fire control officer who trained the new crew described the women as "green, but their enthusiasm and determination will help them develop into a tough unit." He also issued this warning to the "girls": "[Y]ou might as well accept it. There is going to be some tough woods-boss who doesn't think much of the idea of women's lib."

While some men probably resented women's presence on the fireline, the concept of all-female crews spread from Missoula to other Forest Service regions, and by the late 1970s women were being integrated into male fire crews. Still, women encountered suspicion and resistance to integration. Kim Maynard, who started as a firefighter and worked as a smokejumper in Missoula from 1982 to 1984, recalled the atmosphere of anxiety when she and Wendy Kamm arrived for smokejumper training: "[T]hey had a sexual harassment class . . . and they discussed, 'Well, fellas, things are changing. Now when you have to take a pee, you have to go behind the bushes. . . . And you have to watch out for sexual harassment because you could easily get sued.' . . . And people were just scared of us. Nobody would talk to us. . . . They thought, any second, that we were going to sue them."

The transition of women into male-dominated field positions in the 1970s and 1980s was essential for those who wanted a career in forestry. Clerical and office-based jobs had not served as stepping-stones to positions of leadership in the agency. As women moved within the Forest Service into

A female lookout stands outside the Morrell Mountain Lookout in August 1922. Although the Forest Service hired women to staff lookouts, they were not supposed to fight fires. K. D. Swan, photographer, Forest History Society, Durham, N.C.

traditionally masculine fields like law enforcement and firefighting, they gained experience that allowed them to move up the ranks. In 2007, Abigail Kimbell—then in charge of the Forest Service's Northern Region head-quartered in Missoula—was elevated to the position of chief forester, the first woman to hold the office.

Pretty Shield's Success: Raising "Grandmother's Grandchild"

Laura Ferguson

THE LEGACY of a nineteenth-century Apsáalooke grandmother lives on in the traditions of the Crow people today. Born in 1856, Pretty Shield belonged to the last generation of children raised in an intact Apsáalooke culture. Just thirty years later, the tribe faced the loss of their indigenous identities and cultural heritage as well as their lands. Thus, by the 1920s and 1930s, as she raised her grandchildren, Pretty Shield confronted a twofold challenge: first, to bring them up in the poverty of the early reservation years; second, to instill in them a strong Apsáalooke identity during the era of assimilation. She was well aware of the difficulty—and importance—of her task.

Pretty Shield herself had enjoyed a happy childhood. Her elders taught her how to harvest plants, preserve meat, cook, and sew. They guided her spiritually, educated her, and brought her up according to the traditions of the Apsáalooke worldview. Too soon, these happy years gave way to the destructive forces of American colonization.

In 1872, smallpox killed hundreds of Crow people, including Pretty Shield's beloved father, Kills In The Night. At the same time, American military campaigns against other Plains tribes threatened all intertribal trade and safety, while the extinction of the bison destroyed tribal economies. Reduced to poverty and starvation, tribes were forced to relinquish more and more of their homelands. Between 1851 and 1904, the Crows themselves lost 35 million acres. The U.S. government outlawed indigenous ceremonies, mandated that Native children attend government or mission schools, and sent emissaries of assimilation onto the reservations to enforce American policies. Many Crows converted to Christianity, took up farming, and sent their children to be raised at boarding schools, where their Apsáalooke identity succumbed to white American values and a wholly different relationship to the natural world.

Pretty Shield refused to surrender the Apsáalooke way of life. When her daughter, Helen Goes Ahead, died in 1924 of an untreated infection, Pretty Shield accepted the responsibility of caring for her grandchildren, including one-year-old Alma. She was determined to raise Alma as she herself had been raised and surrounded her with other traditional women. She also kept Alma out of the government school as long as possible, having Alma feign illness whenever school officials visited. While teaching Alma the practical means of survival, Pretty Shield also shared a worldview that was at risk of dying with her generation.

"I became what the Crows call *káalisbaapite*—a 'grandmother's grandchild,'" Alma recalled in later years. "I learned how to do things in the old ways. While the mothers of my friends changed to modern ways of preparing things, Pretty Shield stuck to her old ways. . . . While my grandmother was teaching me her ways of the past, how they survived and their traditional and cultural values, mothers of other girls were teaching them to adapt."

Eventually, Pretty Shield was forced to send Alma to school, where the girl enjoyed literature and drama. She learned to sing arias from operas, tap dance, and play basketball. She joined the Girl Scouts. But when Alma reached seventh grade, the principal sent her to Flandreau Indian School in South Dakota. There, she spoke only English, attended Christian church services, and could not follow the customs Pretty Shield had taught her. She adopted the clothing, hairstyle, and behavior of white American teenagers.

Author of *A Taste of Heritage: Crow Indian Recipes and Herbal Medicines* and *Grandmother's Grandchild: My Crow Indian Life,* Alma Snell poses in her kitchen, ca. 1998. © Kristin Loudis 2013

It seemed that each year Alma lost more of her Apsáalooke identity, and Pretty Shield grieved: "They want *all* our children to be educated in their way. . . . That makes me sad," she said, "because I am going to have to let the old ways go and push my children into this new way. . . . It hurts and I feel so helpless. It's just as if I am nothing. . . . I am at the brink of no more."

When Pretty Shield passed away in 1944, doctors told Alma that her eighty-eight-year-old grandmother had died of old age, but Alma believed her grandmother had died of a broken heart, grieving the destruction of the Apsáalooke way of life.

In 1946, Alma moved to Fort Belknap, where she married Bill Snell, an Assiniboine. Caught up in the day-to-day work of ranch life and raising children in the 1950s and 1960s, she began to lose sight of her cultural heritage. Then she had a dream that helped her recognize the value of Pretty Shield's teachings. In the dream, a young and radiant Pretty Shield appeared to her, surrounded by light. When Alma awoke, she held a freshly dug wild turnip in her hand and realized that Pretty Shield had entrusted her with knowledge that had to be shared if Apsáalooke culture was to remain alive.

Snell devoted the rest of her life to teaching others what she had learned about medicinal plants, healing, and Crow culture. "I have a push in my heart to keep up the Indian cultural values. I'm sure Pretty Shield is the source of that push," she wrote in 2006 in a book on Native herbal medicine. Among the book's botanical descriptions and recipes are vivid recollections of her grandmother—testimony to Pretty Shield's importance in her life.

Before her death in 2008, Montana State University awarded Alma Snell an honorary doctorate, testimony to the knowledge she had shared with the world.

More Than Just a Happy Housewife: Home Demonstration Clubs in Post–World War II Montana

Annie Hanshew

HOME DEMONSTRATION clubs—also known as Homemakers clubs—were created in 1914 as part of the U.S. Department of Agriculture's Cooperative Extension Service. Their goal was to bring "expert" instruction on the subjects of home economics and agriculture to rural women. Originally intended to "uplift" rural women through professional instruction, Home Demonstration clubs became a way for Montana women to socialize and

Members of the Fort Peck Friendly Homemakers Club prepare to serve food at a fund-raiser for a children's Christmas party, ca. 1948. Early clubs on the Fort Peck Indian Reservation were segregated by race, but the Extension Office worked to integrate clubs in the 1960s. Roosevelt County Extension Service, "Annual Report of Cooperative Extension Work, 1949," 22

learn from one another and to serve their communities. While the clubs attempted to reinforce conservative domestic values, the experiences of clubwomen in the post–World War II era suggest that farm women adapted them to their own ends.

At their inception, Homemakers clubs reflected a Progressive Era faith that expertise and government intervention could improve American society. Targeting women who were unable to attend college, Home Demonstration agents instructed women in "scientific" methods of child-rearing, food preservation, cooking, consumerism, nutrition, women's and family health, and home and farm management. Department of Agriculture employee Mary E. Creswell expressed optimism that proper instruction would improve the lives—and character—of rural women: "With increased opportunity for training . . . and with the opportunity for permanent service in her county, the work of the county woman agent will continue to be the most potent influence for progressive and happy country homes."

Home Demonstration clubs became especially popular in Montana after World War II, in part because Montana women were seeking such expert advice. Alene Stoner of Great Falls said that she and other "young and new mothers" enrolled because "we just thought maybe the Extension Office could teach us some things, and we'd have fun doing it as a group." Other women who participated pointed out that much of this "expert" instruction offered nothing new for rural women. Margaret Bradley of Richland County recalled that the meetings included "a lot of stuff we already knew. . . . Well, town people probably didn't know much about the gardening and canning . . . like country people would have known."

Rather than joining Home Demonstration clubs to gain new knowledge, women like Bradley reshaped the clubs into female spaces for community outreach. Club members sent flowers to people who were hospitalized, raised funds for charities fighting polio and tuberculosis, sent money to Shodair Children's Hospital in Helena, and volunteered for Red Cross blood drives. The clubs were also valuable for women looking to gather together and share domestic knowledge. Doris Goebel of Sidney explained, "[A]t that time that was our support, really. You know when you are raising little kids, if you had problems, why you'd talk to other homemakers." The sense of community that the clubs provided proved more important than the instruction that agents offered. As Betty Norby of the Girard Homemakers Club put it, "It was just a special time."

According to historian Amy McKinney, Montana's Home Demonstration clubwomen defied post–World War II gender stereotypes. The ideal for 1950s women was one of a happy housewife, but agricultural women's lives rarely resembled this "Leave-It-to-Beaver" stereotype. Rural women did, of course, cook, clean, and raise their children, but they were also intimately involved in the productive labor of the farm. They raised produce and chickens to sell in town, did the bookkeeping, and worked in the fields. Home Demonstration instruction complemented farm and ranch women's traditional role as economic participants in the family enterprise. Do-it-herself canning and sewing meant that less of the family income had to be spent on consumer goods.

Paradoxically, the postwar rise of agribusiness, increased farm mechanization, and the falling cost of consumer goods decreased the importance of women's productive agricultural labor. To supplement their families' incomes, increasing numbers of rural women took paid employment off the farm in the 1950s. This left less time for voluntary activities like the Home Demonstration clubs. By the 1960s, club participation was falling. New economic realities spelled the end of that "special time" during which clubs had served as an important space for building rural female communities.

Nannie Alderson: Pioneer Ranchwoman

Annie Hanshew

When Nannie Alderson and her husband, Walt, immigrated to Montana Territory in 1883, they were among the first wave of settlers in eastern Montana's nascent cattle kingdom. *A Bride Goes West*, Alderson's memoir of her years as a rancher's wife, is consistently listed as one of the best books about the state. In it, she famously paraphrased Theodore Roosevelt, stating that Montana was "a great country for men and horses, but hell on women and cattle." The story of her transition from a life of Southern privilege to the hardships of ranching on the northern plains has come to symbolize the experience of the pioneer woman in Montana.

Alderson grew up in a wealthy West Virginia family. She met Walt while visiting relatives in Kansas in 1882, and they were married in the spring of 1883. Possessed by a "feverish optimism" about the prospects of cattle ranching in Montana, the couple settled on a homestead south of Miles City. In her memoir, Alderson recalls an overwhelming sense of possibility: "Everyone, it seemed, was making fabulous sums of money or was about to make them; no one thought of losses; and for the next year my husband and I were to breathe that air of optimism and share all those rose-colored expectations."

The Aldersons arrived in Montana during a period of rapid change. The Northern Cheyennes considered the area around the Rosebud River theirs by treaty right, even after they had lost a bitter war and faced temporary exile to Indian Territory (present-day Oklahoma). Thus, the Aldersons settled on lands still occupied by the increasingly desperate Northern Cheyennes, who would not gain their own reservation until 1884.

Ecological changes were also occurring. Not only had the buffalo been systematically removed, but the tall, rich buffalo grass that had made the area seem like ideal cattle country had almost disappeared—victim of three short years of overgrazing. These demographic and environmental upheavals set the stage for a series of disasters that would soon undercut the optimistic assumptions of ranchers like the Aldersons.

Nannie Alderson's description of her first year on the ranch details a series of cultural shocks and adjustments. Her model of femininity was her mother, "a southern lady of the floweriest tradition," and her upbringing reflected the expectation that she would live in similar circumstances. The world she encountered in Montana could not have been further from her comfortable Southern home. She recalled being "both fascinated and embarrassed" by the crudeness of masculine conversations, awestruck by the "vast monotony" of the landscape, and, especially, dismayed by the "primitive and uninviting" log shacks that served as housing for aspiring ranchers.

Alderson also had to adjust to the dramatically different gender roles and expectations of pioneer life. She was shocked to learn that men in Montana could cook, but grateful, since she admitted that she knew "no more of cooking than I did of Greek" when she first married. Although they taught her to cook, the men were less helpful when it came to lessons in how to do laundry, clean house, and polish scuffed boots, tasks that had always been done by black servants in her childhood.

The first year, though challenging, was also a bit romantic for Alderson, especially because she and her husband both believed that their stay in Montana would be temporary and that they would move back East after

Chapter XIX

THERE WAS AN OLD AND RATHER BRUTAL SAYING out west, to the effect that this was a great country for men and horses, but hell on women and cattle. Without going into the latter part of that statement, I should like to amend the first part. It was a great country for men and children. Especially for children.

Mine spent a fair share of their lives on their favorite perch at the corral, watching a show which

221

Nannie Alderson worked with writer Helena Huntington Smith to record her iconic story of frontier hardship in *A Bride Goes West*. MHS Library

amassing wealth from their cattle operation. However, their dreams of get-ting rich quick were soon frustrated. In March of 1884, on the same day that Nannie gave birth to the couple's first child in Miles City, a group of Northern Cheyennes burned down their ranch house in retaliation for the actions of a hired hand who had shot at a prominent tribal member. Tellingly, in this and subsequent conflicts with the Cheyennes, Alderson described it as being "no fault of their [the ranchers'] own," reflecting a lack of empathy typical of contemporary Euro-Americans.

The Aldersons rebuilt, but thereafter they had to, as Nannie termed it, "pioneer in earnest," having abandoned the idea that cattle ranching was a path to quick riches. A decade after moving to Montana, and no closer to the wealth they had once dreamed of, the Aldersons gave up ranching and moved to Miles City. Walt died in an accident in 1895, leaving Nannie to raise four young children.

Alderson's account of ranch life, as told to writer Helena Huntington Smith and published in 1939, is rich and informative. The isolation of homesteading life, the hardships of child-rearing and housekeeping on the frontier, the anxieties of poverty, and her frustration at being excluded from the more interesting "men's work" on the ranch are all themes that surface in the account.

It would be a mistake, however, to assume that Alderson's experience represents the ranchwoman's experience writ large. Her relatively privileged upbringing and lack of farming background made her especially ill-suited for the challenges of pioneer life. While the hardships described were undoubt-edly very real, other Montana women found satisfaction and fulfillment on the agricultural frontier. But not Alderson, whose model of feminin-ity was her Southern belle mother, and who never fully reconciled herself to the hard work and sometimes meager rewards of her life on the ranch.

Feminism Personified: Judy Smith and the Women's Movement

Anya Jabour

JUDY SMITH was a fixture in Montana's feminist community from her arrival in the state in 1973 until her death in 2013. Her four decades of activ-ism in Missoula encapsulated the "second wave" of American feminism.

Like many of her contemporaries, Smith followed the "classic" trajectory from the student protest, civil rights, and anti–Vietnam War movements of the 1960s into the women's movement of the 1970s. While pursuing a PhD at the University of Texas, Smith joined a reproductive rights group. Because abortion was banned in the United States, she sometimes ferried desperate women over the border to Mexico to procure abortions. Knowing her actions were illegal, Smith consulted a local lawyer, Sarah Weddington. These informal conversations sparked the idea of challenging Texas's anti-abortion statutes, culminating in the landmark U.S. Supreme Court case *Roe v. Wade*. From this success, Smith learned that "any action that you take . . . can build into something."

Smith brought her conviction that grassroots activism was the key to social change with her to Missoula. As she later characterized her approach, she simply looked around her adopted hometown and demanded, "What do women need here? Let's get it going. Get it done."

Smith's first step was to revitalize the University of Montana's struggling feminist organization, the Women's Resource Center (WRC). In addition to finding new space and obtaining increased funding for the WRC, Smith expanded the group's activities to include weekly films, brown bag discussions, and hands-on workshops. The WRC's newsletter circulated throughout Montana, fostering a statewide feminist network.

Smith forged links between local activists and the national movement. With University of Montana graduate and WRC member Diane Sands, she initiated an annual women's conference, bringing nationally renowned feminists to Missoula and encouraging Montanans to imagine a "feminist future."

Smith educated and empowered generations of women. Using her academic credentials, she attained faculty affiliate status and taught women's studies courses—off the books and open to all—for over a decade, introducing hundreds of college students and community members to "Feminism 101." Smith also shared her knowledge of grassroots organizing and her grant-writing skills with future activists.

For Smith, who identified herself as a radical feminist, grassroots activism was always "steeped in feminist theory." "Feminism to me isn't just about women[;] it's also about oppression," she maintained. "Women are a class and they're oppressed in certain ways and power is the issue. It's not enough just to provide services[;] even though that's important, it doesn't ask the fundamental question of why is the situation the way it is, and what can you do about that situation. . . . It's a systems analysis as well as a service analysis."

Bringing together university students and community activists, Smith

Members of the Women's Resource Center, pictured here, were the nucleus of feminist activism in Missoula in the 1970s and 1980s. Among other services, the WRC provided free classes for women on everything from auto mechanics to assertiveness training. Judy Smith is seated third from the left; the others are unidentified.
Diane Sands Papers, Series 1, Box 2, Folder 19 (Women's Resource Center Photographs, 1975–1983), UM

established new feminist organizations, most notably Blue Mountain Women's Clinic, which provided a full range of health care, including abortion, and Women's Place, a rape crisis center. Missoula's feminist organizations mirrored the national women's movement. As Smith acknowledged, "feminism . . . was always a national movement" even though much of the work occurred locally.

Usually spontaneously and almost simultaneously, women's groups addressing similar issues sprang up around the country in the 1970s and 1980s. They also developed similar group dynamics, struggling to reconcile their ideological commitment to equality with real power differences.

An imposing figure who stood six feet tall, Smith inspired many but intimidated others. Her forceful personality ran counter to the prevailing philosophy of feminist collectivism. Smith "never belonged to a group she did not control," comments Sands. But unlike some second wave feminists, she avoided "trashing" her colleagues. When conflict escalated, she simply moved on. She had "the courage to be innovative," reflects colleague Terry Kendrick, "to pick herself up the next day and get started on something else."

Many second wave feminist organizations were fraught with conflict. As early as 1978, the WRC membership registered "concern and confusion" about "power holders" whose "knowledge and skills" granted them unofficial authority and decision-making power in a group that prized "consensus" and "dialogue." By the mid-1980s, Missoula's feminists were bitterly divided.

Smith also confronted growing opposition from campus officials worried that the WRC's radio program on the UM station openly discussed both lesbianism and witchcraft. "She needed to find another institutional base," explains Sands. That base was Women's Opportunity and Resource Development (WORD), which Smith created by writing a grant for a program that used welfare funding to provide higher education and vocational training to low-income women.

Under Smith's guidance, WORD became an incubator for new organizations. One of WORD's earliest projects, providing small grants for local businesses, later became the Montana Community Development Organization. HomeWORD, an affordable and sustainable housing program, also had its origins at WORD.

Once these projects were launched, Smith turned her attention to public policy, dedicating the last decade of her life to promoting a living wage, affordable housing, and sustainable development through her work with Montana Women Vote, a voter-education group.

Smith was a visionary with "an uncanny ability . . . to see what the next wave of the [women's] movement was going to be," marvels Kendrick. Smith herself attributed progress to collaboration, insisting, "the women's movement did this work."

Convinced that only collective action could create meaningful change, Smith encouraged young women to get involved. Only if successive generations of women engaged in political activism could feminism be what Smith called "a living tradition."

Smith lived the women's liberation mantra "the personal is political." Despite occasional differences with others, she also believed another second wave maxim, "sisterhood is powerful." Judy Smith truly embodied second wave feminism.

Julia Ereaux Schultz, Health Advocate and Cultural Champion

Laura Ferguson

BORN IN 1872 on the South Fork of the Sun River, Julia Ereaux was the daughter of a French immigrant, Lazare "Curley" Ereaux, and his A'a Ni

Nin (White Clay—also known as Gros Ventre) wife, Pipe Woman. Julia, whose White Clay name was Sweet Pine, grew up in a bicultural family and was fluent in French, English, and Gros Ventre. She became a rancher and a newspaper correspondent even as she served as a Fort Belknap tribal council member, promoted traditional indigenous arts, and worked to prevent the spread of tuberculosis on the reservation. A founding member of one of the first Indian women's clubs in Montana, Schultz devoted her life to the well-being of the A'a Ni Nin people.

By the time Julia was born, her parents had already lost two children to a smallpox epidemic that took the lives of hundreds of American Indians in what is now north-central Montana. Along with several other mixed-heritage families, the Ereaux family settled near Augusta and took up farming. They were so poor, Julia later recalled, that her mother had to cut and thresh the grain by hand.

Julia received her schooling at St. Peter's Mission School, an Indian boarding school in the Sun River Valley that was attended by many Blackfeet and Métis children. Run by Ursuline nuns, the school also employed two famous Montanans during Julia's years there: Mary Fields, a former slave who worked as handyman and gardener for the school and who became Montana's first female postal carrier, and Louis Riel, one of the Métis leaders of the Northwest Rebellion of 1885.

After finishing her education, Julia helped her family build a ranch on her mother's allotment on the Fort Belknap Reservation and assisted at St. Paul's Mission School, where her sisters were educated. Then, in 1890, she married German immigrant Al Schultz, and the couple moved with her parents to a ranch near Dodson.

Julia Schultz spent her life working to improve conditions on the Fort Belknap Reservation, particularly, combatting the spread of tuberculosis. From the 1880s through the 1950s, Montana's tribes experienced an extended epidemic of tuberculosis. The overcrowding in many Indian families' single-room cabins, combined with widespread malnutrition and lack of medical care on the reservation, created fertile ground for the disease.

With Montana's public health nurse, Henrietta Crockett, Schultz formed an Indian women's club at Fort Belknap, one of only two such clubs in the state in the 1920s, and through the club, she spearheaded projects to educate tribal members about the causes and spread of TB. It was a cause she also championed during her three years on the tribal council in the mid-1930s.

Schultz also served on the Indian Welfare Committee of the Montana

Shown here celebrating her 100th birthday, Julia Schultz lived to be 104. MHS Photo Archives 944-893

Federation of Woman's Clubs, seeking to bring statewide attention to the dire living conditions on the reservations. With members of the Crow Indian Women's Club, Schultz gathered information about the prevalence of tuberculosis on the reservations and then presented the data to the Montana State Tuberculosis Association. Henrietta Crockett and members of other Montana women's clubs joined the Indian clubwomen in lobbying for hospitals on the reservations. The nearest hospitals were generally too far to be of use to tribal members—and some hospitals did not admit Indians.

Schultz also shared the history and culture of the Gros Ventre people with non-Indians, particularly members of non-Indian women's clubs. In 1930, she won a national essay contest sponsored by the General Federation of Women's Clubs for her essay on Gros Ventre history and culture. The essay ended with a reminder to Euro-Americans of the many kindnesses shown to their ancestors by indigenous people and an impassioned plea for reciprocal compassion.

During the Great Depression, Schultz used her creativity and resourcefulness to help American Indian families survive the hard times. She taught gardening and food-preservation techniques, possibly learned from Mary Fields at St. Peter's Mission, to women on the Fort Belknap Reservation, and she and other women collected the discarded army uniforms that were shipped in boxcars to the Indian reservations. They washed, repaired, and distributed the uniforms that were still in good condition; the remainder they recycled into wool quilts to be shared with families who needed them. Schultz said she once washed, dried, and mended an entire boxcar's worth of uniforms by herself, a task that must have taken weeks.

From 1936 until 1942, Schultz also led a Works Progress Administration program to revive traditional arts and crafts of the White Clay and Assiniboine tribes. The Indian Arts and Crafts Act, passed in 1934, inspired a renewed investment in the traditional artistic skills of indigenous people and created a market for authentic Indian-made products. At Fort Belknap, she organized elderly women, who still retained the skills and knowledge of traditional designs, to share this information with younger women. These efforts enabled the women to sell their creations—such as beadwork, quill-work, parfleche containers, and leather goods—for much-needed cash.

At age seventy, Schultz joined the reporting staff of the *Phillips County News*, where she worked for the next twenty years. During this time, she continued to advocate for tuberculosis education and improved medical services for Montana's Indian population and to promote Native arts and cultural preservation. Celebrated by Indians and non-Indians alike as a cultural and community leader, Julia Schultz lived to be 104 years old.

Elizabeth Clare Prophet, the Church Universal and Triumphant, and the Creation of Utopia in Montana's Paradise Valley

Annie Hanshew

ELIZABETH CLARE PROPHET was a magnetic—and polarizing—New Age religious leader based in Montana's Paradise Valley. At the height of her career, her teachings attracted an estimated fifty thousand adherents, her predictions of a coming nuclear apocalypse garnered national media attention, and her survivalist approach alienated many of her Paradise Valley neighbors. The story of Prophet and the Church Universal and Triumphant illustrates the growing popularity of New Age mysticism in the late twentieth century. It also serves as an interesting (if somewhat sensational) case study for how the Montana landscape can be imbued with spiritual meaning.

Elizabeth Clare Wulf was born in New Jersey in 1940. Though raised by nonreligious parents, she became a Christian Scientist at the age of nine. While attending Boston University in 1959, she met Mark Prophet, who, through his group The Summit Lighthouse, held seminars on ideas about spiritual enlightenment that dated back to the late 1800s. After marrying Prophet, Elizabeth joined her husband as a leader of The Summit Lighthouse, then took control of the group after his death. In 1975, she founded the Church Universal and Triumphant (CUT), which was based on Lighthouse teachings and combined elements of mysticism, Christianity, Eastern spirituality, self-sufficiency, patriotism, and anticommunism.

In the late 1970s and 1980s, Prophet attracted thousands of followers with her message of personal enlightenment. Church members lovingly referred to her as "Mother," and they believed that she was a messenger of "the ascended masters" such as Buddha and Jesus. During her time as CUT president, Prophet exercised almost total control over the church and its property. As the highly visible leader of the church, she also attracted a great deal of controversy, most notably in 1989 and 1990 when she prophesied, and CUT prepared for, a nuclear apocalypse that did not transpire.

Under Prophet's direction, in 1986 the Church Universal and Triumphant moved its operations from Southern California to a ranch south of

Elizabeth Clare Prophet poses in Paradise Valley on Church Universal and Triumphant property in this early 1990s photograph. *Bozeman Chronicle*

Livingston. According to her daughter, Erin, Prophet envisioned the Montana headquarters as an "Inner Retreat," where church members could "escape from the dark energy that pervaded 'the world.'" She also thought the land would provide an important agricultural base that would enable church members to survive in case of economic collapse. At its height, CUT owned over thirty thousand acres.

Geographers Paul Starrs and John Wright emphasize the importance of place—in this case, Montana's Paradise Valley—to Prophet's utopian vision. They situate Prophet in a long tradition of primitivism, the idea that contemporary society is flawed and that people need to return to a simpler way of life. Because it is impossible to go back in time, primitivists instead try to create an ideal community on earth, one that is carefully planned so as to create a superior society.

The importance of the Montana setting is apparent in the church's literature. A mid-1990s brochure advertising the group's summer retreat invited readers to "Imagine waking up in a tent, high in the Rocky Mountains, with an eagle high overhead. Imagine spending your mornings hiking or fishing or practicing T'ai Chi or yoga under a canopy of blue skies." The promise of the retreat, aptly titled "The Environment of Your Soul," was that the landscape of the Paradise Valley would facilitate enlightenment: "This 10-day retreat will help you create the environment your soul needs. Just being in the beautiful mountains on the ranch—and breathing the mountain air—will revivify your aura."

If Montana's natural spaces provided the perfect atmosphere for "aura revivification," the vast tracts of land acquired by the Church Universal and Triumphant also facilitated the development of Prophet's utopian community, although, as John Wright points out, the CUT headquarters was, by most standards, a "strange utopia." In light of Prophet's vision of an imminent nuclear apocalypse, the CUT compound was dotted with exclusive subdivisions, a massive fallout shelter, armored vehicles, and sizable weapons stashes. To outsiders, this "ideal" community appeared hostile and threatening.

The apocalyptic rhetoric of the church moderated in the 1990s, and Prophet relinquished her role as president of CUT in 1996. Two years later, she revealed that she was suffering from early-onset Alzheimer's, a disease that took her life in 2009. Without Prophet's magnetic leadership, CUT membership dwindled, but the remaining group still practices her teachings in the Paradise Valley haven she created for them.

"Be Creative and Be Resourceful": Rural Teachers in the Early Twentieth Century

Laura Ferguson

WHEN BLANCHE MCMANUS arrived to teach at a one-room schoolhouse on the South Fork of the Yaak River in 1928, the school contained a table, boards painted black for a chalkboard, and a log for her to sit on. She had four students: a seventh-grade boy who quit when he turned sixteen later that year; a thirteen-year-old girl who completed the entire seventh- and eighth-grade curriculum in just four months; a sweet-natured first grader; and a lazy fifth-grade boy whose mother expected McManus to give him good grades. "I used to teach arithmetic and then go out behind the schoolhouse and cry," McManus remembered. Like other teachers across Montana's rural landscape in the early twentieth century, McManus relied on her own resourcefulness and creativity to succeed while facing innumerable challenges.

In the early 1900s, an aspiring teacher could obtain a two-year rural teaching certificate provided she was a high school graduate, unmarried, and passed competency exams in various subjects. Some high schools provided limited teacher training during the junior and senior years. Rural district trustees, some of whom had little formal education themselves, assumed students would become miners, wives, or farmers like their parents and therefore needed only a rudimentary education. They frequently hired two-year certified teachers fresh out of high school.

Nonetheless, when eighteen-year-old Loretta Jarussi applied for her first teaching position at Plainview School in Carbon County in 1917, the school board initially balked at her lack of experience. Then one board member declared they ought to hire Jarussi because she had red hair and "the best teacher I ever had was a redhead." Jarussi got the job. Once employed, Jarussi felt she was "getting rich fast." A female teacher in a rural school could earn sixty to eighty dollars per month at that time; a male teacher earned roughly 20 percent more.

Teaching in rural schools presented numerous challenges. Rural districts had limited budgets, and the length of a school year varied greatly, even among neighboring schools. Seldom did a teacher stay at the same school for more than two consecutive years, making it hard to track student progress. Additionally, inconsistent curricula and the high number of non-English-speaking immigrant children in Montana's rural schools meant teachers could not count on a student's age to determine his or her

Eastern Montana photographer L. A. Huffman captured this rural schoolteacher sometime between 1890 and 1920. Note the school's log construction and improvised wall covering. MHS Photo Archives 981-1196

grade level. Invariably, some older students left midyear to help on home-steads, to find wage work, or because their parents felt they did not need additional education.

In addition to teaching, rural teachers cleaned and maintained their schools. Rural schools lacked indoor plumbing and were heated by wood-stoves, so teachers carried water and chopped firewood. The caboose-like "little red schoolhouse" in Lincoln County, where Blanche McManus taught in the 1930s, was built on wheels so it could be moved with the logging camp. Cold air drifted through the floorboards in winter, forcing McManus and her twenty-five students to wear their coats, hats, and mittens to stay warm.

McManus believed that having empathy for students was essential to a teacher's success. She once taught a family of students whose mother had recently died. The older siblings brought their three-year-old brother to school so that none of them would miss out on an education. Recognizing that the children had made the best of their situation, McManus quietly integrated the youngster into the classroom.

Young women teachers frequently boarded with their students' families—an arrangement that had both advantages and drawbacks. McManus fondly remembered that two young students "called me Blanche at home and treated me as if I were a sister . . . but the minute school started, I was 'Miss McManus!'" Loretta Jarussi, however, felt as if she were "on display all the time" when she boarded at one trustee's home. Later that year, she shared a bed with a former teacher's elderly mother. Her next "room" was a fold-out cot that she shared with her host family's daughter. She was relieved when she obtained a one-room cabin of her own at Huntley Butte the following year.

At work and at home, female teachers were held to gender-specific behavioral standards or risked losing their jobs. They could be fired for smoking (even at home), for having unsupervised male visitors, or for any action that generated dissatisfaction among trustees (who, very often, were students' parents). A trustee who did not like the grades Loretta Jarussi gave his son—a mediocre student at best—refused to hire her the following year. Many teacher contracts stipulated that a female teacher who married would be fired within thirty days. During the Great Depression, when married women could teach in some districts, they were let go if their husbands were employed.

Even under the roughest conditions, Montana's women teachers persisted in their vocation. A two-year certificate did not permit teaching at urban public schools, so ambitious rural teachers, like Loretta Jarussi and her sister, Lillian, spent several summers working toward a college degree at the State Normal College in Dillon, one of the few Montana institutions that offered teacher education. Both Jarussi sisters took better-paying positions in urban schools and taught for over forty years. Neither one married. "We needed the job," Loretta said.

Despite biased hiring practices and innumerable challenges, many female rural teachers appreciated the autonomy of working in what one called "this little kingdom all my own." While some women retired to start families, many others became fully certified teachers, principals, or superintendents. After several years teaching in rural schools, Blanche McManus taught high school in Sunburst and then at Western Montana College, where she trained future teachers.

Although she likened her experiences teaching in Lincoln County's remote one-room schools to running a three-ring circus, McManus also believed it was "the most important job in the world."

The Watchers: Montana Women Care
for the Sick and Dying

Marcella Sherfy Walter

IN LATE AUGUST and early September of 1927, Daniel Slayton, a Lavina businessman and farmer, lay dying of bone cancer. During the final three weeks of his life, he spent no moment alone. Daughters, daughters-in-law, his cousin Mary, the community midwife, a nurse hired from Billings, and Slayton's wife Lizzie cared for him and kept vigil. Though Slayton's adult sons had earlier helped him seek treatment and, in the end, came to say their goodbyes, the women in his life watched over him in his final hours.

In serving as family caregivers, Montana women have joined a legion of women across time. Before 1900, hospitals typically cared for soldiers, the poor, and the homeless. On the frontier, where single men far out-numbered women, churches underwrote Montana's earliest hospitals. Soon self-supporting matrons converted boarding houses into private hospitals. In the first half of the twentieth century, Montana pest houses, poor farms, and, finally, state institutions such as the Montana State Tuberculosis Sanatorium at Galen provided some long-term care for Montanans with-out families. Nevertheless, a family's women—its mothers, wives, sisters, aunts, daughters, and cousins—typically assumed responsibility for the care of relatives. Into the 1960s, and beyond, women performed this work out of necessity, longstanding tradition, and, often, love.

Caregiving has always been hard work, especially when added to the routine domestic labor that kept homes and farms going. Although the Slaytons had enough money to hire laundry and chore help in 1927, they were otherwise struggling financially. To further their income, they boarded schoolteachers, who arrived in the final weeks of Daniel's life. A haying crew came through as usual in late August and expected meals—a task that Daniel himself had often managed. All extra family members and caregivers needed feeding, too. In other words, hectic household patterns—including financial worries—continued throughout Daniel's final illness.

Until Daniel's cancer emerged, the couple had worried more about Lizzie's health. She was sixty-nine and struggling with rheumatism and other illnesses. Her frailness may explain why the family hired Eunice Randall once Slayton became bedridden. Though called a midwife, Randall also worked as a private community home-health aide, attending to recu-perations, births, and deaths. Randall took over the more difficult and distasteful parts of nursing—enemas and poultices, for instance. Then, as Daniel struggled with intense pain, the family hired a trained private duty nurse, Harriet O'Day, from Billings.

Still, Daniel relied on Lizzie for comfort, conversation, prayer, singing, attention to legal details, and companionship. At the end of August, Lizzie began keeping Daniel's forty-year diary current. For a few days, she wrote in Daniel's voice, but soon observed and recorded Daniel's approaching death in her own, noting when his limbs grew cold, when he slept more, as well as when she took to her own bed "played out" with exhaustion.

Daniel Slayton's family—and especially the women of his family—cared for him during his illness and final days. Pictured here in a happier time are Daniel and son Ernest (front seat), sons Bert and Daniel (middle seat), and daughter Lydia, wife Lizzie, and daughter Ruth (back seat). MHS Photo Archives PAc 88-75

This scene has a thousand variations. In 1887, Montana pioneer Pamelia Fergus died of metastasized breast cancer on a hospital bed in her daughter Luella's Helena parlor while husband James tended ranch business near Fort McGinnis and son Andrew sold cattle in Chicago. In fact, her daughter had overseen Fergus's mastectomy in the same bed a year earlier. In 1923, in the southeastern Montana coal boomtown of Bearcreek, twelve-year-old Rose Naglich cared for her dying mother. "I missed a lot of school," Naglich remembered, "in order to care for my mom and to help with the cooking and taking care of the kids." Rose, whose father already had miner's consumption, endured enormous emotional loss as well: "I cried while my mother held me in her arms. I knew she was going to die, and there was nothing I could do."

Daniel Slayton died the night of September 8, 1927. Nurse O'Day called the family to his bedside as he slipped away. Lizzie read him Psalm 103 and sang "Simply Trusting Every Day." At his death, the three weeks of "night watching," administering pain medicine, being present for Daniel's requests, and supervising all household activities ended for the ensemble of women—aided by his sons—who'd attended him so closely. The women of Lavina, already generous in small gifts and visits, rallied the next day, bringing doughnuts, providing supper for the boarding teachers, and offering help with funeral preparations.

At no point during Slayton's dying months did Lizzie, her daughters, other family members, or the community question the gift and obligation they faced in caring for Daniel. Across Montana, across time, women like those of the Naglich, Fergus, and Slayton families carried out that same attendance. They orchestrated their vigils and the intense demands of nursing around daily routines, outside work, children, financial straits, and their own emotional and physical travails to provide succor in illnesses that ended joyfully in good health or with grief, and relief, in death.

Cultivating Female Reform: The Montana Woman's Christian Temperance Union

Annie Hanshew

FOUNDED IN 1883, the Montana chapter of the Woman's Christian Temperance Union (WCTU) was a popular, well-organized women's club focused on reducing the consumption of alcohol in the state. Part of a broad series of reform movements that swept the country at the turn of the century, the WCTU was witness to women's growing political power in the area of social reform.

The national WCTU was founded in Ohio in 1873 and quickly gained a broad base of support around the country. Like their national counterparts, Montana women joined the WCTU because they believed that limiting access to alcohol would, in turn, reduce the incidence of social ills such as gambling, prostitution, and public and domestic violence. In addition to advocating temperance (and later complete prohibition), Montana WCTU members also worked for a broad range of social reforms. At their 1910 state convention in Billings, for example, the members voted for resolutions that "urged enforcement of juvenile court law [and] government aid to destitute mothers, . . . condemned the use of coca-cola, and recommended sanitary fountains."

In her study of the WCTU and similar women's clubs in this period, historian Stephenie Ambrose Tubbs argues that Montana women enjoyed a "growing sense of social and political power through their clubs' active participation in social and civil affairs." By asserting their role as reformers, the middle-class women involved in the Montana WCTU were restructuring ideas about femininity and women's roles in the public sphere. They challenged the traditional idea that a woman's place was in the home, suggesting instead that society had become so morally corrupt that it required women's political participation. They drew on the Victorian idea of women's natural moral superiority to make the case that women had to take the lead in reform.

Elizabeth Fisk, wife of the editor of the *Helena Herald*, Robert Emmett Fisk, expressed the idea that "perfect womanhood" required moral uprightness and self-sacrifice: "I never yet fully realized what it is to be a true, whole-souled, woman," she said. "Such capacities of doing, being, and suffering, such striving for the good and pure, not only, or chiefly, for ourselves, but for those whom we love."

Like many Montana women, Fisk's belief in the social responsibility that came with women's moral superiority drove her to become actively

The WCTU remained active even after the repeal of Prohibition. The photo of this billboard was taken from the 1951–1957 minute book of the WCTU's Kalispell chapter.
MHS Photo Archives PAc 83-55.22

involved in the temperance movement. She was especially enraged after the wedding of Irish businessman Thomas Cruse, where free-flowing liquor led to incidents of public drunkenness around Helena. She wrote of the rowdy fete, "It ought to arouse every mother in the city to fight for her boys, her 'God and Home and Native Land.'"

To enable female reform, the WCTU included suffrage as part of its political agenda. The organization's leaders believed that the vote was a crucial tool for enacting social change and that reforms like prohibition would have a greater chance of success if women had the franchise. Thus, they argued for women's right to vote as a social necessity rather than a natural right.

In spite of the WCTU's pro-suffrage stance, historian Paula Petrik points out, some Montana suffragists actually worked to distance their cause from the temperance movement. Knowing that prohibition was a controversial issue, leaders of the Montana Equal Suffrage Association hoped to avoid alienating men (and some women) who might otherwise be inclined to support the vote. This rift did not go unnoticed by Montana WCTU members. Mary Alderson Long, leader of the organization's suffrage campaign, later recalled, "We had another suffrage organization auxiliary to the National Woman Suffrage Society. Its leader told me not to dare to bring prohibition into the campaign. I was not taking orders." "And," she added, somewhat smugly, "the records . . . showed better results where the temperance issue was not camouflaged."

The WCTU followed its success in the 1914 suffrage campaign with a reinvigorated push for statewide prohibition. The organization joined forces with the Montana chapter of the Anti-Saloon League to demand a referendum on prohibition. With a strong base of support among homestead communities, the referendum passed overwhelmingly in November 1916, and the law went into effect at the end of 1918.

Thanks to the efforts of the members of the state's WCTU, Montana was officially "dry" a full year before national Prohibition became the law of the land.

World-Class Champions: Lady Bronc-Busters

Ellen Baumler

MONTANA COWBOYS say that rodeos weren't born; "they just growed" out of custom and necessity. Montana has bred some of the best cowboys and

Fannie Sperry Steele on Dismal Dick at Windham, Montana, roundup,
August 20–21, 1920 MHS Photo Archives 952-169

wiliest mounts as well as some of the West's most famous women riders.
Four bucked their way to renown. Fannie Sperry Steele, Marie Gibson, and
Alice and Marge Greenough were world-class champions, and each wore
her laurels with a grace and dignity that belied her chosen path.

Fannie Sperry was born in the Prickly Pear Valley in 1887. Her mother
taught her to ride almost before she could walk. Sperry cast aside Victorian
decorum and rode astride in a divided skirt, rounding up wild horses. Local
ranch kids gathered on Sunday afternoons for neighborly competitions. In
1903, sixteen-year-old Sperry awed spectators with such an impressive ride
on a bucking white stallion that onlookers passed the hat.

Fannie Sperry earned a reputation for courage, skill, grit, and sticking
power on the backs of the wildest broncos, and in 1907 she began to ride in
women's bucking horse competitions. At the Calgary Stampede in 1912, her
ride on the killer bronc Red Wing earned her the title "Lady Bucking Horse
Champion of the World." She earned the title again in 1913.

Unlike most other bronc-busting women of the time, Fannie Sperry
rode "slick." Most female contestants rode hobbled, their stirrups tied
together beneath the horse's belly for greater stability in the saddle. But hob-
bling was dangerous in the event of a tumble because the rider could not
kick free. Slick riding demanded precision, balance, courage, and unusual
strength. Sperry was the only woman rider among her contemporaries to
ride slick her entire career, just like her male counterparts.

Sperry married bronc rider and rodeo clown Bill Steele in 1913, and she rode exhibition broncs until she was in her fifties. Widowed in 1940, she ran the couple's Helmville ranch alone for another twenty-five years. She was the first woman in Montana to receive a packer's license, and with her string of pintos, she guided hunters on trips into the mountains.

Other courageous Montana women made for stiff competition during the 1910s and 1920s. Paris Williams of Billings, Violet and Margaret Brander of Avon, Peggy Warren of Victor, Princess Red Bird of Arlee, and Marie Gibson of Havre all rode unbroken broncos with remarkable courage. Any ride could end badly, as Havre legend Marie Gibson's story illustrates.

Gibson, born Marie Massoz in 1894, first married at sixteen but left her husband to join her parents in Havre in 1914. Marie began trick riding for prize money to support her children. Her professional debut came in 1917 at Havre's Great Stampede. Two years later, divorced from her first husband, she married rodeo veteran Tom Gibson. Her husband retired to the homestead, and Gibson went on to travel widely, busting broncs overseas and back East. Her many titles included "World Champion Cowgirl Bronc Rider" in 1924 and 1927.

Gibson had just made a successful ride on a bronc in Idaho in 1933. The horse was still bucking as the pickup man approached to help her off. When the two horses collided, Gibson's horse lost his balance and fell on her, fatally fracturing her skull. Her hobbled stirrups prevented her from kicking free.

After World War I, rodeo became its own genre. Fannie Sperry Steele and Marie Gibson were the first generation of professional Montana cowgirls. They witnessed the transition as rodeo matured into a profession and communities established their own rodeo events.

As the first national professional rodeo organization—the Rodeo Association of America (RAA)—formed in 1929 with men and women members, Marge and Alice Greenough of Red Lodge bridged the transition, ushering in modern rodeo. Their father, "Packsaddle Ben" Greenough, was a local character who guided sportsmen into the Beartooth Mountains. The Greenoughs kept horses by the hundreds, and a rock-littered corral served as a playground. Ben expected his children to gentle the wildest horses. They learned their craft out of necessity. "Nobody," Marge reflected, "could get bucked off in those rocks and live."

Alice was seventeen when she rode her first bucking horse in public at the Forsyth rodeo in 1919. Marge, five years younger, won a fifteen-dollar purse for the half-mile cowgirl race at the Red Lodge rodeo in 1924. Marge jockeyed and later rode bareback broncs and steers, while Alice did exceptional trick riding. Both sisters eventually rode bucking horses and bulls and won many championships across the United States. Alice traveled worldwide demonstrating her skills.

The Greenough sisters were refined, well spoken, and dressed like ladies when they were not riding. They carried their sewing machine on the road and made their own clothes. They endured the same struggles as their male counterparts, suffered the same injuries, and rode the same horses.

These four spirited, independent women are all members of the National Cowboy Hall of Fame. Among the 266 members, 33 are women and only 12 rode broncs. Fannie Sperry Steele was honored in 1975, Alice and Marge Greenough in 1983, and Marie Gibson posthumously in 2006. These quintessential Montana women take their places among the best of the best.

Women rarely ride broncs anymore. Today's horses are bred to be larger and more powerful, and it takes a large frame to ride them. Women do have the opportunity, but most choose to focus on other skills. All-girl rodeos offer roping and riding events for women, but the only women's event currently

Alice Greenough traveled the world as a trick rider and rodeo star. MHS Photo Archives 942-480

sanctioned by the Professional Rodeo Cowboy Association (PRCA) is barrel racing. Credit goes to Alice Greenough for forming her own rodeo company in order to feature the first women's barrel racing competitions.

Speaking for Those Who Could Not Speak for Themselves: The Journalism and Activism of Gretchen Garber Billings

Annie Hanshew

GRETCHEN GARBER BILLINGS was a journalist and activist who dedicated her career to advancing progressive causes in Montana. Born in Whitefish but raised in the Seattle area, Billings returned to her native state after World War II to work as a journalist and editor for the *People's Voice*, an independent, cooperatively owned, left-leaning newspaper based in Helena. At the *Voice*, Billings spent almost two decades fighting for those she believed were underrepresented in politics and government: "We felt the mandate was to defend the general welfare," she said, "to be the devil's advocate, and to speak for people who had no voice: for prisoners, for civil rights, and for people who had no strong organizational structures to defend them."

The *People's Voice* was created at the end of the New Deal as an alternative to the Anaconda Company–controlled dailies that then dominated Montana's news industry. Among the paper's "founding fathers" were prominent Montana politicians James E. Murray and Lee Metcalf, and its values reflected what historians Michael Malone and Dianne G. Dougherty termed the "farmer-labor brand of progressivism" that thrived in the state in the first half of the twentieth century.

Gretchen's husband, Harry Billings, joined the staff of the *People's Voice* in 1946, and Gretchen came on board two years later. Together, they built the paper into a mouthpiece for progressive causes and a watchdog of the state government in Helena. Leon Billings remembered his mother as a "crusading journalist" who was a passionate activist when it came to issues she cared about, such as abolishing capital punishment. The Billingses frequently crusaded for causes that pitted them against the Anaconda Company and the Montana Power Company, often called the Montana Twins. These causes included support for union issues, worker's compensation, and public ownership of utilities. They also advocated for public health reform and Native American rights.

Gretchen Billings, shown here addressing an unidentified national convention, spoke "for people who had no voice," through the aptly named *People's Voice*, the Helena-based newspaper she ran with her husband Harry.
MSU Archives, Coll. 2095, Series 8, Box 18

Harry Billings was also an uncompromising opponent of the Vietnam War, a stance that would eventually lose him the support of the *People's Voice*'s governing board, which consisted of representatives of organized labor and the Montana Farmers Union. After Harry left the paper in the summer of 1968 (Gretchen had resigned earlier that year), the *People's Voice* quickly went out of business.

Gretchen supported her husband's controversial stance on the war. Nor was she herself one to shy away from unpopular topics. Indeed, she argued that controversy was an important function of the *People's Voice*. "We were intentionally contentious," she explained, "because unless there's controversy, people aren't thinking." At the same time, Gretchen had a softer, more amiable style than did her husband, and she worked to build good relationships with the conservative politicians and businessmen that the newspaper so frequently criticized.

The paper also benefitted from what Harry called his wife's "accurate reporting and lovely literary style." Journalist Anne Pettinger suggested that Gretchen "wrote articles as though she were writing letters to old friends" and that this style made her especially popular with readers.

Unfortunately, Gretchen's commitment to journalism and progressive activism brought her both physical and mental stress. The Billings family, which grew to include three boys, was frequently the subject of vitriolic attacks. In the mid-1950s, at the height of the "Red Scare," the family even received an anonymous phone call threatening damage to their home.

The years of vehement opposition, combined with the pushback Gretchen and Harry were getting for his editorials on Vietnam, took their toll. "When I finally quit," Gretchen recalled in 1986, "it was purely and simply because I had become so bitter. I was suffering physically, and I couldn't allow myself to become a permanently embittered woman."

The sad irony is that many of their friends would later come to agree with the antiwar position, but the damage to the *People's Voice* and to Gretchen personally had already been done. She went on to work as the secretary of a carpenters' union and eventually served as the executive director of the Montana Rural Electric Cooperatives Association.

Even after the paper folded, the *People's Voice*'s legacy could be felt in Montana. Journalist Charles S. Johnson noted that its brand of progressivism is evident in the 1972 Montana constitution: "A lot of the causes [Harry and Gretchen] fought for over the years are embedded in that document," he said. Moreover, few would doubt that Gretchen fulfilled her goal of giving people a voice. "As a citizen and as a journalist," her obituary notes, "Gretchen spent most of her life representing those who could not speak for themselves."

Behind Every Man: Nancy Cooper Russell

Kirby Lambert

THE ADAGE "behind every successful man stands a good woman" has become an outmoded cliché. Nonetheless, it remains remarkably true for Montana's favorite son, cowboy artist Charlie Russell, whose wife, Nancy Cooper Russell, was instrumental in his success. In fact, while Nancy "stood behind" her husband in terms of providing nurturance and support, when it came to managing the business aspects of his career—and earning him international fame in the process—she was fully out front. As Charlie's nephew, Austin Russell, noted, "[S]uccess came tapping at the [Russells'] door or, rather, Nancy dragged success in, hog-tied and branded."

Nancy Cooper Russell's story would in many ways befit a Horatio Alger novel. She was born in 1878 into meager circumstances on a Kentucky tobacco farm after her father, James Cooper, had abandoned her then-pregnant mother, Texas Annie Mann. In 1890, Nancy moved to Helena, Montana, with her mother, half-sister, and her mother's second husband, James Allen. Thereafter, Allen was most often absent, so Texas supported her daughters by taking in sewing and laundry.

Eventually, Nancy hired out as a housekeeper as well. Texas died in 1894 following a lengthy illness. After the funeral, which Nancy arranged and paid for, Allen returned to Helena, staying only long enough to claim Nancy's half-sister, Ella. He left sixteen-year-old Nancy to fend for herself.

At the recommendation of one of her mother's former customers, Ben and Lela Roberts—a Helena couple who had relocated to Cascade—hired Nancy to serve as their live-in housekeeper and help care for their three young children. Years later, Nancy would recall her excitement when, in the fall of 1895, she learned that the Robertses were expecting a special dinner guest: a former cowboy who had an established reputation as both an artist and a hellion. Eleven months later, Charlie and "Mame," as he always called Nancy, were married in a ceremony held in the Robertses' home. The following year, the newlyweds moved permanently to Great Falls, believing that the larger city would offer them greater opportunities.

Charlie's marriage to Nancy marked a turning point in the artist's career. Uncomfortable selling his art, Charlie had historically undercharged customers for his work. Nancy did not share his discomfort and, with Charlie's encouragement, soon took control of the business aspects of his career. As Montana poet Grace Stone Coates observed, "Russell didn't want to . . . run after moneyed people to buy his pictures; and Nancy wanted to cash in on her husband's talent; both were right." Within a few short years, Nancy was demanding, and receiving, thousands of dollars for Russell's oil paintings, sums Charlie decried as "dead men's prices."

In addition to courting individual collectors, Nancy arranged exhibitions in such distant venues as Calgary, Winnipeg, Washington, D.C., Los Angeles, London, and New York. For Nancy, art was business, and she left nothing to chance. According to Russell scholar Brian Dippie, in addition to locating willing galleries and working with their owners, Nancy organized "advance publicity . . . planted [articles] in the local papers" and held her own "in business negotiations over commissions, copyrights and prices for direct sales."

The drive that made Nancy so successful professionally did not serve her as well in her personal life. She refused to associate with Charlie's closest friends—cowboys and drinking buddies from his early years on the range—whom she viewed as a hindrance to his career. In response, these men resented Nancy and were vocal in their disapproval of the young woman whom Austin Russell described as "smart as a steel trap and as quick as the lash of a whip." In turn, although she longed to be accepted in the elite social circles of Great Falls, society matrons snubbed Nancy for her unprivileged beginnings. She suffered bouts of depression throughout her life, and her demanding nature ultimately alienated her only child, Jack Cooper Russell, whom she and Charlie adopted as an infant in 1916.

Following Charlie's death in 1926, Nancy moved permanently to Southern California, where she, Jack, and Charlie had been wintering since 1920. She devoted her efforts to promoting Russell's legacy, organizing memorial exhibits of his work, and publishing two books of his writings—*Trails Plowed Under*, an anthology of cowboy yarns, in 1927, and *Good Medicine*, a compilation of his illustrated letters, in 1929. And she donated Russell's beloved log-cabin studio and its contents to the City of Great Falls to serve, in her words, "as a permanent record . . . [memorializing] the love of a great man for a big country and its people." She died in Pasadena in 1940 after several years of ill health.

Nancy Russell, whose business acumen made Montana's favorite cowboy artist a financial success, poses here with husband Charlie at Chico Hot Springs, 1908. MHS Photo Archives PAc 77-86.2

Nancy was by no means singular in terms of being a woman who played a critical role in her husband's success. The obstacles that she overcame in her youth and the status that she helped Charlie achieve, however, make her story truly notable. While she had many detractors among those who did not appreciate the changes that marriage brought to the former cowboy's life, Charlie himself fully realized "Mame's" contributions to his career. "My wife has been an inspiration to my work," he once told a newspaper reporter. "Without her I would probably have never attempted to soar or reach any height, further than to make a few pictures for my friends and old acquaintances. . . . I still love and long for the old west, and everything that goes with it. But I would sacrifice it all for Mrs. Russell."

"Lifting as We Climb": The Activism of the Montana Federation of Colored Women's Clubs

Annie Hanshew

In 1921, the Montana Federation of Colored Women's Clubs (MFCWC) organized "to encourage true womanhood . . . [and] to promote interest in social uplift." While its members engaged in many traditional women's club activities—raising money for scholarships, creating opportunities for children, and providing aid to the sick—advancing the cause of civil rights in Montana was one of the organization's most important legacies.

MFCWC (originally the Montana Federation of Negro Women's Clubs) held its inaugural meeting in Butte, where members agreed on five organizing principles: "Courtesy—Justice—The Rights of Minority—one thing at a time, and a rule of majority." At the local level, member clubs engaged in a variety of volunteer work, from bringing flowers to hospital patients to adding works by African American authors to local libraries. But

This photo captured the women (and children) of the first Montana Federation of Colored Women's Clubs annual convention, which took place in Butte on August 3, 1921. Zubick Art Studio, photographer, MHS Photo Archives PAc 96-25.2

at both the local and the state levels, MFCWC members also concentrated on racial politics, taking positions on abolishing the poll tax and upholding anti-lynching laws, and raising funds for the National Association for the Advancement of Colored People.

The MFCWC's legislative committee became especially active after World War II, and from 1949 to 1955, it led the campaign to pass civil rights legislation in Montana. The committee's efforts reflected Montana's complicated racial climate. As its members advocated for legislative change, the MFCWC often encountered resistance from white Montanans, who simultaneously asserted that Montana did not have a "racial problem" and that, where prejudice did exist, it could not "be changed by passing a law."

Nevertheless, MFCWC members persevered. Between 1951 and 1955, its legislative committee worked with Montana lawmakers to introduce a bill banning segregation in places of public accommodation. The committee's main support came from the MFCWC delegates of Cascade County, who saw the discrimination faced by African American airmen stationed at the Great Falls base. Supporters of the bill were given several talking points, ranging from the idea that Montanans "take pride in our reputation for friendliness and hospitality" to the biblical edict "love thy neighbor." The most compelling argument advanced, however, was that segregation was especially unjust to men serving their country during wartime. Following the club's script, one legislative proponent of the bill argued that African American soldiers "didn't ask to be sent to Montana. But I think a man who is good enough to serve in the Army is good enough to have public accommodations."

The civil rights bill passed the house easily in 1953 but ran up against powerful opposition in the senate, where it died in committee. Interestingly, racial prejudice against other minority groups ultimately doomed the bill that session. Senator W. B. Spear, representing Big Horn County but originally from North Carolina, spearheaded the charge to defeat the bill. According to one observer, Spear's position was that in "a county heavily populated with Indians, his white constituents would expect him to defeat any legislative attempt to enforce the extension of full rights of public accommodation to the Indians, and that his failure to do so could well result in his political death. Sufficient henchmen then rose to Senator Spear's bidding to jeopardize the bill." Similarly, a Yellowstone County senator was reluctant to support the bill because of the "Mexican Problem" in his county.

The MFCWC legislative committee regrouped in 1955. This time, they recruited allies from organized labor, the Montana Farmers Union, churches, and white women's organizations, demonstrating that segregation was not just an issue for black voters. The bill, guaranteeing "equal accommodations in public places to all people, regardless of race, creed, or color," passed but only after the state senate stripped the penalties for violating the law. With no enforcement mechanism, the law was mostly a symbolic victory for the MFCWC, but an important one nonetheless.

The MFCWC's commitment to legislative change in the 1950s came at a time when the club's membership was dwindling. Lucrative industry and armed services jobs had drawn many African Americans away from Montana during World War II, and the declining population left many of the local clubs struggling to maintain membership. In 1949, the MFCWC had only fifty members in five clubs, down from over ninety members in fifteen clubs in the mid-1920s.

By the late 1960s, racial politics was at the forefront of Americans' social consciousness, but the Montana Federation of Colored Women's Clubs—the group that had led the initial push for civil rights legislation in Montana—was struggling to survive. Part of the MFCWC's decline could be attributed to African Americans' success at integrating. By 1971, the MFCWC had become a member of the General Federation of Women's Clubs. At that time, president Marie Lacey, reflecting on the MFCWC's fifty-year history, suggested that "[i]ntegration has limited the need for an all-black club. Junior clubs for the youthful blacks are no longer needed." The next year, the club voted to disband, leaving as its lasting legacy its work to secure equal rights for Montana's racial minorities.

Empowering Women: The Helena YWCA

Ellen Baumler

THE Young Women's Christian Association (YWCA) took root during the Industrial Revolution when women's roles began to change and young women left their families to work or to attend school. The YWCA first opened women's residences in New York City and Boston in the mid-1800s. By the early twentieth century, the organization had reached across the country "to draw together women and girls of diverse experience and faiths to open their lives to new understanding and deeper relationships in order that they may struggle for peace and justice, freedom and dignity for all people."

During the Victorian era, strict social rules constrained women's lives.

It was scandalous for a woman to go out alone, eat in a restaurant without a companion, or travel without a chaperone. Women were expected to stay at home and attend to domestic duties. Thus, those who left their homes for employment or educational opportunities in urban areas faced major obstacles. A young woman in an unfamiliar city often had nowhere to turn for housing, support, or advice. In the early twentieth century, YWCAs began to fill this need in Montana. Billings, Missoula, Great Falls, and Helena all had YWCA chapters.

In Helena, physician Dr. Maria Dean had become keenly aware that women and girls needed safe places to live. Young women came to town seeking employment and to attend the Helena Business College. Younger girls from rural communities also came to Helena to attend high school. Dr. Dean saw the YWCA as a solution and became the driving force behind organizing the Helena Y. The first members met in January 1911. They chose two young women from every church in Helena, including the Jewish Temple Emanu-El, to solicit new members. And they began greeting passenger trains at the depot, offering assistance to young female travelers who stepped off those trains.

The forty-three-room Helena YWCA has provided women with a place to stay, and organizations with a place to meet, since 1919. L. H. Jorud, photographer, MHS Photo Archives PAc 2003-48, Box 41, 1957 YWCA

By the end of March, three hundred members had paid their dues. They raised funds and rented a one-room office downtown. Dr. Dean hired Frieda Fligelman, a young and prominent member of the Jewish community, as the first secretary. It was her job to find safe lodging for girls and women and to counsel girls away from home. The Helena YWCA soon rented a house at 220 Fifth Avenue, and tenants immediately filled its nine sleeping rooms. Members opened a public cafeteria in the dining room, which became a popular, income-generating venture. A variety of lectures and classes in painting, cooking, and life skills brought diverse women and girls together in fellowship.

The Helena YWCA incorporated in 1912. Its purpose was to "serve all Helena women by offering them an opportunity to help themselves and others." In one sense, the chapter was unique: in a bold expression of tolerance, it incorporated as an independent chapter, going beyond the implicit restriction in the national Y's charter that allowed only Christian members to participate in chapter management. Helena Y members could not imagine restricting chapter leadership by faith, especially since Frieda Fligelman was doing such tremendous work for them. Until 1987, it remained the only independent chapter in the United States.

Girls and women came to board at the YWCA for a variety of reasons. Parents wanted safe housing for their daughters. Working women sometimes found their salaries inadequate and needed inexpensive lodging. One early resident was broke and wanted someone to listen to her troubles. Another left her home because of family differences. "I have a good home," she said, "but nobody understands me. . . . I'm making my own money now and I want to live my own life."

Concerned family members sometimes asked the Y for help. "My sister will attend school in your town," said a worried brother. "She is not a Christian and may not choose good associates. Can you get her under the influence of the YWCA?"

In 1918, under the able leadership of association president Mary Prescott, members broke ground for a new facility. Built on donated land with substantial monetary donations from the community, the new YWCA opened in February of 1919, and the first women moved into its forty-three rooms. Throughout its long history, the home has sheltered hundreds of women, served as a gathering place for service clubs, housed dance studios and a preschool, and offered occupational classes.

Although the national YWCA long ago relaxed its management rules, a visiting advisor noted in 1972 that the Helena chapter remained the nation's only independent YWCA. National affiliation came in 1987. Today, the organization still operates from its ninety-year-old landmark building. It provides shelter for women transitioning from homelessness to permanent housing and remains true to its original tenets to eliminate racism, empower women, and promote peace, justice, freedom, and dignity for all.

From Poultry to Poetry: The Life and Letters of Harriette E. Cushman

Laura Ferguson

In 1922, the Cooperative Extension Service at Montana State College in Bozeman hired Harriette Cushman to be Montana's poultry specialist. Over the next thirty-two years, Cushman worked to build a profitable poultry industry that proved an economic godsend during Montana's prolonged economic depression. A woman of many interests, Cushman also championed the Indian Center at Montana State University and advocated for libraries, museums, and the arts. She was also a lifelong supporter of 4-H, an environmental advocate, and a prolific writer.

Harriette Eliza Cushman was born in Alabama in 1890. She graduated from Cornell University in 1914 with a degree in bacteriology and chemistry. In 1918, she earned a poultry specialist degree from Rutgers University and became one of the few women pursuing a career as a poultry scientist.

As Montana's poultry specialist, Cushman traveled the state, educating farmers on breeding, culling, egg and bird grading, poultry housing, proper feed, and poultry health. She authored numerous seminal poultry-raising manuals that emphasized the application of scientific methods and utilized local demonstration flocks for hands-on instruction.

Montana's poultry industry expanded significantly under Cushman's guidance. Prior to Cushman's tenure as state poultry specialist, individual poultry growers worked independently, selling birds locally for whatever price they could get. In the 1920s, Cushman helped to form the nation's first egg and turkey wholesale cooperatives, enabling Montana poultry growers to negotiate top prices. As the first poultry grader for the newly formed Northwest Turkey Federation, Cushman secured nationwide markets for Montana's premium quality "Norbest" turkeys, making Montana's turkey industry the most profitable in the nation during the Great Depression.

What was profitable for farmers, however, meant exhausting work for the solitary poultry specialist, who had to coordinate poultry grading and shipping schedules so that farmers could get their poultry to market. November and December were especially busy months. On November 18, 1933, Cushman wrote to her parents from Columbus: "This has been one of the wildest weeks that has ever happened in my life. . . . When I crossed the tracks I saw the line . . . stringing . . . back four or five blocks, to the Yellowstone River bridge." It took Cushman and her assistants twelve hours to grade and pack the sixty thousand pounds of turkey. By noon the next day, the temperatures in the railroad cars were rapidly rising, and Cushman still had more birds waiting in Laurel and Roberts. "I just wanted to sit right down and cry," her letter continued, but instead she solicited help from the railroad crew to cool down the cars. Working around the clock, Cushman and her assistants graded and packed five train cars with over 144,000 pounds of turkey. "We were really shaking when the . . . switch engine man came in. . . . He called the yards: 'Hold the fast fruit express, and have the icing crew ready to get this poultry car out in a hurry!'"

Cushman regularly worked six and a half days a week, even after the Extension Service's budget was slashed during the 1930s. Much of her time was spent traveling, often by train, to meet with poultry growers. Between January and August of 1942, Montana's poultry specialist logged over ten thousand miles—a distance she repeated year after year.

Cushman inspired many new poultry growers in Montana. She introduced poultry production into Montana's 4-H clubs, teaching youngsters how to raise exceptional flocks, grade eggs, and judge poultry. She particularly liked working on Montana's Indian reservations, where profound poverty and lack of economic opportunity were most persistent and where poultry raising made tangible positive impacts. Cushman was deeply pleased when the Blackfeet, in gratitude, made her an honorary tribal member.

Despite her exhausting schedule, Cushman found time for other interests. She spent her free time camping, hiking, and photographing Montana's mountains with friends. For over thirty years, she penned intimate weekly letters to her parents, detailing her work, her social activities, and her views on political events. She and her mother both enjoyed writing, especially poetry. "Your poems are better than mine," Harriette told her mother in 1932. "You write of human relationships. They are what others want to hear about. Somehow I feel embarrassed when I write of human relationships. Nature seems easier."

Despite her own small income, Harriette Cushman regularly sent her mother money to alleviate her parents' financial hardships. Her generosity

When she wasn't working, Harriette Cushman was an avid outdoorswoman and an outspoken environmentalist. In 1973, she lobbied against strip mining for coal in eastern Montana, saying, "We just can't have another Appalachia."
MSU Archives, Parc-001264

extended beyond her immediate family, however, and she devoted much of her life to the betterment of her community. In 1948, she helped found the Montana Institute for the Arts to promote the arts throughout the state. She also actively supported Montana's libraries and the development of the McGill Museum (now the Museum of the Rockies), founded by Bozeman physician Dr. Caroline McGill in 1957.

After retiring in 1954, Cushman devoted herself to promoting the success of Indian students at Montana State University. In 1969, nine years before her death in 1978, Cushman sent out six hundred handwritten invitations to her own post-life celebration and asked her many friends to contribute to the Indian Center in lieu of mourning. She willed her estate to the university, providing funds for both the Indian Center and a scholarship for outstanding American Indian students.

Cushman earned numerous awards during her lifetime, including three writing awards from the Montana Institute of the Arts. She was named a fellow of that organization in 1954. She was inducted into Mu Beta Beta, a 4-H honorary society, in 1959; a decade later the Cooperative Extension Service awarded her the Epsilon Sigma Phi "Ruby Award" for distinguished service. Montana State University dedicated its Little International Stock Show to Cushman in 1962 and bestowed an honorary Doctorate of Agriculture on her in 1963. In 1973, she received the Blue and Gold Award from the university for her lifetime of service to Montana.

Family Planning and Companionate Marriage in Early Twentieth-Century Montana

Annie Hanshew

LIKE THEIR national counterparts, Montana women in the early twentieth century generally considered marriage, childbirth, and motherhood to be natural (and expected) elements of womanhood. Nonetheless, they did attempt to control their fertility. Conservative attitudes about sex, religious prescriptions against artificial contraception, and isolation and scarcity of medical care all conspired to limit Montana women's access to birth control. Nevertheless, through female social networks and activism, the women of the state were able to exercise a degree of control over reproduction.

Montana women had a variety of reasons for seeking contraception. Many could sympathize with the anonymous ranch wife who, when interviewed, said that she limited her family to two children "because when you had so much work to do, you can't do all of it. So the children were the minor thing." Other women, struggling with the hard times that hit Montana in the 1920s, sought to delay pregnancy until they were on better financial footing.

Women interested in family planning, especially those in rural areas, typically turned to other women for advice. Girls learned about sex and reproduction from their mothers or other female relatives, and homesteading women came together to discuss a range of topics related to childbearing and motherhood, including contraception. Before the widespread availability of medically sanctioned birth control devices, women used folk methods such as homemade sponges, douches, and spermicides. As a last

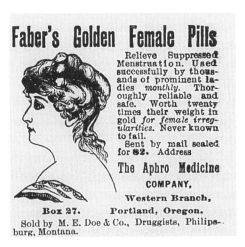

Faber's Golden Female Pills claimed to be "worth twenty times their weight in gold for female irregularities. Never known to fail." This coded ad for an abortifacient ran in the *Philipsburg Mail*, August 17, 1893. Pregnancy was the main cause of "suppressed menstruation" or "irregularity," and cures were commonly advertised. *Philipsburg Mail, August 17, 1893*

resort, they would also turn to abortion, although that method was both illegal and often dangerous in the early twentieth century.

The Comstock Law of 1873 made it illegal to advertise, sell, or import contraceptive medicines and devices, and Montana law prohibited the publication or advertisement of information about contraception. Nevertheless, the national birth control movement, most famously championed by Margaret Sanger, who coined the term in 1915, slowly made its way to Montana. One Helena feminist who supported birth control was Belle Fligelman Winestine. In the early 1920s, she urged the national leaders of the League of Women Voters to take a position on the issue. For her advocacy, some of the other league members labeled her a "zealot."

Edna Rankin McKinnon, youngest sister of Jeannette Rankin, took the matter further, making birth control education her personal mission. A graduate of the University of Montana's law school, McKinnon met Margaret Sanger in 1936. That same year, a federal appeals court decision ruled that the Comstock Law did not apply to contraceptive materials "which might intelligently be employed by conscientious and competent physicians." Buoyed by this decision, McKinnon returned to Montana in 1937 to crusade for birth control education.

She encountered significant opposition. According to biographer Wilma Dykeman, "Catholic doctrine and Protestant prudery combined with traditional frontier values (masculine virility and large families . . .) to keep birth control a taboo subject." Moreover, Montana women "found it shocking that a lady of Edna's background . . . would discuss diaphragms and jellies and foam powders in public meetings." Doctors also were reluctant to help. Ultimately, McKinnon's brother, prominent Montana lawyer Wellington Rankin, forced her to abandon her effort in the state because he was worried that it would embarrass the family.

Nevertheless, national attitudes about sexuality had started to shift. Around 1900, writers, scholars, and feminists began to argue that "respectable" women could find fulfillment in sex (as long as it was in the confines of heterosexual marriage). This idea of "companionate marriage," in which both husband and wife sought mutual pleasure, meant that some couples no longer perceived sex within marriage as strictly for producing children.

Family planning was an important component of companionate marriage, as birth control allowed couples to have sex without fear of pregnancy. In 1926, Margaret Sanger argued for the link between family planning and marital happiness, writing, "When the young wife is forced into maternity too soon, both [partners] are cheated out of marital adjustment and harmony that require time to mature and develop. The plunge into parenthood prematurely with all its problems and disturbances, is like the lighting of a bud before it has been given time to blossom."

In Montana, conservative forces, including the Catholic Church, resisted this shift in attitude. According to historian Mary Murphy, Margaret Sanger was advised not to visit heavily Catholic Butte during her tour of Montana in the 1930s: "Butte would be futile, I'm afraid," wrote Belle Winestine, "on account of the great preponderance of citizens who are opposed even to *listening* to birth control propaganda, on account of religious convictions."

Even if Montanans were uncomfortable with public discussions about birth control, it seems that women were using it. Between 1915 and 1933, Montana's birth rate steadily declined. The onset of the Great Depression in the 1930s brought additional economic strain to Montana, making family planning even more important. And when birth control was inaccessible or failed, women were more likely to turn to abortion. One Montana woman anonymously confessed that she had three abortions during the Great Depression because she and her husband felt it was "unethical" to have children they could not provide for economically. In fact, historians estimate that as many as one in four pregnancies were terminated during the Depression.

Despite such grim statistics, the times—and the laws—were changing. By the late 1930s, Montana's physicians and pharmacists could sell and distribute birth control. While obscenity statutes still prohibited advertising or distributing information about contraception, patients now could, and did, request prescriptions for birth control without violating the law.

The Life and Legend of Mary Fields

Annie Hanshew

BORN A SLAVE in the American South, Mary Fields died a legendary figure in Montana's mythic pioneer past. Sometimes referred to as "Black Mary" or "Stagecoach Mary," Fields is interesting both for the life she led in and around Cascade and for the tall tales her life inspired. Fields's race and her gender complicate her role as a symbol of Montana's pioneer days, and the myths that have developed around her life lend insights into the prevailing racial hierarchies that shaped life for African Americans in Montana's early history.

Born around 1832, possibly in Tennessee, Mary Fields celebrated her

An avid baseball fan, Mary Fields (standing at far right) regularly rewarded Cascade team members who hit home runs with bouquets from her garden. Wedsworth Memorial Library, Cascade, Montana

birthday on March 15. The details of her life before she came to Montana Territory in 1885 are difficult to trace, complicated by her birth into slavery and the fact that, although she was literate, she left no written record. According to one biographer, Fields's mother was a house slave and her father was a field slave. After the Civil War, Fields worked as a chambermaid on the *Robert E. Lee*, a Mississippi River steamboat. According to some accounts, she met Judge Edmund Dunne while working on the *Robert E. Lee* and eventually became a servant in his household.

In the 1870s, Fields began working at the Ursuline Convent in Toledo, Ohio, where Dunne's sister, Mother Mary Amadeus, was the superior. In 1884, Mother Amadeus traveled to Montana to join the Jesuits at St. Peter's Mission. The next year, she wrote to request that the convent send more people to staff the struggling mission and boarding school. Mary Fields traveled upriver with the nuns sent by the order.

Thus, Mary Fields began her new life among the sisters in Montana. She worked at the mission for the next ten years, raising chickens, growing vegetables, and freighting supplies from nearby Cascade. She developed a reputation for having "the temperament of a grizzly bear," but tales also spread about her toughness and devotion to the nuns and students.

Because of her tendency to smoke, swear, and bicker with other hired hands at the mission, Fields drew the ire of Bishop Brondell, of Great Falls, who banned her from the mission around 1894. Though the nuns defended Fields, they had no choice but to follow the bishop's orders, and Fields, reportedly devastated, moved into Cascade.

After two failed attempts at running a restaurant, Fields secured a contract to deliver mail to St. Peter's Mission. She earned the nickname "Stagecoach Mary" for her reliability and speed, and she drove the fifteen-mile route between the mission and Cascade from 1895 to 1903. She was around seventy years old when she finally "retired" in town and ran a laundry out of her home. She died in Great Falls in 1914.

In many ways, Fields transcended the traditional gender boundaries for women of the era. She neither married nor depended on the support of the church. Handy with a gun, she smoked, drank, and swore and took a "man's job" delivering mail. Because she was a large woman, she wore men's shirts and jackets. She also socialized with men at the baseball field and in the saloon. In a 1959 issue of *Ebony*, Montana-born film star Gary Cooper reminisced that Fields could "whip any two men in the territory" and "had a fondness for hard liquor that was matched only by her capacity to put it away."

The Mary Fields of legend is a masculine figure; her traditionally feminine attributes are typically underplayed. Yet Fields generally wore skirts, loved to grow flowers, and babysat many of Cascade's children. A subtle racism may explain this discrepancy. The people of Cascade accepted Fields while she was alive and celebrated her after death, but historian Dee Garceau-Hagen points to nicknames like "Black Mary," "Colored Mary," and "Nigger Mary" and argues that Cascade residents "affirmed a caste system based on race, even as they celebrated Fields' notoriety."

As the sole African American in Cascade, Fields did not have the benefit of a close-knit black community, like those that developed in Helena, Great Falls, Butte, and Fort Benton. And because she was also "outside the boundaries of respectable womanhood," Fields was in some ways on her own. It is hard to imagine that Fields did not feel the sting of prejudice, or at least the "friendly contempt" described by African American musician W. C. Handy on a visit to Helena in 1897. Nevertheless, she certainly lived an inspirational life—and one forged on her own terms. A writer for *Negro*

Digest in 1950 cast her as a role model: "She was, in the best sense, a pioneer woman. She was rough and she was tough." And as Gary Cooper opined, she was born a slave but "lived to become one of the freest souls ever to draw a breath or a .38."

The Long Campaign: The Fight for Women's Suffrage

Martha Kohl

ON NOVEMBER 3, 1914, Montana men went to the polls, where they voted 53 to 47 percent in favor of women's suffrage. Along with Nevada, which also passed a suffrage amendment that year, Montana joined nine other western states in extending voting rights to non-Native women. (Indian women would have to wait until passage of the 1924 Indian Citizenship Act to gain the ballot.) Montana suffrage supporters rejoiced, and in 1916 followed up their victory by electing Maggie Smith Hathaway (D) and Emma Ingalls (R) to the state legislature and Jeannette Rankin (I) to the U.S. Congress. In this

The *Suffrage Daily News,* the short-lived paper in which this photo ran on November 2, 1914, identified these suffrage campaigners only by their husband's names while noting that the women had campaigned for the vote in four different Montana counties. Left to right: Mrs. R. F. Foote, Mrs. J. B. Ellis, chairman, Silver Bow County, Mrs. H. Salholm, Mrs. A. Obermyer, and Mrs. E. G. Clinch. MHS Photo Archives 951-821

seeming wave of feminism, May Trumper (I) also became the state superintendent of public instruction.

An air of inevitability surrounded the victory, but it had not come easily. Montana women's rights advocates first proposed equal suffrage twenty-five years earlier at the 1889 state constitutional convention. Fergus County delegate Perry McAdow (I), husband of successful businesswoman and feminist Clara McAdow, championed the cause. He even recruited longtime Massachusetts suffrage proponent Henry Blackwell to address the convention.

Blackwell was an articulate orator, but he did not have the backing of a well-organized, grassroots movement. "There has never been a woman suffrage meeting held in Montana," he lamented. Nevertheless, Blackwell hoped to convince the delegates to include constitutional language allowing the legislature to grant equal suffrage through a simple majority vote instead of requiring a constitutional amendment. That proposal failed on a tie ballot.

Although the constitutional convention did not grant them equal suffrage, Montana women did retain the right to vote in school elections (first ceded to them by the 1887 territorial legislature). The new constitution also granted all tax-paying women the right to vote on questions concerning taxpayers. For Montana feminists, however, the goal was equality in voting rights. It proved a difficult target. Suffrage clubs formed and disbanded as the movement lurched between periods of concentrated effort and years of "discouragement and apathy." The state legislature voted on equal suffrage during almost every session between 1895 and 1911. Suffrage questions sometimes passed in the House but never by the required two-thirds—and never in the Senate. Without the two-thirds majority in both houses, the question could not be put to a simple vote of the people.

After the 1911 session, however, a sophisticated and multifaceted organizing campaign changed the momentum. The first step toward victory came when suffrage advocates convinced both the Democratic and Republican parties to write equal suffrage into their platforms. Then, in January 1913, the legislature passed a women's suffrage bill by large majorities (26 to 2 in the Senate and 74 to 2 in the House). This left the 1914 popular vote as the last hurdle to amending the state constitution.

Jeannette Rankin is undoubtedly Montana's most famous suffragist, but the movement's final triumph involved hundreds of women across the state. Belle Fligelman, of Helena, shocked her mother by speaking on street corners and in front of saloons. Margaret Smith Hathaway, of Stevensville, traveled over fifty-seven hundred miles promoting the cause and earning the nickname "The Whirlwind." The Missoula Teachers' Suffrage Committee published and distributed thirty thousand copies of its leaflet, "Women Teachers of Montana Should Have the Vote."

The campaign found arguments for every interest group, bringing in outside talent as necessary. New York laundry worker Margaret Hinchey proved particularly popular. The plainspoken Irish immigrant undoubtedly converted at least some of Montana's class-conscious miners and loggers with her fiery speeches advocating equal suffrage as a tool for advancing the cause of working women.

From its headquarters in Butte, the Montana Equal Suffrage Association (MESA) "mailed letters to women's clubs, labor unions, granges, and other farm organizations, asking for pro-suffrage resolutions." During the state fair, MESA published a daily paper, underlining its dual argument for suffrage. The first was simple justice: "those who must obey the laws should have a voice in making them." The second asserted that women's ingrained morality would reduce political corruption and make it easier to pass humane legislation.

Women voters as a moral force was the prime argument of the state's oldest suffrage organization, the Woman's Christian Temperance Union (WCTU). The WCTU had over fifteen hundred members and fifty chapters in Montana and ran its own campaign. State president Mary Alderson Long, of Bozeman, traveled forty-five hundred miles and effectively mobilized her members to engage in neighbor-to-neighbor campaigns. Nevertheless, MESA did not allow WCTU members a float in its grand suffrage parade for fear of tarring the suffrage movement with the temperance brush.

The campaign emerged victorious despite such disagreements on tactics and the inevitable interpersonal rivalries. Ravalli County voted 70 percent in favor of equal voting rights, Missoula County 64 percent, and Yellowstone County 57 percent. The suffragists squeaked out a narrow victory in Hill County but lost Silver Bow (home to Butte) by a mere thirty-four votes. In general, farming counties supported suffrage, while mining counties opposed it—possibly out of fear that women would vote in prohibition.

With the passage of equal suffrage, women had won the battle for justice. The promise that they would make politics more moral remained an open question. As the *Harlem Enterprise* editorialized after the votes were counted: "Evidently Montana has a better educated body of men who recognize the intelligence of their women. . . . Now we will see whether politics in the state will be more 'rotten' than under the control of men."

After Suffrage: Women Politicians at the Montana Capitol

Ellen Baumler

On November 3, 1914, Montana became the tenth state to empower women with the right to vote. Two years later, newly enfranchised Montana women helped elect Jeannette Rankin to the U.S. House of Representatives. She took her seat as the first woman to serve in Congress four years before women achieved national suffrage. Rankin's victory largely eclipsed another, equally significant 1916 victory: that year, Montana seated the first two women in the state's House of Representatives. These women opened the door for those who followed in the political arena.

Emma Ingalls, a Republican from Flathead County, and Maggie Smith Hathaway, a Democrat from Ravalli County, represented opposing parties, but they both championed the cause of women's suffrage and spoke out for the disenfranchised. Conscious of their role as female reformers, both championed child welfare and women's rights in the legislature. Emma Ingalls served two terms and Maggie Hathaway served three. Both made valuable contributions and earned the respect of, and courtesy from, their male colleagues.

Lifelong feminist Emma Ingalls used the newspaper she and her husband founded, the Kalispell *Inter Lake*, to editorialize for civic reform. A rival editor said she was a clever and interesting writer who "occasionally wielded a caustic pen." During her first term in 1917, Ingalls introduced the national suffrage amendment when it came before the Montana House for ratification. During her second term, Ingalls sponsored a bill establishing the Mountain View Vocational School for Girls. Before that time, courts sent both boys and girls to the state reform school at Miles City. Separation of boys and girls was an important step in the care of delinquent juveniles.

After serving a second term, Ingalls became the first woman to work with the State Bureau of Child and Animal Protection, chairing the northwest district under Governor Joseph Dixon. Despite her accomplishments, Ingalls believed her life was unremarkable. "God put me on his anvil and hammered me into shape," she once said. "The things that seemed so hard to bear at the time have proven to be the stepping stones to a larger, richer life."

Maggie Smith Hathaway, acclaimed for translating ethics into action, also blazed a long and noteworthy trail. Hathaway traveled thousands of miles campaigning vigorously for women's suffrage before the 1914 election. She did the same for Prohibition in 1916, speaking in every neighborhood

Mrs. Maggie Smith Hathaway
Democratic Candidate
FOR STATE REPRESENTATIVE
PRIMARY ELECTION AUGUST 29th.

Experience in Montana Legislative Work---

Clerk in House in 1913

Lobbyist for Montana Women's Organization in 1915 and deserves credit for passage of Mother's Pension and Equal Guardianship Laws.

"Emir at Women Plead for Vote."

"Mrs. Hathaway's Manner Is Clear and Convincing"
---Helena Independent, July 28, 1914.

"A Logical Speaker."
---Lewistown Democrat, 1914.

To Women Voters---
She helped to get you the Vote. Why not send her to the Legislature?

Financially Interested in a Ravalli County Ranch

For Prohibition, a Workable Farm Loan Law Child Welfare, Efficiency, Economy, and Protection of Home Industry.

Paid for by M. S. Hathaway
Printed by Tribune, Stevensville

Maggie Smith Hathaway outlined her positions on Prohibition, child welfare, and a "Workable Farm Loan Law" in this 1916 campaign flier. UM Archives, Hathaway Coll., Mss 224

in Ravalli County. Hathaway's fellow male legislators affectionately, but pointedly, called her "Mrs. Has-Her-Way" for her power of persuasion. She drafted Montana's Mother's Pension Bill, fought to create the state's Child Welfare Division, and made the speech that won the eight-hour workday for women. A male legislator said of the diminutive redhead, "She is the biggest man in the House."

During World War I, with nearly 10 percent of Montana's men serving in the military, Hathaway recognized women's capabilities to serve on the home front. She employed only women on her "manless" ranch so more men could join the armed services. She herself gathered apples, hitched up her own plow, and turned furrows as straight as any man's.

There were other political firsts for Montana women. Dolly Cusker Akers was the first Native American elected to the Montana House of Representatives. Akers, active in tribal politics, was the only woman elected to the legislature in 1932. She chaired the Federal Relations Committee that handled Indian affairs. She also oversaw passage of legislation that allowed Indians to send their children to schools run by their own communities and not by the federal government.

A significant milestone came in 1939, when the three female Democratic state representatives—Minnie Beadle, Clare Martin, and Marian Melin—carried a bill amending the definition of "jury." Women did not usually serve on juries because the law defined the term as "a body of men." Changing the definition of jury to "a body of people" gave women equal responsibility to serve. Another milestone came in 1945 when Ellenore Bridenstine was the first woman elected to the Montana Senate.

Women have prompted some of the legislature's most memorable moments, and some were not above shenanigans when the occasion suited. The late Polly Holmes, a Democrat beloved by veteran lawmakers for her outspoken views, served during the 1970s. She sponsored the first Montana bill to ban smoking in public places. When she rose to read her bill, opponents all lit up cigars. Unfazed, Holmes put on a medical mask and wore it while she read.

Women who have served Montana have given much of themselves to the state. Emma Ingalls and Maggie Hathaway each made a name for herself by courageously acting on her convictions, and they left a legacy for other women to follow. Those mentioned here and others paved the way for today's women who have carved a career in Montana politics.

Freda Augusta Beazley and the Rise of American Indian Political Power

Laura Ferguson

IN THE mid-twentieth century, American Indian tribes faced crippling poverty, enormous land loss, and attacks on their status as semi-sovereign nations. One Montanan integrally involved in the efforts to fight these injustices was Freda Beazley, an Assiniboine woman from Klein and the widow of a former state legislator. Beazley served on the advisory council to Montana's Office of Indian Affairs, the first such agency in the nation. She was an officer on the Montana Intertribal Policy Board (MIPB), the National Congress of American Indians (NCAI), and the Affiliated Tribes of Northwest Indians. She was also the first coordinator of Rural and Indian Programs for Montana's Office of Economic Opportunity (OEO). Throughout the 1950s and 1960s, Beazley worked steadfastly at state and federal levels to protect tribal sovereignty, end poverty, and improve Indians' education and employment opportunities.

The post–World War II era was a precarious time for American Indian tribes. In 1953, the Eisenhower administration resurrected nineteenth-century assimilationist goals by enacting a policy to terminate tribal sovereignty. Euphemistically called "liberation," Termination severed federal-tribal relations, ended trust status for Indian lands, and withdrew all federal services previously guaranteed in treaties. The policy's blatant dismissal of tribal sovereignty and treaty rights galvanized emergent multi-tribal advocacy coalitions like the NCAI and the Affiliated Tribes.

The Flathead Reservation was one of the first reservations slated for Termination, but the Bureau of Indian Affairs faced strong opposition from Montanans. As secretary for both the MIPB and the NCAI, Beazley urged Montana's legislature and its congressional representatives to unite against Termination. Kept abreast of tribes' concerns by Beazley and the MIPB, Congressman Lee Metcalf exposed Termination as a "land-grab" aimed at divesting tribes of natural resources such as hydroelectric power, oil, gas, and uranium.

With high unemployment and virtually no industry, most western tribes were already extremely impoverished. Energy companies took advantage of the Indians' vulnerability. In Montana alone, Indian landowners lost over 1.5 million acres between 1953 and 1958—even without Termination. Beazley realized that accelerating land loss through Termination would only exacerbate Indians' poverty. "Nobody will believe us about the starving and the pressure to sell our lands," testified a Rocky Boy tribal member before a congressional committee in 1957. "Is it necessary that we sell out to get the services that the Federal government bargained with in the treaty days?" Those federal services, promised in exchange for the lands ceded by tribes in treaties, included food, education, and assistance with economic development. Beazley pressed the government to fulfill its treaty obligations and advocated for both long-term economic development assistance and short-term aid.

As a voice for Montana's tribes, she often interceded on their behalf. When overall unemployment in Montana reached 16 percent in 1958, it stood at 84 percent on the Blackfeet Reservation. "Their people are without food and without transportation," Beazley reported while petitioning the government to provide surplus food to Montana's Indians. Despite support from the Montana Farmers Union, the Railroad Commission, and the AFL-CIO, tribes were denied surplus commodities year after year.

Freda Beazley, a member of the Assiniboine tribe of the Fort Peck Reservation, attended the fifteenth annual meeting of the National Congress of American Indians held in Missoula, Montana, September 14–19, 1958. MHS Photo Archives Lot 31, Box 5, Folder 2

In December 1963, schools on the Blackfeet Reservation withheld lunches from children of less than one-quarter Indian ancestry, even though these lunches were often the children's only sustenance. Parents turned to the tribal council, only to be denied assistance. A tribal member wrote to Beazley for help, saying, "Poor people were begging for money or purchase orders to get food for their children. The councilmen took off, leaving the poor needy people behind. . . . We have gone through all the proper channels, but we need help. The Blackfeet Indians are starving."

Beazley and Montana's coordinator for Indian Affairs, Knute Bergan, discovered that Congress had delayed sending federal aid that should have subsidized the lunches. Furthermore, Blackfeet tribal funds were depleted. Beazley and Bergan contacted Montana's congressmen to appropriate the overdue aid. Although their intervention was successful, ever-deepening tribal poverty remained a pressing issue.

Working with the NCAI in the early 1960s, Beazley helped draft specific measures aimed at improving conditions on the reservations and ensured their incorporation into President Lyndon Johnson's War on Poverty legislation. Most notably, the Economic Opportunity Act of 1964 benefited American Indian communities by enabling tribes, for the first time, to develop and operate their own independent federally funded programs.

Because of Beazley's experience with governmental programs, Governor Tim Babcock appointed her administrative assistant to the state's War on Poverty office in 1965 and, a year later, made her the Rural and Indian Programs coordinator for Montana's Office of Economic Opportunity. Beazley helped teach tribal representatives how to apply for OEO grants and how to implement OEO programs—such as VISTA, full-day Head Start, Job Corps, Upward Bound, and Community Action Programs. In 1966, Beazley gave the commencement address to Montana's first class of Upward Bound graduates.

Beazley frequently addressed civic and religious organizations about women's rights, civil rights, and Indian affairs. A member of the League of Women Voters, a Democratic congressional committeewoman, and a feminist, she passionately believed that women had to be actively engaged in politics and economics. In 1966, she was elected the first woman vice president of the Affiliated Tribes of Northwest Indians, an organization working to protect treaty rights. That same year, President Johnson named Freda Beazley among America's "Forty Outstanding Women" for her dedication to fighting poverty and inequality.

In 1970, Freda Beazley and the Indian affairs organizations she served celebrated a victory they helped bring about when President Richard Nixon officially ended Termination and pledged support for Indians' self-determination through tribal autonomy. Beazley continued to demonstrate her dedication to Indians' well-being, civil rights, and women's equality for the remainder of her career. She died in Helena in 1982, just shy of seventy-five years of age.

Champions: The Girls of Fort Shaw Basketball

Laura Ferguson

AMID THE RUINS of the Fort Shaw Government Industrial Indian Boarding School, a metal arch and granite monument honor ten Native American girls who overcame separation from their families and forced estrangement from their Native cultures to become some of the finest female basketball players in the country. Declared the "World Basket Ball Champions" in 1904, the girls from Fort Shaw also deserve praise for having triumphed over extraordinary life challenges.

In 1892, the federal government opened the Fort Shaw Indian boarding school. Such off-reservation schools were designed to break the chain of cultural continuity by removing children from their tribal communities. The schools' paramount educational objectives were cultural assimilation and English language fluency. Students were trained for employment in domestic services, industrial labor, and farming. Classes in music, theater, and physical education rounded out their instruction.

The girls who formed Fort Shaw's famous team had much in common. Although they came from several different tribes, nearly all of them were daughters of indigenous women and white men. Many of the girls were multilingual, several spoke English conversantly, and several had siblings at Fort Shaw.

Many of the girls had also known tragedy in their lives. Four of the girls had lost their mothers, and two had lost their fathers. While attending Fort Shaw, two were orphaned and yet another girl lost her father. Two had sisters who died from infectious diseases at school, and several had brothers or male cousins who ran away from Fort Shaw, one who froze to death in the attempt.

Boarding school demanded that the girls relinquish their indigenous cultural identities, at least outwardly, and adopt white cultural behaviors. While discovering friendship and support from one another, each of these girls also drew on her own inner strength, courage, and intelligence to surpass expectations and to excel as a student and as an athlete.

When Josephine Langley, their physical culture instructor, introduced basketball at Fort Shaw in 1896, the sport was in its infancy. The strenuous game instantly delighted the female students, whose physical activities were generally more restricted at school than they had been at home. When the Fort Shaw girls gave their initial intramural basketball demonstration in 1897 at the year-end closing ceremonies, the three hundred spectators responded with enthusiasm to the first high school basketball program in Montana.

However, lack of funding and lack of opposing teams kept the Fort Shaw girls from playing competitive basketball until the fall of 1902, when intramural coach Josie Langley (Blackfeet) joined Emma Sansaver (Chippewa-Cree), Belle Johnson (Blackfeet), Nettie Wirth (Assiniboine), and Minnie

Burton (Lemhi Shoshone) to form that first team. Fort Shaw won its first competitive game, against Butte, but lost against Helena High a few days later. Despite the loss, the *Montana Daily Record* ran a front-page article complimenting the Indian team's talent. In January 1903, Butte Parochial High School handed Fort Shaw its second—and last—defeat.

Montanans' enthusiastic support for the Fort Shaw team grew with each competition. Unable to host a game at their own school, the Fort Shaw team played "home" games at Luther Hall in Great Falls, the only place big enough to accommodate several hundred fans. By the end of 1903, the team, now expanded in numbers as well as fame, had even defeated Missoula and Bozeman's college teams as well as the reigning state champions, Helena High.

Fort Shaw superintendent Fred Campbell quickly grasped the benefits of a competitive basketball team. The girls were mastering teamwork, building physical agility, and gaining self-confidence. Anti-Indian prejudices seemed to be fading as white Montanans' exposure to team members

Jessie Tarbox took this picture of the Fort Shaw girls' basketball team in 1904 during their visit to St. Louis. Standing, from left: Rose LaRose, Flora Lucero, Katie Snell, Minnie Burton, Genevieve Healy, Sarah Mitchell. Seated, from left: Emma Sansaver, Gennie Butch, Belle Johnson, Nettie Wirth. Missouri History Museum, St. Louis

and their accomplishments increased. Fort Shaw's band and its mandolin orchestra entertained spectators before games, and newspapers gushed about the girls' talent in ballroom dancing at after-game assemblies. The team's fame soon opened up even greater opportunities to showcase the school's successful, and transformative, education of indigenous children.

In 1903, Campbell received an invitation to send students to participate in the Model Indian School at the 1904 World's Fair in St. Louis. The model school contrasted with exhibitions of indigenous peoples' traditional life-ways and was intended to validate America's policy of forced assimilation. Campbell didn't hesitate to choose the ten girls on the basketball team as his delegates. Four of the members of the 1902 team—Belle Johnson, Emma Sansaver, Minnie Burton, and Nettie Wirth—joined the girls who had since rounded out the team: Gen Healy (Gros Ventre), Katie Snell (Assiniboine), Gennie Butch (Assiniboine), Rose LaRose (Shoshone-Bannock), Flora Lucero (Chippewa), and Sarah Mitchell (Assiniboine). Nettie's older sister, Lizzie Wirth, accompanied them as chaperone and substitute player.

The girls played fund-raising games en route to St. Louis, often encountering anti-Indian attitudes among the spectators. At the fair, they divided up for five-on-five exhibition games before captivated audiences, while across the street male athletes competed for medals at the Third Olympiad. Late in the summer, when they received an invitation to stage an exhibition game at the Olympics, the girls played before thousands of cheering spectators. By the close of the fair, the girls were being celebrated as the basketball champions of the world. They sealed that title with back-to-back victories against a Missouri all-star team, the only team to brave a competition.

With all they had to overcome, and all they had to leave behind, the girls' glory was well earned. Their achievements demonstrated their ability to excel despite personal tragedies, destructive federal Indian policies, and limitations imposed on them as Indian women in turn-of-the-century America. Even today, their victories in life and in basketball continue to inspire us and make us cheer.

Early Social Service Was Women's Work

Ellen Baumler

PAROCHIAL institutions in nineteenth- and early twentieth-century Montana, which were almost exclusively under the supervision of women, were the forerunners of our modern social services. Catholic nuns,

Methodist deaconesses, and nondenominational Christian women offered comfort, sanctuary, and stability to the lost, the desperate, and the destitute. Their contributions were far-reaching, and some of their pioneering services evolved and remain viable today.

Sisters of Charity of Leavenworth (Kansas) came to Helena in 1869 at the invitation of Jesuit priests who saw a dire need for feminine influence in the rough-and-tumble gold camp. The sisters' mission was threefold—to teach youth, care for orphans, and minister to the sick—and it fit in with the real needs of the frontier community. St. Vincent's Academy, the first boarding school for non-Indian girls, opened in 1870 and educated girls until 1935.

St. Joseph's Home for Orphans fulfilled one of the missions of the Sisters of Charity of Leavenworth. Earthquakes in 1935 left the children homeless, and they spent nearly two years as the guests of wealthy U.S. senator James E. Murray at Boulder Hot Springs. L. H. Jorud, photographer, *Helena Independent Record*

The sisters cared for the indigent mentally ill until the founding of a hospital in Warm Springs in 1877. There was no other place for these people, and their care was a dangerous undertaking. On one occasion, a violent patient escaped his restraints and overpowered a hired man and a priest. Sister Patricia calmly threw a mattress over the patient so that others could rush in and restrain him.

The Sisters of Charity also founded St. Joseph's Home for Orphans, the territory's first orphanage. In 1881, the Sullivan brothers of Butte (ages three, five, and six) were the first of hundreds of needy children to enter their care. After the boys' mother died, their miner father could not care for them, so the sisters took the children in and nurtured them. In time, Stephen and Ambrose would enter the priesthood and John would become a doctor.

Because Helena was the seat of the Catholic diocese, the largest population center, and the capital, many social service institutions were first located there, especially during the reform movements of the 1890s. Sisters of the House of the Good Shepherd arrived in 1889 to open a sanctuary and school for "fallen women and wayward girls." In 1896, members of the Woman's Christian Temperance Union were among the founders of the Florence Crittenton Home, which complemented the work of Good Shepherd. Longtime matron Lena Cullum and the Crittenton board developed a close reciprocity with the Sisters of the House of the Good Shepherd, whose mission, although similar to that of the Crittenton Home, did not include the care of pregnant girls.

The Montana Children's Home Society, also founded in Helena in 1896, was a Protestant nondenominational alternative to the Catholic St. Joseph's Home. Dr. Elizabeth Holden, who specialized in women's and children's health in private practice, gave her home for use as the first facility. The organization took in children from the orphan trains, babies up for adoption from the Crittenton Home, and other needy children.

Parochial education also evolved under the auspices of women in Montana, and it was often intertwined with social services. Various orders of Catholic sisters opened schools in many Montana communities, including Helena, Missoula, Great Falls, and Billings. By 1908, Catholic schools were serving 5,536 of the 61,928 children enrolled in Montana schools, not including those on reservations.

Protestants, concerned that there was no alternative private education, brought deaconesses from the Chicago Training School to open the Montana Deaconess Preparatory School in the Helena valley in 1909. The school was the only Protestant boarding school west of the Mississippi, and it accepted children ages five to fourteen. The deaconesses were trained teachers and social workers. The school had many charity cases and sometimes took in Protestant children originally placed at St. Joseph's orphanage. Although the school was not an orphanage, the community perceived it as such. Consequently, donations helped sustain the school.

Networking among the women of these early institutions, established before child welfare systems and other social services were in place, speaks to the heart of those who strove to do the best they could for those under their care. Lila Schroeder Anderson serves as one example of a lost child who benefitted greatly. Anderson was the third of six children of an eastern Montana rancher. In the 1920s, when her mother died and her father split up the family, she was the only sibling sent to the Deaconess Home at Helena. Soon thereafter, Crittenton Home matron Lena Cullum, en route to a meeting at the home, saw ten-year-old Anderson marching down the sidewalk with her belongings in a pillowcase. Cullum stopped and asked the child where she was headed. "I will find my brothers somehow," Anderson recalled saying. Cullum then made arrangements to take her in at the Crittenton Home. While Anderson had an unconventional childhood at the maternity home, she went to public school, where she excelled. Cullum gave her away when she married.

Child welfare services and the foster care system eventually replaced the early children's homes. Most Catholic institutions closed in the 1960s and 1970s, but some of the early institutions continue to serve needy Montanans. The Deaconess Home, now Intermountain, serves children under severe mental distress. The Florence Crittenton Home continues to accept unwed teens and focuses on parenting skills. The Children's Home Society evolved into Shodair Hospital, which provides genetic testing and psychiatric services.

The institutions that took root in Helena for the good of Montana residents speak to the caring groups and individuals who left important sustainable legacies. Their contributions have been monumental and their influence far-reaching.

Saving Girls: Montana State Vocational School for Girls

Ellen Baumler

IMAGINE an eight-year-old child thrown into a prison cell with a hardened criminal. Until the late nineteenth century, any child over the age of seven who broke the law was normally sentenced to an adult penal institution. However, after psychologists realized that, for children especially, rehabilitation was more effective than punishment, states began to establish juvenile reformatories. Then, as women took up the cause of child labor laws, juvenile court systems, and separate women's correctional institutions, they also began a campaign to separate delinquent girls and boys in reformatories.

In 1893, the Montana legislature established the Pine Hills Boys and Girls Industrial School at Miles City. The court could commit any boy or girl between the ages of eight and twenty-one to Pine Hills for any crime other than murder or manslaughter. Judges could also remand a child who "is growing up in mendicancy, or vagrancy, or is incorrigible" to the reform school. Girls were generally sentenced "to punish petty larceny; to supply a home; to effect moral salvation; to prevent further 'lewd' acts; and to provide protection from physical abuse." Boys, on the other hand, were sentenced for more criminal behaviors.

As women gained a voice in government, "saving girls" was one of their first concerns. Female reformers saw creating an all-girls reformatory as a moral issue, especially since many of the girls sentenced to the coeducational

Matrons put students at the Mountain View Vocational School for Girls to work, believing that "Satan finds some mischief still for idle hands to do." The girls' farm labor helped support the school. Here, five residents clean the barnyard, ca. 1920.
MHS Photo Archives PAc 96-9.3

Pine Hills facility were simply homeless or orphans, not criminals. Women's organizations, including the State Federation of Women's Clubs and the Good Government Club, took up the cause. Jeannette Rankin, a trained social worker, joined in advocating for a separate girls' facility. So did Helena physician and humanitarian Dr. Maria Dean, who tirelessly lobbied the Montana legislature to establish a girls' reform school.

It took women's suffrage—and the election of female legislators—to create the Mountain View Vocational School for Girls. When Emma Ingalls joined Maggie Hathaway as Montana's first female state representatives in 1917, she immediately proposed a bill to create a state industrial school for girls. Her first attempt failed, but when she reintroduced the bill in 1919, it passed. The primary function of the school was "the care, education, training, treatment and rehabilitation of girls ten (10) years of age or older and under twenty-one (21) years of age who [were] committed to the school by a court as provided by law."

In April 1920, the first six girls were transferred from Miles City to the new facility seven miles north of Helena. Ten months later, twenty-eight girls occupied the new dormitory, aptly named the Maria Dean Cottage after Dr. Dean, who had died just weeks after the legislature authorized the school. Agriculture and hygiene were the only classes offered at first, and the girls spent much of their time helping the facility become a self-sustaining agricultural venture. By 1922, the campus was already overcrowded with sixty-six girls.

The school's inmates varied markedly. Some of the girls were orphans, others had behavioral problems, and still others were labeled incorrigible because they had run away from home. No matter why girls were sentenced to the school, they all faced harsh discipline from the early matrons—despite reformers' caring rhetoric. Until the 1950s, punishment included lockup or solitary confinement, deprivation of one of the three daily meals, loss of privileges such as letter writing, and physical chastisement. Matrons often made girls stand for long periods of time, sometimes with a piece of soap in their mouths.

Administrator Ruby Miller, who took over school management in 1950, instituted welcome changes. In 1951, the school's four-year high school program was accredited. Miller brought in instructors to teach a variety of classes, including music, acting, and beauty culture, and she introduced swimming and softball, dances, and other extracurricular activities. These reforms led some officials to criticize the facility as a finishing school rather than a detention facility.

Although the state added maximum security units after Miller died in 1960, her emphasis on education and rehabilitation rather than punishment remained the norm, at least for a time. In 1967, the name changed to Mountain View School for girls. In 1971, the school's male administrator noted that a girl "would never be any good if she doesn't like herself." His policy of solitary confinement, however, hardly encouraged self-esteem. A 1993 investigation revealed violations of the girls' rights under the 1980 Civil Rights of Institutionalized Persons Act. The investigatory report noted inadequate staff training, excessive use of seclusion and restraints, and a facility "grossly deficient" in terms of environmental and fire safety. The school subsequently closed in 1996.

The Mountain View campus now houses the Montana Law Enforcement Academy, but poignant traces of the girls remain in the graffiti, much of it dated to the 1930s, scrawled on the walls of a forgotten attic. Messages and doodles on the peeling plaster tell of the misery some girls endured at Mountain View. Tick marks count days of confinement, looping hearts symbolize a girl's wishful dream, and sassy quips speak to the insolence of youthful offenders.

Mountain View was a vision whose time had run its course. Today, judges have options such as treatment facilities, group homes, and alternatives to lockup. The system was never, and still is not, perfect. However, contemporary services would not have evolved without the actions of the women of the Progressive Era who advocated for the troubled girls of their time.

"She Really Believed in Families": The Medical Career of Sadie Lindeberg

Annie Hanshew

Dr. Sadie Lindeberg of Miles City had an exceptional career by any standard. She became a doctor in 1907, a time when there were perhaps as few as three women physicians in all of Montana. She practiced well into her eighties and delivered, by her own count, over eight thousand babies in a career that spanned more than half a century. These accomplishments alone make Lindeberg a notable figure in Montana history, but her work helping girls and women through unwanted pregnancies—at a time when pregnancy out of wedlock was shameful and abortion was illegal—makes Dr. Lindeberg's story truly extraordinary.

Born in 1884 to Swedish immigrants Nels and Hanna Lindeberg, who homesteaded a few miles west of Miles City, Lindeberg claimed to have been the first white baby born in the area. She graduated from high school in Miles City in 1901. After working for a few years as a substitute teacher, Lindeberg enrolled in medical school at the University of Michigan. Graduating in 1907, she took a yearlong internship at the Women and Children's Hospital in Chicago, then returned home to establish a private practice.

Dr. Sadie Lindeberg opened her practice in 1908, two years before the construction of Miles City's Holy Rosary Hospital (above), where Lindeberg later delivered many babies. MHS Photo Archives PAc 96-83 33

Maternal care was hard to come by in Montana in the early twentieth century, and Dr. Lindeberg's services were in high demand. For at least one family, she was at the births of three generations: Eleanor Drake Harbaugh, born in 1910; Eleanor's son Loren, born in 1942; and Loren's daughter Mianne, born in 1964.

In addition to helping happy families grow, Dr. Lindeberg also helped women who found themselves unhappily pregnant, facilitating adoptions and providing safe abortions. Many of Lindeberg's adoption records were lost, and those that remain appear to have been forged to protect the privacy and reputations of the unwed mothers. Thus, it is impossible to know how many adoptions she facilitated.

Marijane Morin discovered that she was one of "Sadie's babies" when she was sixty-three years old. By that time, her adoptive parents had died, but she was able to discover the identity of her birth parents by talking to longtime residents of Miles City and looking through school yearbooks. Lindeberg's own adopted daughters, Hanna Lindeberg Reynolds and Jean Lindeberg Stenken, were more typical in that they never knew anything about the circumstances of their births.

Lindeberg is perhaps best (and most controversially) remembered as "one of the state's leading abortionists." Abortion was illegal in Montana from the territorial period until the U.S. Supreme Court voided anti-abortion statutes in 1973. Nonetheless, all Montana's major towns had professional abortionists, many of whom were physicians. Before 1973, some women experienced dangerous "back-alley" procedures—but others found their way to physicians like Dr. Lindeberg, whose reputation for safety and discretion became widespread.

While other Montana doctors did not necessarily approve of Lindeberg's practice, they also did not take measures to stop her. One Miles City physician, Dr. Sidney Pratt, recalled that he "got all hot and bothered" when he first learned that abortions were being offered in his community, but he eventually had to admit to himself that Lindeberg "fulfilled a social need, that was going to be met by a person who was capable of doing it, or a person who was not." Pratt, who at one point served as the director of the Maternal, Family and Child Health Bureau of Montana's Department of Health and Environmental Sciences, acknowledged the need for safety: "There were a lot of coat-hanger abortions being done and we ran into a lot of problems with that, infections and all sorts of things. We decided Sadie was doing a good job. Let's let her do it, rather than all these quacks."

Anecdotal evidence supports Lindeberg's reputation for safety and compassion. Anna Dunbar received an abortion from Dr. Lindeberg in 1963. She later told an interviewer, "Dr. Sadie was like a little old lady doctor, and I found it quite remarkable that she was doing what she was doing with such fervor. She described everything that was going to happen and what could not happen. She was very fair about the whole thing."

Interestingly, Dunbar also recalled that Lindeberg first refused to help her because she was married. Dunbar was able to convince her to perform the abortion only after promising that she would obtain a divorce and revealing that her husband was African American (which indicates both a possible prejudice on Lindeberg's part and the general discrimination that families with mixed-race children could expect in that era). "She was principled," remembered Dunbar. "She really believed in families. I think she felt if you were married there was no reason to have an abortion. She didn't like that at all."

Like many abortionists of the period, Lindeberg was never prosecuted for her actions, and the open secret of Lindeberg's abortion practice did not seem to tarnish her reputation. The Miles City Business and Professional Women's Club honored her as Woman of the Year in 1953. She was also honored by the Montana Medical Association in 1957 and by the American Medical Association in 1960.

Lindeberg expressed no regrets for her career path. Speaking to the *Great Falls Tribune* in 1965, she said, "I've enjoyed my work, every bit of it. And if I had the choice I certainly would ask for a refill of the same." She died four years later, in 1969, at the age of eighty-four.

Mary Ann Pierre Topsseh Coombs and the Bitterroot Salish

Laura Ferguson

MARY ANN PIERRE was about ten years old in October 1891 when American soldiers arrived to "escort" the Salish people out of the Bitterroot region and to the Jocko (now Flathead) Reservation. With her family and three hundred members of her tribe, Mary Ann tearfully bid goodbye to the homeland where her people had lived for millennia. The Salish left behind farms, log homes, and the St. Mary's Mission church—evidence of all they had done to adjust to an Anglo-American lifestyle. Nearly eighty-five years later, Mary Ann Pierre Coombs returned to the Bitterroot to rekindle her people's historical and cultural connections to their homeland.

The Bitterroot region and the Salish people share a long mutual history. Salish travel routes to and from the Bitterroot testify to centuries of use as they moved seasonally to hunt bison and trade with regional tribes in well-established trading centers. Linguistic studies of the inland Salish language reveal ten-thousand-year-old words that described specific sites in the Bitterroot region and testify to the tribe's knowledge of the region's geography and resources.

When Lewis and Clark entered the Bitterroot in 1805 in destitute

Ellen Bigsam, Mary Ann Coombs, Victor Vanderburg, and Sophie Moise were children when the Salish were force marched out of the Bitterroot. Salish-Pend d'Oreille Culture Committee, Confederated Salish and Kootenai Tribes, SPCC c-0582

condition, the hospitable Salish presented the bedraggled strangers with food, shelter, blankets, good horses, and travel advice. In 1841, Jesuit missionaries established St. Mary's Mission at present-day Stevensville, and many Salish adopted Catholicism alongside their Native beliefs.

In 1855, Washington territorial governor Isaac Stevens negotiated the Hell Gate Treaty with the Salish, Pend d'Oreille, and Kootenai tribes. The necessity of translating everything into multiple languages made the negotiations problematic. One Jesuit observer said the translations were so poor that "not a tenth . . . was actually understood by either party." While the Kootenai and Pend d'Oreille tribes retained tribal lands at the southern end of Flathead Lake, the fate of the Bitterroot was not clear. Chief Victor believed the treaty protected his Salish tribe from dispossession, as it indicated a future survey for a reservation and precluded American trespass. However, the Americans claimed the treaty permitted the eventual eviction of the Salish at the president's discretion.

Following Chief Victor's death in 1870, President U. S. Grant issued an executive order demanding the Salish remove to the Flathead and sent General James Garfield in 1872 to force their consent. When Victor's son,

Chief Charlo, refused to sign the "agreement," Garfield forged Charlo's "X" on the document and the United States seized most of the tribe's land. Three hundred Salish people refused to leave and instead worked hard to maintain peace with the increasing number of intruding whites. Many Salish families, including Mary Ann's, built log homes, took up farming, planted orchards and vegetable gardens, and minimized their traditional seasonal travels. Her family got along well with their white neighbors. The Salish even refused aid to their allies, the Nez Perce, during that tribe's conflicts with the United States in 1877. The Salish hoped that such efforts to maintain good relations would appease the Americans' determination to drive them from their homeland.

Over the next twenty years, however, Americans continued to trespass into the disputed territory, establishing new towns and building a railroad for the timber industry. Just after Montana became a state, Congress ordered General Henry Carrington and his soldiers to remove Chief Charlo's tribe to the Flathead. On October 14, 1891, armed soldiers evicted three hundred Salish, some of whom left on foot. Later, Mary Ann recalled that "everyone was in tears, even the men," and said the procession was like "a funeral march." Other elders who had been children at the time of the removal remembered women weeping as troops marched them through Stevensville in front of white onlookers.

The federal government promised to compensate the Bitterroot Salish for the homes, crops, and livestock they left behind, but it was an empty promise. So, too, was the government's promise to provide for their survival on the Flathead Reservation. Mary Ann's family lived in poverty on the new reservation, where the rocky soil made farming difficult.

Mary Ann attended two years at the Jocko agency school but never learned to speak English fluently. As a teenager, she worked as a laundry maid for Indian agent Peter Ronan's family. While working for the Ronans, she met Louis Topsseh Coombs, whom she later married. They raised a family on the Flathead Reservation, and many years passed before Mary Ann Coombs returned to the Bitterroot.

By the 1970s, only three of the hundreds of Salish people who had made the trek from the Bitterroot to the Flathead were still alive, among them Mary Ann Coombs. In 1975, those three joined several descendants on a trip back to the Bitterroot. During the journey, the elders recounted childhood memories and tribal histories associated with particular places. They visited the graves of ancestors and showed younger relatives places where generations of Salish people had gone to receive medicine through visions.

Recently, Montana Fish, Wildlife and Parks and the Metcalf Wildlife Refuge relied on oral histories passed down by Coombs and her peers to create interpretive signs describing Salish history throughout the Bitter-root. The tribe has created an extensive project to map and record historical Salish sites using ancient place-names. Although Mary Ann Pierre Topsseh Coombs—who once woke up to see the rosy tops of the mountains of her homeland—is gone, Salish people's connections to the Bitterroot remain.

Childbirth and Maternal Health in Early Twentieth-Century Montana

Annie Hanshew

FOR WOMEN in the early twentieth century, pregnancy and childbirth were natural facts of life. But because of economic, cultural, and demographic circumstances, pregnancy and childbirth could also present great risks. Women, especially rural homesteaders in eastern and central Montana, often lacked access to reliable care and information. Remoteness, harsh weather, poverty, and cultural taboos against openly discussing pregnancy made childbirth unusually hazardous in Montana.

Maternal and infant mortality in the state were serious problems in the first decades of the twentieth century, especially among rural women. Viola Paradise, the author of a 1917 survey of an eastern county, found that, compared with other rural states, Montana had a "very bad record of maternal losses." Two years later, according to historian Dawn Nickel, the state was in the "'unenviable position' of having the highest reported infant mortality rate" in the Northwest. For Native Americans, the statistics were even more grim. A 1927 report found that "in Montana the infant mortality rate among Native Americans was 185.4 [per 1,000 births], compared to only 69.1 for whites."

Several factors contributed to the high risk of pregnancy. The economic realities meant that rural women had limited access to prenatal care and education and had to continue to work no matter their condition. Hazel Dorr of Eaton recalled being kicked in the stomach by a cow during her pregnancy. Fortunately, she "recovered after a visit to the doctor."

Women in remote areas also had trouble finding qualified physicians or midwives. Paradise, who conducted her survey for the Children's Bureau of the U.S. Department of Labor, described the "inaccessibility of medical care in confinement" as her "most striking finding." Working in an area roughly the size of the state of Connecticut, Paradise noted that there was no hospital and only three registered physicians, although "two or three others, not registered," had been "drawn into practice . . . because in emergencies their neighbors called upon them and they could not refuse to go."

While many rural Montana women tried to arrange for professional care at the time of delivery, plans could, and did, fall through. One woman recalled that she and her husband "had planned to have a physician, but the snow was so bad it was impossible to send for him." One nineteen-year-old mother gave birth alone while her husband was away seeking help. She delivered the baby, cut and tied the cord, cared for her infant, and "did all of her own cooking and housework until her husband arrived with help two days later." She and the baby survived, but she was too weak to work for the next six months. Other women were less lucky. Historian Mary Melcher recounts the story of one woman who hemorrhaged throughout her pregnancy due to an unrepaired laceration from "a previous confinement"; both mother and infant died.

Some communities had women who, though they lacked formal training, had extensive practical experience. Catherine Hayes Murphy was a midwife "whose only training was having ten children herself." She acquired most of her skills herself. "You learn as you go along," Murphy said. "You feel the pulse in the cord, and when it quits pulsating, you tie it. . . . You tried to make it so there wouldn't be infection." Almost 40 percent of the women Paradise surveyed had a neighbor or a family member help them deliver. Those who helped

Maternity supporters, such as this one from around 1920, helped support a pregnant woman's belly, making it easier for her to continue with her regular work. MHS Museum 2009.56.15a

often did so "with fear and misgivings," and only because a woman "can't be left alone in such a time."

Murphy did not receive pay for her work, but many larger Montana communities had midwives who charged for their services. Aino Hamalainen Puutio was a trained Finnish midwife who practiced around Butte and then Red Lodge. She worked with her patients during pregnancy, instructing them on proper diet, rest, and physical activity and gave advice as the women prepared for delivery. The day of the delivery she worked alone with the mother, keeping family members out of the room. She stayed until the next day, bathing the baby and providing bed care, then visited the mother and newborn in the days that followed.

Starting in the 1920s, women more often began to opt for hospital births. Hospitals were seen to offer the "newest technological and scientific methods to aid women giving birth while affording patients comfort and freedom from domestic duties." As obstetric practices became regulated in the 1930s, and antibiotics and transfusions were used to treat the problems of infection and hemorrhaging, maternal death rates dropped.

However, as the process of birth was professionalized and doctors replaced midwives, women lost a degree of control over the birthing process. According to historian Rima Apple, an increasing emphasis on "scientific motherhood" took away women's agency as mothers: "Mothers were pictured as passive learners, taking their direction from experts . . . usually a male physician . . . who insists that female patients must heed his every instruction."

Some Montana women resented this loss of control, and in the second half of the century, they reasserted their right to evaluate scientific evidence and decide their own course for motherhood. The "natural childbirth" movement and the La Leche League reflect this reassertion. So too did the successful fight in the 1980s to legalize midwifery in Montana.

A "Witty, Gritty Little Bobcat of a Woman": The Western Writings of Dorothy M. Johnson

Annie Hanshew

DOROTHY M. JOHNSON was Montana's most successful writer of Western fiction. Born in Iowa in 1905, Johnson grew up in Whitefish. Her love of the West and nineteenth-century frontier history and folklore inspired her to write seventeen books, more than fifty short stories, and myriad magazine

Dorothy Johnson spent most of her childhood in Whitefish. After a short stint on the East Coast, she returned to Montana, where she lived in Whitefish and Missoula. She is pictured here, ca. 1953, second from left, attending the Montana Library Association banquet at the Big Mountain Ski Resort in Whitefish. MHS Photo Archives PAc 86-97

articles. On the basis of her publishing success and numerous awards, scholars Sue Mathews and Jim Healey have called Johnson the "dean of women writers of Western fiction."

Johnson's family moved to Montana in 1909 and settled in Whitefish in 1913. She graduated from Whitefish High School in 1922 and studied premed at Montana State College (Bozeman) before transferring to Montana State University in Missoula. By the time she graduated with a degree in English in 1928, she had already published her first poem.

After college, Johnson left Montana and worked as an editor in New York for several years. In 1950, she returned to Montana and became editor of the *Whitefish Pilot*. Three years later, she relocated to Missoula to teach at the university and work for the Montana Press Association. She lived in Missoula until her death in 1983.

Ironically, many people who might not know Johnson's name are, nevertheless, familiar with her work. Three of her stories—"The Hanging Tree," "A Man Called Horse," and "The Man Who Shot Liberty Valance"— were made into motion pictures. *The Man Who Shot Liberty Valance*, a 1949 John Ford film starring Jimmy Stewart and John Wayne, has the honor of being listed on the National Film Registry for its cultural significance to American cinema. Johnson recalled that she conceived of the story while questioning the western myth of manly bravado: "I asked myself, what if one of these big, bold gunmen who are having the traditional walkdown is *not* fearless, and what if he can't even shoot. Then what have you got?"

Johnson's work modifies the formula of the strong, stoic western male. In her work, westerners (both male and female) are tough but not invincible. Speaking of the real westerners who inspired her characters, Johnson explained, "I think the people who headed West were a different kind of people. Somebody said in a long poem that the cowards never started and the weaklings fell by the way. That doesn't mean that everyone who went West was noble, brave, courageous, and admirable because some of them were utter skunks, but they were strong, and I like strong people."

Johnson focused on women's stories as well as men's. Women in Johnson's stories tend to be strong and loyal. Scholar Sue Hart notes that love and sacrifice are common themes in Johnson's work: "'I believe in love,' Johnson says—and her finest characters reflect that belief." Johnson also attempted to incorporate the perspectives of Indian women. Her novel *Buffalo Woman* focuses on the story of Whirlwind, an Oglala Sioux woman living in the aftermath of the Battle of Little Bighorn. Johnson considered *Buffalo Woman* to be one of her best books, and the National Cowboy Hall of Fame honored the work with its prestigious Western Heritage Award.

In her later life, Johnson published several articles about her childhood in *Montana The Magazine of Western History*. Her nonfiction expresses her love of Montana and her sense of the West's meaning. She described Whitefish as a "raw new town" filled with opportunity thanks to the jobs created by the Great Northern Railway. For the workers drawn to Whitefish, it was "the anteroom of paradise . . . the promised land, flowing with milk and honey. All they had to do to enjoy it was work."

The hardworking men and women of Whitefish stood in contrast to the "rich people and Eastern dudes" Johnson encountered in Glacier National Park. Interestingly, when she wrote of the social stratification she noticed among visitors to the park, she framed it in terms of an East-West divide: "We unrich Westerners were suspicious of the whole lot of them. We looked down on them because we thought they looked down on us. But they didn't even *see* us, which made the situation even more irritating. Years later, when I lived in a big Eastern city, I learned not to see strangers. . . . But in the uncrowded West, in *my* country, it's bad manners, and on the trail it's proper to acknowledge the existence of other human beings and say hello."

Above all, Johnson was a consummate westerner, and this helped her excel in a literary genre that tended to be associated with men. Johnson defended women's ability to write Westerns: "After all, men who write about the Frontier West weren't there either. We all get our historical background material from the same printed sources. An inclination to write about the frontier is not a sex-linked characteristic, like hair on the chest." Though Johnson never grew hair on her chest, she was, according to one friend, a "witty, gritty little bobcat of a woman," and her writings reflect her western spirit.

Progressive Reform and Women's Advocacy for Public Libraries in Montana

Annie Hanshew

AT THE January 24, 1914, meeting of the Hamilton Woman's Club, the club president "presented the idea of the Club boosting for [a] Carnegie Library building here." Club members concurred and appointed a committee to urge city officials to act. Mrs. J. F. Sullivan, head of the club's newly formed library committee, approached Hamilton's city council about asking industrialist and library benefactor Andrew Carnegie for funds. After Marcus Daly's widow, Margaret, donated the land for the building site, Carnegie's secretary approved the city's request. Two years later, the Hamilton Woman's Club moved its meetings to a specially designated room in the town's new Carnegie Library, an institution that owed its existence to the clubwomen's hard work.

The Hamilton Woman's Club's instrumental role in the library's construction is not an isolated case. During the Progressive Era, women's voluntary organizations frequently led community efforts to build public libraries. In 1933, the American Library Association estimated that three-quarters of the country's public libraries "owed their creation to women." More recently, scholars Kay Ann Cassell and Kathleen Weibel have argued that "women's organizations may well have been as influential in the development of public libraries as Andrew Carnegie," whose name is carved into thousands of library transoms across the United States.

Since the time of white settlement, Montanans seem to have been unusually passionate about books and libraries. In an 1877 edition of the *Butte Miner,* one writer noted, "The need for a library was felt here last winter, when aside from dancing there was no amusement whatever to help pass the long, dreary evenings. Dancing, in moderation, will do very well, but it is generally allowed to have been somewhat overdone last winter. . . . [T]his library scheme . . . will furnish a means of recreation . . . that is more intellectual and more to be desired in every respect."

Rising to the call, women's clubs founded libraries in communities

This 1901 postcard from the Union Circle of the King's Daughters was used to solicit books for the Virginia City library. MHS Archives, MC 262, Box 13.8

> Virginia City, Montana,_____1901.
> Dear
>   The Union Circle of the King's Daughters
> are organizing a Public Library. Will you
> assist to the extent of donating a book
> by mail? The name and address of donor
> should accompany each gift.
>   Yours Respectfully,
>
>   Address:
> For Public Library, Virginia City, Montana.

across Montana. Most of these libraries started small: club members donated books, and a local milliner, dressmaker, or hotelier would offer shelf space. As the library (and the community) grew, it often moved to a room in city hall before, finally, opening in a separate building. By 1896, Montana could boast seven public libraries with collections of a thousand volumes or more, and the State Federation of Women's Clubs maintained a system of traveling libraries.

At the turn of the century, library advocates in Montana received a boost from the Carnegie library grant program, which made funds available for library buildings if communities could prove they would provide a building site and tax support for the library's ongoing operation. In the first two decades of the twentieth century, seventeen Montana communities built public libraries using Carnegie funds.

The history of Carnegie libraries has been well documented, and this focus has led historians to emphasize the mayors and city council members who submitted the grant requests to the Carnegie Foundation. While Daniel Ring, for example, acknowledges women's contributions, he also underestimates their significance. "At least 50 percent of the pre-Carnegie Montana libraries owed their founding to the civic-minded women," according to Ring, and "When the Carnegie libraries came on the scene, it was usually women's clubs that alerted the city's power structure to the idea of obtaining a grant." However, Ring emphasizes, "the women could not act alone. Without the support of the male business elite, they were powerless." Thus, he delegitimizes women's political activism.

Truly, both men and women worked to establish libraries. However, their motives for engaging in the effort often differed. According to Ring, male politicians who promoted library development typically cared little about libraries as "educational institutions. Rather, the towns' elites used the libraries as a mechanism to control the new settlers socially, to boost the towns' fortunes, to exude a sense of permanence, and to bond the new-founded communities socially." By contrast, the clubwomen who founded public libraries had other intentions. Gender historian Anne Firor Scott concludes that "[w]omen's work for libraries was closely related to their work for public education." Members of women's voluntary associations linked education to self-improvement, and over the course of the twentieth century they increasingly viewed access to education as a key to "breaking the cycle of poverty."

Like many scholars of women's history, Scott recognizes that "Historians, looking at the past, do not see all that is there." Until recently, historians have overlooked and underestimated women's contributions to library development—in Montana and elsewhere—as well as to their work sustaining libraries after construction. Members of the Miles City Woman's Club, for example, made fund-raising for the town's Carnegie Library their "main objective" after the building was completed in 1902. And they were not alone. Today, East Glacier still relies on women's club volunteers to staff its library.

Montana's clubwomen played a crucial role in community improvement and educational development in the early twentieth century. Putting women back at the center of the state's library history sheds light on their achievements and offers recognition that is long overdue.

Queens of the Clouds: Montana's Pioneering Aviatrixes

Kate Hampton

WORKING FOR the Grace Shannon Balloon Company from 1893 through 1895, fearless Rubie Deveau thrilled crowds with her aerial acrobatics, ascending in a hot-air balloon until she "looked like a speck in the sky" and then parachuting back to earth. Like many other aerial pioneers, however, her career was short-lived. After 175 successful jumps, she was caught in an unexpected air current during her final descent and landed against a brick chimney, breaking her back. She was just eighteen. After she recovered, Deveau homesteaded in McIntosh, South Dakota, before marrying and moving to Missoula in 1925.

Early aerialists, including Rubie Deveau Owen, possessed an adventurous spirit that often overwhelmed reason. The list of those hurt and killed is distressingly long. Nevertheless, flight remained an exciting curiosity, with airplane manufacturers feeding the public's interest through exhibitions at fairs and other events.

Both men and women participated in these exhibitions. In 1913, just three years after Bud Mars made Montana's first recorded flight in an airplane, Katherine Stinson performed at the Helena fairgrounds. On a tour promoting the idea that the U.S. Postal Service could use airplanes, she thrilled crowds at the Montana State Fair, not only by performing stunts but also by flying bags of mail from the fairgrounds and dropping them onto Helena's downtown post office. Officially designated "the postmaster of the fairgrounds," she thus became the first to deliver airmail in Montana.

Barnstormer Katherine Stinson performed at the Montana State Fair in 1913. Among other stunts, she flew bags of mail from the fairgrounds to Helena's downtown post office, thus becoming the first person to deliver airmail in Montana. R. H. McKay, photographer, MHS Photo Archives 949-885

Montana women soon got into the act. Born in Billings in 1901, the headstrong only child of a prominent family, Maurine Allen loved mechanized travel, often taking her father's car on trips through the countryside. In 1927, she enrolled in a five-month flying course at Rogers Aviation School in Los Angeles. According to the *Billings Gazette*, she was one of the first women to earn her pilot's license in California. Allen returned to Billings in March 1928 to great fanfare, with local newspapers reporting that her skills as a female pilot, stunt flier, and even wing-walker had captured the interest of movie executives.

Desiring to be more than a stunt pilot, Allen hoped to earn a commercial license so she could work for the fledgling Yellowstone Air. It is unclear if she achieved her goal. Her boldness may have derailed her, for she had five forced landings during the next four years, and her flying career ended soon after.

Esther Combes Vance was the first aviatrix to receive her pilot's license in Montana. Born on August 19, 1903, in Clinton, Indiana, Esther moved as a young girl to Sidney, Montana. In 1921, she graduated from Sidney High School; four years later, she married a former World War I combat pilot and barnstormer Earl Vance. On July 17, 1928, the U.S. Department of Commerce issued Esther Vance private pilot license number 3,180. A year later, she became the twenty-second woman in the nation to receive a limited commercial license, which allowed her to carry passengers for Vance Air Service.

In an effort to connect professionally and socially and to advance their cause in aviation, in 1929 female pilots across the country formed the Ninety-Nines. As a charter member and regional chapter chair, Vance actively served the organization. The records she kept indicate that, even by the mid-1930s, Montana had only three licensed female pilots—commercial and personal. Vance remained connected to the Ninety-Nines throughout her life and established an organization scholarship for aspiring female Montana pilots that is still offered.

Like Esther Vance, Ruth Marie Hladik Nelson Dean embraced aviation during the late 1920s, not only as an exciting pastime but also as a practical career. Born in Iowa, Ruth grew up in Harlowton and Missoula. In 1926, she married Frank H. Nelson and moved to Butte. Tragically, Frank died on January 15, 1928, and at age twenty-four, she found herself widowed.

A month later, in February 1928, Ruth Nelson had her first airplane ride. She felt sick as pilot Robert Johnson, of the Johnson Flying School in Missoula, "indulged in dips and rolls." Despite this inauspicious beginning, she returned to the sky, logging two hundred flights, including twenty-five solos, by November of the same year. In addition to the art of flying, she "familiarized herself with . . . every department of airplane operation, with a view to fitting herself for the life of a first class pilot." Although she briefly managed a flying school, her flying career proved short-lived. By 1933, she was working in a more traditional profession for women: as a corsetiere at Fisher's Millinery in Helena.

Like their counterparts throughout the nation, Montana's early "Queens of the Clouds" received public accolades and attention from the press. They realized a freedom in flying that released them from social expectations. Their celebrated achievements, however, were presented as curiosities and only rarely resulted in long-term careers. Airplane manufacturers promoted female pilots to prove that "anybody" could learn to fly a plane. However, once they achieved their licenses, many women pilots found the industry inhospitable. In 1930, licensed female pilots nationwide numbered about two hundred, and through that decade their numbers only slowly increased.

With World War II, women's role in aviation took off as women proved to be vital to the war effort as pilots and mechanics. However, by the late 1940s, women experienced pressure to embrace more traditional roles and leave flying to the men. Today, the airline industry continues to be a male-dominated profession; of the fifty-three thousand members of the Air Line Pilots Association, only 5 percent are women.

"Men Were My Friends, but Women Were My Cause": The Career and Feminism of Frances Elge

Annie Hanshew

Frances Elge is notable as the first female county attorney in Montana, but her legacy to Montana's women goes far beyond that historic first. Described as "feisty," "outspoken," "blunt," and a "chic and wise magistrate," Elge once told a reporter, "Men were my friends, but women were my cause." Her work has had a real and lasting impact on women's political and legal rights in Montana.

Born in Helena in 1906, Elge attended that city's public schools and went on to graduate from law school at the State University of Montana in 1930. Reflecting on her time at the university and her subsequent career as an attorney, Elge recalled, "I was a novelty when I went through law school. The men helped me along because they didn't see me as competition. Men today know better."

After law school, she returned to Helena, where Wellington Rankin—a prominent Helena attorney and public official and brother of former congresswoman Jeannette Rankin—allowed her to use his library and office and gave her ten cases with which to start a private practice. She continued in private practice until 1932, when she was elected to the position of public

Frances Elge cultivated a deliberately ladylike style as she made her way up the ranks of the male-dominated legal profession. Montana's first woman elected county attorney, Elge was later one of the few women Indian probate judges for the Department of the Interior.
MHS Archives, Frances C. Elge Papers

FRANCES C. ELGE
FOR
COUNTY ATTORNEY
REPUBLICAN

administrator in Lewis and Clark County. Two years later, the voters elected her county attorney, the first woman to serve in that office.

After a single term, Elge left to work on Jeannette Rankin's second campaign for Congress and acted as the congresswoman's administrative assistant in Washington, D.C. During World War II, she worked for the War Shipping Administration and Maritime Commission. In 1954, she became an Indian probate judge for the Department of Interior, one of the only women in that position, and served until her retirement in 1977.

Elge's political activism was as noteworthy as her legal career. One of her early victories was to successfully lobby for jury service for women. Even though Montana women had attained the vote in 1914, they did not have the right to sit on juries. Supporters of women's jury service framed the argument in terms of equality. In a 1923 issue of the *Helena Independent*, one advocate wrote, "This obstacle should be removed for [women have] now . . . attained equal rights in all activities, the law, medicine, business, and the various professions. . . . [We] even have lady bootleggers."

Elge became interested in the issue after serving as county attorney and encountering all-male juries. Along with friend and fellow activist Belle Fligelman Winestine, Elge took up the cause through the League of Women Voters and National Federation of Business and Professional Women's Clubs. Winestine and Elge also created a coalition of support among organized labor and the Montana Farmers Union. Persuaded by their lobbying efforts, Montana passed the Women's Jury Service Act in 1939.

Elge continued to champion women's rights in Montana well past her retirement. She was "an omnipresent force" during the debate over Montana's ratification of the Equal Rights Amendment (ERA) in the early 1970s and again when anti-ERA forces mobilized to rescind ratification. A charter member of the Montana Council for the Equal Rights Amendment, she actively lobbied against nullification at the 1975, 1977, and 1979 legislative sessions.

Elge adopted a deliberately feminine style of politics that might have seemed old-fashioned in the second half of the twentieth century, but it was an approach that nonetheless served her well in her career and activism. Rather than acting and behaving "like a man" to succeed in the worlds of the law and politics, Elge remained, in her own words, "positive and aggressive without being abrasive." "I always played the game," she told a reporter in 1974. "I dressed in a feminine manner and I put up with the prejudice. Quietly but surely, I made my way up through the ranks."

Elge passed away in 1991 at the age of eighty-four. After her death, the Montana Supreme Court issued a resolution in her honor, crediting her with "a legacy of spirited advocacy on behalf of women, and ultimately on behalf of all humankind."

Oshanee Cullooyah Kenmille: A Joyful Spirit

Laura Ferguson

OSHANEE KENMILLE dedicated eight decades of her life to making beaded gloves, moccasins, cradleboards, and other leatherwork for family, friends, tribal members, celebrities, and dignitaries. She had very little formal education but learned from the Salish and Kootenai women in her life how to tan hides, sew buckskin clothing, and do beadwork. Kenmille then applied her expertise toward teaching others both these skills and the Salish and Kootenai languages, ensuring this cultural knowledge will continue with future generations. In spite of the many challenges and tragedies in her life, Oshanee Kenmille inspired others with her strength, her joyful spirit, and her commitment to preserving traditional tribal culture.

Oshanee's parents, Annie and Paul Cullooyah, maintained their traditional Salish way of life on the Flathead Reservation. Oshanee, who was born in 1916, began beading at age eleven while watching her mother, whose praise for Oshanee's first efforts inspired the child to develop her beading skills. Annie, who died in 1928 when Oshanee was only twelve years old, did not live long enough to see how well Oshanee succeeded.

Like many other American Indian children of her generation, Oshanee was sent away from her home in Arlee to a boarding school. At the Villa Ursuline School in St. Ignatius, the nuns cut Oshanee's long hair, dressed her in a school uniform, and called her Agnes. Soon Oshanee and a handful of other homesick students ran away, walking home over the mountain pass to Arlee. Forced to return to the boarding school, Oshanee continued to run away. Finally, the agent on the Flathead Reservation had her sent to a boarding school in DeSmet, Idaho, hoping the distance from home would keep her in school. Within a year, Oshanee returned home, and her brother recruited her to help pick sugar beets that summer. That fall, instead of returning to school, Oshanee got married. She was fourteen years old.

Oshanee's husband, Edward Stasso, was Kootenai and did not speak Salish. Oshanee did not yet speak Kootenai. Her husband communicated largely in sign language because he was hard of hearing, so she learned to sign. She also learned the laborious traditional methods of hide tanning from Edward's mother and beading from his sisters. A year and a half into their marriage, Edward died from tuberculosis. Within a couple of years, Oshanee married again, this time to Joe Mathias, another Kootenai, who encouraged her interest in tanning and leatherwork. Again, however, tragedy broke apart her family when Joe was killed in a construction accident at the Kerr Dam, leaving Oshanee to raise their young daughters.

To support her children, Oshanee relied on her developing talents as a hide tanner and beadwork artisan to create moccasins, gloves, and beaded clothing she could sell to earn a living on the reservation, where jobs were scarce. Over time, she became an expert at brain-tanning hides and produced soft, supple hides of superior quality, which she then made into regalia, clothing, cradleboards, and handbags decorated with beadwork. Her excellent workmanship made her products very popular among local residents, tourists, and collectors. She raised her family, which had grown to four more children after her marriage to Camille Kenmille, on the proceeds from her work, which she supplemented with seasonal income from picking apples in Washington.

Tanning and beadwork offered Oshanee Kenmille a means for becoming self-reliant, and she worked hard to perfect these skills. As her products became increasingly popular, Kenmille recognized that she had valuable cultural knowledge to share with the world. For over twenty years, she taught hide tanning and beadwork at the tribal college in Pablo, an endeavor that brought her great happiness. Her students learned that it took hard work to perfect these skills and came to appreciate their cultural heritage. They also learned that a person could suffer great personal tragedies and still radiate a joyful outlook on life.

Through her example, Kenmille demonstrated that challenges—in her case the lack of formal education, the loss of her parents and husbands, and single motherhood—did not have to become barriers that prevented a person from achieving happiness or meeting their responsibilities. When she could no longer tan hides, her granddaughter, Gigi Caye, stepped in to teach at the college.

Oshanee Kenmille earned much-deserved recognition for her work and her cultural leadership, including a Montana Indian Educator of the Year award, a Governor's Award for Lifetime Achievement, and a National Heritage Fellowship from the National Endowment for the Arts. Celebrities, governors, foreign dignitaries, and presidents are among the recipients of her artistic work. For years, she was the head woman dancer at the annual Arlee powwow, where other dancers and tribal members proudly continue to wear items she made. Her gifts to the world are not just physical and

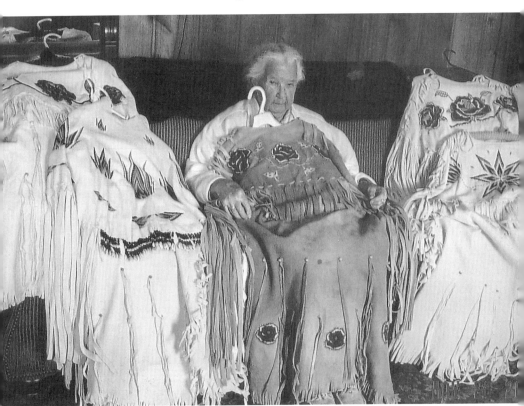

Oshanee Kenmille poses with some examples of her work, ca. 2007. Courtesy Gigi Caye

aesthetic; she also shared her joyful spirit. "Few people have eyes that literally sparkled like Oshanee's did," her friend Germaine White recalls, "and
that sparkle went all the way to her heart and came from her heart."

Sister Providencia: Advocate for Landless Indians

Laura Ferguson

IN 1952, a nun teaching sociology at the College of Great Falls committed
herself to alleviating poverty among the city's Indians. What began as an
effort to solve a local problem grew into a twenty-year crusade on behalf
of all American Indians, taking Sister Providencia Tolan from Great Falls
to the halls of Congress. In the process, she collaborated with charitable
organizations and Indian advocates to change the course of federal Indian
policy.

Great Falls's Indian residents lived primarily in makeshift communities
like Hill 57 on the edge of town. Their overcrowded shacks lacked utilities.
Many were unskilled, undereducated seasonal laborers who struggled to
provide for their families. For years, concerned citizens donated necessities
to provide stopgap assistance. While supporting these efforts, Sister Providencia also approached the matter as a sociologist: studying the problem,
ascertaining its root causes, and advocating social and political solutions.

One cause of the urban Indians' plight was the matter of jurisdiction.
The federal government denied responsibility for unenrolled, non-
recognized, or off-reservation Indians. City, county, and state agencies
frequently refused assistance out of the misconception that all Indians were
wards of the federal government.

Compounding the jurisdictional conundrum were two federal Indian
policies instituted in the 1950s that increased Indian landlessness and poverty: Termination and Relocation. Under Termination, the federal government dissolved its trust responsibilities to certain tribes. Deprived of
services and annuities promised them in treaties, terminated tribes liq-
uidated their assets for immediate survival. When the Turtle Mountain
Chippewa tribe was terminated in 1953, some families moved to Great Falls
to live with their already impoverished relatives on Hill 57. The Relocation
policy moved Indian families to cities without ensuring that they had the
means for long-term survival. Meanwhile, the government did not increase
aid to states or counties so that they could cope with the expanding numbers of people in need.

"The restricting of Bureau welfare programs and the present hardship situation . . . are cause and consequence," Sister Providencia concluded. She contended that policies that dismantled tribes also eroded tribal values and broke down Indian families. The nun witnessed this disintegration in Great Falls, where teenage Indian girls became prostitutes to earn money for food and desperate young men committed suicide. Sister Providencia encountered a boy from a Chippewa family who "stood crying at the reception desk of the hospital, his pockets full of leaves. He told me that they were his only food for two days."

Sister Providencia insisted that Montanans had to "spearhead the drive aimed at reaching a solution" to Indian poverty. She urged local institutions to increase their contributions of goods and services and rallied the press for greater coverage of the issue. Her students conducted comprehensive sociological studies of poverty among Great Falls's Indian population and then went on the radio to ask why "Uncle Sam should forget his treaty obligations to these Indian people, just because they have been forced to leave their reservations?"

Sister Providencia realized that Indians who were repeatedly denied relief, medical services, and aid believed that white society did not care if they survived, so she worked with the Community Council of Cascade County to hold public forums on Termination and off-reservation Indian poverty. The College of Great Falls and the Friends of Hill 57 sponsored "Workshops in Understanding" to build empathy among non-Indians. Testimony from women who had provided educational assistance, secured donations of food and clothing, and arranged to bring utilities to Hill 57 revealed the severity of the problem and underscored the need for federal involvement.

Sister Providencia found allies in the Montana Intertribal Policy Board (MT-IPB) and Montana's Advisory Council on Indian Affairs, two groups fighting reservation poverty and Termination. Beginning in 1953, officers of the MT-IPB were elected to the National Congress of American Indians (NCAI)—the most influential Indian policy organization in the country. Sister Providencia became an advisor to both the MT-IPB and the NCAI.

Together, they pressured the government to uphold its obligations. In 1957, Montana's legislature passed four joint memorials demanding restoration of federal obligation in matters of Indian welfare, education, employment, and health care. Montana's Senator James Murray and Representative Lee Metcalf introduced reform legislation in Congress. Encouraged by

Sister Providencia, the Great Falls Business and Professional Women sponsored a woman from Hill 57 to travel to Washington to testify in favor of the proposals.

Despite an abundance of testimony supporting the reforms, the Interior Department blocked their passage. Commissioner of Indian Affairs Glenn Emmons also refused an offer by Great Falls landowners to donate Hill 57 lots for a landless Indian reservation, insisting the Indians should apply for relocation assistance through their reservations—assistance for which non-recognized or terminated Indians were ineligible.

A breakthrough in their efforts came when Sister Providencia invited broadcaster Robert McCormick to visit Hill 57 and provided him with material for a documentary. Broadcast by NBC in November 1958, *The American*

Sister Providencia, shown here with Eleanor Roosevelt, brought crafts from nine Northwest tribes to display in the House Indian Affairs committee room at the U.S. Capitol in 1941. Providence Archives, Seattle, Washington

Stranger exposed the government's neglect of its indigenous citizens. Sister Providencia convinced NBC to make copies of the documentary available for rebroadcast around Montana and elsewhere. Within days, NBC, Metcalf, and the Bureau of Indian Affairs received thousands of letters from Americans faulting the Interior Department.

Sister Providencia never stopped lobbying. When vice-presidential candidate Lyndon Johnson campaigned in Great Falls in 1959, the nun reminded him of the government's obligations to American Indians. Johnson agreed that their condition was "a federal responsibility."

The tide finally turned in the 1960s when President Johnson launched the War on Poverty. Sister Providencia, the NCAI, and Indian leaders worked closely with Metcalf to ensure War on Poverty programs addressed Indians' need for educational assistance, welfare, medical services, and job training. Together, they helped end Termination and ushered in self-determination policies that restored the nation-to-nation relationship between tribes and the federal government.

Number, Please: Women Telephone Operators

Ellen Arguimbau

THE FIRST TELEPHONE arrived in Montana in 1876, the same year Alexander Graham Bell patented his invention, and by the 1890s many Montana cities had telephone exchanges. Early telephones needed to be connected directly by wire. To facilitate that connection, telephone companies established exchanges, staffed almost entirely by young female operators. "The caller telephoned the operator and asked to be connected to someone. The operator then plugged the wire into the call recipient's slot."

"Number, Please," an article published in *Montana The Magazine of Western History,* describes the working conditions of these female employees:

> Often a maze of cords and sockets, switchboards were attended by one operator in a small exchange or by a roomful of operators in the larger towns, usually all young women. According to a 1902 U.S. Census Bureau report: "For many years it has been recognized that operators' work in telephone exchanges attracts a superior class of women. It has been demonstrated beyond all doubt that the work of operating is better handled by women than by men or

Telephone operators worked at hotels as well as at exchanges. Photographed here is Helen (last name unknown), an operator at Many Glacier Hotel in Glacier National Park in 1925. At the time, park concessionaires often required their Blackfeet employees—including bus drivers and telephone operators—to dress in "traditional" clothing to appeal to tourists. Bain News Service, Library of Congress Prints and Photographs Division, Washington, D.C.

boys and that trained and well-bred women operators perform the most satisfactory service.

Although female telephone operators may have been recognized for their abilities, they often worked long hours for very low pay. For example, in 1907 Rocky Mountain Bell operators' wages were frequently as low as thirty to forty dollars per month for a ten- to twelve-hour day. That year, Butte operators struck for higher wages and an eight-hour day, and the company, in recognition of their united strength, almost immediately agreed to a minimum wage of fifty dollars per month, an eight-hour day, and a closed shop. That same year, the legislature enacted a law banning the employment of girls under the age of sixteen as telephone operators and in 1909 limited the hours of telephone operators to nine hours per day in cities and towns of more than three thousand people, except under special circumstances of illness or emergency.

Dorothy Johnson worked as an operator in Whitefish starting in 1919. She described her experience:

> The board was a vast expanse of eyes, with, at the base, a dozen or so pairs of plugs on cords for connecting and an equal number of keys for talking, listening, and ringing. On a busy day these cords were woven across the board in a constantly changing, confusing pattern; half the people using telephones were convinced that Central was incompetent or hated them, and Central—flipping plugs into holes, ringing numbers, trying to remember whether 44 wanted 170-K or 170-L, because if she went back and asked him, he'd be sure she was stupid—was close to hysterics. It was every operator's dream that when her ship came in she would open all the keys on a busy board, yell "To hell with you," pull all the plugs, and march out in triumph, leaving everything in total chaos. Nobody ever did. We felt an awful responsibility toward our little corner of the world. We really helped keep it running, one girl at a time all by herself at the board.

"You Had to Pretend It Never Happened": Illegal Abortion in Montana

Annie Hanshew

TERMINATING A PREGNANCY was illegal in Montana until 1973, when the U.S. Supreme Court ruled in the case of *Roe v. Wade* that abortion was a constitutionally protected right. Nevertheless, the practice of abortion was still commonplace. The stories of Montana women who obtained illegal abortions reveal the uncertainty, fear, shame, and danger they experienced.

Abortion before "quickening" (fetal movement) was legal in the United States prior to the 1860s, but around 1860 politicians and members of the American Medical Association campaigned to outlaw the practice. During Montana's territorial period, it was illegal to induce abortions with either medicine or instruments except in cases where the life of the mother was at risk. By 1895, the woman receiving the abortion as well as the person performing it were subject to prosecution.

The criminalization of abortion did not mean the end of the practice, and Montana women continued to seek professional help, or in some cases, to help each other, when they wanted to terminate a pregnancy. The practice decreased as women had greater access to contraceptives in the twentieth century, but a variety of factors—ranging from fear of complications during pregnancy to the shame of childbirth out of wedlock—meant that there was continued demand for underground abortions.

Anna Dunbar grew up in Bozeman and was married and living in New York City when she became pregnant in the summer of 1963 at the age of twenty-two. Her husband had children from a previous marriage and "wasn't really terribly interested in having any more." Dunbar recalled how agonizing the decision was: "I didn't want children at that time either, but somehow when you find yourself pregnant and you're married and it sort of . . . it was a very, very difficult decision for me to make." Dunbar had the support of her parents; she remembered her father saying, "In civilized countries, they do this in the hospitals." Consequently, she returned to Montana to seek an abortion with Dr. Sadie Lindeberg in Miles City.

Dunbar was fortunate to have found a safe and reputable physician to perform her surgery. Other Montana women were not as lucky. One recalled her horrific experience with an abortion provider in Shelby after becoming pregnant at the age of sixteen:

> I looked around, and, God, it was just a stainless steel basin . . . with these instruments in it. . . . [T]he water was bloody, and there was a sort of film of crud over the instruments. And . . . there was blood on the floor, and there was another bowl that had these sort of bloody looking sponges in it. . . . I'd heard terrible stories . . . how these women just, you know, died. They got infections and they hemorrhaged and they died. And I sat there and I realized, God, this is going to happen to me.

In this case, the provider seems to have been an elderly doctor, but in other instances women received abortions from prostitutes or even performed the procedure themselves with the help of a trusted friend. Almost always the abortion was performed without anesthesia.

Despite moral and religious objections, poverty was frequently the impetus for ending a pregnancy. Historians estimate that during the Great Depression as many as one in four pregnancies was terminated. A woman who identified herself as E.M. had multiple abortions in the early 1930s. She

238

EDWIN S. KELLOGG, M. D.,
SURGEON.

HARRIET A. THAYER, M. D.,
RESIDENT PHYSICIAN AND MANAGER.

KELLOGG SANITARIUM.

20 N. Benton Avenue, HELENA, MONTANA.

>+FOR THE TREATMENT OF+<

**Surgical Diseases, Obstetrics, Diseases of Women and all
CHRONIC AILMENTS**

The only Private Hospital in the city. New and complete in all its appointments, with Faradic Electric Baths. Established Exclusively for the sick, affording careful nursing and the comforts of a home.

>+ALSO A COMPLETE X-RAY APPARATUS+<

Terms Reasonable.   Correspondence Solicited

Although he was never convicted, Helena homeopath Edwin Kellogg, whose 1898 advertisement is shown here, had at least seven encounters with the law between 1893 and 1915 over allegations that he performed abortions. At least two of his alleged patients died from the procedure. Polk's *Helena City Directory* (Helena, Mont., 1898), 238

was married, but she and her husband felt it was "unethical" to have children that they could not provide for. They attempted a variety of birth control methods—cold water and turpentine douches, condoms, diaphragms—but she still became pregnant three times and, in each case, decided to terminate the pregnancy. In the 1940s, when their farm was more economically stable, E.M. and her husband had two daughters. She later told an interviewer that she felt her daughters grew up to enjoy successful lives because they were "planned."

For women who obtained illegal abortions, the secrecy, shame, and horrific conditions all had a lasting effect. One woman recalled, "Now I'm aware of how demeaning that was, that the whole thing was so shameful. . . .

[Y]ou had to keep it a secret. You had to pretend it never happened. It's just denying such a part of yourself." Some women were politicized by their experiences and joined the women's rights movement of the late 1960s. One interviewee even began to assist a doctor who performed abortions: "When it was over, I just said, 'God, that is never going to happen to me again, ever. If I have anything to do about it, it's never going to happen to anybody that I know ever again.'"

Expanding Their Sphere: Montana Women in Education Administration and Public Health

Laura Ferguson

As MOTHERS and homemakers, women have historically presided over child and family welfare. By extension, their purview has included education and health care. Before the mid-twentieth century, teaching and nursing were the socially acceptable occupations providing avenues for women to expand their influence in public affairs. Making the most of limited opportunities, many teachers and nurses became school superintendents or public health nurses. Often collaborating to achieve their goals, these leaders in education and community health significantly improved Montanans' lives.

Montana's women did not obtain full suffrage until 1914, but they had participated in school elections since the 1880s. In 1882, Helen Clarke and Alice Nichols became the first two women elected to public office in Montana, both of them as county school superintendents. Their duties included visiting schools, recommending necessary improvements to buildings and curricula, and creating teacher licensure exams. They also coordinated teacher institutes to advance teachers' skills. By 1890, twelve of Montana's sixteen county superintendents were women. Since that time, the majority of the state's county superintendents have been women.

Coinciding with the ascendance of women county school super-intendents was the rise of public health nurses. The Montana State Board of Health, formed in 1901, employed four field nurses in an effort to decrease high infant and maternal mortality rates and to curb the spread of infectious diseases. Serving a population spread across hundreds of square miles, these field nurses traveled extensively to educate the public about disease transmission, hygiene, nutrition, and infant care. "These women supervise the work of all nurses in their districts," reported the director of the state's Child Welfare Division. "In conjunction with the county super-intendent of schools and women's organizations, they . . . hold children's health conferences in schools . . . and advise prospective mothers concern-ing the importance of securing medical supervision." One of these field nurses, Henrietta Crockett, established the first infant health clinic on a Montana Indian reservation in 1925 and engaged tribal members in the public health campaign.

The goals of public health and education often intersected. Schools were essential to the success of public health efforts because they were ideal locations for evaluating children's health, counseling maturing girls, and holding vaccination drives. Although the federal Sheppard-Towner Act of 1920 provided limited funds for states to hire school nurses, public health nurses often filled this duty until statewide school funding improved. Their school visits coincided with well-baby clinics (often also held in schools), presentations on maternity care, and home health visits. Public health nurses supported superintendents' crusades for indoor plumbing, adequate light-ing, and better ventilation in schools. They also backed superintendents' efforts to retain nurses in each district.

Many women who became educators or nurses did so because of the career limitations placed on them in other fields. "I learned that I wasn't equal when I was thirteen years old," recalled Virginia Kenyon. Excluded from the vocational agriculture courses offered to boys in the late 1920s, Kenyon decided to become a nurse. Then, after she completed nurse's train-ing in Great Falls, she took advantage of the 1935 Social Security Act to fund her education in public health nursing. During her twenty-one-year career in rural Montana, Kenyon observed the discrimination public health nurses faced. "I would like to have had physicians accept the nurses in the field for what they could do, and not fight them as they had! We just had a battle with them all the time!" Kenyon believed that male county physicians resented the challenges to their authority that public health nurses represented.

Female county superintendents encountered similar resistance from male trustees, who often opposed reforms and seemed indifferent to the educational needs of children. Noting that trustees repeatedly failed to budget adequately for teachers, supplies, and schools, Dawson County superintendent Alice Cavanaugh declared in her annual report in 1890: "There is one thing we need in our country schools, and that is a more competent and energetic class of Trustees and Clerks who will look after the financial affairs of our districts."

The wage gap between men and women in skilled professions reveals one of the most significant aspects of the gendered discrimination faced by female educators and nurses, who received 50 to 80 percent of what men earned. As late as 1949, public health nurses were among the lowest-paid professionals in the state.

Despite such difficulties, women superintendents and public health nurses made significant gains for the public and in their careers. The election of May Trumper as Montana's first female state superintendent of Public Instruction in 1916 began an era of statewide school reform. During her twelve-year tenure, Trumper instituted many of the reforms that women county superintendents had been recommending for decades: a 180-day school term statewide, better teacher training and more rigorous certification exams, more school nurses, better teacher pay, vocational training programs in high schools, and the first statewide equalization of district funding. Since Trumper's election nearly a century ago, all but one of Montana's state superintendents have been women.

By 1950, Montana had one public health nurse for almost each of its fifty-six counties. Many became leaders in their field and influenced public health policies. Pioneering public health nurse Henrietta Crockett was also executive secretary for the Montana Tuberculosis Association and led the state's efforts to eradicate that disease. Virginia Kenyon became the Public

Public health nurse Margaret Thomas (shown here ca. 1925, back left) traveled throughout western Montana organizing well-baby clinics, lecturing on nutrition, caring for the sick, and sponsoring school health contests. MHS Photo Archives Lot 30, Box 2, Folder 9

Health Division director for the State Board of Health and represented Montana's nurses in state and national professional organizations.

Montana owes much of the improvements in education and public health to its women school superintendents and public health nurses. Their dedication to the well-being of children and communities stimulated important local and statewide accomplishments, including a decline in the spread of infectious diseases, significant reforms in public schools, and expanded educational and public health services throughout the state.

Laura Howey, the Montana Historical Society, and Sex Discrimination in Early Twentieth-Century Montana

Annie Hanshew

LAURA SPENCER HOWEY was a prominent Helena pioneer and activist. Her work as librarian of the Historical and Miscellaneous Department of the Montana State Library (now the Montana Historical Society) is her enduring legacy, as she ensured the preservation of thousands of books, documents, and artifacts relevant to Montana's early history. Her abrupt dismissal from that position in 1907 shows one way that sex discrimination operated in the early twentieth century.

Laura was born in Cadiz, Ohio, in 1851. Her father died when she was young, and her mother taught school to support herself and two young children. A biography of Howey credits her mother as "one of the foremost and best female teachers in that part of Ohio" and a "remarkably well read woman" who raised her children "in the refining atmosphere of books and music." Laura attended Beaver College, a prominent women's college in Pennsylvania, where she studied music, French, and drama. While teaching at Harlem Springs College in Ohio, she met fellow professor and her future husband Robert E. Howey.

The Howeys moved to Helena in 1879 so that Robert could take a position as superintendent of schools. Both Laura and Robert were ardent Progressives who supported a number of reforms, ranging from women's education to prostitution reform. Laura was especially active in the temperance movement. She served as the president of the Montana Woman's Christian Temperance Union and was friends with national president Frances Willard.

In 1898, Laura Howey was appointed to the position of head librarian of the Historical and Miscellaneous Department of the Montana State Library.

Laura Howey was instrumental in building the Montana Historical Society, known during her tenure as the Historical and Miscellaneous Department of the Montana State Library. Pictured here is the library's reference room, then located in the basement of the Capitol. MHS Photo Archives 952-768

The Montana territorial legislature had approved the establishment of a historical society in 1865, making it the second oldest institution of its kind west of the Mississippi. However, the society had languished in its first three decades. Howey, college-educated and a former trustee of the Helena city library, brought a new sense of professionalism to the library. She created a card catalog, bound the library's historic newspaper collection, collected and organized state documents, published four volumes of recollections and diaries from Montana's pioneers, and actively lobbied for funding from both the state legislature and private donors.

But Howey's tenure as head librarian ended abruptly in 1907 when Montana's attorney general, Albert Galen, published an opinion finding that a woman could not serve in that position because women did not have the right to vote. He argued, "It being apparent that the Librarian of the Historical Library of the State is a public officer, it necessarily follows that, in order for a person to be eligible to hold such office, he must be qualified to vote at general elections and for state officers in this State, as provided by Section 11, Article IX, of the State Constitution."

Howey was a prominent and popular figure, and Galen's opinion drew immediate criticism. The *Sheridan Enterprise* advised Galen to "Leave Mrs. Howey alone and get busy on your own affairs." The *Joliet Journal* jokingly suggested that Howey should replace Galen: "From our observation, Montana would now be much better equipped in her law department had she elected a woman like Mrs. Howie [*sic*] to the office of attorney general." One of the most scathing critiques came from a writer at the *Stockgrowers Journal*, who (also jokingly) wrote that the injustice of Howey's dismissal was almost enough to sway him to the cause of women's suffrage:

> If there is one argument, or one condition of affairs, that could move this paper to change its views as to the terrible inexpediency and absolute error of the granting the electorate to the fair but fickle sex, it might be found in this obnoxious ruling of the attorney general. In order that the important office Mrs. Howey now so admirably fills should be hers till she chose to resign it, we would almost consent to fraternize with that awful [Carrie Chapman] Catt woman and urge female suffrage on a people already blighted through a too wide diffusion of this inestimable privilege. That shows what we think of Mrs. Howey as a public official.

In spite of its unpopularity, Galen's decision stood. Even as the board of trustees chose her replacement, they adopted a resolution stating their regret that they were legally prevented from rehiring Mrs. Howey and "their high appreciation of the eminent services rendered by Mrs. Howey as Librarian." According to historian Brian Shovers, the loss of Howey's leadership was extremely detrimental: "During the next twenty-five years, funding stagnated, collecting slowed, [and] library space gave way to other state offices."

After her dismissal, Howey continued to be active in the Helena community. She taught civics and mathematics at Helena's Montana Wesleyan University and engaged in charitable work. She died in 1911 from ongoing heart trouble. Her obituary in the *Helena Independent* described her as "one of the best known women in the state" and "a woman of marked executive ability" whose "death came as a great shock to hundreds of admiring friends here and many more throughout the state of Montana." Howey died just three years before women gained the right to vote—and therefore hold office—in Montana.

Susie Walking Bear Yellowtail: "Our Bright Morning Star"

Laura Ferguson

Susie Walking Bear Yellowtail was among the first Apsáalooke (Crow) people to achieve a higher education. Like many Native children of her generation, she attended mission boarding schools where students were expected to give up their indigenous languages, beliefs, and cultural ways. Instead, Yellowtail maintained her Apsáalooke identity and, guided by her cultural heritage, used her education to improve the lives of American Indian people.

Born in 1903 and orphaned as a child, Susie grew up in Pryor and attended a boarding school on the Crow Reservation. As the only child who spoke English, Susie translated for the other students. With her missionary foster parents, Susie soon left the reservation for Oklahoma, where she briefly attended a Baptist school. Her guardian, Mrs. C. A. Field, then sent Susie to Northfield Seminary in Massachusetts. Mrs. Field paid Susie's

In 1927, Susie Walking Bear (back row, center, with her graduating class from the Boston City Hospital's School of Nursing) became the first member of the Crow Nation and one of the first Indians in the country to become a registered nurse. MHS Photo Archives PAc 87-70

tuition, but Susie earned her room and board by working as a housemaid and babysitter.

After graduation, Susie continued her education by enrolling at Boston City Hospital's School of Nursing. She graduated with honors in 1923 and finished her training at Franklin County Public Hospital in Greenfield, Massachusetts. In 1927, Susie Walking Bear became the first registered nurse of Crow descent and one of the first degreed registered nurses of American Indian ancestry in the United States.

After working with other tribes for a few years, Susie returned to the Crow Reservation and married Thomas Yellowtail, a fellow Crow who also continued to practice Apsáalooke spiritual and cultural traditions. Susie Yellowtail worked first at the government-run hospital at Crow Agency and then traveled to other reservations as a consultant for the Public Health Service. Wherever she went, she observed similar problems: appalling living conditions and unmet health-care needs on the reservations, the need for cultural competency among medical professionals working with indigenous people, and the need for immediate reforms in the Indian Health Service.

Yellowtail documented instances of Indian children dying from lack of access to medical care, Indian women being sterilized without consent, and tribal elders unable to communicate their health concerns to doctors. She also pushed for effective improvements to the Indian Health Service, such as allowing traditional tribal healers to attend Indian patients and creating the Community Health Representatives outreach program on reservations. In the words of her daughter, Connie, "She became a watchdog on health care for Indians."

Throughout her career, Yellowtail served on Indian health and education councils at the tribal, state, and federal levels, including as an appointee to the President's Council on Indian Education and Nutrition and the U.S. Department of Health, Education and Welfare's Council on Indian Health under three different administrations. In each of these positions, she advocated for improved health care, better access to care, and better living conditions for American Indians. "When she talked, people—both Indian and non-Indian—listened. Why? Because this woman spoke with experience, knowledge and conviction about the poor health conditions of the Indians and how to make the Indian healthy and strong once again. She also had great concern for the education of her people," said her friend, tribal historian Joe Medicine Crow.

Yellowtail knew that education could help Indians improve their situation, not by taking something essential from them, but by giving them a chance to apply their cultural values in ways that built up their communities. While she advocated for formal education, she also promoted Crow culture through involvement in events such as the annual All-American Indian Days and by serving as chaperone for the Miss Indian America contestants. Susie and Thomas Yellowtail were among the federal government's American Indian goodwill ambassadors to several foreign nations in the 1950s, cheerfully sharing their cultural heritage and Susie's fine beadwork with people around the world.

At home, Yellowtail exemplified Apsáalooke maternal commitment to the well-being of children. She raised three of her own as well as several other youngsters and took in other people in need. Joe Medicine Crow observed that Yellowtail became increasingly concerned with child welfare: "She realized that the modern Crow family is no longer strong and stable and that young parents often neglected, abused and even abandoned their children. She wanted to establish a children's home and orphanage on the Crow Reservation." Although she did not live to accomplish this goal, Yellowtail's adherence to Crow values, her pride in her Crow identity, and her devotion to her community serve as models for present and future generations.

Deservedly, Susie Walking Bear Yellowtail received the President's Award for Outstanding Nursing Health Care and is included among the honorees in the Gallery of Outstanding Montanans in the Capitol Rotunda in Helena. Among the Crow, she will forever remain "our bright morning star."

Minnie Two Shoes: American Indian Journalist

Laura Ferguson

IN 2009, the Native American Journalists Association (NAJA) honored Minnie Eder Two Shoes of Fort Peck with an award for journalistic excellence. A cofounder of the association, Two Shoes was known for her journalistic integrity and her hallmark sense of humor. Two Shoes worked as writer, assistant editor, and columnist for the *Wotanin Wowapi* of Poplar. She served as an editor for *Native Peoples*; as an editor, writer, and producer for *Aboriginal Voices*, a Canadian magazine and radio show; and as a contributor to *News from Indian Country*. As a journalist, she helped reinvestigate the 1975 murder of AIM member Anna Mae Aquash. Throughout her career, Two Shoes blended humor with serious inquiry into matters affecting Indian Country.

Minnie Two Shoes (third from right, standing) is pictured with other founding members of the Native American Press Association at Penn State in 1984. Ronnie Washines memorialized Two Shoes in 2010, writing, "[S]he was a sincere advocate of free press, free speech, and free food for everyone." Sequoyah National Research Center, Little Rock, Arkansas

Born Minnie Eder in Poplar in 1950, Two Shoes began her career in 1970 as a publicist for the American Indian Movement (AIM). Founded in 1968 as an advocacy organization for American Indian prisoners, AIM coordinated several highly publicized protests in the early 1970s, including the nineteen-month occupation of Alcatraz Island in 1969–1971, the occupation of the Bureau of Indian Affairs building in Washington, D.C., in 1972, and the occupation of Wounded Knee, South Dakota, in 1973.

AIM's goal was to bring national attention to the political, economic, and social injustices facing American Indians, but the FBI considered AIM an "agitator" organization. In an attempt to sabotage AIM, the FBI planted informants in the organization, fracturing the trust between its members. In early 1975, AIM leaders questioned Two Shoes about providing information to the FBI and exiled her, despite her claims of innocence. That summer, two male AIM leaders interrogated Two Shoes's friend, Anna Mae Aquash, at gunpoint. A Mi'kmaq from Canada and one of AIM's most dedicated participants, Aquash was murdered six months later.

In 1980, Two Shoes started a women's traditional society at Wolf Point and in 1983 earned a BA in community development. She began contributing articles to the *Wotanin Wowapi*, then an all-women-run newspaper. From 1987 to 1990, she studied at the School of Journalism at the University of Missouri and continued writing for the *Wotanin Wowapi* through the 1990s.

Two Shoes's column, "Red Road Home," reflected her ability to inject humor into almost any topic. A classic example is Two Shoes's story about getting pulled over by a gloved cop and asked to perform a sobriety test. "As I got out of the car, my mind was racing. WHAT IS a drunk test? . . . I thought it had something to do with blowing up a balloon, but was I ever wrong! It was like a college exam, with more than one section." So startled was Two Shoes that she "forgot to tell Black Leather Glove Man about the bad tires" that made it difficult to steer her dilapidated car, Rez Bomb. She passed the test and ended her article with a jab at the economic disparities between reservation Indians and non-Indians living elsewhere, stating that she drove Rez Bomb "for the sake of recycling." "That's what I tell my kids when they ask why the cars on the reservation are older models. . . . We're using up our cars all the way, like the old Indians did with the buffalo."

A fellow journalist observed that Two Shoes "could stir emotion by pointing out society's cruel injustices, but lampoon them in the next breath with her hilarious quips. It was her way of pushing people out of their comfort zones. . . . In the process, she provoked them to think about issues that mainstream America would rather ignore." In addition to reporting on reservation poverty, Two Shoes wrote about safe houses for domestic violence victims, environmental contamination on reservations, and the high rates of cancer-related deaths among American Indian women.

Two Shoes was not afraid to speak against injustice wherever she found it. She criticized male AIM members who got drunk, slept around, and fathered children they did not raise. At a NAJA convention in the 1970s, she responded to a non-Indian feminist's criticism that women in AIM let the men take all the credit for AIM's accomplishments by asserting that anonymity enabled AIM women to carry out their work with less scrutiny from the FBI.

In fact, the FBI's attempt to co-opt highly visible AIM women like

Anna Mae Aquash made them objects of suspicion. When Aquash, who led extensive community-building and educational efforts, was killed in late 1975, the FBI claimed she died of exposure. A second autopsy revealed that she had been shot in the head.

In the 1990s, Two Shoes played a crucial role in the NAJA's reinvestigation of Aquash's murder. Two Shoes contacted AIM participants she knew from the 1970s, reviewed FBI files, and helped piece together what happened in 1975. In 2004, two AIM members were tried and convicted of Aquash's murder. Many former AIM activists, including Two Shoes, attributed Aquash's death, ultimately, to the paranoia created by the FBI's infiltration of AIM.

After the Aquash investigation, Two Shoes moved to Minneapolis, where she continued her journalism career and mentored younger Native journalists. At the 2009 NAJA conference, she noted that when the association was first founded, it boasted only a handful of members; by its twenty-fifth year, there were nearly five hundred. "Part of what we said years ago was that we wanted to create journalists to take our places," Two Shoes said. "And I've got some really tiny shoes to fill!"

Using humor and her "rapier-like wit" to expose the often serious matters facing Indian Country was Two Shoes's journalistic specialty. A year before she died of cancer in 2010, Two Shoes reflected on her twenty-five-year career: "[As] journalists we [are] very special people, and we have a very serious responsibility, but that doesn't mean we can't have fun along the way!" And she did.

A Department of One's Own: Women's Studies at the University of Montana

Kayla Blackman

IN THE 1970S, women activists across the nation experienced growing dissatisfaction. As participants in the civil rights and antiwar movements, they had learned to question the status quo. Nevertheless, many of these women felt as if their own concerns—from unequal pay, sexual harassment, and the lack of recognition for women's contributions to social movements— went unnoticed. Eager to challenge gender discrimination, these women formed groups that would become the bedrock of "second wave" feminism. In Missoula, one such group blended activism and scholarship to create the University of Montana's Women's Studies Program.

The program began after a 1974 symposium on women featuring speakers from various university departments, when English professor Carolyn Wheeler circulated a handwritten memo to other women faculty members, asking if they would teach a class focused on women. History professor Maxine Van de Wetering initially resisted the idea, saying she "couldn't even imagine what that would be." However, according to Wheeler, Van de Wetering quickly changed her mind when "she just started thinking what it could mean to . . . history."

The response from other faculty members was electric. Joan Watson, a liberal studies professor and later director of the Women's Studies Program, observed, "The contributions of women have been hidden from history. . . . [W]omen, like people of color, have been largely absent from the texts we study." For many students, correcting that omission seemed to be both a revelation and a revolution.

In addition to for-credit classes like "Women in American History" and a social work course titled "Liberation and Oppression of Women," women's studies faculty invited community women to offer nonacademic classes in home and auto repair. Taking their cue from consciousness-raising groups, which had become popular during the era, these classes often lacked the formalized teacher-student relationship and employed a more organic, egalitarian approach to learning. The "free-school" model operated out of a campus building that also housed the School of Social Work, the Black Student Union, and the Women's Resource Center (where women could receive counseling for sexual assault and obtain other health-related resources). Over two hundred people in the Missoula community participated in these informal classes.

To those active in the program, disseminating information proved more important than following university regulations. Campaigns to provide students with birth control information and abortion referrals met with backlash from university officials and provoked the ire of resident hall matrons, many of whom confiscated the materials wherever they were found.

The university's traditional women's studies courses encouraged women to develop an analytical framework that could be used to tackle real-life issues such as poverty, racism, and sexism. Inside of class, students read New Left tracts published by groups such as the Student Nonviolent Coordination Committee (SNCC), Students for a Democratic Society (SDS), and the women of the Black Panthers. Outside class, students hosted group meetings to share their experiences, their discontents, and their ideas. "These were community and campus [groups]. There was no distinction between them," organizer Diane Sands recalled. There was also considerable overlap between Missoula's early feminist community—which often used the term "women's liberation" rather than "feminist"—and other activist movements such as the fledgling Native American and African American studies programs. "All those political movements come out of a common tie, and for a common reason," Sands remarked, "because all of them question the structures of society."

This questioning led to action as students chafed against restrictive, discriminatory university policies. Female students, for example, answered not to the dean of students but to the dean of women, a distinction that subjected them to rules and regulations based on gender. The university required women to live on campus until their senior year or until they were twenty-one, and residents of all-female dorms had to obey curfews or answer to a "standards board." Behavior such as drinking or sneaking out could result in expulsion. The double standard proved infuriating to many women students, some of whom resisted the mandatory live-in policy by pitching tents on the dorm lawn.

When Professor Wheeler first encouraged female faculty members to offer women's studies courses within their disciplines, the goal was not to establish an independent department, but rather to create an informal alliance of teachers working together across departments. Still, as the field matured and more professors began offering relevant courses, the goal changed. And yet, the Women's Studies Program did not become a formal program until 1991, almost fifteen years after the National American Women's Studies Association was founded.

One reason for the long delay is that the program's early efforts were as focused on activism as on academics. Once activists achieved some of their aims—such as an end to the dean of women's position and to curfews for women students—classes became more formalized. Petitions to University of Montana administrators revealed a desire to earn traditional credits that could be counted toward graduation and a degree.

By 2002, the Women's Studies Program had become the Women and Gender Studies Program, offering an average of twenty-five different courses a semester, including "Introduction to Feminist Theory," "Women and War," and "Twentieth-Century Lesbian and Gay Fiction." In 2014, the program was renamed Women's, Gender, and Sexuality Studies. Students still cannot graduate with a degree in WGS, but the university does offer a liberal arts degree with an emphasis on women's, gender, and sexuality studies, a minor, and a graduate certificate.

At the same time, a capstone course and sponsored lectures attempt to encourage the same culture of activism that inspired the program's inception. But the program itself is largely focused on academic inquiry even as its mission statement encourages students to "envision justice for all peoples," a goal that would have resonated with the program's founders.

Legalized Midwifery: Montana Leads the Way

Jennifer Hill

ALTHOUGH Montana midwives had a long history of working with doctors to serve the needs of women in their communities, their profession—and especially the idea of home birth—faded from mainstream acceptance as the hospital replaced the home as the "normal" birthing location. By the 1950s, a majority of women across the United States delivered their babies in hospitals. Even as hospital births became more common, midwives continued to assume that pregnancy and delivery were nonmedical events. Physicians, on the other hand, began to insist that medical assistance and access to technology were necessary for safe deliveries.

The conflict crystalized in 1988 when the Montana Board of Medical Examiners, at the request of a Missoula physician, pressed charges against a Montana midwife, Dolly Browder, and initiated a court case accusing her of violating the Medical Practice Act by practicing medicine without a license.

After a three-day civil trial, the Missoula judge ruled against Browder. He concluded that she was practicing medicine and banned her from assisting pregnant women. The case concluded in January 1989, just as the Fifty-first session of the Montana legislature convened. With the looming threat of additional lawsuits, the Montana Midwifery Association hired a lobbyist, raised funds, and organized supporters. Their goal: to change the Montana Medical Practice Act to exempt home birth midwifery.

Midwifery supporters encountered organized, well-funded, and authoritative opposition from the Montana Medical Association, the Montana Nurses Association, the Montana Hospital Association, and individual hospitals and physicians. Mona Jamison, lobbyist for the Montana Midwifery Association, explained that midwifery advocates found themselves "against the establishment" and in direct confrontation with the medical profession.

Midwifery Bill proponents countered the influence of health-care providers and institutions by emphasizing the long-standing importance of midwifery throughout Montana history. They also mobilized a large, grass-roots support network to communicate with senators and representatives, and a committed group of home birth advocates traveled to the legislature to be present for testimony on the bill. Midwifery supporters drove to Helena during the Montana winter "in storms and caravans of cars" to attend hearings. For each hearing on the Midwifery Bill, supporters "filled the room with mothers and with babies," demonstrating by sheer numbers the importance of home birth to Montana voters.

Home birth supporters made much of Montana's geographic isolation and the ability of midwifery to provide adequate medical care to a rural and scattered population. They also provided statistics demonstrating the safety

Midwifery on trial in Montana

Doctor: woman's care is inadequate

By MICHAEL MOORE
of the Missoulian

A Missoula physician who dealt with four clients of lay midwife Dolly Browder testified Wednesday that Browder, who has delivered 300 babies, is not competent to do home births.

Dr. Valerie Knudsen told District Judge John Henson that while Browder is a "great coach" for women going through labor, much of her care for pregnant women is inadequate.

Knudsen, who practices at the Western Montana Clinic, testified on behalf of the state Board of Medical Examiners.

The board, acting on a complaint from Missoula physician R.D. Marks, has asked Henson to halt Browder's midwifery business on the grounds that she practices medicine.

Initial testimony in the case was Nov. 30, but the hearing was not completed and had to be rescheduled because of Henson's court calendar. Further testimony is scheduled Thursday.

Called to the witness stand by board attorney Patricia England, Browder repeatedly said that she does not practice medicine, despite evidence that she has administered prescription drugs to clients.

"I don't practice medicine," she said. "I practice midwifery." Much of Wednesday's testimony focused on case histories of Browder's clients, with England defending her work and Knudsen criticizing it.

WHILE ON the witness stand Wednesday, lay midwife Dolly Browder looks over a document being shown to her by Patricia England, attorney for the State Board of Medical Examiners.

The case, which may set precedent in Montana, has raised interesting debate over what constitutes the practice of medicine or midwifery, particularly in matters of diagnosis and treatment. While Montana law openly recognizes nurse midwives, who are licensed, lay midwifery appears to fall in a gray area.

Although their arguments run counter to one another, both the Montana Midwifery Association and the board are preparing legislative campaigns designed to clear up the legal status of lay midwifery.

In the meantime, however, Henson must grapple in the gray with Browder's midwifery practice.

During direct questioning of Knudsen and Browder, England steadfastly portrayed measures taken by Browder during prenatal, birth and postpartum as either diagnosis or treatment.

Among those were blood-pressure and weight monitoring, analysis of urine samples, checking of fetal heart rates, examination of placentas and giving shots.

Knudsen, who is opposed to home birth, testified that such actions are either diagnosis and treatment, and thus constitute the practice of medicine.

Knudsen was particularly critical of a case where Browder admittedly dispensed Methergine

pills to one of her clients. The drug, used to prevent and control postpartum hemorrhaging, had been prescribed for someone else.

"When you prescribe a drug, it's for a specific person," said Knudsen, who said the woman possibly could have had an allergic reaction to the medication.

Browder said dispensing the Methergine was a mistake she won't make again.

"I don't feel that it was good practice on my part," she said.

Knudsen's testimony about Browder's competence was sharply countered by testimony from Pam Luoma, who had two of her children at home under Browder's care.

When asked by one of Browder's attorneys, Jack Tuholske, about Browder's care, Luoma said, "It was excellent."

Contributing to that excellence, Luoma said, was Browder's attention to her emotional condition as well as her physical condition.

That, of course, goes to the heart of why many people turn to midwives in the face of the high-tech medical world, midwife supporters say.

Catherine Goodman, testifying on Browder's behalf, described the birth of her first child at Missoula Community Medical Center as "torture."

Goodman said her requests were ignored by a doctor and nurses, and that decisions were made and acted upon without consideration of her wishes.

"I was very angry, very demoralized, angry," Goodman said of her hospital birthing experience.

Goodman and Luoma said they plan to have their next children at home under Browder's care, provided she still can practice.

The argument over home birth midwifery played out in the newspapers as well as in the court and the legislature. The *Missoulian* published this article on January 4, 1989.

of home birth and trumpeted the rights of Montanans to determine the circumstances of their individual birthing experiences.

Despite intense opposition, Montana home birth supporters secured successful passage of the Midwifery Bill, HB 458, with strong legislative approval. Many legislators supported the bill because they believed it provided health-care options to the state's rural population. Midwifery advocates won the day by focusing on issues specific to Montana—its long history of home birth midwifery, limited rural medical services, and individual choice.

Nevertheless, for midwifery supporters the battle was about a much more fundamental issue: a woman's right to control her own health-care decisions. According to Jamison, the legislation "was really a reflection of the greater societal view on who's in charge, and who's in charge of women's bodies. So this was . . . a breakthrough on a greater issue than just the issue of home birth." By exempting home birth midwifery from the Medical Practice Act, legislators endorsed the notion that Montana women should be able to birth at home and that Montana parents could choose how and where their children would be born. The Montana legislature placed parents in charge of birth and supported women's individual birthing preferences.

On April 11, 1989, Governor Stan Stephens signed the Midwifery Bill into law, guaranteeing Montana midwives an exemption from the Medical Practice Act. During the following session, legislators passed a bill to formally regulate the profession of home birth midwifery. At that time, only ten other states licensed midwives to assist with home deliveries, marking Montana as an early supporter of legalized midwifery.

Hospital and home births have shown comparable success rates for low-risk births since 1989, and Montana women continue to choose midwifery care. The decades since legalization have vindicated the legitimacy of home birth as an option for pregnant women.

Since legalization, Montana midwives have practiced with state sanction, even as women in North and South Dakota, Wyoming, and Idaho could not access legal midwifery care. Idaho legalized home birth midwifery only in 2009 and Wyoming in 2010, while mothers desiring midwifery assistance to deliver at home in North and South Dakota must still do so illegally.

Montana midwives' fight for licensure created an environment supportive of birth options for Montana women. Montana's home birth rate topped national rankings in 2009 and continues to surpass national home birth statistics. Early midwifery legalization and sustained home birth practices put Montana midwives at the forefront of the national home birth movement.

Work Done by Muscle Power or Grit: Anna Dahl, Rural Electrification, and the Transformation of Rural Women's Work

Annie Hanshew

IN THE TWENTIETH CENTURY, rural women faced a different—and arguably more rigorous—set of gender expectations than did their urban sisters. They did, of course, preserve and cook food, mend and wash clothes, care for children, and clean their homes, but they were also intimately involved in farm labor. Rural women raised produce, chickens, and pigs; kept the farms' books; and worked in the fields. Their work was so essential that historian Richard Roeder called women the "economic linchpins" of the state's farms and ranches.

Even more amazing than the number of tasks rural women performed is the fact that, before World War II, they largely completed their work without electricity. Anna Dahl, a farm wife from Sheridan County, helped change this. A key community activist promoting rural electrification in eastern Montana, Dahl helped bring power to six hundred families in Sheridan, Roosevelt, and Daniels Counties. Her efforts significantly altered life on the farm, especially for Montana women.

Anna Boe Dahl arrived in Plentywood, Montana, with her brother in 1917. She taught school in Dagmar for two years before marrying Andrew Dahl in 1919 and moving to a 640-acre farm near Coalridge. There, she and Andrew raised five children. During the Great Depression, Anna also taught English and farm economics for the Works Progress Administration to supplement the family income.

It is a myth that ruggedly independent, self-sufficient individualists populated the West. Like many of their neighbors, the Dahls worked cooperatively to improve their lives and their communities. Active in the Montana Farmers Union, they participated in a variety of collective endeavors ranging from digging wells to cooperative coal mining. After the dry years of the Depression had ended, the Dahls used their knowledge of community organizing to build grassroots support for rural electrification.

Federal assistance made rural electrification possible. In 1936, Congress

Posed here in October 1946 with the Sheridan County Electric Cooperative's first board of trustees, Anna Dahl became used to being the only woman at the table. She went on to become the second woman in the United States elected president of the board of a rural electric co-op, the first woman member of the board of directors of the Montana State REA, and the first woman trustee of Northwest Public Power Association. MHS Archives, Anna Dahl Scrapbook, SC 909

passed a bill to create the Rural Electrification Administration (REA), an agency that offered liberal federal loans for rural electrification and gave preference to state and local governments, cooperatives, and nonprofits over private utilities.

Local efforts were also essential. In August 1941, Anna Dahl and her neighbors formed the Sheridan County Electric Cooperative, to which she was elected secretary. The co-op received an REA loan in 1945, and the power came on in 1948. Writer David Long attributes the cooperative's success to Dahl, describing her as the "nuts and bolts of the Sheridan project, its unfailing center of energy for years." In 1956, she became the president of the co-op, only the second woman in the United States to serve in that role.

Anna Dahl's background as an educator was particularly useful as she worked to build local support for electrification. She spoke passionately about the benefits of electricity to farm families as she persuaded her neighbors to support the co-op.

Among Dahl's most powerful arguments was that electricity would ease women's burdens. She vividly described farm life before electrification: "[T]he best years of our lives have been spent carrying coal, wood, ashes, and water, and . . . all the work within and without the home was done by muscle power—if you had it—and by grit if you didn't." She exclaimed, "[T]he change to cooking, cleaning, washing and ironing with electricity . . . is almost beyond comprehension."

Electricity did transform rural women's work dramatically. Access to hot running water and the ability to use such technologies as electric stoves, washing machines, and vacuum cleaners reduced the "muscle power" housekeeping required. However, these "labor-saving" technologies did not necessarily save women time. Paradoxically, electrification may have actually increased women's workload because standards for cleanliness became more rigorous. Historian Ronald Kline finds that in the 1950s and 1960s, home economists promoted technology to farm women not as a way to create more leisure time, but rather "as a means to increase the quality and productivity of 'home-making.'" Once women could wash clothes more easily, they were expected to wash them more often. And the free time women earned using a vacuum was now supposed to be spent on child-care or home management.

Still, for many rural women the trade-offs were worth it. Certainly Anna Dahl believed that electrification improved rural women's lives. In 1957, she had the honor of being the first woman to speak at the National Rural Electric Cooperative Association. "I raised five children in the pre-REA days," she noted, "and while the little gray home in the West is a good thing to sing about, if you have to live in it, it can be very rugged."

Dahl continued to believe that by working together to bring electricity to rural Montana, she and her neighbors "could get away from the drudgery that attends work on the farm," she said. "And, I believe that for the most part, we have done just that."

"Women . . . on the Level with Their White Sisters": Rose Hum Lee and Butte's Chinese Women in the Early Twentieth Century

Annie Hanshew

BORN IN BUTTE in 1904, Rose Hum Lee earned a BS in social work from Pittsburgh's Carnegie Institute of Technology and completed a doctorate in sociology at the University of Chicago. Her dissertation—"The Growth and Decline of Rocky Mountain Chinatowns"—was published in 1978. Because Lee's work was largely based on the experiences of her own family and childhood, her scholarship offers invaluable insights into the lives of Chinese women and families in Butte during the first four decades of the twentieth century.

The daughter of merchant Hum Wah Long and his wife, Lin Fong, Rose Hum Lee, like many other Chinese American children, attended Butte's grammar and high schools, where she distinguished herself academically. Additionally, the fact that her father was one of the city's most prominent Chinese businessmen conferred a level of respect on the Hum family.

Nevertheless, Lee, like other Chinese women of Butte, encountered the common racist assumption that equated Chinese women with prostitution. The *Montana Standard* reflected that stereotype while defending the wives of Butte's merchants in a 1942 article about the city's Chinese history. "While the Chinese men of Butte were, as a rule, good law-abiding citizens . . . the less said about the Chinese women of that day the better," the *Standard* noted. "The exception among the women were the wives of Chinese doctors and merchants, women who were on the level with their white sisters and who have left many estimable children." Certainly, those estimable children—like Lee—contended with pressure to maintain their respectability.

Lee herself came from a family of seven, and her research noted that the families of Butte's first-generation Chinese tended to be large, with an average of five children. Lee found no childless couples in her study. The premium placed on family size was due in part to the fact that immigrants "brought with them village mores, [and] regarded large families as a symbol of status." Families and extended kinship groups helped create social stability in the face of frontier life, and births were celebrated both in Butte and by extended families back in China.

According to Lee, the first-generation Chinese women who lived in Butte in the early twentieth century generally came to Montana directly from China or from other Chinese communities in the West. Many were part of arranged marriages, and in some cases they did not even meet their husbands before traveling to the United States. One bride remembered that her aunt had arranged for her to marry a Butte merchant who was "too busy taking care of [his business] to leave and find himself a wife." The marriage ceremony was held in the groom's absence, and when the young woman arrived by boat in America, her escort (a new cousin) "pointed to a figure . . . [and] said, 'See that man smoking a big cigar? He is your husband!'"

Prior to the Chinese Revolution of 1911, married women's lives, even in the United States, were carefully supervised and restricted. One Butte woman recalled, "Until the Revolution, I was allowed out of the house but once a year. That was during New Year's when families exchanged New Year calls and feasts. . . . The father of my children hired a closed carriage to take me and the children calling . . . even if we went around the corner, for no family women walked." The isolation and limited contact with

Pictured here in 1945, Rose Hum Lee (left) became a sociologist who used her academic training to document Butte's Chinese community. Roosevelt University Archives 3048

other women made life in Butte particularly difficult, but after 1911 attitudes about women venturing into the public sphere slowly shifted: "When the father of my children cut his queue he adopted new habits; I discarded my Chinese clothes and began to wear American clothes," one of Lee's sources said. "Gradually the other women followed my example. We began to go out more frequently and since then I go out all the time."

According to Lee, only three Chinese families remained in Butte by 1945. Drawn away in search of economic opportunities during the Depression and World War II, Montana's Chinese population dwindled. Lee was among those who left. She finished her doctorate in 1947 and distinguished herself in 1956 at Chicago's Roosevelt University by becoming the first woman, and the first Chinese American, to head an American sociology department. Though she never again lived in her home state, her dissertation continues to be one of the most important resources on the Chinese in Montana.

A Farm of Her Own: Women Homesteaders in Montana

Ellen Baumler

HISTORIANS estimate that up to 18 percent of homesteaders in Montana were single women. Passage of the Homestead Act of 1862 allowed any twenty-one-year-old head of household the right to homestead federal land. Single, widowed, and divorced women fit this description, and they crossed the country to file homestead claims of 160 acres. After the turn of the century, when the Enlarged Homestead Act doubled the acreage to 320, even more single women took up free land in Montana. While not all succeeded, those who did proved that women were up to the task.

Gwenllian Evans was Montana's first female homesteader. A widow from Wales, she immigrated to the United States in 1868. Her son, Morgan Evans, was Marcus Daly's land agent and a well-known Deer Lodge Valley rancher. In 1870, Gwenllian Evans filed on land that later became the town of Opportunity; she received her patent in 1872. She was one of the territory's first postmistresses and lived on her homestead until her death in 1892.

The Enlarged Homestead Act of 1909 marked the beginning of Montana's homesteading boom and brought many more single women to Montana. Women, like men, homesteaded for a variety of reasons and did not always intend to stay. Grace Binks, Ina Dana, and Margaret Majors homesteaded together in the Sumatra area in Rosebud County in 1911. The three women from Ottumwa, Iowa, along with Dana's mother, came for the adventure. They claimed land, used one another as witnesses for final proof of occupancy, and then commuted their patents by buying their properties. Dana and Binks each paid two hundred dollars for their land titles. All three women left their claims after a year. A photo album documents the pride they felt in their accomplishments on the land, detailing the homes they made and the neighbors they enjoyed.

Some women homesteaded in partnership with other family members to accumulate large holdings. The Scherlie family claimed land in a desolate

In 1911, thirty-nine-year-old Grace Binks (left) and twenty-nine-year-old Margaret Majors (right) came to the Sumatra area (northwestern Rosebud County) as part of a group of Iowa homesteaders. The women stayed only a year, paying cash to "commute" their homesteads into purchased land. MHS Photo Archives PAc 92-62 p. 19C

area in Blaine County called the Big Flat. Thirty-two-year-old Anna Scherlie filed in 1913 on land adjacent to two of her brothers' claims and three of her sisters'. At that time, women made up about one-fourth of the total home-stead applicants in the four surrounding townships.

By 1916, Anna Scherlie had forty acres planted in wheat, oats, and flax. Isolation on the Big Flat led many settlers to winter elsewhere, and Scherlie was no exception. Legend has it that during the winters she went to St. Paul to work for the family of railroad magnate James J. Hill. Over the decades, Scherlie made few changes to her small, wood-frame shack, adding only a vestibule she used as a summer kitchen, storage shed, and laundry. She remained in that shack on her land until 1968.

Many homesteading women came to Montana from Canada, where single women could not claim land until the 1930s. They often filed on claims in Montana but continued to work in Canada while they proved up. One of these independent women was teacher Laura Etta Smalley, who arrived from Edmonton, Alberta, in 1910. Smalley had a meticulous plan, and luck was with her all the way. Over the long Easter weekend, Smalley packed her bag and boarded the train for Inverness, Montana. She arrived in the middle of the night. The hotel was under construction, but the clerk rented her an unfinished room.

The next morning, the land locator took her out to view available claims. Smalley found the land she wanted and took the night train to Havre to file. Because it was deemed unsafe for a single woman to travel alone, the locator's secretary kindly accompanied her. Smalley arrived at the Havre land office on April 1, 1910, the first day a person could file under the new Enlarged Homestead Act. She was the first in line. Within two minutes, many other land seekers were in line behind her.

Smalley returned to Canada, finished out the school year, and then returned to Montana. In Havre, she bought a ready-made shack to fill with furniture and supplies. Men then transported the shack on two wagons twenty-six miles out to her claim and dropped her off. That fall, Smalley returned to teach in Edmonton, but by the opening of the 1911–1912 school year, she had secured a teaching position in Inverness.

In 1914, Laura Smalley married Will Bangs. Smalley moved to her husband's homestead but kept her own. And that was a good thing since Bangs lost his farm in 1926. The family, which then included four children, moved to Smalley's tiny claim shack, and their home grew around it. Laura Smalley Bangs died at eighty-seven in 1973. Sadly, her death occurred before she could see her grandson work the land she claimed.

These and other women take their place alongside their male counterparts who came to Montana for the opportunities the land offered. Like their counterparts, not all of them succeeded. But those who stayed and prospered with their land, like Gwenllian Evans, Anna Scherlie, and Laura Smalley Bangs, made significant contributions to Montana's agricultural history.

Womanhood on Trial: Examining Domestic Violence in Butte, Montana

Natalie F. Scheidler

SHORTLY BEFORE eleven on February 8, 1946, as Hazel Kauf stepped off the Aero Club's dance floor, she was confronted by her ex-husband, Howard Kauf, who had entered the club a few minutes earlier. Grabbing Hazel by the arm, Howard "spun her around . . . and in the spin just . . . blasted that first one [shot]." As Hazel lay on the floor, Howard, standing over her, fired a second shot into her chest. According to the *Montana Standard*, the horrific event quickly drew a crowd, and "within a few minutes traffic at Park and Main [just outside the club] was virtually at a standstill."

This assault was not an isolated incident. Following World War II, rates of violence increased nationally, and rates of wife assault and wife homicide, like other forms of violence, peaked in postwar Butte. Hazel's case, however, represents more than a historically persistent crime that was often addressed only in whispers. It demonstrates that even as social constraints on women lifted, cultural beliefs that dictated women's and wives' behaviors remained firmly intact. These beliefs perpetuated the narrative that assault on wives could, in some situations, be justified.

The lives of Hazel and Howard Kauf in many ways resembled the lives of couples across Montana and the United States during World War II. Philipsburg native Hazel Alda Henri married Howard Kauf, a local manganese miner in 1936. Howard spent the early war years laboring in that strategic industry. In 1945, however, he enlisted in the U.S. Navy, joining fifty-seven thousand other Montanans in the armed services. Shortly after Howard's deployment, Hazel and the couple's four-year-old son moved to Butte, where Hazel, like over a million other military wives nationwide, entered the workforce.

For many women, World War II offered emancipation on an unparalleled scale as they gained greater access to education, employment, and economic independence. Hazel, too, seems to have been fulfilled by the opportunities she found in Butte. Working as a waitress and in a Park Street store, she formed a close group of female friends with whom she participated in the city's entertainment. Howard recalled that Hazel aspired to open a dress shop. When she asked for a divorce—the rates of which peaked immediately following the war—he reported, "She just said she wanted to be alone." She wanted "to be free." Hazel momentarily secured her freedom when the Kaufs' divorce was finalized on February 8, 1946, hours before her murder.

Hazel's death—and the manner in which it was interpreted—reflected the experiences of thousands of women. At the coroner's inquest, a Mr. Sullivan, counsel for the defendant, attempted to justify Howard's actions by focusing on Hazel's behavior, particularly her "failure" to conform to feminine and wifely standards. Sullivan inquired about Hazel's drinking habits, the "places of amusement" she frequented, and the parties she attended, and he drew attention to the fact that she and her female friends often attended these events without their husbands—all while Howard was serving his country. Similarly, he cast aspersions on the female friends who had witnessed Hazel's murder. To undermine their testimony, and Hazel's character by association, Sullivan asked each of them about their marital status and their drinking habits. He also pointed out that, on the night of Hazel's death, none of them had objected when several men asked them to dance without first securing proper introductions.

Officers Continue Probe of Kauf Slaying; Ex-Sailor Being Held

(Continued From Page 1)

quarters. He returned to the room and then telephoned St. James hospital, but when he came back she apparently was dead.

Police said Augusta told them Mrs. Kauf was dancing with an Anaconda man when Kauf entered from the street, spun her around and fired a shot. The woman screamed and fell, he said, and Kauf fired a second time.

The proprietor, John J. Duggan, ran up the stairs and summoned Officer Holman from the corner. Holman placed Kauf under arrest and he and other officers, including Capt. Emett Sullivan, Del Rodda, Larry Tromly, John Maguire, Alex Cuthill, John McCallum and Ed O'Keefe took the names of approximately 15 witnesses.

Despite the lateness of the hour, a large crowd assembled quickly outside the place, and traffic at Park and Main, the city's busiest corner, was snarled in a standstill.

County Attorney Roe and Police Chief Bart Riley said Kauf, a native of Butte, had told them he returned home from the Navy Jan. 28, and sensed immediately that his wife had become estranged.

"I don't know what caused it,"

Chief Riley quoted him as saying. "When I was home on leave last May, we were together all the time, went places together, had a wonderful time."

She had written regularly to him, he said, but finally the letters stopped coming. He was discharged at Farragut, Idaho, after having served 11 months and 11 days as a seaman, first class, and came to Butte by train the next day.

"I went to her address but found she had moved," he told the chief. "I met her, though, in a West Park street bar and we talked things over as we went from place to place."

Several times in succeeding days, he said, they met downtown by pre-arrangement and went from one establishment to another or had dinner together. Sometimes Mrs. Kauf took a cab home, her husband said, and he did not learn where she was staying.

Kauf said his wife insisted she wanted a divorce "to be free" and asked for a divorce.

"I asked her if there was another man, but she wouldn't say there was," Chief Riley quoted him as saying "She just said she wanted to be alone.",

Friday Kauf acquiesced and met his wife in the office of an attorney, where he signed papers consenting to a divorce.

Friday night Kauf met his wife in a West Park street tavern. Afterward they had dinner together at a restaurant. From that point, Chief Riley said, Kauf insisted he remembered nothing.

"I had brought my rifle and pistol from Philipsburg when I came here, but I don't remember going back to the hotel last (Friday) night to get it," he told the chief. "In fact, I don't remember a thing until I was being questioned in jail (by County Attorney Roe). It's all a blank."

County Attorney Roe said that when he first started to question Kauf early Saturday morning, the former serviceman said:

"Let's get this over with fast. I'm not going to plead insanity or anything like that."

The county attorney added that Kauf, when questioned concerning the actual shooting, said, "I don't remember the shooting." Roe said that all witnesses questioned agreed that Mrs. Kauf had been in the bar at least 10 or 15 minutes before

BERTOGLIO

HOME APPLIANCE STORE
Dealers for the

DOMESTIC or
WHITE
SEWING MACHINE

DEMONSTRATING MODELS
on Our Showroom Foor

BERTOGLIO

HOME APPLIANCE STORE
200 N. Main   Ph. 5924

Finest Food . . .

MRS. HAZEL KAUF

HOWARD KAUF

IN BUTTE SLAYING — Mrs. Hazel Kauf, 26, was fatally wounded Friday night in a night club on Butte's main intersection. Her husband, Howard K. Kauf, 33, formerly sailor whom she divorced a few hours before the tragedy, is being held by county authorities for questioning.

Hazel Kauf's murder received press attention, with a large story published in the *Montana Standard* on February 10, 1946.

The narrative that women were potentially at fault for their own victimization was also present in *State of Montana v. Howard Kauf*. Jury instruction 45 ordered the jury to consider Howard's sanity at the time on the basis of "his temper, jealousy, shattered hopes, desires, and troubles of all kinds," insinuating that Hazel may have actually driven Howard to murder and that violence was an understandable reaction to her wifely shortcomings.

The coroner's jury deliberated for five hours before determining that Howard was at fault for Hazel's death and that the crime should go to trial. The first trial jury reached a stalemate. The second sentenced Howard to the minimum sentence of ten years. While Howard was found guilty, the scrutiny of Hazel's behavior throughout the inquest and trial demonstrates the pervasive belief that women, if they "misbehaved," might give their husbands just cause to respond violently.

Despite ongoing bias in the courts, women did not passively accept the patriarchal worldview that undermined their ability to escape violent relationships. Nor were they ever merely victims. On the contrary, these women were friends, sisters, mothers, and integral parts of their community. They were women who participated in activism, resisting legal and cultural biases by filing assault charges against violent husbands, acting as legal guardians for women under eighteen years of age so that they could secure divorces from violent husbands, and, as evidenced in the Kauf trial, testifying on one another's behalf.

Individual activism became organized in Butte in the 1970s when women set up a network of "safe houses," worked to educate the public about domestic violence, and established a Woman's Referral Center at the local YMCA. After years of work by individuals and organizations alike, the State of Montana formally adopted a law explicitly addressing intimate partner violence in 1985.

Violence against women, however, is not a phenomenon of the past. Contemporary data indicates that annually, in the United States alone, 1.3 million women are injured and more than three women a day are killed in domestic altercations, illustrating the need for continued resistance.

Alma Smith Jacobs: Beloved Librarian, Tireless Activist

Annie Hanshew

ALMA SMITH JACOBS served as the head librarian of the Great Falls Public Library for almost twenty years before becoming the Montana state librarian in 1973. Both of these achievements were historic firsts for an African American woman. Throughout her life, Jacobs demonstrated a passion for education and for community building and a commitment to working for racial justice in Montana.

Alma Smith was born in 1916 in Lewistown to Martin and Emma Riley Smith, members of the wave of African American migrants who had been drawn to the Pacific Northwest between 1865 and 1910. Although Montana now has a reputation for being predominantly white, in the early twentieth century, there were sizable black communities in the state, especially in larger cities like Helena, Butte, Missoula, and Great Falls.

The Smith family moved to Great Falls when Alma was a child. After graduating from Great Falls High School, Alma took advantage of scholarships to achieve an impressive education, first at Talladega College in Alabama and then at Columbia University, where she completed a degree in library science. Credentials in hand, and newly married to World War II–veteran Marcus Jacobs, she returned to Great Falls, where she found a position at the public library in 1946. Eight years later, she became head librarian. From that position, she worked to build the presence of the library throughout the city and central Montana.

Jacobs recognized the powerful role that public libraries could play in a community. She believed that a good library was a community center and a place for educational opportunities. The idea of self-education was particularly important to her. She wanted the library to be a place where people could pursue the knowledge they needed to learn a new vocation or advance their career. As she would often say, "The public library is the poor man's university."

As a member of a minority group in a state with a large white majority, Jacobs's racial identity was complicated. On the one hand, she was a native of Montana and lived in the state for most of her life. Her tireless effort to better her community through her library work is evidence of her love for her hometown and her state, and she seems to have wanted that work to define her. In a 1967 interview with the *Great Falls Tribune,* she underplayed the importance of her racial identity to her professional career: "I don't consider myself the Negro authority in Great Falls or anyplace else. I resent being thought of as a Negro librarian. I would rather concentrate on being a good librarian."

On the other hand, Jacobs's race was undoubtedly important. She continued to live in Montana after much of the state's African American population had moved on to larger metropolitan areas, and as a member of this shrinking minority, she worked to advance civil rights and racial justice. She served as president of the Montana Federation of Colored Women's Clubs and sat on the Montana Advisory Committee to the U.S. Civil Rights Commission. She spoke out against segregation in Great Falls at a time when it was unpopular to do so. Together with her sister, Lucille Smith Thompson, she also worked to document the history of African Americans in the state, an effort that resulted in the 1970 publication of *The Negro in Montana, 1800–1945: A Selective Bibliography.*

In a way, Jacobs's professional excellence and prominent stature had the effect she hoped for. As Great Falls architect William Hess once wrote of her, "Her personality is such that after even a one minute meeting you are no longer aware of a race difference." Yet the very fact that Hess felt the need to comment on her race indicates the extent to which racial difference

Alma Jacobs's tireless effort to better her community through her library work culminated in the construction of a state-of-the-art facility for the Great Falls Public Library. Here, Jacobs (right) poses with other dignitaries at the building's dedication in 1967. MHS Photo Archives Pac 2002-3, Box 1

still clearly defined the African American experience in twentieth-century Montana.

Jacobs died in 1997, but her work to build the Great Falls Public Library has not been forgotten. The city officially proclaimed the week of June 16 to 22, 2009, Alma Jacobs Week, and during that week, the Alma Jacobs Plaza at the library was dedicated in her memory.

The Power of Strong, Able Women: The League of Women Voters of Montana and Constitutional Reform

Marcella Sherfy Walter

IN 1972, Grace Bates, a Gallatin Valley delegate to Montana's Constitutional Convention, identified herself in the required biographical sketch as "farmer's wife, public servant." A member of the League of Women Voters of Montana (LWV), she represented, literally, a league of midcentury Montana women whose capacity for informed and skilled political action changed the state's governance.

Nationally, the LWV began in 1920, following passage of the Nineteenth Amendment granting women the vote. Though Montana women joined in the 1920s, the organization did not take ordered shape until after World War II. By 1952, Billings, Butte, Great Falls, Havre, Helena, and Missoula had chapters.

The league championed educated, vigorous citizen engagement in government. National rules prohibited members from supporting or opposing political parties or candidates. Instead, they investigated issues affecting government and citizens' well-being, promoted informed political participation, and campaigned for the positions they reached after careful research.

"I enjoyed people who were talking about issues and not recipes and baby formulas," said Bozeman member Dorothy Eck. She personified membership during the Montana LWV's strongest years; it was largely made up of urban, middle-class, homemaking wives of professionals and businessmen who were eager to use their knowledge and skills for important causes. Between 1955 and 1980, women in the Flathead, the Bitterroot, Bozeman, Liberty County, and Lincoln County created new chapters. Statewide membership ranged from 325 to 450.

League work focused first on public-meeting participation and voter education. Members served as formal "observers" at planning, school board, and city and county commission meetings. They prepared and distributed pamphlets on state and local government organization and function. They orchestrated candidates' forums, get-out-the-vote efforts, poll-watching, and served as precinct reporters under contract to *ABC News*.

As important, members conducted in-depth research on current topics: model cities, child-care, equal rights, social justice, land use, water quality, state custodial institutions, rural development, civic beautification, mental health, school quality, taxation, hunger, coal mining, campaign finance, senior services, fair housing, the United Nations, and wilderness. As 1972 Montana League president Jean Anderson said, "LWV is the cheapest education you can buy. . . . The more you apply yourself, the better the education."

Action followed study. In 1975, Butte LWV leader Lydia Wideman reminded potential members that the league was "not for armchair philosophers or the impatient." Following research, members discussed each topic, reached consensus, and then lobbied for the outcomes they had charted and in so doing, became public relations masters. "No one would listen to scholarly discussion," Dorothy Eck recalled. "We learned to find a simple message—a few words—eye-catching."

In 1967, LWV members Eck and Daphne Bugbee became full-time, unpaid citizen lobbyists at the Montana legislature, committed to communicating clearly and sidestepping party politics. Two years later, the league put its nonpartisan lobbying success, statewide connections, and respected reputation to work supporting the call to revise Montana's 1889 constitution, a dated document crafted by mining interests to achieve statehood. The LWV identified constitutional reform as the most critical step toward more open, efficient, and democratic state government as Montana emerged from corporate dominance. As the organization's members hoped, the 1969 legislature approved a statewide constitutional convention referendum. League members then created extensive constitutional studies and issue lists, and—cooperating with an array of other organizations—they campaigned successfully for voter approval for a convention.

Nine of the nineteen female delegates elected to the 1972 convention were LWV members, including Bates, Bugbee, and Eck, the convention's Western District vice president. League experience gave all nine clarity and fearlessness. "Most of the League issues went into our discussions," Eck recalled. "Local government, environmentalism, human rights . . . the right to know, the right to privacy, the right to participate."

Perhaps as important, the LWV's emphasis on nonpartisanship and realistic, substantive change shaped the convention and its outcome. Midway through the sixty-day process, league president Anderson wrote to

Montana League of Women Voters members joined in world peace efforts in the 1930s. Photographer Edward Reinig captured this image of Blackfeet chief Eagle Cap signing a petition for reduction of world armaments at the Montana League of Women Voters booth at the Montana State Fair. Staffing the LWV booth were (left to right) Agnes Webster, secretary of the College League; Helen Seth, president of the College League; Charlotte Bowman; and Mrs. E. K. Bowman, International Relations chairwoman of the Montana League. MHS Photo Archives PAc 87-103, Box 1, Folder 4

each of the hundred delegates, "[W]e urge you to keep your courage high and allow us to vote for a really improved Constitution. Do not be misled by the few loud voices which say, 'Favor us, or we will not vote for your new Constitution.'" A dozen delegates wrote to thank Anderson. "I am hoping to retain my ideals and 'dream the impossible dream' [to] . . . get a new constitution free from special interests," responded Missoula delegate Mae Nan Robinson.

The Montana League of Women Voters then campaigned hard for adoption of the new constitution. Three months before the statewide vote, Anderson rallied local chapters: "We are counting on member participation and the knowledge you all should now have after three years of study. . . . If you are shaky, bone up. The next two months will make all our previous efforts worthwhile ONLY IF IT PASSES." It did.

Montana's LWV soon evolved. By 1974, men could join, although a state newsletter that year mused, "We have built something special in the

League—and men, God bless 'em, may not be ready for it. . . . They're not used to submerging occupational prejudices and concentrat[ing] on issues instead of political considerations." Simultaneously, women moved steadily into the paid workforce—taking with them the time and skill they had invested in volunteer leadership.

Still, in the years beyond 1972, LWV members answered the call for public service. "I'm an optimist," retired State Senator Eck said in 2011. "My philosophy has always been if you see something that isn't working well, don't just complain. See if you can do something about it." She and her League of Women Voters sisters lived that premise. Montana's landmark constitution stands tribute.

Defining Gender Equality: The Debate over the Equal Rights Amendment in Montana

Annie Hanshew

WHEN THE U.S. Senate approved the Equal Rights Amendment (ERA) in March 1972, the next step—passage by two-thirds of state legislatures—seemed a formality. However, over the next decade, the battle over ratification of the Equal Rights Amendment revealed that the United States was still divided over equality between the sexes. In Montana, the controversy over the ERA suggests similar unease.

The Equal Rights Amendment read simply, "Equality of rights under the law shall not be denied or abridged by the United States or by any State on account of sex." First proposed in 1923, the amendment passed out of Congress in 1972. It then went to the states for approval. In theory, Montana's ratification should have been easy; the recently passed 1972 Montana Constitution's "individual dignity" clause already guaranteed Montana women equal rights. In fact, ERA proponents argued that ratification was a way for Montanans to ensure that "their loved ones in other states . . . enjoy the same benefits and protections which we have under our state laws."

In reality, ratification was controversial from the beginning. The amendment "breezed through the house by a 73-23 vote" in 1973, but, despite the fact that forty out of Montana's fifty state senators had signed on as sponsors of the bill, anti-ERA activists managed to convince the senate to table discussion.

The topic proved "emotionally explosive" when ratification came up again in 1974. According to the *Billings Gazette,* "the Equal Rights Amendment has triggered more public response than any other issue before the legislature." In a debate published in the Kalispell *Daily Inter Lake,* Elizabeth McNamer, wife of a senator who had led the fight against the ERA the previous year, averred that while she was "all for women's rights," she opposed the amendment because it would "strip all women of certain legal benefits in order to give some women needed rights." She also appealed to traditional arguments about women's role in society: "Women are the gentler sex. . . . We are the civilizers. Women are better at raising children. I speak from personal experience. My mother, the original women's libber, worked and my father stayed at home. It doesn't work." Supporters of ratification claimed the "argument . . . that the Equal Rights Amendment would destroy home life and force women into servitude . . . is preposterous," but McNamer's statement reflected a widely expressed fear that women would lose their "privileged" position in society if the ERA passed.

Amid heated debate, ratification ultimately eked through the senate in 1974, making Montana the thirty-second state to approve the ERA. The controversy, however, did not die with ratification. Passage of the amendment required ratification by thirty-eight states, and by 1974 the amendment's political momentum had stalled. A coalition of social conservatives and religious institutions mounted a well-organized and highly visible campaign against the amendment. Groups like Phyllis Schlafly's Stop ERA mobilized members

National Organization for Women members Dee Adams (holding the banner) and Doris Brander (Malta ERA T-shirt) are pictured here at a pro-ERA "Failure Is Impossible" rally in Helena in 1982. MHS Photo Archives PAc 89-65

to oppose ratification in states considering ERA and to fight for rescission in states that had already ratified.

In Montana, a group calling itself Montana Citizens to Rescind ERA organized almost immediately after ratification. Marcella Warila of Butte joined the club because she wanted "to keep our right to stay home and be homemakers." Anti-ERA advocates also appealed to fears that the amendment would promote homosexuality, facilitate on-demand abortions, lead to unisex bathrooms, and make women subject to military conscription. After the Montana Supreme Court struck down Rescind ERA's attempt to bring the issue to Montana voters in a 1974 referendum, they instead focused on lobbying the Montana legislature, and bills to rescind were introduced in the 1975, 1977, and 1979 sessions.

The issue was especially heated in 1979. The previous year, Congress had voted to extend the deadline for ratification from March 1979 to June 1982 to give ERA supporters more time to get the amendment through recalcitrant state legislatures. By the time Montana's 1979 legislature convened, three states—Idaho, Nebraska, and Tennessee—had already rescinded, and one state—South Dakota—had stipulated that its ratification would end with the original 1979 deadline.

Montana conservatives decided to follow South Dakota's lead. Backed by Betty Babcock, the former first lady and 1972 constitutional convention delegate, and Patrick Sherrill, a lobbyist employed by the Church of Jesus Christ of Latter-day Saints, Senator Jack Galt introduced a resolution affirming the March 1979 deadline. While Galt claimed that the resolution was simply meant to "reaffirm Montana's respect for the Constitution and the time-tested process of amending it," ERA proponents argued that the resolution was "cheap rescission." Hundreds of people came to the committee hearing on the resolution, which "squeaked through" the senate by a vote of 26–24 but ultimately died in the house.

In the end, Montana's ratification of the Equal Rights Amendment stood, suggesting that Montanans had an ideological commitment—albeit an uneasy one—to gender equality. Ultimately, however, the debate was moot. No states ratified the ERA after 1977, leaving the amendment stalled three states short of the thirty-eight needed for ratification. Speaking in March 1982, when defeat of the amendment seemed inevitable, ERA proponent and state legislator Dorothy Bradley encouraged her audience to focus on all that they had accomplished. "If it hadn't been for the nationwide ERA campaign," she argued, "it is unlikely Montana would have created its own Constitutional provision for equal rights." "We probably won't have the

ERA on June 30," she continued, "but look around yourself and you know our work will leave a mark. . . . [T]he efforts on behalf of equal rights, and on behalf of women, will continue."

Working to Give Women "Individual Dignity": Equal Protection of the Laws under Montana's Constitution

Annie Hanshew

In 1972, Americans were engaged in a national debate over whether to ratify the Equal Rights Amendment (ERA) to the U.S. Constitution. That debate informed discussion during Montana's 1972 constitutional convention, and convention delegates enshrined equal protection in the "individual dignity" clause of its Declaration of Rights. Backed by this promise of equality, women's rights advocates and members of the newly formed Montana Women's Political Caucus, an organization of female state legislators, worked to reform Montana's laws to erase sex discrimination. Through their efforts, the 1970s saw important steps toward equalization of Montana's laws; however, the Montana Supreme Court's conservative application of the individual dignity clause to sex discrimination undercut the potential for radical strides toward legal equality.

The Declaration of Rights in Montana's 1889 constitution stated that "all persons are born equally free," but the 1972 constitution went far beyond that vague provision in its individual dignity clause. Working on the language for the state's new constitution, delegate Virginia Blend of Great Falls proposed that the actual language of the Equal Rights Amendment be included in the Declaration of Rights. Instead the 1972 constitution addressed the issue of gender equity in the "individual dignity" clause, which guaranteed equal protection of the laws. Notable for its expansiveness, Article II, Section 4, of the 1972 constitution promised that "neither the state nor any person, firm, corporation, or institution shall discriminate against any person in the exercise of his civil or political rights on account of race, color, sex, culture, social origin or condition, or political or religious ideas." The clause linked equality to human dignity and included a long list of protected classes, making it, according to scholars Larry Elison and Fritz Snyder, the "most inclusive scheme of 'equal rights' of any known constitution."

Though many of the delegates to the state constitutional convention assumed that the ERA would soon pass nationally, they specifically decided to include "sex" in the list of protected classes because they "saw no reason

An active member of the Montana Women's Political Caucus, Geraldine Travis was elected to the Montana House of Representatives from House District 43 in 1974. She is pictured here with Governor Thomas Judge (seated) and other politicians as Judge signs her first bill into law. Courtesy Geraldine Travis

for the state to wait for the adoption of the federal equal rights amendment." In light of the national failure to ratify the ERA, Montana's statement of its commitment to gender equality became even more important.

Once the constitution was ratified, Montana lawmakers—particularly women lawmakers—began a push to align state laws and institutions with the new guarantee of equality. The forty-third Montana legislature (1973–1974) created three new state agencies to monitor discrimination: the Human Rights Bureau, the Equal Employment Opportunity (EEO) Bureau, and the Women's Bureau. The Human Rights Bureau, the administrative arm of the newly created Montana Human Rights Commission, was given the power to handle discrimination complaints. The EEO and Women's Bureaus helped place women and minorities in state jobs and spread information about opportunities for women, but both agencies lacked enforcement powers.

In the forty-fourth Montana Legislature (1975), members of the Montana Women's Political Caucus undertook a concerted effort to eliminate legal sex discrimination in Montana. Caucus members proposed bills, including ones that prohibited discrimination in government employment, reformed divorce and custody laws, and equalized the obligations of support between spouses. Not all of their proposals passed. For example, a bill making it illegal to patronize a prostitute died on the floor. However, other efforts to remove sex discrimination from property and criminal laws moved through and quickly were signed into law.

Two key factors facilitated the push for legislating legal equality. Reapportionment shifted political power to Montana's urban areas, which led to the election of more progressive Democrats. Accompanying that change, a surge of female legislators helped shift the agenda to shed light on sex discrimination. In 1971, only one woman, Dorothy Bradley, served in the state legislature. In 1975, there were ten women in the house and four in the senate, including Geraldine Travis, Montana's first and only African American state legislator. These numbers meant that women comprised 9.3 percent of the legislature.

As legislators worked to rewrite Montana's laws one at a time, the Montana Supreme Court could have facilitated the process by invoking the individual dignity clause to chip away at sex discrimination. In other areas of constitutional law, notably the right to privacy, which is also guaranteed by the 1972 constitution, the court used the new constitution to forward a much broader set of protections than existed federally. By contrast, in the area of sex discrimination, the court tended to overlook the Montana constitution's equal rights provisions, relying instead on federal equal protection decisions to justify its determinations.

In spite of women's gains in the legislative arena, the process of eliminating sex discrimination from the law through legislative action was slow, piecemeal, and ongoing, and the Montana Supreme Court's reluctance to facilitate the process undercut the radical potential of the individual dignity clause. As attorney Jeanne M. Koester noted, "The Montana equal rights provision calls for an *unequivocal* 'eradication of public and private discrimination based on . . . sex.' Sex discrimination can be eradicated only if the Montana courts fully recognize this new right."

Writing a Rough-and-Tumble World: Caroline Lockhart and B. M. Bower

Annie Hanshew

FOLLOWING the publication of Owen Wister's *The Virginian* in 1902, Western novels became extremely popular, and several Montana women became successful genre writers. These writers, including Caroline Lockhart and Bertha Muzzy Sinclair Cowan (best known as B. M. Bower), drew inspiration from the life, land, and folklore of Montana. Their stories suggest the enduring place that Montana has in the imagined, symbolic West of the past. They also reveal the role gender discrimination played in popular expectations about Westerns and their creators.

Scholar Jane Tompkins has explored the power of the Western—both in novels and on film—in the American psyche. She argues, "The West functions as a symbol of freedom and of the opportunity for conquest. It seems to offer escape from the condition of life in modern industrial society. . . . [T]he creak of saddle leather and the sun beating down, the horses' energy and force—these things promise a translation of the self into something purer and more authentic, more intense, more real." This version of the West was decidedly masculine. And while largely mythic, it was an idea that was wildly popular—especially among the country's young men—from 1900 to 1975.

Montana's women writers both capitalized on this western myth and modified it. Caroline Lockhart was often quoted as saying she was "born on a horse," and her Westerns reflect her deep affection for both the West and the ranching way of life. Born in Illinois in 1871, Lockhart grew up in Kansas. Her father farmed and later traded cattle, so Lockhart had early experience with rural farm life. At eighteen, she moved east to become the first female reporter for the *Boston Globe*. She later moved to Philadelphia to work for the *Philadelphia Bulletin*. In 1901, the paper sent her to Montana to write a story about the Blackfeet Indians. During the trip, Lockhart fell in love with the West; in 1904, she moved to Cody, Wyoming, and launched her new career as a Western novelist.

Caroline Lockhart's first book was *Me-Smith*. Published in 1911, it became a national hit and was compared favorably with the writings of Owen Wister. One reviewer praised its realistic portrayal of western life: "[*Me-Smith*] is a photograph of the actual life of the West. You see and grasp the life of this country." Her second novel, *The Lady Doc*, became even more popular nationally, though it drew significant criticism in Cody for its close resemblance to (and unsympathetic portrayal of) actual townspeople. *The Lady Doc* cemented Lockhart's reputation as a novelist who excelled at creating strong characters in a "realistic"—at least in the minds of easterners—western setting.

Lockhart's love of the West was lifelong, and she worked hard to preserve what she believed was the authentic frontier. In 1925, she retired to

Western author Bertha M. Bower (left) rides along the Tongue River in 1917, accompanied by Nancy Russell's sister, Ella Ironside. MHS Photo Archives 941-206.

an eastern Montana ranch situated on the Bighorn River near the Pryor Mountains. Taking the position that "petticoats are no bar to progress in either writing or ranching," Lockhart developed a working homestead and eventually acquired cattle.

Explaining her willingness to take up the difficult life of ranching when she was already economically successful, Lockhart wrote in a press release to the *Cody Enterprise*: "Miss Lockhart is a lover of the old west, and made her home in Cody for many years until the dudes and the march of progress made this an altogether too citified atmosphere for her tastes. In the Dryhead country she has found just the haven which she desires. . . . [There] the drone of the motor car is unknown." Lockhart's final novel expressed a similar nostalgia for the primitivism of an Old West that she feared was disappearing. Published in 1933, it was aptly titled *The Old West and the New*.

Dorothy Johnson (perhaps Montana's most beloved female author) suggested that it was harder for women to write Westerns because "a woman's name on a Western book scares off a number of readers. . . . [T]hey think women can't write what they want to read." Caroline Lockhart enjoyed publishing success in spite of her gender. Unlike Lockhart, Bertha Muzzy Sinclair Cowan excelled in the masculine genre of the Western in part because she published under the name B. M. Bower, allowing her audience to assume that she was a man.

Born in Minnesota in 1871, Bertha Muzzy (B.M.) moved with her family to a ranch near Big Sandy in 1889. She married three times but published under Bower, her first husband's name. Bower's stories took place at the fictitious Flying U ranch in north-central Montana. Readers were drawn in by Bower's convincing portrait of ranch life, which was based in part on her experiences. Her readers' assumptions that she must be a man—because only a man could know that much about cows and cowboys—also contributed to Bower's success.

Bower's career as a writer reveals the extent to which audiences expected the world of Westerns to be a masculine one. One western historian, upon learning Bower was a woman, reportedly said, "I have skulked in the shadows ever since. It broke my heart." Female fans were more generous. Dorothy Johnson credited Bower with first inspiring her to become a doctor—because Bower's hero Chip Fuzzy fell for one—and later a writer. She joked, "It's a good thing that such books as *Vanity Fair* and *Anna Karenina* didn't have as much impact on me as *Chip of the Flying U.*"

Biased Justice: Women in Prison

Ellen Baumler

ACROSS THE frontier West, abandonment, poverty, domestic abuse, and poor education led some women to crime. When women stood accused of serious crimes in all-male courtrooms, gender, race, and social status worked against them. And, once incarcerated, women served their time neglected and forgotten in prisons built for men. The Montana Territorial Penitentiary at Deer Lodge, built in 1871, was no exception.

In 1878, Hispanic prostitute Felicita Sanchez became the first female inmate at Montana's prison. True to form, her ethnicity, profession, and gender were factors in her three-year sentence for manslaughter. As the warden led her to an empty cell within the men's cell house, three guards stated that they would not attend a female prisoner and resigned.

A year later, Mary Angeline Drouillard was the second woman sentenced to Deer Lodge. Drouillard sat in the Missoula County jail for a year awaiting trial for the shooting death of her abusive husband. At twenty-four, she was three times married and twice divorced, a battered woman whose multiple partners implied loose morals. These factors and her French

Canadian heritage guaranteed conviction. Although Mary's young daughter had witnessed the crime and could have corroborated her mother's story, no one questioned her, and the judge sentenced Drouillard to fifteen years in the penitentiary.

Nineteenth-century society saw Sanchez and Drouillard as fallen women whose ethnicity and sexual conduct made them unredeemable. Guilt or innocence hardly mattered in courtrooms where all-male juries often based their verdicts on social bias. Jury demographics changed little in the early twentieth century, even after Montana women won suffrage in 1914. Women began serving on juries only after the state legislature redefined the term "jury" as a "body of persons" instead of "a body of men" in 1939.

Wealthy Missoula madam Mary Gleim was one of the few who beat the system. Charged with dynamiting the home of a rival, she was convicted of assault with intent to commit murder. She began her fourteen-year sentence in 1894, but expensive attorneys won her a new trial. Witnesses disappeared, the victim died, and the judge dismissed her case. Before year's end, Mary Gleim paid her bond and walked out of prison.

Bessie Fisher was not so lucky in 1901. When "Big Eva" Frye drew a knife and lunged at her, Fisher fired her gun. The coroner ruled it self-defense, but because she was black, addicted to morphine, and a common prostitute, nineteen-year-old Fisher had three strikes against her. The jury found Fisher guilty, and the judge sentenced her to twenty years at Deer Lodge.

Deer Lodge was a men's prison, where female inmates were never allowed to leave their cells. Believing that hard work rehabilitated prisoners, Warden Frank Conley put his convicts to work building a massive wall, a cell house, an exercise yard, and female quarters. Conley's work ethic, however, did not include women. Confined inside the men's domain, women languished in their cells.

In 1908, women inmates moved to their own small facility, but they could access their own enclosure only through the men's yard. A female matron replaced male guards, but women still had no educational or work opportunities. In 1910, the state's three female inmates—including Bessie Fisher—were afterthoughts of the judicial system.

In 1918, half of all prisoners at Deer Lodge were listed as "mentally insane." Edith Colby of Thompson Falls was one of them. An aspiring newspaperwoman in 1916, Colby traded insults with a local politician before shooting him three times. Throughout the trial, Colby maintained that her editor had taught her to shoot a gun and had encouraged her to use it.

Burton K. Wheeler of Butte viciously prosecuted the case. Defense attorneys tried to prove insanity, but the jury found her guilty, and Colby served three years in prison.

Lucy Cornforth's pathetic case came before a Miles City judge in 1929. Contemplating suicide, Cornforth had purchased strychnine, mixed it in a cup, and told her eight-year-old daughter of her plans. But Cornforth changed her mind and set the cup aside. The child cried out, "I want to go too!" She seized the cup, drank the poison, and died minutes later.

Cornforth pled guilty to first-degree premeditated murder. Her attorney argued that she was "intellectually deficient," and the judge agreed to life in prison instead of the death penalty. Cornforth was a model prisoner, and after she had served fifteen years, a sponsor agreed to employ her in his home. However, the judge refused parole, maintaining that Cornforth still posed a threat to herself and society. Ten years later, in 1954, a retired teacher again requested a parole board's review for Cornforth, but to no avail.

In 1959, a prison riot and an earthquake forced the state to remove women inmates from Deer Lodge. For the next thirty-five years, they were shuffled from one makeshift facility to another until, in 1994, a retrofitted treatment center in Billings became the women's prison. It currently accommodates more than 265 inmates.

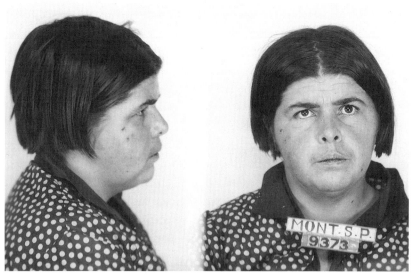

Poor, uneducated, and unmarried, Lucy Cornforth, shown here in her mug shot, was convicted of murdering her daughter in 1929. She spent the remainder of her life either in prison or in Warm Springs State Hospital. MHS Photo Archives Pac 85-91 9373

When Bessie Fisher did her time in the early years of the twentieth century, African Americans were the largest minority among Montana women inmates. This figure is astounding given that black women were so few in Montana in 1910 (only 776 out of Montana's 149,181 female population). Today, a different minority group makes up the majority of women inmates. Only 6 percent of Montana's population is Native American, but Indians make up 27 percent of the state's women inmates.

Although positive changes separate Bessie Fisher's experiences from those of today's prisoners, there is need for improvement. Gender, ethnicity, and poverty are controlling issues behind incarceration, and mental illness and abuse are still common threads. Until there are better solutions, incarcerated women will remain afterthoughts of the judicial system.

Helen Piotopowaka Clarke and the Persistence of Prejudice

Laura Ferguson

IN 1909, the *Anaconda Standard* ran an article called "The Uplift of the Indians." It argued that Indians could be brought from their "untutored, childlike state" and transformed—through education, private property ownership, and conversion to Christianity—into productive American citizens. Perhaps no Montanan of her generation better exemplified this assimilationist ideal than Blackfeet descendent Helen Piotopowaka Clarke. While Clarke's remarkable personal and professional accomplishments earned her great respect and admiration, they also revealed the persistence of anti-Indian prejudices at the turn of the twentieth century.

Helen was born in 1846 to a prominent Scottish American, Malcolm Clarke, and his Blackfeet wife, Cothcocoma. She spent most of her childhood at a convent school in Cincinnati and returned to Montana just a few years before a group of Blackfeet men murdered her father in 1869. Later that year, Helen's brothers participated in the Baker Massacre, during which troops, ostensibly on a mission to capture Malcolm Clarke's killers, slaughtered a peaceful and unassociated Blackfeet camp.

Following these tragic events, Helen Clarke moved back east and had a brief but successful acting career in New York. In 1875, she returned to Montana, where attorney and family friend Wilbur Sanders found her a teaching position in Helena. Not everyone in Helena was happy with her hire. Elizabeth Chester Fisk, whose husband edited the *Helena Herald*, withdrew her children from school because she objected so strenuously to Helen's mixed ancestry. However, enough Helenans were accepting of the refined, devoutly Catholic, and talented woman that they elected Clarke county superintendent of schools in 1882. She held the position for three terms—one of the first two women (and only person of Indian descent) to hold elective office in Montana Territory.

In 1889, Clarke left Montana to work for the Office of Indian Affairs. Two years earlier, Congress had passed the General Allotment Act mandating the allotment of tribal lands to individual Indians and allowing the government to sell "surplus" reservation land to whites. Allotment began in Oklahoma, where Otoes and Poncas—who had purchased their tribal lands outright—stood in strong opposition to allotment. Hoping her Indian ancestry might help her persuade the Otoes and Poncas to cooperate, the bureau hired Clarke as an allotment agent. "Being identified with the Indian race, it is probable that she would be able to exert a greater influence with them than one who is not so identified," the commissioner of Indian Affairs suggested.

Clarke was one of the first two women to serve as an allotment agent. She attempted to carry out her duties, against the tribes' firm opposition, but found her work thwarted by men from the Department of the Interior. She reported, "After two or three weeks . . . it looked as if the work would succeed, when along came officials pretty high in the [Interior] Department to tell the Indians that a woman has no business at this work, which the Indians construe to mean that she has no legal right to do the work."

After four years among the Otoes and Poncas, Clarke moved to San Francisco, where she established herself as a tutor of "artes, elocution and dramatic art." Unfortunately, anti-Indian prejudices followed her to California. In 1901, a "special correspondent" from the *Helena Herald* to the *San Francisco Chronicle* submitted an article that took aim at Clarke's mixed-blood status, declaring, "Miss Clarke was proud, and when it was demonstrated to her humiliation that her birth prevented her from taking the place in society her education and refinement warranted, she decided to leave Helena." The article asserted that, although she was beautiful, "Miss Clarke was known to be the daughter of a Piegan Indian woman, and this fact caused for her to be looked down upon socially." The article alienated Clarke from some of San Francisco's high society, and she left the city in 1903.

Clarke returned to Helena just long enough to grant the *Helena Daily Record* an interview in which she asserted there was no shame in having mixed ancestry. She then moved to the Blackfeet Reservation, where her arrival came at a fortuitous time for the tribe. In an effort to strong-arm the Blackfeet into accepting allotments, the agent there had struck over 90 percent of tribal members from the ration rolls. The Blackfeet hoped Clarke, as an educated woman with some standing with the federal government, could help. She pursued charges of mal-administration against the agent, eventually succeeding in getting him removed from his position. In 1909, Helen and her brother Horace were granted tribal membership and allotments, but, ironically, the Interior Department still required her to prove her ancestry as well as her "competency" so that she could own her allotment outright.

New York photographer Napoleon Sarony, well known for his celebrity portraits, took this picture of Helen Clarke, ca. 1895. MHS Photo Archives 941-745

Dwelling on the pervasiveness of anti-Indian racism, Clarke wrote in 1911, "This very nation looks with eyes askance upon the cultured, the intelligent, intel-lectual half-breeds of mixed-bloods who reside either off or on the reservations. Such inconsistencies in character or principles belong not to a great people." An idealistic advocate of assimilation in her youth, Clarke, by the end of her remarkable life, had proved through experience a bitter truth: no matter how accomplished a woman was, no matter how assimilated a person of indigenous ancestry, early twentieth-century America was largely unwilling to let go of its prejudices against both women and Indians.

A Glamorous Façade: Red-Light Women of Butte

Ellen Baumler

"THE GIRLS range in age from jail bait to battle ax," wrote Monroe Fry of Butte prostitutes in 1953. "[They] sit and tap on the windows. They are ready for business around the clock." Fry named Butte one of the three "most

Although Butte had Montana's largest and most notorious red-light district, prostitutes worked in almost every sizable community. These prostitutes, posing ca. 1905 with potential customers in Miles City, are wearing "Mother Hubbard" dresses, loose gowns designed to be worn without corsets. By the 1880s, these "easy access" dresses had become a prostitute's standard uniform. MHS Photo Archives PAc 95-70, Box 11, Folder 18, Robert C. Morrison Coll.

wide-open towns" in the United States. The other two—Galveston, Texas, and Phenix City, Alabama—existed solely to serve nearby military bases, but Butte's district depended upon hometown customers. Butte earned the designation "wide open"—a place where vice went unchecked—largely because of its flamboyant, very public red-light district and the women who worked there.

For more than a century, these pioneers of a different ilk, highly transient and frustratingly anonymous, molded their business practices to survive changes and reforms. As elsewhere, the fines they paid fattened city coffers, and businesses depended upon their patronage. Reasons for Butte's far-famed reputation went deeper, however, as these women filled an additional role. Miners who spent money, time, and energy on public women were less likely to organize against the powerful Anaconda Copper Mining Company. As long as the mines operated, public women served the company by deflecting men's interest.

Today, the architectural layers of Butte's last intact nineteenth-century parlor house, the Dumas Hotel, now a museum, visually illustrate a changing economy and shifts in clientele. The second floor retains the original suites where Butte's elite spent lavish sums in the high-rolling 1890s. But the ground floor's elegant spaces, where staged soirees preceded upstairs "business," were later converted to cribs, one-room offices where women served their clients.

As the elegant parlor house declined at the end of the nineteenth century, the women began to solicit more blatantly, lounging in the windows of houses and cribs along the district thoroughfares. Scantily clad in wrappers called "shady-go-nakeds," they tapped on their windows, rudely addressing passersby. Small brothels and cribs, reeking of disinfectant, lined the streets and alleyways where thieves loitered. Butte's public women called it the "burnt district," and the widely read, company-owned *Butte Miner* relished reporting on the district's crime and tragedies.

In 1902, the *Miner* issued a special Sunday section on the red-light district that addressed solicitation, unhealthy conditions, urban blight, alcoholism, and the graft city officials openly demanded from public women. While some citizens proposed eliminating or moving the district, the *Miner* presented both sides of the argument. The exposé further advertised Butte's wide-open image, luring even more miners to Butte.

Public women responded to subsequent ordinances. They willingly paid crib rents and monthly fines, but orders to lengthen their dresses, don high-necked blouses, and draw their blinds left them outraged. The women cut holes in the blinds for their faces and organized a protest. In Butte, the heart of the labor movement, prostitutes banded together just this once, loudly tapping on their windows in solidarity. Even so, the city banned solicitation from public thoroughfares, at which point the women cut doors and windows in the backs of the cribs, creating the labyrinth known as Pleasant Alley.

In January 1916, the district expanded as copper rose to a high of twenty cents a pound. At the back of the Dumas, new brick cribs opened onto Pleasant Alley. Activity, however, was short-lived. In 1917, federal law closed red-light districts in an effort to protect World War I enlistees from rampant venereal disease. Prostitution in Butte—including at the Dumas—then moved to dingy basement cribs. In 1990, demolition of the nearby Copper Block revealed tiny, dirt-floored, cave-like cribs where women worked underground under deplorable conditions.

Pleasant Alley reopened in the 1930s as Venus Alley, but federal law closed the district as a wartime measure again in 1943. After World War II, several madams worked out of antique-filled, dilapidated houses. Most of the legendary cribs of Venus Alley, known to Butte's last madams as Piss Alley, fell to the wrecking ball in 1954. At the Dumas today, orange shag carpeting, a pay phone, and red trim reflect its 1960s remodeling.

In 1968, arson closed the Windsor Hotel, which had also served as a parlor house. Its irate madam, Beverly Snodgrass, went to Washington, D.C., to complain to her senators about the loss of her business. She claimed that she had been paying seven hundred dollars monthly as protection money to Butte policemen since 1963 and that uniformed officers frequently demanded free services of her employees. Senator Mike Mansfield determined, however, that this was a local matter.

After an eight-part series on Butte vice in the *Great Falls Tribune*, Butte's three remaining houses closed. Only Ruby Garrett at the Dumas reopened. Customers paid about twenty dollars for the services of her several employees, and Garrett, too, claimed she paid Butte police monthly protection money. She had already been robbed twice when a third brutal holdup in 1981 prompted unwanted publicity. Charged with federal income tax evasion, Garrett promised not to reopen and served six months in federal detention. It was no accident that the Dumas's 1982 closure coincided with the final shutdown of Butte's mines.

Charlie Chaplin claimed that Butte's public women were the most beautiful, the best treated, and the luckiest. In reality, Butte's red-light district was compelling because of the disparity between its glamorous façade and its true underbelly. Women were at the heart of this double image. Today, metal figures—the work of local high school shop students—quietly commemorate the anonymous women who worked along the brick-paved alleyways. The prostitutes' presence also lingers in Butte's historic "wide-open" mythology.

Doris Brander and the Fight to Honor Women's Military Service

Jodie Foley

"EVEN NOW there's that feeling of bitterness. . . . [W]e tend to forget that we were way out of line back there in the '40s to even venture to join the service, because it just wasn't done. We really were rebels." This is how Doris

Brander, a World War II veteran from Avon, Montana, described the sexism she experienced during her military service.

Born in Malta, Montana, on August 29, 1921, Doris I. Palm Brander graduated from Malta High School, joined the Navy's Women's Accepted for Voluntary Emergency Service (WAVES) in 1942, shortly after Pearl Harbor, and attended the U.S. Naval Training School in New York.

Like most of her compatriots, Brander enlisted in the Navy out of the dual desires for adventure and to contribute to the war effort. As she recalled, "I think most of us women that volunteered in the Army, Navy, Marine Corps, and Coast Guard did it out of a sense of adventure, but also because we knew that until the war was over, both in Europe and in Asia, things would not go back to normal. So by pitching in and helping, we felt we would get things back to normal faster. We wanted to do what we could to stop the war."

As reasonable as she found these goals, she discovered that her male comrades often questioned her motives and abilities. "Because we were cutting a new path in history with our volunteering for the service, we were really looked at with question marks as to what our purpose was, what our motive was, what our morals were," she recalled.

Doris Brander, shown here in her enlistment photo, joined the Navy's Women's Accepted for Voluntary Emergency Service (WAVES) in 1942, shortly after Pearl Harbor. Courtesy Linda Brander

After the war, Brander settled on a ranch near Avon. She returned to college in her fifties, ultimately becoming the medical records manager for Warm Springs State Hospital. However, she never forgot her military experience, and through oral histories, essays, and presentations, she gave voice to feelings shared by women veterans of the World War II era, and well beyond.

Brander's commitment to promoting women's military service extended long after World War II ended. "Women love their country as much as men," she explained, "and I am really proud to have been part of the forerunners who opened up the way for the young women of today to serve in more areas than we were allowed."

Even as women continued to serve in the military, however, no monuments or memorials in Washington, D.C., recognized their sacrifices. Determined to see that women veterans received appropriate recognition, Brander joined the Women in Military Service for American Memorial Foundation (WIMSA) in 1990. Founded five years earlier, in 1985, the organization promoted the building of a monument at Arlington National Cemetery to honor all women who served in the U.S. military.

Brander led the campaign for Montana's participation in the national effort. She convinced Montana governor Stan Stephens, the tribal councils of Montana's seven Indian reservations, and each of Montana's fifty-six counties to issue resolutions in support of the memorial. She also successfully petitioned the governor's office to establish a Women Veterans Day.

Brander raised over fifty thousand dollars to support the memorial. And she recruited an army of volunteers to document as many as possible of the estimated forty-eight hundred female veterans in Montana. Those volunteers copied discharge papers from county records, obtained enlistment records from the adjutant general's file at the Montana Historical Society, and appealed to friends and relatives of veterans to provide information. All in all, Brander's efforts played an important role in making WIMSA a success.

Designed by Marion Gail Weiss and Michael Manfredi, the Women in Military Service for America Memorial at the ceremonial entrance to Arlington National Cemetery opened to the public in October 1997. Annually, over two hundred thousand people now visit the site that honors "all military women—past, present and future."

As important as Brander's contributions toward the creation of the national monument were, so too is the rich collection of records she gathered in the course of that work. These records explore the experiences of Montana women who served in the military in the two world wars, the Korean War, the Vietnam War, and in peacetime. Today, they reside at the Montana Historical Society, where they are available to researchers.

"I Am a Very Necessary Evil": The Political Career of Dolly Smith Cusker Akers

Laura Ferguson

MONTANA'S FIRST Native American legislator and the first woman to chair the executive board of the Assiniboine and Sioux tribes was not a women's liberation advocate because she refused to acknowledge women's limits. The fight Dolly Smith Cusker Akers did champion, however, was that of American Indians to determine their own destinies free from federal oversight and interference. Assertive and self-reliant—as she believed tribes should be—Akers achieved many notable accomplishments in her lifetime, but not without conflict and criticism.

Born in 1901 in Wolf Point, Dolly Smith was the daughter of Nellie Trexler, an Assiniboine, and William Smith, an Irish American. She attended school on the Fort Peck Reservation and at the all-Indian Sherman Institute in California. Graduating at age sixteen, she returned to Montana and married George Cusker in 1917.

In the early 1920s, the Fort Peck tribes sent two elders to Washington, D.C., to lobby for school funding. Neither elder spoke English, so Dolly accompanied them as interpreter. The articulate young woman impressed the congressmen, whom she then lobbied in favor of universal citizenship for American Indians—an issue that had been debated for many years. In 1924, the Indian Citizenship Act became law, establishing the basis for American Indian suffrage and furthering the government's long-term goal of gradual absorption of American Indians into American society.

At Fort Peck, Cusker frequently attended tribal executive board meetings on behalf of her husband, who was often debilitated by alcoholism. In time, the board appointed her the first woman on the tribal executive board, a position she held on and off for many years.

Concerned with the economic difficulties affecting Montana's tribes during the Great Depression, Dolly Cusker ran as a Democrat for the state legislature in 1932 and received almost 100 percent of the vote in Roosevelt County, where whites outnumbered Indians by nearly ten to one. The

Elected to the Montana House in 1932, with almost 100 percent of the vote, Dolly Cusker Akers was the first Native American to serve in the Montana legislature and the only woman serving during her two-year term. She was also the first woman to serve on the Fort Peck Tribal Executive Board. MHS Photo Archives, Legislative Coll.

first Native American person to be elected to the Montana legislature and just thirty-one, she was the only female legislator during the 1933–1934 session.

In 1934, Governor Frank Cooney named Cusker the state's first coordinator for Indian welfare and asked her to represent Montana's Indians to the secretary of the Interior. American Indians were treated differently from non-Indians with regard to relief during the Great Depression because states and counties did not want to assume responsibility for these new American citizens. In Washington, D.C., Cusker succeeded in securing federal relief for tribal members.

Dolly remarried to John Akers in 1944 and invested in their ranch while maintaining her involvement in tribal matters. Now a Republican, she opposed the management of tribal affairs by the Bureau of Indian Affairs (BIA), especially policies that prevented tribes from independently negotiating the development of their own natural resources and the sale or lease of Indian lands. "Why should Indian people," she asked in 1952, "be forced to live under a law made some eighty years ago? That is the year in which the Indian Commissioner referred to Indians as 'wild beasts!'"

Akers charged that the BIA sold land and mineral rights out from under tribes, robbing Indians of royalties that could have provided essential income. "There can be no real solution of the so-called 'Indian problem' unless the Interior Department embraces the principle of self-determination of Indian people by actual practice," argued Akers. "The archaic protective rules and laws merely tend to hamper the Indian people from attaining their final goal of self-sufficiency, which is the goal of Congress for the Interior Department to foster."

In 1953, the Republican-led Congress and Interior Department enacted their version of tribal "self-sufficiency" through Public Law 108, or Termination, which ended the federal government's treaty obligations to tribes and left "terminated" tribes to sink or swim on their own. Akers, a supporter of the principles behind Termination, was elected the first female chair of the Fort Peck executive board in 1956. Her critics accused Chairwoman Akers of only serving her own interests and doing so in an underhanded manner. Alleging misuse of tribal funds, her adversaries voted to impeach her in 1958.

Nonetheless, Akers continued to exert her influence in Indian issues, briefly becoming vice president of the National Congress of American Indians in the 1960s and later serving on the Montana Intertribal Policy Board. As chair of the Fort Peck Tribal Housing Authority in the 1970s, Akers succeeded in acquiring federal funds for much-needed housing on the Fort Peck Reservation. However, the tribal council voted to remove her from the housing authority, complaining that she unfairly used her authority to secure houses for her supporters rather than treating all applicants equitably. In Aker's defense, one woman reminded the council that Akers was the only person who "had the guts" to confront the BIA when it owed tribal members money from land sales.

Over the course of six decades, Akers made numerous trips to D.C. to voice her views on Indian matters and to influence politicians. Among the improvements she was most proud of having supported were a regulation permitting tribes to hire their own legal counsel and the 1968 Indian Civil Rights Act—both of which removed inequities that had hampered the autonomy of American Indian people. Reflecting on her career, this remarkable woman said, "I am a very necessary evil. I try to stay in the background, but every now and then I have to come out and kick somebody in the shins." Kick she did, and Dolly Akers will be remembered differently by those who benefited from her actions and those whose shins got bruised.

A Young Mother at the Rosebud and Little Bighorn Battles

Laura Ferguson

In 1876, the Lakota, Cheyenne, and Arapaho people defended their sovereignty, their land, and their lives against the United States. The Rosebud and Little Bighorn battles proved the tribes' military strength but ultimately contributed to tragic consequences for the victors. A young Cheyenne mother, Buffalo Calf Road Woman, fought alongside her brother and husband at both battles in defense of Cheyenne freedom.

Buffalo Calf Road Woman lived during the Indian wars, an era of extreme violence against the Native inhabitants of the West. American settlers frequently trespassed onto tribal lands, and tribes retaliated by raiding settler camps. Several brutal massacres of peaceful tribal groups by whites led to widespread fear among the tribes and shocked the American public. Such violence increased tensions in the region.

After Lakota chief Red Cloud decisively defeated the U.S. military in 1864 to close the Bozeman Trail, the United States negotiated a peace treaty with the Lakota. The 1868 Fort Laramie Treaty established the Great Sioux Reservation, a huge area encompassing present-day western South Dakota, and designated the unceded lands between the Black Hills and the Bighorn Mountains, including the Powder River country, for the Indians' "absolute and undisturbed use." Northern Cheyenne and Arapaho bands also occupied this region.

In 1874 the U.S. government sent Lieutenant Colonel George Custer, who had led a massacre against the Southern Cheyenne four years earlier, to explore the Black Hills. When the expedition found gold, the government sought to buy the Black Hills, but the Lakota refused. Fearing conflict, the government ordered all Indians who remained on this unceded tract to go to the Sioux reservation by January 1876, declaring that troops would deal forcibly with any who refused. However, the region was critical to the Lakotas' existence since it remained prime hunting ground for what was left of the once vast buffalo herds.

The tribes were caught in a double bind: retreat to the reservation and possibly starve or continue to occupy their full territory and risk attack. In the summer of 1876, several hundred Cheyennes and Lakotas camped in the Powder River and Little Bighorn valleys. Buffalo Calf Road Woman, her husband Black Coyote, their daughter, and Buffalo Calf Road Woman's brother, Comes In Sight, were among the Cheyennes in these unceded lands west of the reservation when Brigadier General George Crook's troops arrived in the area.

Earlier that year, Crook's men had burned a Cheyenne village. Not wanting to face the same fate, Cheyenne and Lakota warriors attacked Crook's troops at the Rosebud on June 17. When soldiers shot Comes In Sight's horse and he fell, Buffalo Calf Road Woman rode into the heart of the battle. Amid a shower of arrows and bullets, she helped her brother cling to her horse and carried him to safety. At the end of the day, Crook's command withdrew, unable to defeat the tribes. The Lakotas and Cheyennes fled, some joining those camped on the Little Bighorn.

Eight days later, Custer's regiment attacked the Cheyenne and Lakota families at the Little Bighorn. Most of the women took their children and retreated to safety, but some rode onto the battlefield, singing "strong heart" songs of encouragement as they watched for fallen or injured men. One of these women was Antelope (Kate Bighead), who later recalled seeing the lone woman warrior:

Calf Trail Woman had a six-shooter, with bullets and powder, and she fired many shots at the soldiers. She was the only woman there who had a gun. She stayed on her pony all the time, but she kept not far from her husband, Black Coyote. . . . At one time she was about to give her pony to a young Cheyenne who had lost his own, but I called out to them, "Our women have plenty of good horses for you down at the river." . . . She took the young Cheyenne up behind her on her own pony and they rode away toward the river. This same woman was also with the warriors when they went from the Reno creek camp to fight the soldiers far up Rosebud creek

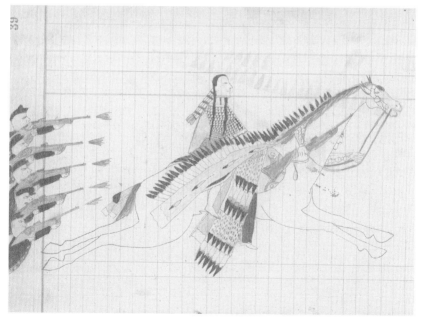

This drawing, from the Spotted Wolf–Yellow Nose Ledger, shows Buffalo Calf Road Woman rescuing her brother through a hail of bullets. Buffalo Calf Road Woman wears an elk tooth dress. Her brother, Comes In Sight, wears a war bonnet. According to the book *We, The Northern Cheyenne People*, the horse's split ears indicate that it is a fast one. Smithsonian Institution, National Anthropological Archives, Bureau of American Ethnology, ms 166.032

about a week before. . . . She was the only woman I know of who went with the warriors to that fight.

Following the tribes' victory at Little Bighorn, the United States redoubled its efforts to hunt down off-reservation Indians. Over twelve hundred Cheyennes took to the hills, pursued by U.S. troops. For many months, several Cheyenne bands eluded capture, fleeing their camps as the soldiers attacked. It was during this period and under these conditions that Buffalo Calf Road Woman had a second child.

By the summer of 1877, the Cheyennes, facing starvation, surrendered. Instead of returning them to the Sioux reservation, however, troops forced-marched them fifteen hundred miles to Indian Territory (present-day Oklahoma) and imprisoned them at Fort Reno. Nearly fifty Cheyennes died en route, and many more succumbed to malaria and exhaustion in the extreme Oklahoma heat. In September 1878, some three hundred Cheyennes led by chiefs Dull Knife and Little Wolf escaped and headed north toward home.

The leaders separated near Fort Robinson, Nebraska, and Buffalo Calf Road Woman's family continued north with Little Wolf. In a rash act, Black Coyote killed a soldier. He and his family were captured and taken to Fort Keogh in Montana, where nearly three hundred Cheyennes were already imprisoned. There, Buffalo Calf Road Woman died from diphtheria in the winter of 1879. In his grief, Black Coyote committed suicide.

Cheyenne warriors recorded Buffalo Calf Road Woman's courageous ride into the Rosebud battle in a ledger drawing. Today, the Cheyenne people still call the battle site "Where the Girl Saved Her Brother." Each January since 1999, Cheyenne runners have participated in a four-hundred-mile memorial run from Fort Robinson to the Northern Cheyenne Reservation in honor of their ancestors who fought for their freedom and sovereignty, including Buffalo Calf Road Woman.

"Things to Be Done Which Money and Men Will Never Provide": The Activism of Montana's AAUW

Laura Ferguson

THE AMERICAN ASSOCIATION of University Women (AAUW) has always aspired to the promotion of women as fully contributing, educated members of society. Until the 1960s, this organization of female college graduates remained largely apolitical. At the division (state) level, Montana's AAUW created the highly successful AAUW Education Foundation to provide college fellowships for women, while local branches focused primarily on community-building projects. However, the social, economic, and political changes during the 1960s and 1970s spurred a transformation in the AAUW. "There are things to be done which money and men will never provide," said one Montana member. Under the leadership of courageous feminists, the AAUW evolved into a prominent activist organization that brought women to the forefront of public-policy making.

In 1960, most AAUW members were homemakers or held traditionally female occupations in teaching or clerical work. Few Montana women had attained professional careers or advanced to leadership positions; fewer still worked in the public-policy arena. When Governor Tim Babcock created a state Commission on the Status of Women in 1965, the AAUW seized the chance to initiate policy changes and secured the appointment of several of its members to the commission.

In 1967, Montana's AAUW formed its own Status of Women Committee. That same year, the Billings branch organized a unique Inter-club Committee on the Status of Women that included two members from each of the participating groups: AAUW, Soroptimists, Altrusa, Zonta, and the National Federation of Business and Professional Women's Clubs. Its goals were to get more women into local, county, and statewide appointed offices; to encourage women to stand for state elective office; and to keep women in office as state superintendent of schools.

The inter-club committee adopted a strategy of solidarity: they committed to being nonpartisan, providing constructive support to women candidates, and not voicing opposition to any woman nominee chosen by members. Within a year, one of the coalition's nominees was appointed to the Montana Selective Service Board (the first woman ever in this position) and another to the State Milk Control Board. "By pooling our efforts we could exert more influence on the appointing administrators than if we, or our clubs, had attempted this individually," reported the Billings AAUW president. Following Billings's lead, Helena women from AAUW, Zonta, League of Women Voters, Soroptimists, and the Helena Graduate Home Economists joined forces to create the Capital City Status of Women Committee.

The Status of Women committees nominated qualified AAUW women to fill Montana's many appointed public positions, and AAUW members wrote letters supporting women candidates. AAUW branches also sent

AAUW members concerned themselves with a broad range of issues. At this Great Falls workshop in 1965, members heard from a panel that included Alma Jacobs, far right, the Special Chair for Implementing Library Resolution, as well as from the Legislative Program Chair, Division Publicity Chair, Special Chairman for Mental Health, and I.C. for Science. MHS Photo Archives PAc 90-20, Folder 10

observers to local government and school board meetings, educated both men and women on the need for having qualified women in public office, and created local leadership development programs for women.

Several prominent AAUW leaders gained appointments to state offices during the 1960s and 1970s, including Bozeman's Geraldine Fenn to the Montana Council on Human Resources, Billings's Doris Davies to the Montana Library Commission, and Helena's Harriett Meloy to the Board of Public Education. Women in state-level appointments gained valuable experience that often opened doors to higher positions. Fenn later represented Montana and the AAUW at the White House Conference on Children; Meloy served eight years on the National Committee for Support of Public Schools.

While the inter-club committees achieved great success in securing nonpartisan public appointments for women, women were still nearly absent from the policy arena. In 1969, for example, only one woman served in Montana's legislature—giving women just 1.6 percent representation.

"AAUW members can and should be the key activators in most communities!" the Montana Division's Status of Women chairperson, Natalie Cannon, told branch presidents. "Legislators must be convinced that we and our issues are serious; they must be stripped of their condescending attitude, and they must be made to realize that human values are worthy of higher priorities."

To combat inadequate representation and to familiarize women with legislative processes, in 1965 the AAUW began sponsoring a Legislative Day during each session. This groundwork produced many legislative triumphs in the late 1960s and 1970s. The Missoula branch earned one of the AAUW's earliest policy victories with the passage of a bill requiring day-care licensure. Anaconda AAUW conducted a statewide survey of mental health needs and presented the findings as recommendations to the state legislature. Billings and Helena branches led a well-organized, seven-year campaign to create state-funded public kindergartens. AAUW members Louise Cross of Glendive and Harriett Meloy of Helena organized tours of strip mines in eastern Montana and helped create reclamation regulations. The Governor's Commission on the Status of Women, chaired by AAUW's Maxine Johnson, introduced family planning and pro-choice legislation drafted by the Helena, Miles City, and Bozeman branches. AAUW members' lobbying efforts contributed significantly to the passage of these key pieces of legislation.

Another of AAUW's priorities in the early 1970s was to ensure that women were included in Montana's constitutional convention. Three AAUW members became delegates to the "Con-Con": Mae Nan Robinson (Missoula), Lynn Sparks (Butte), and Louise Cross (Glendive). The AAUW delegates ensured that the 1972 constitution included Montanans' "right to a clean and healthful environment," equal rights language, and the mandate to teach about Montana's Indian tribes in public schools.

Since the 1970s, AAUW has continued to expand educational and political opportunities for women while keeping issues of importance to women before the legislature. Through the Montana Women's Lobby, established in 1982, the AAUW and its sister organizations continue to advocate for women's rights and against the erosion of past achievements. Today, the AAUW remains an active supporter of fully funded public education, women's reproductive rights, equal pay, the implementation of Indian Education for All and Title IX, voting rights, fair elections, and equal rights for all citizens.

"We Are No Longer Criminals": The Fight to Repeal Deviate Sexual Misconduct Laws

Kayla Blackman

IN 1993, Linda Gryczan told her neighbors she was suing the State of Montana to overturn a law that criminalized gay sex. Though she "was afraid that someone might burn down her house," her neighbors—and activists across the state—rallied to her cause. Those who believed homosexuality should remain a crime also mobilized. Women took leading roles on both sides of the decades-long fight over Montana's deviate sexual misconduct law.

Passed in 1973, Statute 45-5-505 of the Montana Annotated Code defined "deviate sexual relations" as "sexual contact or sexual intercourse between two persons of the same sex or any form of sexual intercourse with an animal." Though rarely enforced, the law carried a fine of up to fifty thousand dollars as well as ten years in prison and made same-sex consensual intimacy a felony.

At the urging of gay and lesbian rights advocates, Montana state representative Vivian Brooke (D-Missoula) introduced a bill in both 1991 and 1993 to strike the law from the books. The bill failed in both sessions. Many legislators agreed with Representative Tom Lee, who argued that "[God] has declared homosexual activity to be wrong, and I don't think we serve the other people of this state by contradicting him." Others, noting that the law was not enforced, wished to avoid political fallout over what they saw as a symbolic vote.

Frustrated by their lack of progress in the legislature, repeal advocates decided to take their fight to the courts. On December 6, 1993, six lesbian and gay Montanans sued the State: lead plaintiff Linda Gryczan of Clancy was joined by William Summers of Missoula, Doyle Forister of Billings, Stacey Haugland of Bozeman, Donn Farward of Kalispell, and Anne Gehr of Helena. Attorney Rosemary Daszkiewicz of the Seattle-based, feminist Northwest Women's Law Center represented the six activists. She argued that the law led to discriminatory practices in housing and employment, violated the privacy of individuals, and insulted the fundamental dignity of Montana citizens.

The State's attorneys took a two-pronged approach to defending the law. First, they maintained that since the law had never been enforced, none of the plaintiffs had ever suffered direct injury from it, and they therefore lacked "standing" to challenge the statute. However, District Judge Jeffrey

Sherlock rejected the State's request for a dismissal, noting "the fact that the law has never been enforced does not mean it is immune to a court challenge." Secondly, while acknowledging that Montana's constitution guaranteed a right to privacy, the State argued that the right did "not immunize adult same-gender sexual conduct from state regulation."

To prove they had legal standing, the plaintiffs presented evidence of the discrimination they had experienced. They also showcased the social and emotional toll of living under Statute 45-5-505. Stacey Haugland testified, "Every time I've filled out a job application, they would ask, 'Have you been convicted of a felony?' and I had to sit there and say, in my mind, well, not convicted." Anne Gehr, the mother of a young son, expressed her fear that Statute 45-5-505 could be used by social service agencies to remove children from their homes. Psychologists also confirmed that laws such as Statute 45-5-505 created a culture of fear. Dr. Janet Allison testified that "living in a state of knowing that you can be prosecuted anytime simply for being who you are is a terrifying experience."

Supporters of repealing Statute 45-5-505 produced and distributed this pin that featured a pink triangle, the gay rights symbol. Courtesy Linda Gryczan

The debate continued in the court of public opinion. Laurie Koutnik, executive director of the Christian Coalition of Montana, claimed that to repeal the act "would be to cast aside millennia of moral teaching." Arlette Randash, a spokesperson for the Eagle Forum, suggested that legalizing same-sex intimacy would encourage children to experiment with promiscuity and increase AIDS among young people.

On December 8, 1995, Judge Sherlock handed down his decision in favor of the plaintiffs. He issued an immediate injunction with his ruling, pointing out that "[i]f, as has been suggested, the statute is an attempt to protect public morality, the statute is not doing a very good job since no one has ever enforced it."

The State appealed the case, but two years later, on July 2, 1997, the Montana Supreme Court unanimously upheld Judge Sherlock's ruling. In issuing its opinion, the court explained that the Montana constitution guarantees "individual privacy" except where there is "a compelling state interest," and that the State had failed to show any such "compelling interest."

Justice James Nelson said in summary, "Quite simply, consenting adults expect that neither the state nor their neighbors will be cohabitants in their bedrooms."

Repeal advocates were overjoyed. Diane Sands, Montana's first openly gay legislator, called the ruling "a glorious Fourth of July reaffirmation of the constitution." Plaintiff Donn Farward hoped the victory was the first step toward "attaining the rights that everyone else takes for granted." On the other hand, opponents feared that legalizing same-sex intimacy opened "the door to the entire homosexual agenda."

At first, both hopes and fears seemed overblown. In 2004, a majority of Montana voters, 67 percent, supported a constitutional amendment defining marriage as "between one man and one woman." Missoula and Helena did pass ordinances prohibiting discrimination on the basis of sexual orientation in 2010 and 2012, respectively, but Statute 45-05-505 remained on the law books—no longer enforceable but retaining symbolic power.

That changed in 2013, when the Republican-led Montana state legislature passed Senate Bill 107, removing the law the Montana Supreme Court had declared unconstitutional sixteen years earlier. As lesbian and gay rights advocates rejoiced in their victory, Gryczan's remarks from 1997 finally echoed true: "We are no longer called criminals for whom we love. We are at last legal citizens."

Gifts of Love and Gratitude: Belle Highwalking

Laura Ferguson

A CUSTOM among many tribes, the giveaway—and the love and gratitude it represents—strengthens social bonds through reciprocal acts of generosity. Similarly, the tribal tradition of adoption to replace lost family members helps heal broken hearts and builds family ties. These culturally prescribed acts of generosity and love were central to the life of Belle Highwalking, a Northern Cheyenne woman.

Belle's mother died giving birth to her in 1892. The Cheyennes pitied the motherless child and considered Belle poor, for a mother provided material and emotional sustenance. Belle's grandmother took the infant to nursing mothers to be fed until Belle was able to drink canned milk.

As a young girl, Belle traveled on horseback with her grandmother to visit relatives on the Crow Reservation, where she recalled first experiencing a giveaway: "They gave us many fine gifts. . . . They sang songs for the different Cheyennes and gave out the gifts—shawls, quilts and dress goods. Some received horses. . . . When I arrived home, an old man, Braided Locks, gave me a beautiful shawl. He said, 'My granddaughter helped me drive the horses very well and I will give her a shawl that I received as a gift.'"

By the time Belle was a young woman, her grandmother was very frail. Belle wanted to marry so that she could provide for the old woman, but Belle's father, a tribal policeman, advised his daughter to stay single as long as she could. Even so, on a snowy night in 1912, the twenty-year-old girl eloped with her sweetheart from a New Year's dance. A few days later, tribal police took the couple to court to be punished for living together in the recently outlawed Cheyenne way of marriage. Promising to become married legally, Belle and Floyd Highwalking were released.

"I remember what a hard life I had when I was young. But when I chose my husband, I must have used my head," Belle told a friend. On the couple's wedding day, Floyd's grandmother announced, "We brought my daughter-in-law home. Do not speak harsh to her or ever scold her. Treat her well and take care of her," while Floyd's father reminded his family to treat Belle kindly because she "didn't have any mother." Floyd's mother brought her daughter-in-law her meals and cut up Belle's meat for her in an expression of motherly tenderness. Floyd's family later held a feast and a giveaway on Belle's behalf, giving clothing, household goods, and horses to her family and to friends who had given the couple wedding presents.

Belle and her husband worked as hired hands—haying, picking beets, hauling freight by wagon between the Northern Cheyenne and Crow Indian agencies—and raised their own produce and horses. Over the years, they sponsored numerous giveaways on behalf of their children, Floyd's sisters, and their grandchildren. Such giveaways were a customary part of important family events such as weddings, births, funerals, and adoptions. Giveaways did not depend on how well-off a person or a family was; rather, Cheyennes gave to express love and gratitude for others.

Pictured here in her late seventies, Belle Highwalking lived most of her life on the Northern Cheyenne Reservation. She died October 30, 1971. Courtesy Jerry Mader, photographer

Belle had inherited horses—considered an especially fine gift—from her mother. She gave away colts when her brother got married. When her first child, George, was born, Belle and George's grandmothers gave horses to those people who had blessed them with gifts. Belle and Floyd also gave away a horse to have baby George's ear pierced, a custom that showed their love for the child. "This is how my son first gave away. . . . This is when I learned to love the giveaways, and I still like to give," Belle said.

In the 1920s, Belle and Floyd traveled to Oklahoma, where the Southern Cheyennes treated them to a Christmas feast. "After everyone finished," Belle said, "the other people left, but we were asked to stay. This woman who asked us also invited all her relatives to come meet us. When they came, they hugged me and cried. I guess that this woman's daughter had just died and I looked like her. . . . Then they gave-away to me, and this is how I was adopted by these Oklahoma people."

Years later, Belle met a North Dakota man who reminded her of a grown son she had lost. She gave him and his wife many fine gifts. The younger couple reciprocated with money, blankets, quilts, and a war bonnet. In this way, Belle and Floyd Highwalking adopted the man and his wife as their own son and daughter.

A year after Floyd died, Belle and her sons held a feast and giveaway for his friends and the people who had come to his funeral. Belle gave away seven tables of gifts, saying, "This is the way you show your respect for the person who has died. . . . It comforts you to give away."

By 1970, when Belle began recording her life's story, the Northern Cheyenne tribe had become one of the most impoverished populations in the United States. The government had slaughtered their once-great horse herds to force the Indians to lease their lands for cash. Cultural fragmentation, unemployment, and a high rate of alcoholism had taken heavy tolls on Cheyenne society. Yet Belle continued to give away in honor of her relatives and to show her love for them. "In the past, I owned horses, but now I don't. . . . All I have to give my relatives anymore are prayers for good health. That's the thing I like [to give] now."

"The Men Would Never Have Survived": Women, Union Activism, and Community Survival in Butte

Annie Hanshew

ALTHOUGH EXCLUDED from most jobs in the mines and smelters of Butte and Anaconda (with the short-lived exception of female smelter workers in World War II), women played integral roles in the survival of these company towns. The success of each community depended on the wages of laborers who toiled for the Anaconda Copper Mining Company. When those wages were threatened—either through company actions or because of union strikes—the entire community mobilized. During periods of conflict, women's contributions to the household economy became especially significant, as women pinched pennies and took on paid employment to help their families survive. These and other activities in support of labor were crucial to community survival, but men's resistance to women's full participation in union efforts also reveals the prevalence of conservative gender ideals in midcentury Butte and Anaconda.

Historian Janet Finn argues that "women's paid and unpaid labors have made a significant, if undervalued, contribution to the social fabric and economic stability of Butte." This was especially true during strikes. Women focused on saving up money around the time that union contracts were renegotiated in case their family income was disrupted. In the event of strikes, women took jobs outside the home to supplement the family savings, stretched their household budgets as far as possible, and relied on the community for support. One woman remembered the strikes vividly: "I don't really know how we got by. You just tried to make it day by day with coupons and strike funds and turning to your neighbors and family for help."

Mutual female support became especially important. Another miner's wife recalled, "It was people recognizing needs and helping one another. I know that I could go to my friends and say, 'I'm out of this. Can I have some of this?' We traded and borrowed and handed down clothing. . . . That's far from union work, but it's all a part of it."

Women in Butte and Anaconda also tried to further the interests of miners by participating in local union efforts, but here they were more likely to be marginalized or excluded. Local 117 of the International Union of Mine, Mill, and Smelter Workers (or Mine-Mill) established a women's auxiliary in 1939. The auxiliary's goals were to educate women and children about the labor movement and assist the local union during strikes and legislative sessions.

At the national level, Mine-Mill leadership placed a strong emphasis on equality, and the inclusion of women in the union was in keeping with this rhetoric. In practice, however, the activities of the Mine-Mill auxiliary in Butte reflected the prevailing conservative gender ideologies. According to historian Laurie Mercier, the women of Butte and Anaconda were "excluded

Betty Jo Houchin and Ruby Larson used their informal network to organize a picket of St. James Hospital in July 1971. Their husbands were both on strike when the women decided to protest the hospital's decision to treat strikers and their families "only on an emergency basis" because striking workers were not covered by the Anaconda Company's health insurance. Photo courtesy the *Montana Standard*, July 4, 1971

from the workplace and discouraged by male unionists from participating in substantive local affairs." As a result, the auxiliary's activities were "traditional rather than liberating."

Mercier points to the militant masculine culture of the union as the main reason for the auxiliary's limited success. The men of Butte and Anaconda clung to a breadwinner ideal in which the men were the single wage earner in a family and women were tethered to the world of domesticity and reproduction. Women's attempts to become more active in union efforts—or to gain employment in the mines and smelters—were seen as an affront to this family model. According to Mercier, this ideology ultimately hamstrung the efforts of the women's auxiliary: "[E]xcluded from the workplace and discouraged by male unionists from participating in substantive local affairs, they fell back on traditional activities of middle-class women's groups."

Ultimately, the Mine-Mill auxiliary did not offer a comfortable home for Butte and Anaconda's working-class women who wanted to further the interests of labor. Thus, women returned to the strategy of helping from the home and within the community. Though not always acknowledged as official contributors to union efforts, women were nonetheless crucial to community survival during times of labor unrest. Some women, at least, were able to recognize their contributions. As one daughter of a miner noted, "It's ironic, here after all these years in the mines, my father is a trim and healthy man, and it's my mother who suffers from health problems. . . . She was the one who had to do all the worrying and make sure the family got by. If it weren't for the women in Butte, like my mother, the men would never have survived."

The Work Was Never Done: Farm and Ranch Wives and Mothers

Ellen Baumler

UPON STATEHOOD in 1889, 5,600 farms spread across Montana. By 1910, that number had jumped to 26,000. The Enlarged Homestead Act of 1909 was one reason thousands flooded into Montana, including many married couples. Although federal census records consistently note that women whose husbands were involved in agriculture had no occupations, women were often the linchpins of the family economy and played key roles in building their communities.

Helena Hagadone, Janet Smith, Lilly B. "Ma" Smith, Ruth Garfield, and others represent different experiences but share a unique sisterhood. What women brought to the marriage influenced the success, and sometimes failure, of the partnership. They were neither as frail nor as frightened as they have sometimes been portrayed.

Frank and Helena Hagadone married in 1913. In 1917, the Hagadones homesteaded with their three children in a hostile place in the Missouri Breaks called the Devil's Pocket. The Missouri River bottomlands were unbearably hot in summer and cruelly cold in winter. The family grew vegetables and caught fish, but they had no well. They carried river water to the house, let the silt settle, and boiled it for cooking and drinking. Rattlesnakes were everywhere, and one of the children survived a near-fatal bite. After four years, the Hagadones separated. Mrs. Hagadone sent the young girls to board in town and paid for their schooling by working the homestead alone. The girls were glad to leave because their mother had become a mean woman.

Partnerships were sometimes uneven. "I was just like a hired man," recalled Katie Adams of Hill County. "I was right there. I helped harness the horses and unharness them and hitch them up. And I followed the plow more than once and the harrow and the rake, raked the fields." Women worked alongside men in haying, threshing, and branding. But they also did the cooking, the washing, and raised the children.

Adams made every minute count. "You'd go to bed about eleven-thirty, twelve o'clock, you'd get up at four, and you go out and help harness the horses, you milked the cows, get breakfast, strain your milk and put it away. Wash up your dishes, feed your chickens, and slop the pigs. If there was any time left, you would start your washing, maybe carry your water . . . heat your water in a boiler, get your washboard and your tub. . . . Wasn't many times I'd fool around."

Husbands perceived that women had more leisure time, and so it often fell to them to supplement the family income. "Cream checks" and other financial ventures like selling produce, teaching school, raising chickens and sheep, even mining small claims or taking pictures helped the household survive.

Rose Weaver Lorenson of Drummond said, "The cream check covered everything. That was the bank account. . . . Lots of times, that was the only money we had. . . . If it hadn't been for the chickens, we'd have starved."

Women's work made an essential contribution, and, according to Jewell Peterson Wolk of Glacier County, many marriages were born of necessity: "There were darn few marriages of love out here among these early beginners. . . . A man just couldn't work out in the field all day and then come in and start the beans boiling—it didn't work. . . . You realize that washing clothes was almost a two-day operation in the wintertime. . . . Just running the household was a full-time job, so you went out looking for a woman and you went out fast. . . . I don't think I've ever heard a homestead wife tell how much she loved her husband. That wasn't part of it. It was survival."

Outspoken Janet Smith, the only woman in Montana convicted of sedition, ranched with her husband in the Powder River country. During World War I, she called the Red Cross a fake and bragged that if Americans revolted, she would shoulder a gun and get the president. Both Mrs. Smith and her husband served more than two years at the Deer Lodge penitentiary. The isolation of ranchers like the Smiths made them particularly vulnerable. They did not realize the serious implications of their casual talk.

Lilly Smith, affectionately known as "Ma," was a ranch wife in Garfield County and a woman who made difficult choices and material sacrifices. In addition to proving up her own homestead in partnership with her husband, Smith was a practical nurse who helped elderly Dr. Lon Keith deliver scores of babies and assisted him in countless cases. She was by his side when he died of pneumonia in 1918. Smith took charge of the doctor's household, pressed his black suit, and laid out the body. She took a dress length of fine gray silk—a Christmas gift from her son—from her hastily packed suitcase. New dresses did not come often, but Smith had instinctively known that it would make the perfect lining for Doc Keith's coffin.

Ruth Garfield was a ranching wife with a young son whose husband was sheriff of newly created Golden Valley County in 1920. Sheriff Garfield had just been elected to a second term when he was fatally shot. Mrs. Garfield set aside her grief to assist the community and serve out her husband's term. She was Montana's first female sheriff and served two years.

Despite hardships, many women loved the land and took time to appreciate it. According to Anna Dahl, "It wasn't just drab, drab work all

Pearl Unglesbee Danniel homesteaded in the badlands of eastern Montana with her husband Clarence Unglesbee. Her caption for this photograph read, "Our little home where the Crickets used to make me feel that it was always summer. They sang in the walls all winter." This photo was taken ca. 1930. After Clarence died in 1927, Pearl transferred the property to her daughters and took out another homestead nearby. MHS Photo Archives PAc 95-7 1.

the time." Women had to be strong and resilient, and most did more than their part. They played active roles in the history of the agricultural frontier.

A "Compassionate Heart" and "Keen Mind": The Life of Dr. Caroline McGill

Annie Hanshew

BORN ON A FARM near Mansfield, Ohio, in 1879, Caroline McGill devoted her life to the people of Montana, her adopted state. In her work as a physician, she earned the love and respect of the people of Butte, but her role in the creation of the Museum of the Rockies in Bozeman is her enduring legacy to all Montanans.

McGill's family moved to Missouri when she was five, and at the age of seventeen she acquired a teaching certificate so she could support herself

From 1916 to 1956, Dr. Caroline McGill, pictured here in 1953, served the families of Butte, becoming one of Montana's most beloved physicians.
MHS Photo Archives 943-656

and complete high school. She achieved that goal in 1901 and continued her education at the University of Missouri. By 1908, she had a BA in science, an MA in zoology, and a PhD in anatomy and physiology, thereby becoming the first woman to receive a doctorate from that school. She taught at her alma mater until 1911, and former students later "aver[ed] that she was the finest medical school instructor" they had had.

Although the University of Missouri offered McGill a full professorship, she decided to shift career paths and accepted a position as pathologist at Murray Hospital in Butte. In a letter to a family member, she explained her decision to move to Montana: "I'll tell you right now I am making the biggest fool mistake to go . . . but I'm going. . . . Feels sort of funny to stand off and serenely watch myself commit suicide, [but] I'll just have to let her rip."

McGill moved to Butte in 1911, but after a year in Montana, she decided to pursue a medical degree at Johns Hopkins University. For the next four years, she split time between Butte and Baltimore while earning her MD. In

1916, she turned down a residency offer from Johns Hopkins and settled in Butte to establish a private practice.

At that time, Butte was still a "wide open" mining town frequently marked by roughness and vice. McGill ministered to "victims of knifings, shootings, knock-downs and dragouts all over Copper Hill's dark alleys, bawdy houses and teeming saloons." She cared for Butte's diverse citizenry —from miners and their families to residents of the town's red-light district—and her patients were deeply devoted to her. One reporter covering McGill's career wrote of her: "How the miners and their families loved Dr. McGill! With many European backgrounds, often left but recently, these families counted her the special guest for whom the best of food and manners must be provided." A family practitioner, McGill was described by one Butte resident as "ardent for babies" and "against the small families so common around here." Yet McGill also openly educated Butte's residents about birth control and family planning at a time when those subjects were still largely taboo.

In 1956, McGill "retired" to her beloved 320 Ranch in the Gallatin Canyon. She had first seen the ranch in November 1911 "from the back of a bobsled" and had purchased it twenty-five years later. For her, the 320 represented the restorative value of nature: "To get out into God's mountains, whether to ride, walk, or just sit, will cure more ills than all the medicine or medical knowledge in existence." Committed to conservation, McGill was a charter member of the Montana Wilderness Association and acquired over four thousand acres of land to preserve habitat and access around Yellowstone National Park.

After retiring from the practice of medicine, McGill did not "relax and rest"; rather, she turned her energies to her vast collection of antiques, pioneer artifacts, and documents related to Montana's history. This collection, which she donated to Montana State University, became the basis for what is now the Museum of the Rockies.

This gift, like her career as a physician, reflected McGill's generosity. Mary McWhorter, McGill's niece, recalled her aunt's kindness and strength of character: "All her life, Aunt Caroline gathered amazing people around her. She was a woman who valued those of us related to her by blood, but her compassionate heart, keen mind and sense of humor drew an extended family of friends, patients, doctors, publishers, Indian Tribal members, hunters, fishermen, artists, editors, writers, and interesting travelers. . . . To each she gave herself," McWhorter concluded, "without pretension or self-consciousness."

The Education of Josephine Pease Russell

Laura Ferguson

In 1937, Josephine Pease became one of the first Crow (Apsáalooke) people to graduate from college. Cultural and linguistic differences made obtaining an education challenging, but even greater were the difficulties that came with being a Crow woman who wanted a career in the mid-twentieth century. Crows discouraged women from being more successful than men, while some whites refused to hire Indians. Nevertheless, Pease persisted in her dreams to become a teacher, blazing a trail for future generations of Crow women.

The oldest of five children, Josephine was born in 1914 and grew up near Lodge Grass. Her parents wanted her to go to school because neither of them had had a chance at an education. There was a missionary school in Lodge Grass, but Josephine's parents wanted her at the public school. For two years, Josephine was the only Crow child at the school. The rest were "English" (white) children who wouldn't play with her. She remembered feeling as if she were "in a foreign country."

Many local white residents did not want Crow children attending the public schools on the reservation because tribal members did not pay property taxes. Then, in 1920, Congress passed the Crow Act, which specified the tribe's land grants for schools and opened Montana's public schools to Crow students.

For Apsáalooke children, going to school presented many challenges. While the girls kept to themselves, the Crow and "English" boys fought with each other. In Apsáalooke culture, girls and boys played separately from one another, but at school their teachers taught them games that included all of the children. In the classroom, the Crow students, who had been raised to be very modest, found it hard to "put themselves forward" as their teachers expected them to.

The Crow students' greatest difficulty, however, was language. Josephine's friend Joe Medicine Crow started school in 1924 and was still in first grade five years later because he found it so hard to learn English. "We were there to get an education, to learn to speak English, so we were discouraged from speaking Crow," Pease recalled. It would have made their education easier, she thought, if the teachers had been bilingual, as was her high school English teacher, Genevieve Fitzgerald.

The daughter of Baptist missionary Dr. W. A. Pedzoldt, Genevieve Pedzoldt Fitzgerald had grown up in Lodge Grass, where she learned Crow. Her

Shown here with her grandchildren, Josephine Pease Russell was one of the first Crow women to graduate from college. On her return to the reservation, she persevered in the face of discrimination to become a trailblazing educator. Courtesy Kathleen Wescott, photographer

willingness to explain ideas in their language enabled Crow students to gain fluency in English and thus improve in all subjects.

Pease credited her teachers for giving her "a push forward to become educated." Both Mrs. Fitzgerald and Mrs. Stevens, her science teacher, encouraged her to attend college. Her mother also advised her to get a college degree and a good-paying job. "I want you to go into this world and have a place somewhere that you can call your own where you will be making money," she told Josephine. With help from Dr. Pedzoldt, Josephine applied to Linfield College in McMinnville, Oregon. Pedzoldt and the Baptists paid her tuition.

For the first two weeks at Linfield, Josephine was so homesick that her father sent her a return ticket, but the college president and his wife convinced her to stay another week. Then she met two girls from China. Realizing how far they had come for a college education, Josephine decided to stay.

Josephine Pease graduated in 1937 with a major in business and a minor in English. One of the first three Crow college graduates (all of whom were women), she returned to the reservation, hoping to find a job as a high school business teacher. She soon became frustrated with the lack of employment opportunities for educated Crows, who were overlooked in favor of whites for jobs on the reservation. The fact that she was a woman also seemed to count against her. During the next three years, she worked at menial office jobs, married briefly, and had a daughter.

Eventually, Pease secured a teaching post at a small country school at Soap Creek. Her mother came to live with her and cooked for her eight students. Pease said her two years at Soap Creek were a "hard life" of poverty.

In 1942, opportunities opened up at Crow Agency School as teachers left for the war. For the next seventeen years, Pease taught young students who did not speak English. She then spent two years in the Teacher Corps, training teachers to work with Native students.

After two decades of teaching, Pease became director of the Head Start program on the reservation. As a Crow woman in a leadership position, Pease faced discrimination and prejudice from both the white and Crow communities. Non-Indians resented having an Indian person in charge, while many Crows, particularly men, did not want a Crow woman to achieve something beyond what they themselves had achieved. Reluctantly, Pease retired after two years. "Our own people can get really tough. . . . It was really difficult," she recalled. Even in the late 1980s, Pease observed that Crow women were still expected to do less than they were capable of so as not to surpass the men.

Josephine Pease Russell showed that Crow women could achieve an education, support themselves, and rise to leadership positions. She set the stage for the next generation, when her niece, Janine Pease—the first Crow to earn a doctoral degree—became the founding president of Little Big Horn College.

Mamie and Octavia Bridgewater and Montana's African American Community

Ellen Baumler

MAMIE ANDERSON BRIDGEWATER and her daughter, Octavia, were strong African American women who lived under the veil of racism in Helena during the first half of the twentieth century. Each earned the respect of the Helena community, and each helped to make a difference in the lives of other African Americans.

Mamie was born at Gallatin, Tennessee, in September 1872, one of eight children. In 1892, she married a career "buffalo soldier," Samuel

Bridgewater, at Fort Huachuca, Arizona Territory. In 1903, she followed her husband to Fort Harrison, Montana, where he was stationed after the Spanish-American War. There, she raised five children and worked as a matron at the veterans hospital. All the while, she cared for Samuel during his frequent bouts of illness from wounds received at the Battle of San Juan Hill in 1898.

After her husband's death in 1912, Mamie Bridgewater worked as a domestic in private homes, always scraping together enough to care for her children and grandchildren whenever they needed her assistance. She was a leader of Helena's black Baptist congregation and was heavily involved in fund-raising for Helena's Second Baptist Church, completed circa 1914. She was also a founder of the local Pleasant Hour Club, which organized in 1916 and became the Helena chapter of the Montana Federation of Colored Women's Clubs. At her death in 1950 at age seventy-seven, she was serving as chaplain of the Pleasant Hour Club.

Throughout her adult life, Mamie Bridgewater instilled pride in her children, and her home was always open to family and friends. She was a bulwark in times of trouble, including a son's severe mental illness and a grandson's tragic drowning. She also prepared her daughter, Octavia, for the work that she was to accomplish.

Mamie Anderson Bridgewater and her daughter Octavia were strong African American women who lived under the veil of racism in Helena during the first half of the twentieth century. Above (left to right) are Leon, Octavia, Herbert, and Mamie Bridgewater at their Helena home in 1925. MHS State Historic Preservation Office

Octavia Bridgewater was, without doubt, a product of her mother's encouragement. She graduated from Helena High School in 1925 and attended the Lincoln School of Nursing in New York City, which was, at the time, one of only two nursing schools exclusively for African Americans. After graduating in August 1930, she attended the University of the State of New York, where, a month later, she received her registered nurse's degree. Returning home to Helena, Octavia discovered that Montana hospitals did not hire African American nurses, and so she worked as a private-duty nurse.

In 1941, the U.S. Army Nurse Corps began accepting a small number of African American nurses, and a year later, Octavia was one of fifty-six black nurses accepted for service. This small quota was long in coming, for African American nurses had served throughout all wars, though only as contract nurses rather than as members of the military. At the end of World War I, during the influenza epidemic when there was a severe shortage of nurses, the Army Nurse Corps enlisted eighteen black women. They cared for German prisoners of war and African American soldiers stateside, but they had never served in wartime before 1941.

During World War II, African American nurses slowly began to pierce the barriers within the military system. When Octavia joined the Army in 1942, there were eight thousand black nurses in the United States. These women realized that if they were not allowed to serve in the military, black nurses would never be integrated into the mainstream medical community. Nationally, through the black press, the women mobilized for their cause. They flooded the White House and Congress with telegrams and letters. The Army and Navy lifted the ban against black nurses in 1945. Octavia Bridgewater's voice was one of those that helped bring about the change.

Bridgewater not only fought for the rights of African American nurses, but her service helped improve the status of all nurses. World War II brought a new respect for women nurses, allowing them full status as officers, full employment, and an improved public image. Bridgewater herself earned the rank of first lieutenant, proud to have achieved the rank and to have supported important progress. Her role in the national movement was a life-altering experience.

When Lieutenant Bridgewater returned to Helena in 1945, she found that racial barriers had softened but had not disappeared. When the veterans hospital refused her medical treatment because she was black and a woman, she asked her congressman to intervene and he did so.

After the war, St. Peter's Hospital in Helena began to hire black personnel, and Bridgewater served as a much beloved and long-remembered registered nurse in the maternity department until she retired in the 1960s. Like her mother, Octavia was active in both the city's Baptist church and in the Montana Federation of Colored Women's Clubs, serving as treasurer in 1971. She died at age eighty-two in 1985.

Both Mamie and Octavia Bridgewater lived productive lives through times of great change. Both faced economic, social, and legal barriers, and both worked to overcome them and to improve their communities. Mamie did so through her club and church work and as a supportive mother. Octavia did so through civil rights organizing, club work, and her career as a nurse. Both women made important contributions to Montana's African American community—and to the greater Helena community in which they made their home.

"You Design It and You Make It": The Life and Work of Ceramicist Frances Senska

Laura Ferguson

WHEN THE state college in Bozeman—now Montana State University (MSU)—hired Frances Senska to teach ceramics in 1946, both the college art department and Senska herself were fairly new to the art form. The school's small fine arts program focused primarily on two-dimensional art, and Senska, who had a master's degree in applied art, had taken just two classes in ceramics. Nonetheless, hiring Senska proved fortuitous for the college and for America's burgeon-ing midcentury crafts movement. At Montana State, Senska also met print-maker Jessie Wilber, who became her lifelong companion and with whom she helped cultivate Montana's art community.

Frances Senska believed in a utilitarian approach to art. Her cooperative teaching style endeared her to her students, many of whom went on to be influential artists in their own right. *A Ceramics Continuum, Fifty Years of the Archie Bray Influence,* courtesy Archie Bray Foundation for the Ceramic Arts

Frances Senska was born in 1914 and grew up in Cameroon, where her parents were missionaries. Her father, a cabinet maker and woodworker as well as a doctor, taught Frances how to use woodworking tools. The people of Batanga, Cameroon, also predisposed the girl to appreciate utilitarian crafts. "Everything that was used there was made by the people for the purposes they were going to use it for. It was low-tech. . . . And they were experts at what they did," Senska later recalled.

Senska discovered her own love of clay while stationed in San Francisco with the WAVES during World War II. At a night course taught by Edith Heath at the California Labor School, Senska got her hands into "real, useable clay." She immediately appreciated the autonomy of making utilitarian items by hand. "Clay is such a universal medium," she said in a later interview. "You can do anything with it. . . . It doesn't have to go through a factory system to be converted into a metal structure or something like that. . . . You do the whole thing yourself: you have the clay, you make the pot, you decorate it, you fire it; it's all your work."

As a teacher, Senska applied an approach to ceramics used by her own instructors, particularly László Moholy-Nagy and Marguerite Wildenhain,

Senska's partner, Jessie Wilber, chaired the MSU art department and worked with Senska and others to found the Archie Bray Foundation. This photo of Wilber was from a trip she and Senska took to Africa in 1966. Courtesy Frances Senska and Jessie Wilber Collection

as well as by her father and the people of Cameroon: be low-tech, find local resources, build it by hand, and see if it works. With three hundred dollars from the college art department, she and her students purchased foot-operated pottery wheels for their basement studio on campus. Together they designed and built an electric kiln. "We did things which people would never think of doing now. We went out and dug our clay and prepared it and used it, took it all the way from the hillside to the end product," Senska said in a reminiscence.

She disapproved of the big university ceramics departments where "they had everything and it looked like a factory. And there wasn't anything the students did except go and pick up a piece of clay and make something out of it and have it fired by somebody." Senska similarly objected to the apprenticeship method where students mimicked a master's work. Instead, she wanted her students to discover their own direction. Her method proved true: among her many successful students were Peter Voulkos and Rudy Autio, two men who became world-renowned sculptors and transformed American ceramic arts.

In the early 1950s, Senska and Jessie Wilber, who had become head of the college art department, designed their own house and art studios. On campus, the growing ceramics program finally moved out of the basement, but its graduates needed a place to continue their craft. Senska's former students, Voulkos and Autio, met Archie Bray, the owner of a brickyard in Helena. Bray embraced the idea of transforming the brickyard into a facility where the ceramic arts could flourish. Built by artisans like Senska, Wilber, Voulkos, and Autio, the Archie Bray Foundation is today an internationally recognized institution where ceramicists from around the world come to work in what Senska called a "tradition of cooperation, rather than competition."

That cooperative approach to the arts was also fostered by Professor H. G. Merriam, who helped found the Montana Institute of the Arts in 1948. Senska and Wilber encouraged the growth of the Montana Institute, which included writers and artists of many types. They also supported efforts to bring art to Montana communities so the public could share in its enjoyment and creation. In Bozeman, they helped establish the Beall Park Art Center, which now houses the Senska Studio for community art education and the Jessie Wilber Gallery, where works by both women are on permanent display.

Senska helped Montana emerge as a prominent ceramics arts center by laboriously building the ceramics program at Montana State University, nurturing its students for over twenty-five years, and supporting community arts programs. In 1982, MSU formally acknowledged these contributions by awarding Senska an honorary doctorate in art. When Senska and Wilber were co-recipients of the 1988 Montana Governor's Award for Distinguished Achievement in the Arts, Bozeman's exuberant art community threw a street celebration in their honor.

Yet, despite receiving several prestigious awards, Senska remained humble and unconcerned with fame. While others admired and collected her works, she held on to only a few of her own pieces, keeping instead work made by her students and a little black pot from her childhood in Cameroon. In her artist's statement for a show at Helena's Holter Museum of Art in 2001, Senska simply said, "I make pots." She continued making pots into her nineties. In many ways, her life was very much like her pots: built by her own hands, beneficial to her community, purposeful, and beautifully earthy.

Lucille Otter: Doing Good for Tribe and Country

Laura Ferguson

"POLITICS, one way or another, controls your destiny. Choose yours today," read a 1974 announcement written by Lucille Otter on the front page of the confederated Salish, Kootenai and Pend d'Oreille tribes' newspaper. Empowering tribal members to exercise their right to vote was one of the many ways Lucille Trosper Roullier Otter helped Indian people better their condition.

Lucille Trosper was born in 1916 on the Flathead Reservation to Angeline McCloud, a member of the Salish tribe, and Belford Trosper. She grew up hunting and fishing with her brothers—activities that inspired her dedication to conservation efforts in the Flathead region. She graduated from Ronan High School in 1933. Although Lucille did exceptionally well in school, she did not attend college because her father objected.

Jobs were scarce in Montana during the Great Depression and nearly nonexistent on the reservation. "Life was terrible!" Lucille recalled. She worked briefly for the Works Progress Administration before being hired in 1934 to work at the Dixon headquarters of the Indian Division of the Civilian Conservation Corps (ICCC). The first woman to work in an administrative capacity in the Indian CCC, she was in charge of budgeting ICCC projects, keeping accounts, and overseeing payroll and purchase orders for the ICCC camps. The ICCC enrollees called her "Buddy."

"The CCC was a godsend for the reservation," Lucille observed. Enrollees received training as communication radio operators, mechanics, and heavy equipment operators—skills they later used to find employment with telephone companies, on construction crews, on highway projects, and in industrial manufacturing.

Lucille donated much of her monthly salary to support her brothers' college education in Missoula. That left next to nothing for her to live on, yet she remained self-supporting throughout the Depression, taking additional work as a records clerk and voter registrar at the Bureau of Indian Affairs office on the reservation.

In addition to advocating for voting rights, Lucille Otter encouraged the creation of the Mission Mountains Tribal Wilderness, the first tribally designated wilderness in the country. Courtesy Renee Roullier-Madrigal

Lucille's first husband, Phillip Roullier, died in 1955, leaving her to raise their daughter, Renee, alone in an era of high unemployment on the reservation. Recalling how beneficial the Indian CCC had been for Indian people, Lucille, as a member of the Democratic Central Committee of Lake County, suggested to Montana senator Lee Metcalf the creation of a reservation-based vocational training program similar to the Indian CCC. Metcalf responded with legislation that created the Kicking Horse Jobs Corps in Ronan in 1966.

Lucille's greatest achievement, however, was empowering tribal members to vote. She was only eight years old when the Indian Citizenship Act of 1924 made all members of federally recognized tribes American citizens, ostensibly enfranchising them. Her mother set a precedent by being the first Indian woman on the reservation to register to vote. Angeline Trosper then became the first female juror in Lake County. It wasn't until her mother's death in 1960 that the importance of these "firsts" fully dawned on Lucille.

"I got to thinking how pitiful the Indians were in not voting," she said. Heavily outnumbered by non-Indians, even on the reservation, the few Indians who did vote couldn't influence elections, and elected officials seldom concerned themselves with Indian issues or the impact of legislation on Indian people. Part of the problem stemmed from efforts by the state to curtail the Indian vote. Montana's 1889 constitution permitted only tax-paying individuals to vote, thereby disenfranchising Indians who lived on, or derived income from, trust lands. Later, Montana prohibited individuals who did not pay local taxes from becoming local registrars, effectively suppressing Indian voter registration in reservation counties. By the time the Voting Rights Act passed in 1965 to remove these barriers, many tribal members had given up on trying to vote. Lucille Roullier set out to change this situation.

Her strategy at first was to register Indian women. "I really concentrated on the women, the mothers, because I thought they would encourage their children to vote. I went all over the reservation, to every residence." She took time to teach each new voter how to fill out a ballot correctly so that their votes would count.

Many tribal elders, whose rights had been ignored so long by the government, wouldn't vote even after she had registered them. Lucille persisted. "The Indians are going to be left in the dust if you don't get a hold of what's going on in our government," she told those who wavered. When women complained that their husbands didn't want them at the polls, she showed them how to apply for absentee ballots.

Occasionally, Lucille, who remarried in 1969 to Laurence Otter, faced significant opposition to her efforts from some of the white residents on the Flathead Reservation, but that only motivated her to work harder. She set up registration tables at the commodity distribution warehouse, at local events, and in grocery stores. She carried extra registration cards in her car, and once, while out fishing, even registered a young woman on horseback.

Over time, Lucille Roullier Otter registered well over a thousand voters on the reservation. "I felt as though a tribal member should do something for the tribe, not to be a taker, but to be a giver. I spent a lot of money on gas, and time, but it was worth it. And I renewed my friendships."

In 1988, Salish Kootenai College awarded Lucille Roullier Otter an honorary degree, and in 1992 her daughter set up a scholarship at the college in her name. Many tribal members, including tribal council members and legislative representatives, attribute their political involvement to Lucille Otter, who admonished them, "For heaven's sake, pay attention to what's going on in this country! If you don't get involved, we're going down the river!"

Montana Women of the Ku Klux Klan

Kayla Blackman

IN THE 1920S, a group of women banded together under the auspices of a shared political belief and religious background. They dedicated themselves to installing memorials in their communities, hosting family picnics, and visiting patients at local hospitals. In many ways, they resembled other civic organizations of their time, many of which served a social function by bringing women of similar interests together. Committed to "tenets of the Christian religion," "freedom of speech and press," and "the protection of pure womanhood," the ideology of this group overlapped with other groups such as the Woman's Christian Temperance Union (WCTU). Yet

The Ku Klux Klan had a national membership of 3 to 5 million men during its height in the 1920s, and over 1 million women joined the women's auxiliary. This photo was likely taken near either Billings or Livingston. The lead car sports a Billings license plate. WHC Archives 86.71.01 a, b

their commitment to "white supremacy" separated the Women of the Ku Klux Klan (WKKK) from other women's organizations—and provides a reminder that female participation in politics was not always a progressive force.

At its height, in the 1920s, the Montana Realm of the Ku Klux Klan boasted fifty-one hundred members across more than forty chapters. Committed to what they called "100% Americanism," KKK members espoused xenophobic policies against immigrants and racist policies against nonwhites and fostered hatred toward Jews and Catholics. However, in a Montana suffering from economic downturn, rapid technological advances, drought, labor unrest, and a generally chaotic postwar period, the Klan provided an appealing organization for those looking for scapegoats.

The Klan's anti-vice platform and its promise to protect white womanhood may have particularly attracted the women who joined its ladies' auxiliary. A full-page KKK ad in the *Billings Gazette* declared "our hostility to bootleggers, professional gamblers, and all forms of organized and commercialized lawlessness or vice is unlimited." For members of the WKKK, the recently won right to vote became a tool for promoting both the KKK's nativist policies and the "social housekeeping" agenda they shared with other women's groups like the WCTU. Over 1 million women joined the WKKK nationally, and their rhetoric focused on protecting the home and white womanhood.

In Montana, the KKK and WKKK emphasized anti-Catholicism in their rhetoric and politics. Central to their mission was a campaign for compulsory public education to stem the influence of parochial schools. This focus on education gave WKKK members another reason to support the organization. Women and men alike had long seen education as a "women's issue"; in fact, Montana women had voted in school elections since 1887 (twenty-seven years before they won equal suffrage), and working to influence educational policy continued to provide an appropriate political outlet for Montana women.

The Klan's involvement in social issues was rooted in its racist, anti-Catholic ideology. The WKKK's constitution, for example, declared that the organization "shall ever be true to the maintenance of White supremacy and [members] will strenuously oppose any compromise thereof." Montana's WKKK members embraced this stance. In 1928, Mrs. D. Cohn, a seventy-one-year-old resident of Butte, sent Montana's "Grand Dragon" a token showing the Catholic presidential candidate, Al Smith, in a coffin. Other WKKK members in Billings, Roundup, Harlowton, and Livingston attended cross burnings, organized boycotts, and proudly displayed their Klan affiliation—although the acceptability of women wearing men's regalia came into question during discussions about organizing a 1927 parade in Whitehall. WKKK members also attended Klan rituals such as funerals and, like their national counterparts, took on the traditionally female role of providing costuming and food for social events and secret gatherings.

Klan members met their share of antagonism from other Montanans. In Butte, where immigrants, many of whom were Catholic, made up a considerable portion of the population, Sheriff Jack Duggan reported, "Our men have orders to shoot any Ku Kluxer who appears in Butte." Elsewhere, however, Klanswomen presented themselves as a respectable alternative to other area women's clubs, and reporters were sympathetic; one *Billings Gazette* article recorded the WKKK delivering flowers to the hospital.

By the end of the 1920s, the Klan's influence waned both in Montana and nationally. The Klan had failed to stem Montana's prolific bootlegging, and a national backlash against the KKK hurt local chapters as well. Butte's chapter of the Klan folded in 1929; state Klan records exist only until 1931. Klan propaganda continued to circulate in the state, but membership dwindled to a few isolated groups whose racist rhetoric sporadically appears in Montana communities today, usually in the form of pamphlets and broadsheets.

"Must a Woman . . . Give It All Up When She Marries?" The Debate over Employing Married Women as Teachers

Martha Kohl

IN THE FALL of 1913, Jennie Bell Maynard, a teacher in Plains, married banker Bradley Ernsberger. The couple kept their wedding a secret until Bradley found a job in Lewistown and they moved: "No inkling of the marriage leaked out. . . . Mrs. Ernsberger continued to use her maiden name and teach school." A year later, Butte teacher Adelaide Rowe eloped to Fort Benton with her sweetheart, Theodore Pilger. They hid their marriage for three years. Maynard and Rowe were just two of the many Montana women teachers who married secretly—or didn't marry at all—in order to continue teaching.

The story of "marriage bars," or bans, does not unfold linearly. Livingston lifted its "rule against the employment of married lady teachers" in 1896. The Anaconda school district also allowed married women to teach in the 1890s, but in 1899, facing lower than anticipated enrollment, the superintendent sought the resignation of the district's one married teacher, explaining that Mrs. Foley "is married and is not in need of the salary which she draws from the schools."

The idea that married women did not need the income, and that "hiring married women would deprive single girls of opportunities," was the most common rationale for marriage bars. On the other hand, advocates for married teachers tried unsuccessfully to reframe the debate in terms of student welfare. Mrs. W. J. Christie of Butte argued in 1913 that "[t]he test of employment should be efficiency and nothing else." Mrs. James Floyd

Denison agreed: "When a married woman has the desire to go from her home and to enter the school room . . . it must be because her heart and soul are in the teaching work. Under those circumstances, if she is allowed to teach, the community will be getting her very best service." Unconvinced, Miss Ella Crowley, Silver Bow County superintendent of schools, believed that a married woman's place was at home. While she recognized the value of experience, she also believed that if women taught after marriage, "there never would be any room for new teachers or for girls."

Unlike urban districts, country schools, desperate to fill lower-paid positions, generally welcomed married teachers. In 1924, when Lilian Peterson, a widow with six children, could not find a job in Kalispell or Missoula because their marriage bars extended to widows with children, she signed on at Pine Grove School northeast of Kalispell. Likewise, Maggie Gorman Davis, who homesteaded with her husband, Dennis, in Chouteau County, taught in the four-teacher Carter School in 1911 to supplement their income.

While some districts banned all married teachers, others were willing to employ married women if their husbands were "an invalid in some way."

The Billings Federation of Women's Clubs opposed the 1927 Billings school district's decision to bar married teachers. When the school board refused to reconsider, members recruited candidates to run for the school board on a pro–married teacher platform. All three lost the election. *Billings Gazette*, April 1, 1927

Commenting on the Billings school board's decision to institute a marriage bar in 1927, the editor of the *Helena Independent* argued that exceptions should be made for "married women whose husbands are invalids or insane and unable, therefore, to provide a living for the family." Nevertheless, he averred that men should take care of their wives. "Single women with their living to make should not be penalized by having positions open to them otherwise taken by women who have married failures."

Unsurprisingly, attitudes toward married teachers changed during World War II, with most schools welcoming married women back to the classroom. In 1942, M. P. Moe, the secretary of the Montana Education Association, stated that "1,500 married teachers are in the schools 'for the duration only.'" However, advocates for married women teachers, including the National Education Association, published several editorials asking school boards to remember married teachers after the war, arguing that if they "were good enough . . . in wartime . . . , they're good enough in peace time."

Most, but not all, Montana school districts took this message to heart—helped along by the demand for teachers during the postwar baby boom. The Billings school board lifted its ban against married women teachers in 1953, encouraged by the superintendent who explained that he expected teacher demand to outstrip supply indefinitely. In districts facing declining enrollment or decreasing revenue, however, discrimination continued. In 1953, the Bigfork school board adopted two salary schedules, one for single teachers and a second, lower scale for married women teachers whose husbands worked. "Ideally," Superintendent C. E. Naugle explained, "everyone would be treated in the same manner. However, we are not dealing with an ideal situation, we are dealing with reality," and cuts should be made "where it will hurt the least."

In 1955, Montana attorney general Arnold Olsen declared that "[m]arriage is not a ground for dismissal" and that "teacher contracts could not discriminate against married teachers." Even so, as late as 1964, the superintendent of the Anaconda school district reassured angry residents—worried that single teachers lacked opportunities—that both the district and the Anaconda Teachers Union supported hiring single women and married men over married women. In fact, married women were only offered contracts when qualified single (or male) teachers were unavailable.

Ultimately, the 1964 Civil Rights Act ended discrimination against married women teachers. By outlawing discrimination based on sex, the act forced local school districts to treat married female teachers as they treated their married male counterparts. At last, boards began to follow the course education reformers had recommended fifty years earlier: basing their hiring decisions on ability alone.

Writing Our Lives: Novelist Mildred Walker's Illumination of Montana Women

Marcella Sherfy Walter

"MONTANA WAS SO VAST and strange to me that I didn't dare to write about it for almost ten years," novelist Mildred Walker said during the 1960s, a decade after she had left the state. But three of her best-known works—*Winter Wheat, The Curlew's Cry,* and *If a Lion Could Talk*—are set in Montana. The novels' richly developed female characters reflect Walker's own ambivalence about the state: its traditions, weather, landscape, and capacity to nurture or starve women.

Walker was born in 1905 in Philadelphia to a schoolteacher mother and a preacher father—a family for whom the right words had power. She wrote her way through Wells College in New York and set the terms of her marriage to Michigan-born physician Ferdinand Schemm: that she would write, that he would embrace his profession unstintingly, that she would not do the washing. They started married life in Michigan's Upper Peninsula logging communities but soon moved to Ann Arbor, where Walker earned her MA in creative writing. Her award-winning and first published novel, *Fireweed*, paid for the young couple's move to Great Falls in 1933.

There, they found a craftsman bungalow that gave their two oldest children, Ripley and George, tricycle-riding small-town freedom; Schemm an easy commute to both hospitals; and Walker a niche for her desk. For the next decade, Mildred Walker Schemm intertwined the multiple roles she had established for herself: well-dressed doctor's wife, arms-length mother, friend, and writer.

In 1944, the family moved to a rambling haven south of Great Falls and next to the Missouri River. By then, they had welcomed their third child, Christopher, begun escaping to a rustic cabin on the Rocky Mountain Front, and celebrated Dr. Schemm's growing prominence in heart research. The family's friendships included artist Fra Dana and literary lights Joseph Kinsey Howard and A. B. Guthrie Jr. Household help and a quiet study of her own allowed Walker her most productive writing years before Schemm's death in 1955.

During Walker's twenty-two Montana years, she taught her daughter to clear a table properly; sold Great Falls Junior League state fair tickets; hosted afternoon teas and dinner parties; typed her physician husband's research papers; and published nine of her thirteen novels, including two of the three set in the state. In short, Walker first experienced and then captured the hardship, fellowship, loneliness, and ambiguities that have defined life for many Montana women across time and across the region's topography.

Hence, at the beginning of World War II, *Winter Wheat*'s Ellen Webb heads from her family's farm to school in Minnesota, impatient to gain the grace and erudition missing in her hardscrabble, windswept High Plains life. The college boy she brings home mocks rural Montana and cannot cope. Economic realities require her to take a teaching position in an isolated one-room school. Loss and loneliness force her to wrestle with how she understands her tough Russian immigrant mother, her parents' partnership, and her own choices. Walker ultimately accords Ellen a measure of acceptance and appreciation for Montana's unforgiving wind and her mother's work-reddened hands. She employs winter wheat as a metaphor for how women—and men—grow through tough times.

In *The Curlew's Cry*, Walker again peopled her Montana setting with capable twentieth-century women uncertain about how to live with or live beyond the West's cowboy myths, survive the huge lonely land, and honor their own consciences. Pamela Lacey divorces her eastern husband

and, though ridiculed by the men in her community, makes a go of turning her father's cattle operation into a dude ranch. Small-town milliner Madame Guinard and Pamela's lean, tough-talking friend Rose Morley—described as "a broom with an apron and shawl tied to her" and patterned after one of the Walker family's colorful Missouri River housekeepers—give her relevant

Mildred Walker studiously cultivated the image of a proper doctor's wife even as she dedicated herself to her writing.
Yaw, photographer, MHS Photo Archives 945-467

examples of how to be an independent woman. And still, the curlew's cry—loneliness—defines Pamela's life.

If a Lion Could Talk is Walker's only Montana-based novel set in the nineteenth century. In it, she re-creates the real Fort Union fur magnate Alexander Culbertson and his elegant Blood Indian wife Natawista as Fort Benton's fictional Major Phillips and Eenisskim. When New England missionaries Mark and Harriet Ryegate step into this multicultural frontier world, their lives slowly begin to unravel. Mark's proselytizing fails, he finds himself drawn to the exotic Eenisskim, and Harriet wants only to return to the East and their old lives. Walker allows the foursome to wrestle with the choice of physical and spiritual homes—wild and challenging lands or conventional territories.

Walker left Montana abruptly after her adored husband's death—the memories too powerful to endure—to teach at her alma mater. Later, retired from Wells, she lived for a while in her birth family's Vermont home, traveled, and published two more works. She returned to Montana to summer at the Schemm cabin on the Rocky Mountain Front and later to live near her daughter in Missoula.

Though each of her novels enjoyed measured acclaim on publication, Walker's visibility lagged in later years. Readers know her now through the University of Nebraska Press's mid-1990s reprints, though still not as well as the male authors she entertained around her dining table in Great Falls.

Drawing on her own varied roles—vibrant and confident young matron, easy colleague to Montana's midcentury greats, joyful outdoorswoman, lonely widow—Walker wrote of people and geography from deep within her own life. Even as her health declined, she pushed herself to finish one more novel and to keep up her journal. After her mother's death in 1998, daughter Ripley Schemm recalled Walker's late-in-life admission that she "was writing for her life." In fact, Walker wrote for the lives of twentieth-century Montana women—finding her way word-by-word across the roles and landscapes that faced her female contemporaries.

Sarah Gammon Bickford: From Slave to Businesswoman

Ellen Baumler

ON APRIL 10, 2012, Montana honored Sarah Bickford by inducting her into the Gallery of Outstanding Montanans in the Capitol Rotunda in Helena. A former slave who became one of Montana's most prominent businesswomen, Bickford richly deserved this honor. She was the first and only woman in Montana—and probably the nation's only female African American—to own a utility. Yet despite her public success, Sarah Bickford's life is difficult to piece together. Like most African Americans who came west, she carried the burden of slavery, making her past especially difficult to trace.

Sarah Gammon Bickford was born on Christmas Day in 1852, 1855, or 1856 in North Carolina or Tennessee. Her parents were slaves of John Blair, a wealthy Tennessee attorney and state senator. As was common, Sarah (nicknamed Sallie) and her family took the last name of their owner. At some point Sarah's parents were sold, and she never saw them again.

After the Civil War, freed by the Emancipation Proclamation, Sarah went to Knoxville, Tennessee, to live with Nancy Gammon, who may have been her aunt. While in Knoxville, Sarah took the last name of Gammon. There, she also met John Luttrell Murphy, a local attorney and newly appointed associate justice of the Territorial Supreme Court in Virginia City, Montana Territory. At the time, the judge was looking for someone to tend to his two foster children on the family's journey west. Sarah, then a teenager, exchanged her services as a nanny for her passage.

Murphy took the bench in 1871 but served only briefly before leaving Virginia City. However, Sarah was in Virginia City to stay. Initially, she worked as a chambermaid at the Madison House Hotel and, in 1872, married a miner, John Brown. The couple had three children, two boys and a girl, but the marriage was a difficult one. The boys died of diphtheria, and John Brown proved a miserable husband. Sarah suffered beatings, death threats, and desertion. In 1880, she engaged attorney Samuel Word to sue Brown for divorce on the grounds of abuse and abandonment. This was a courageous move for a woman in the nineteenth century, but in making her private trauma public and risking the stigma of divorce, she sought to protect her remaining child, seven-year-old

Sarah Bickford arrived in Virginia City in 1871. The former slave became the first and only woman in Montana to own a utility company by 1902.
Courtesy Ellen Baumler

Eva. The judge granted Sarah a divorce and awarded her sole custody of the girl.

Again a free woman, Sarah went to work in the French Canadian household of Adaline Laurin. Soon thereafter, she opened a bakery, restaurant, and lodging house on Wallace Street, perhaps with Laurin's financial assistance. Her advertisements for "meals and Lunches at all hours" appeared frequently in the *Madisonian* in 1880 and 1881. Bickford's business endeavors demonstrate the value of traditional women's work in Montana Territory's primarily male mining camps.

In 1882, nine-year-old Eva died of pneumonia. This was not an unusual story at a time when one in every five children died before the age of five, but it was nonetheless heartbreaking to the mother. For Sarah, it meant starting over. In 1883, she married Stephen Bickford, a white miner and farmer. The couple had three girls and a boy. Many years later, her daughters recalled that, when they were growing up, their mother told them poignant stories about her first family and sang to them the French songs that she and Eva had learned in the household of Adaline Laurin.

When Stephen died in 1890, the Bickfords owned two-thirds of the Virginia City Water Company. Left on her own, Sarah Bickford took a business management class by correspondence, purchased the remaining third of the company, and in 1902 became the sole owner of the utility. In another bold move, she purchased the infamous Hangman's Building and converted it into her office. Sarah Bickford not only managed the business, but she personally visited every customer and learned their needs. She was also her own bill collector, keeping after her customers to pay their bills on time. While she earned the respect of the community, it was not always easy to dog her neighbors.

Late in 1917, Bickford raised water rates 10 percent. The rate increase incensed her customers, who had been paying the old rate for forty years. With Prohibition about to claim his livelihood, longtime saloonkeeper Frank McKeen protested, "Here the State of Montana goes dry, and Sallie Bickford boosts the price of water. It is getting to be a hard world in which to live." But business is business, fair is fair, and Bickford did what she had to do.

In fact, Sarah Bickford always did what she had to do. She stepped out of her accepted domestic role to become a top-notch businesswoman. Well respected by her community, she triumphed over tragedy, but she never forgot those she had lost. When she died in 1931, a portrait of Eva was at her bedside. The *Madisonian* expressed the community's sadness, declaring that Virginia City had lost one of its most devoted mothers and loyal pioneer citizens.

Bonnie HeavyRunner: A Warrior for Diversity

Laura Ferguson

"We in the Native American community know that the warrior of old no longer exists. So we ask ourselves, 'What do we have left?' We have individuals who are culturally aware, who realize the value of getting a 'white man's education' and utilizing that to the benefit . . . of the community. They have the ability to turn this whole negative picture of cultural genocide around." Bonnie HeavyRunner spoke these words in praise of her sister, Iris HeavyRunner, but she could have been describing herself.

One of thirteen children, Bonnie HeavyRunner grew up in Browning on the Blackfeet Reservation, where she experienced the daily reality of poverty, relatives struggling with alcohol addiction, and the sudden loss of family members. At a young age, she vowed to stay sober and remain true to her cultural values. Her personal integrity became the foundation of her determination to improve the lives of American Indian people by being an advocate for Native and women's issues while building cross-cultural bridges. As the director of the University of Montana's Native American Studies program, she worked tirelessly to bring about greater cultural awareness of American Indians while making the academic world more hospitable to Indian students.

HeavyRunner earned a bachelor's degree in social work from the University of Montana in 1983 and then a law degree in 1988. One of only a few women in the School of Law in the 1980s, HeavyRunner was also the only American Indian law student in her class. She went on to become a clerk, and then a judge, on the Blackfeet Tribal Court, but she did not forget the cultural isolation she had felt at the university. Many Native students dropped out of school because they experienced such a wide gap between themselves and the non-Indian culture of the university community at large. HeavyRunner wanted to change that.

In 1991, Bonnie HeavyRunner Craig, now married and raising a daughter and son, became the director of the fledgling Native American Studies program at the University of Montana (UM). At the time, the program offered courses to supplement other degrees, but HeavyRunner dreamed of a Native American studies department that offered its own major. She also aspired to create a more welcoming and culturally understanding academic climate for Native students. Despite being diagnosed with ovarian cancer just one year into her new job, HeavyRunner put her full effort into making her goals a reality.

HeavyRunner mentored over three hundred American Indian students in her six years at UM, helping them navigate the world of academia, get scholarships, pay for child-care, and stick to their educational goals. She reached out to the university community to make the campus a more inclusive place, one that recognized and promoted cultural diversity. For her work, she earned numerous community service awards, including the Robert T. Pantzer Award for making UM a more humane, compassionate learning environment and the Joann Youngbear Community Service Award for improving the well-being of the Indian community.

Bonnie HeavyRunner, pictured here a year before her untimely death, was the founding director of the University of Montana's Native American Studies Department. Courtesy Aislinn HeavyRunner-Rioux

In 1996, HeavyRunner triumphed when the university offered an undergraduate major in Native American studies for the first time. HeavyRunner strongly believed that education could build bridges between people and strengthen communities. Having spent many years advocating for American Indian issues and cultural diversity, HeavyRunner knew that making Native American studies its own discipline would generate greater awareness of American Indian cultures, histories, and current events among students and faculty. She hoped this better understanding would also reduce anti-Indian prejudices.

In addition to being the founding director of, and driving force behind, UM's Native American Studies Department, HeavyRunner served on the university's Diversity Council, the board of the National Indian Justice Center, and Montana's advisory committee to the U.S. Civil Rights Commission. She founded the Kyi-yo Native Academic Conference that brought together indigenous scholars during UM's annual Kyi-yo powwow and continued to advocate for Indian people's health and well-being even as her own health was failing.

HeavyRunner never let her struggle with ovarian cancer deter her from her path. While undergoing chemotherapy, she sought help from Native healers to maintain her spiritual health. She openly discussed her condition, allowing her illness and the treatments she chose to become another avenue of advocacy for improved care for American Indians and, indeed, for all cancer victims.

HeavyRunner's dual approach to her health crisis inspired her to speak to humanities classes, in public forums, and to the cancer treatment community about the necessity of holistic care and the value of the indigenous medicine that sustained her spiritually even as her body weakened. She calmly addressed the fear of dying and of death itself, emphasizing the importance of providing culturally appropriate spiritual treatment to terminally ill people.

HeavyRunner died in 1997 at the age of forty-six; however, her dreams continue to become realities. In 2010, the University of Montana opened its new Native American Center on campus, fulfilling HeavyRunner's goal to make the university a "home" to American Indian students and a place where cross-cultural understanding can flourish. Immediately inside the architecturally beautiful building is the Bonnie Heavy Runner Gathering Place—a large, open, sunny space where people can celebrate the continuity of American Indian cultures and begin making their own dreams of cross-cultural acceptance, justice, and well-being into realities.

Me, Me, Me, Me: Butte's Bohemian, Mary MacLane

Mary Murphy

TEMPERANCE ADVOCATE Carrie Nation once pronounced Mary MacLane "the example of a woman who has been unwomanly in everything that she is noted for." MacLane was no doubt delighted with the description. Writer, bohemian, and actress, Mary MacLane (1881–1929) was born in Winnipeg, Manitoba, and grew up in Butte. Best known for her two autobiographical books, *The Story of Mary MacLane* (1902) and *I, Mary MacLane* (1917), she also wrote features for newspapers, starred in a motion picture, and became notorious for her outrageous, unwomanly behavior.

MacLane was the child of failed fortune. Her father died when she was eight; after her mother remarried, her stepfather took the family to Butte in

There is nothing immodest about this 1906 portrait of Mary MacLane, but her self-absorbed autobiography and bohemian lifestyle shocked her hometown of Butte. MHS Photo Archives PAc 77-35.3

search of riches. According to legend, on the eve of Mary's departure for Stanford University, her stepfather confessed that he had lost the family's money in a mining venture and could not afford to send her to college. Whatever the truth, Mary did not attend college after graduating from Butte High School, but spent her days feeling restless and trapped, walking through Butte and recording her thoughts in her diary. In 1902, she sent the handwritten text to a Chicago publisher, Fleming H. Revell Company, under the title *I Await the Devil's Coming*. The editor who read the piece judged it the "most astounding and revealing piece of realism I had ever read." But it was not the kind of material that Revell, "Publishers of Evangelical Literature," brought to the market. Fortunately, the editor sent it to another publisher, Stone & Kimball, who released it as *The Story of Mary MacLane*. Within a few months, the book had sold eighty thousand copies, and MacLane may have earned as much as $20,000 in royalties in 1902 (approximately $500,000 in 2013 dollars).

The book challenged the notions of what proper young, middle-class women were supposed to think and feel. In an age when legs were referred to as limbs, Mary boasted of her strong woman's body; in an era of moral absolutes, she claimed that right, wrong, good, and evil were mere words. She titillated and outraged readers when she claimed that she wanted not merely romance but seduction. And above all, she craved "Experience":

> It is not deaths and murders and plots and wars that make
>   life tragedy.
> It is Nothing that makes life tragedy.
> It is day after day, and year after year, and Nothing.
> It is a sunburned little hand reached out and Nothing put into it.

Declaring herself "earthy, human, sensitive, sensuous, and sensual," she prayed that she would never become "that deformed monstrosity—a virtuous woman."

The book and its author became sensations across the country. The Butte Public Library banned *The Story of Mary MacLane*, and a daily paper denounced it as "inimical to public morality." The *New York Herald* pronounced MacLane mad and demanded that paper and pen be denied her until she regained her senses. The *New York Times* advised a spanking. The book's popularity and Mary's narcissism spawned parodies such as *Damn! The Story of Willie Complain* and *The Devil's Letters to Mary MacLane, By Himself*. A vaudeville team created a popular routine, "The Story of Mary McPaine."

Using royalties from book sales, MacLane left Butte and moved to the East Coast. She was barraged by the press in Chicago and spent time in Greenwich Village, where she reveled in the company of other free-spirited women. She wrote about male lovers and her physical attractions to women. At some time in the late summer or fall of 1902, she met Caroline Branson, the former partner of writer Mary Louise Pool, and began a six-year relationship with her, the only long-term romance MacLane ever had. She published another book in 1903, *My Friend Annabel Lee*, but it received poor reviews and garnered few sales.

Broke and having written nothing of substance for some time, in 1909 she returned to Butte, where she remained for seven years, haunting gambling dens and roadhouses. Betty Horst recalled the time her father, Butte's health officer, rented a hack to take his wife to a roadhouse for dinner. As they walked through the bar toward the dining room, they passed MacLane sitting at a slot machine, smoking and drinking. She invited Mrs. Horst to join her. When Mrs. Horst accepted, her shocked husband continued into the restaurant. When it sank in that his wife actually knew Butte's notorious female writer, Dr. Horst got up and drove home.

While in Butte, MacLane wrote another autobiographical book, *I, Mary MacLane*, released in 1917, and wrote and starred in a silent film, *Men Who Have Made Love to Me*. But what was sensational in 1902 seemed self-indulgent in 1917. Sales of *I, Mary MacLane* were disappointing, Mary had no future as an actress, and she never again published. Deliberately cutting herself off from friends and family, plagued by poverty, she lived quietly in boarding houses and hotels in Chicago until her death in 1929. When the hotel manager discovered her body, clippings and photographs from her glory days surrounded it.

"I Was a Strong Woman": Adeline Abraham Mathias

Laura Ferguson

WHEN THE confederated Salish, Pend d'Oreille, and Kootenai tribes needed more information on historical events, cultural customs, or the Kootenai language, they did not look in a library or on the web; they asked Adeline Abraham Mathias. A member of the Ksanka band of Kootenai—or Ktunaxa—people, Mathias lived her entire life on the Flathead Reservation. Over the span of her lifetime (1910–2007), she witnessed how the influx of non-Indians profoundly altered her people's homeland. The great-granddaughter of a Kootenai chief, Adeline Mathias was the recipient of cultural, spiritual, and historical knowledge, which she, in turn, passed along to the next generation of Kootenai people.

Atliyi "Adeline" Paul Abraham was born near Dayton in 1910, the same year the fertile valleys of the Flathead Reservation were opened to home-steading. The arriving farmers transformed the diverse riparian habitat into a patchwork of fields and altered the course of rivers to meet their irrigation needs.

More profoundly, the newcomers brought different social and cultural ways that, over time, threatened the continuity of the Kootenai, Salish, and Kalispel (Pend d'Oreille) languages and way of life. In just three genera-tions, the number of fluent Kootenai speakers fell to only a handful of indi-viduals, one of whom was Adeline Mathias.

Adeline's first language was Kootenai. Her mother, Lizette Pierre, died in 1915, and Adeline's maternal grandparents, Louie and Mary Ann Pierre, raised her according to Kootenai customs. Her grandmother's father was Eneas Paul Bigknife, one of the last of the Kootenai traditional chiefs. As he had taught Mary Ann, she in, turn, taught Adeline: be kind, generous, and helpful to others.

The Pierres also shared with young Adeline the tribe's history—a his-tory that dates back to over ten thousand years in the region that is now northwestern Montana, northern Idaho, and lower British Columbia. At one time, the Kootenais numbered several thousand, but epidemics of European infectious diseases severely reduced their population. By the early twentieth century, the Ksanka band had only a few hundred members.

Adeline's grandparents were among those Kootenai who strove to retain their cultural identity in changing times. Thus, Adeline learned how to hunt, how to tan hides and sew clothing, and how to find, preserve, and cook the many foods that made up the Kootenai diet. Her grandparents followed the seasonal round that had guided their people's subsistence for generations, and they passed this knowledge—and the history and values it contained—on to Adeline.

The nuns of the Catholic mission in St. Ignatius also inspired Adeline. Despite her grandmother's objections, Adeline attended six years at the Ursuline boarding school, where she learned Latin and English and developed her beautiful singing voice. Adeline found certain parallels between some of the Christian teachings and what her Kootenai grandparents had taught her, including the importance of kindness, hard work, and honesty.

As she grew, Adeline demonstrated the self-reliance and morality her elders had instilled in her. She worked as a jockey in her teens, despite her height of nearly six feet, and, for many years, as a waitress, seasonal agricultural worker, and even a policewoman at regional powwows. Known for her integrity, she expected high standards of behavior. Throughout her lifetime, she remained proud that she never relied on men for sustenance. Adeline hunted deer and skinned, butchered, and preserved the meat by herself, even after she married Mitchell Mathias, the son of Chief Baptiste Mathias, in 1926. "I was a strong woman," Adeline recalled.

As one of the last fluent Kootenai speakers, Adeline Mathias was the repository of much of her tribe's cultural knowledge and history. She understood that the survival of Kootenai culture depends on the preservation of the Kootenai language since the language contains much of the tribe's culture, history, and value system. However, Kootenai is a language isolate; no other related languages exist, so its preservation poses particular challenges. Determined to do her part, Mathias recorded many hours of Kootenai language for educational use, compiled oral histories into books for children, and helped create a Kootenai dictionary.

In the late twentieth century, the Cultural Committee of

One of the last fluent Kootenai speakers, Adeline Mathias spent many hours recording Kootenai language tapes and other instructional material in order to preserve the language.
Courtesy Gigi Caye

the Confederated Salish and Kootenai Tribes began an intensive effort to restore and record their tribal histories. One significant component of their work was the research into the tribal names for places throughout western Montana—the tribes' traditional homelands. They prioritized this work because place-names often encapsulate tribal history, describing specific events or identifying resources the tribes gathered at those places. Mathias's knowledge was instrumental to the project's success, as she recounted numerous place-names and associated histories dating from her lifetime and back into the ancient history of the tribe—information that the committee was able to record. In recognition of her contributions, Salish Kootenai College named its Technology and Computer Sciences building for her, while Adeline Mathias's family created an endowed scholarship at the college in her name.

In addition to her wealth of cultural, linguistic, and historical knowledge, Mathias carried the ceremonial traditions of the Kootenai people. As the keeper of the tribe's spiritual and cultural practices, the elder upheld her obligation to keep the fabric of Kootenai culture intact by mentoring others. "White man's culture was not meant for Indian people," Adeline Mathias often said, fearing that the Kootenais of today would not know their own language, history, or customs. Today, a new generation carries the charge of keeping alive the Kootenai culture, the longest-practiced living culture in Montana.

Head, Heart, Hands, and Health: Montana's Women and Girls in the 4-H Movement

Laura Ferguson

MONTANA'S 4-H CLUBS grew from three thousand youngsters in 1914 to over twenty thousand members a century later. The organization encourages children to develop skills that enable them to better their lives and strengthen their communities. Its emphasis on the economic importance of women's work created leadership opportunities for women and inspired girls to partake in 4-H clubs, camps, and competitions. Women and girls in 4-H have proven their abilities while broadening the organization's objectives and expanding its opportunities for boys and girls alike.

When Montana's Cooperative Extension Service hired Augusta Evans to organize the state's first 4-H clubs in 1914, the nation's agricultural industry was striving to stabilize food production. The Extension Service and experimental agricultural stations engaged 4-H youth in their efforts to apply an industrial approach to farming: maximizing efficiency using new technologies and boosting production by applying scientific methods. Initially, almost all Montana's 4-H members were boys, and these early club members produced corn, peas, potatoes, beef, and sheep. In contrast, the state's first girls' clubs focused on corset making. By 1930, however, the number of girls in Montana's clubs exceeded the number of boys, and their activities had greatly diversified.

Home Demonstration agents effected this change when they brought up-to-date techniques to rural women. Even women already experienced in canning and cooking benefited from the expertise of agents like Helen Mayfield, who demonstrated food preservation for maximum nutritional content. A 4-H leader from Rosebud County noted in the 1930s that farm women were often more bashful than their daughters but just as eager to try the newest technologies. This outreach to rural women stimulated a rapid rise of 4-H club leaders.

Girls in sewing and dressmaking clubs gained proficiency in an eco-nomically valuable trade while introducing their mothers to the latest styles,

Dorothy and Gladys Hill, both Blackfeet tribal members and students at the Cut Bank Boarding School, showcased their project "Furnishing of a Model Indian Home" at the 1930 4-H Club Hi-Line Association Conference at Rocky Boy, Montana. Attendees included residents of the Rocky Boy, Blackfeet, Flathead, Fort Peck, and Fort Belknap Reservations. The conference earned praise from officials who saw 4-H as a valuable tool of education and assimilation. MHS Photo Archives PAc 84-59, Folder 2

tools, and fabrics. Through 4-H, rural girls also developed confidence and etiquette equal to that of their urban counterparts. The prevalence of home economics projects in 4-H had another benefit as well: as early as the 1940s, boys began successfully modeling their self-tailored suits at the dress revues that are a hallmark of 4-H competitions.

Women soon extended 4-H to Montana's Indian reservations. In the 1920s, woman's club member Jessie Roberts organized the Fort Belknap Clothing Club, the first Indian 4-H club in the United States. Like other 4-H clubs, Indian clubs helped girls develop practical skills such as dress-making, gardening, canning, and poultry production. Indian club leaders also taught cultural crafts like beading and leatherwork, and girls success-fully exhibited their handmade traditional-style dresses. Ruth Grainger, a Lakota club member from Poplar, earned over a thousand dollars during the Great Depression through the sale of her crafts, prepared foods, pro-duce, and poultry. In 1939, Grainger won a trip to the national 4-H camp in Washington, D.C., for her outstanding accomplishments during nine years in 4-H.

Along with building young people's skills, 4-H clubs helped them gain proficiency with emerging technologies. When home electrification spread across Montana in the mid-twentieth century, 4-H clubs introduced local communities to new appliances meant to improve women's household effi-ciency. When two fourteen-year-old girls from Teton County entered a statewide cake-baking competition in the early 1940s, they used an electric oven for the first time. Their white cake equaled that of older girls who had the advantage of experience.

For decades, the vast majority of 4-H girls undertook home economics projects, but a few pursued agricultural projects. At the 1920 Montana State Fair, sisters Eula and Hazel Thompson humbled forty-two boys by win-ning first and second place in the baby beef category. Gradually, more girls became involved in agricultural production. Montana's first woman poultry specialist, Harriette Cushman, spearheaded this expansion.

Hired by the Extension Service in 1922, Cushman recognized that poultry—generally overlooked by state 4-H leaders in favor of beef cattle and sheep—was a mainstay of home economies and an essential source of income for women. Cushman educated 4-H members in egg production, poultry health, quality inspection, and marketing, thus ensuring many suc-cessful 4-H projects and enabling Montana youth to attend national poultry industry conferences.

For many Montana children, the opportunity to travel afforded through 4-H was one they could not have experienced otherwise. In 1925, Montana sent its first full delegation to the weeklong national 4-H congress in Chicago. Marie MacDonald of Highwood (one of six female delegates) recalled, "Certainly, after that week, after seeing the richness and complexity of the outside world, we were never again the same."

One of Montana's most devoted 4-H leaders, Peace Corps trainer Geraldine Fenn of Bozeman, recognized that Montana's youth benefited from exposure to new ideas and cultures. Rather than focusing on the 4-H objectives that led to the betterment of one's own life, Fenn advanced the equally important goals of community development and service. In 1948, she established Montana's International Farm Youth Exchange (IFYE), a program that sends experienced 4-H youth to countries around the world where they help communities incorporate tried-and-true 4-H agricultural techniques. The IFYE, now part of clubs throughout the United States, has elevated 4-H's commitment to community well-being to a global level.

Today, girls still make up the majority of Montana's 4-H club members. They continue to learn new skills and find opportunities for leadership, travel, and accomplishment in both conventional "women's work" and in previously male-dominated activities. The program owes much of this success to generations of Montana women who have contributed their expertise, time, and ideas to creating a lasting, viable 4-H legacy.

"She Spoke the Truth": The Childhood and Later Activism of Lula Martinez

Annie Hanshew

BORN TO Mexican immigrants Petra Ortega and Fidencio Acebedo in 1922, Lula Martinez grew up in Butte but left as a teenager for agricultural work in the Pacific Northwest. She returned over forty years later to work on behalf of the city's impoverished and unemployed. Her memories of her childhood in Butte reveal the complex racial dynamic that existed in the mining city in the early twentieth century, and her experiences as an ethnic minority instilled a lifelong commitment to community activism and female empowerment.

Martinez's father worked construction on the railroad, and his job took the family from Texas to Montana. The Acebedos settled in Butte, and Fidencio worked in the mines. The Acebedos were part of Butte's small but significant Hispanic population, drawn to the booming copper mines in the first decades of the twentieth century. By World War II, "several hundred Mexicans and Filipinos" lived in Butte. The majority of the Mexican immigrants worked at the Leonard Mine and lived on the city's east side. Unlike Filipinos, who encountered violence in the mines and tended not to stay, Mexican workers seem to have been generally accepted by the other miners, and Mexican families did not live in segregated neighborhoods. Martinez recalled that growing up "we were surrounded by different nationalities. We had Vankoviches and Joseviches and Biviches, and we had Serbians, and we had Chinese. We had *italianos*, *españolas*, and Mexican people. We had the whole United Nations around on the East Side."

In spite of this ethnic diversity, Martinez did encounter discrimination. As she got older, and especially after she began to attend school, it became clear that she was trapped in a racial hierarchy that discriminated against Mexicans and Mexican Americans. She remembered, "As children we didn't know there was a difference so we got along fine. It was when you're . . . going to school when the teachers started to say, 'Well, you gotta sit over

Lula Acebedo Martinez became a social activist in part because of the discrimination she experienced growing up in Butte. Her mother's determination and generosity also inspired Martinez. "Mama never turned anyone away," she remembered. Courtesy Phyllis Costello

there. All the Mexicans sit on that side.' . . . [A]nd then we found out that there was a difference." Martinez's encounters with racism in her childhood instilled a determination to work for social justice, but they also gave her a "hatred" of Butte that she carried with her into adulthood.

Fidencio Acebedo died in a mining accident in 1928, leaving his wife to raise five children. She remarried Juan Aguilar, a Mexican immigrant who could not read or write English. (Later, Aguilar would also die in the mines.) Martinez credits her mother as a role model for helping others. Petra Aguilar took in boarders even if they could not afford to pay, and she fed neighbors and transients who came through on the train. Martinez recalls that her mother "never gave up. At the time that my dad got killed in the mine, she got a pension [from] the mine. . . . [S]he'd feed everybody. She'd make big pots of stew and feed all the kids. . . . [M]y mother influenced me by . . . my seeing . . . that she never judged."

Martinez left Butte when she was seventeen to pick apples in Washington. As an adult, she became deeply involved in community organizations that served agricultural workers. Her efforts ranged from collecting food commodities to starting health clinics to organizing advocacy groups to help migrant workers collect social services.

Martinez's activism was based in part on her particular brand of feminism that linked womanhood to community betterment. Although raised to follow traditional gender roles in which women kept the home, Martinez saw women as uniquely suited to solve problems in the greater community. She believed that "a woman is the strongest" member of the family. Motherhood, in particular, gave women insights into community problems: "[I]t's women who know how much they need when their children get sick. It's women who know that without a good health clinic or good doctor, they're the ones that suffer. Their children suffer."

In 1984, at age sixty-two, Martinez decided to return to the hometown that she had abandoned as a teenager. She brought her skills as an activist and her insights into racial and class prejudice and began working as an organizer for the Butte Community Union (BCU), a group formed to advocate for the city's lower classes. At BCU, Martinez campaigned for better conditions in public housing and access to affordable heat, among other issues. Sister Kathleen O'Sullivan, a BCU board member, described Martinez as the "wisdom person at BCU." O'Sullivan also noted that Martinez was a highly effective organizer: "[S]he spoke truth, not trying to convince people, but would say something that would focus the discussion, draw your attention to the essence of something."

Martinez left Montana in 1988 to be closer to family in Portland, but her return as an adult had shifted her opinion of Butte. Although she never learned to love the city as ferociously as some, she did come to love the community: "[A]nytime you make friends, long-lasting friends, you've won. . . . I've learned a lot by being here these last years, more about Butte than I did before I left. . . . The hate isn't there, but it's still not . . . a love of Butte. It's the love of people."

Jeannette Rankin: Suffragist, Congresswoman, Pacifist

Mary Murphy

JEANNETTE RANKIN of Missoula was the first woman elected to the U.S. House of Representatives. Unsurprisingly, her election made headlines across the country. People wanted to know who this western upstart was and what this radical change might portend. The *Kentucky Courier-Journal* captured the magnitude of the political quake when it wondered, "Breathes there a man with heart so brave that he would want to become one of a deliberate body made up of 434 women and himself?"

Born on a ranch near Missoula in 1880, Jeannette Rankin was the oldest of John Rankin and Olive Pickering Rankin's seven children. She attended the University of Montana, and in 1908—inspired by the career of Jane Addams, founder of Hull House, the famed Chicago settlement house— she headed to New York to study social work at the New York School of Philanthropy. She worked briefly as a social worker and then as an organizer for the National American Woman Suffrage Association in several states' suffrage campaigns. In 1914, Rankin returned to Montana to help lead her state's suffrage movement to victory. Rankin believed that western conditions, in which men and women had to share the tasks of settlement, encouraged greater gender equality than existed in the East, making it easier to convince Montana men to give women the vote.

Building on the grassroots organization she had created in 1914, she ran for Congress as a Progressive Republican in 1916 and won the seat. When she learned that she had been elected, she said, "I knew the women would stand by me." And indeed, newly enfranchised Montana women went to great lengths to vote for her. Edith Mutchler wrote to Rankin from Chester to tell her that she was eight months pregnant when she "rode 14 mi on a cold windy day" to cast her ballot but testified that she "would gladly do it again."

Rankin's first vote in Congress was on the highly charged issue of whether the United States should enter World War I. Rankin did not respond to the first roll call; on the second, she rose from her seat and stated, "I want to stand by my country, but I cannot vote for war." While many women and men across the country supported her, others declared that her action proved that women did not have the constitution for politics. Such critics conveniently ignored the fifty-five male members of Congress who also voted against war. Rankin's fellow freshman legislator Fiorello La Guardia

When this photograph of Jeannette Rankin was taken in Washington, D.C., in April 1917, she was at the beginning of what appeared to be a very promising political career. Her unpopular votes against the United States' entry into World Wars I and II would end her political aspirations but ultimately earn her widespread respect for adhering to her principles. MHS Photo Archives 944-480

recalled that, when asked if Miss Rankin was crying when she voted, he replied that he could not say, for he had not been able to see through the tears in his own eyes.

During the congressional term, Rankin pursued an agenda of progressive reform. She introduced a bill that protected American women from having their citizenship revoked when they married foreign men. She also supported legislation that sought to provide for maternal and infant health care. While neither of those measures passed, she was able to facilitate improved working conditions for women in the U.S. Bureau of Printing and Engraving. Rankin also used her position to publicize the grievances of Montana miners and farmers. In 1917, she attempted to mediate a bitter dispute between Butte copper miners and the Anaconda Copper Mining Company. The company proved resistant, even more so after she called upon the government to nationalize metal mines essential to the war.

Defeated in a bid for the Senate in 1918, Rankin spent the next twenty-two years working for peace organizations such as the Women's International League for Peace and Freedom, the Women's Peace Union, and the National Council for the Prevention of War. She also created a second home near Athens, Georgia, where she strove to live a simple, self-reliant life and became an active grassroots organizer for the Georgia Peace Society. In 1940, at age sixty, she once again won election as a Republican from Montana to the U.S. House of Representatives. She became the only person in history to vote against U.S. entry into both world wars, but this time she voted alone.

Undaunted by public hostility, Rankin continued to work for peace in semi-retirement. She traveled extensively, making several trips to India. Mahatma Gandhi was assassinated before she was able to meet him, but she believed his theories promised a model for world peace. With the onset of the Vietnam War, Rankin once again entered the political arena. In 1968, she led several thousand women, the Jeannette Rankin Brigade, in a march on Washington, D.C., to protest U.S. involvement in yet another war. Rankin continued an active life of public speaking until her death at age ninety-three in 1973.

Historian Joan Hoff Wilson summed up Rankin's politics in this way: "[S]he consistently pursued a progressive brand of foreign policy that has its roots in Jeffersonian agrarian values, in a nonconsumer oriented life style, in direct, decentralized government, in reform at home before reform of the world, and finally, in the belief that people, especially women, could be educated in the habits of peace."

In 1983, the Montana legislature chose to honor Jeannette Rankin by having her statue placed in the U.S. Capitol's Statuary Hall, where each state may place statues of two individuals notable in that state's history. Rankin's statue joined that of Charlie Russell, making Montana the only state to be represented by an artist and a feminist.

The Right to Procreate: The Montana State Board of Eugenics and Body Politics

Kayla Blackman

IN 1924, headlines across the state decried the "butchery of the helpless" at the Montana State Hospital for the Insane at Warm Springs, where eleven inmates were forcibly sterilized. Hospital staff responded that all sterilizations had received the required approval and that eugenics was "necessary to the future welfare of Montana." Eugenics—the idea that "human perfection could be developed through selective breeding"—grew in popularity in the early twentieth century, including support for forced sterilization. The movement reached its zenith in Montana in the early 1930s, and, despite growing concerns, the practice of forced sterilizations continued into the 1970s.

Montanans' support for forced sterilization was part of a national trend. Eugenics proponent Albert E. Wiggam, a national lecturer and trained psychologist, helped spread the eugenics gospel in Montana through a column in the *Missoulian*. "Already we are taxing ourselves for asylums and hospitals and jails to take care of millions who ought never to have been born," Wiggam wrote. Many Montanans agreed, including the Helena mother who wrote the state hospital in 1924 in support of sterilization policies. "I am a tax payer. That means I wish there was no insane, no feeble minded, and no criminals to support and to fear. . . . The very fact that these people are inmates of state institutions proves that they are morally or mentally unfit to propagate their kind."

Montana institutions began sterilizing selected inmates in the 1910s, but it was not until 1923 that the state legislature created the Montana Board of Eugenics to regulate the practice. The law establishing the board stressed that eugenic sterilization required consent—either from a legal guardian or next of kin or, barring that, from the board itself. The first board, which included several doctors, among them noted Butte physician Caroline McGill, distanced itself from eugenics' most avid proponents by stressing

The Montana Board of Eugenics approved over two hundred sterilizations at the State Hospital for the Insane at Warms Springs. This photo shows the hospital's administration building in 1938. MHS Photo Archives PAc 95-39.20

that sterilization was not to be used as "a punitive measure" but for the "betterment of . . . inmate[s] or to protect society." The board required that sterilizations be performed only at state institutions: primarily, the State Hospital for the Insane at Warm Springs and the State Training School at Boulder, both custodial establishments for those with mental disabilities.

Though in theory the law applied equally to both sexes, in application it disproportionately affected women. Of the 256 Montanans legally sterilized between 1923 and 1963, 184 (or 71 percent) were women. It also disproportionately affected the poor and the unmarried. The first three Montanans sterilized were unmarried "imbeciles" committed to the state hospital multiple times for pregnancy out of wedlock. The hospital staff suggested that, once sterilized and released, none of the women would return because they were capable of supporting themselves; sterilization prevented their readmittance and relieved the state's burden of caring for the women's children, all six of whom were "deficient mentally" and some of whom were already in state custodial care.

Compared with many states, Montana applied its eugenics law infrequently. Oregon sterilized over 2,600 individuals under its eugenics law, while Montana officially reported sterilizing 322. Nevertheless, some bemoaned Montana's low rate of forced sterilization. In 1924, the state hospital reported sterilizing twenty-three individuals but stated that "unquestionably at least four hundred-forty-seven should have been done instead."

By passing eugenics laws, state officials gave themselves the power to control reproduction, and prejudice often influenced their decisions. In 1927, the U.S. Supreme Court ruled in *Buck v. Bell* that forced sterilization was constitutional, infamously declaring that "three generations of imbeciles are enough." However, the classification of "imbecile" often included women who committed petty crimes or were promiscuous. Drug addicts, the homeless, and the unemployed also found themselves targets of eugenic sterilization laws. So did members of Indian tribes.

In the 1970s, women from reservations across the United States discovered that, during the course of standard medical procedures, they had been sterilized without their consent by doctors working for the Indian Health Service (IHS). In Montana, three anonymous women from the Northern Cheyenne Reservation filed a class action lawsuit (ultimately settled out of court) alleging forced sterilization without their knowledge.

Amid a rising outcry, Northern Cheyenne tribal judge Marie Sanchez interviewed women on the reservation and discovered that IHS doctors had sterilized at least twenty-six tribal members. Doctors told two fifteen-year-old Northern Cheyenne girls they were having their tonsils removed; instead, the doctors removed their ovaries. Often, the IHS misled women into thinking the process was reversible or coerced their signatures by threatening to take away medical services or remove children from their homes. "The doctors that come to us are young, often fresh out of medical school," Sanchez told a reporter, "and they want to practice on someone."

According to a federal investigation, between 1973 and 1976, the IHS sterilized 3,406 American Indian women without their permission, intentionally targeting full-blooded Native women for the procedure. At the same time, IHS policies failed to address other health concerns on reservations, including high infant mortality rates. American Indian activists called the sterilization process genocidal. Erasing reproductive ability, many claimed, was an effort to erase the tribes themselves.

As of 2014, seven states have apologized for their role in sterilizing citizens; Montana is not among them. In 1973, the State Eugenics Board approved all twenty-four of the cases presented to it; later in the decade the board quietly dissolved. In 1987, however, the Montana Developmental Disabilities Planning and Advisory Council was still debating the merits of sterilization for citizens with "mental disabilities," a debate about an issue some considered a violation of "a fundamental human right: the right to procreate." The question of compulsory sterilization has not been conclusively resolved; although no statute remains on Montana's law books, neither has any guarantee of reproductive rights been passed. The right to procreate in Montana remains a contested subject.

Montana's Postwar Women Politicians

Annie Hanshew

ACCORDING TO one common narrative, the post–World War II period marked a "return" to traditional gender roles, including breadwinner husbands and homemaker wives. But contrary to this stereotype, in the 1940s and 1950s married women entered the paid workforce in greater numbers than ever before. Women also volunteered with community organizations and were actively involved in both political parties. In Montana, a small but significant number of women even ventured into—and achieved success in—the traditionally masculine world of electoral politics. These postwar politicians achieved a number of important "firsts" and gained political experience that would be invaluable in the push for equal rights in the 1960s and 1970s.

Among these postwar women politicians was Ellenore Bridenstine of Terry, who in 1945 became the first woman elected to the state senate. An active participant in the local Republican Party and the wife of the only physician in Prairie County, Bridenstine recalled her decision to run for office: "Many of my women friends felt that I was crazy to try for it. But I decided to try for it anyway just to see what would happen. The man holding the office had never campaigned, and I am sure that he felt he would not need to against a woman." Bridenstine won her seat by a mere six votes but was reelected in the next cycle.

In the late 1940s and 1950s, several other women won seats in the Montana legislature. Some, like Republican Bertha Streeter of Lake County, elected in 1957, came to the state senate after holding local office. Many others served multiple terms. The number of women active—and successful—in local and state politics suggests that Montanans supported women's political ambitions with their votes. Historian Joanne Meyerowitz has found widespread admiration during the 1950s for "women who exhibited 'devotion to the public good.'" The success of Montana's postwar politicians fit this emphasis on female service.

Once elected, Montana's women politicians were expected to live up to the conservative stereotypes of wife and mother while they worked to better their communities, and their experiences reflect differential treatment based

It's hard to spot State Senator Ellenore Bridenstine (third row back, on the right) amid her male colleagues. When this photo was taken, in 1945, Bridenstine was the first woman to serve in the Montana Senate. MHS Photo Archives PAc 89-59, Senate of the 29th Legislative Assembly

on their gender. Bridenstine "felt really sorry for some of [her] fellow senators because they did not know how to handle working with a woman. . . . Some of them were too polite, jumping to their feet whenever I approached them for advice, while some of them simply ignored me." Antoinette "Toni" Fraser Rosell, a Billings Republican who was elected to the house in 1956 and who remained active in the legislature for the next two decades, recalled that she was treated "fairly" by her colleagues—although she ate sack lunches because she "was not invited out to lunch by lobbyists."

In general, female politicians worked within cultural stereotypes about women's political capacities. During the Progressive Era, American women had carved out distinct niches in politics based on the belief that women were naturally suited to deal with certain social issues like education, maternal and child welfare, and public health. This "female dominion" of American politics, as historian Robyn Muncy has pointed out, was a place where women could exercise significant political power even as their authority was circumscribed by more powerful male politicians and bureaucrats.

The work of Montana's postwar politicians suggests that they operated within a similarly restricted context. Bridenstine, for example, was given the chairmanship of the Sanitary Affairs (later renamed Public Health) Committee and the vice chairmanship of the Education Committee. These committee placements reflected Bridenstine's personal expertise—she was a former educator and the wife of a doctor—but they were also areas traditionally associated with female reformers. Because she was from a rural county, she was also placed on the Agricultural Committee. In this traditionally masculine realm, Bridenstine recalled that she was "promptly ignored." Other female politicians followed a similar pattern. Bess Reed, a Republican from Missoula, also served as chair of the Public Health Committee and worked on public school reform.

Even while working within the context of conservative gender roles, many postwar politicians avidly promoted women's rights. As a member of the Republican state platform committee in 1942, Bridenstine pushed for a rule requiring that women serve as vice chairs on party committees. Bridenstine was also an ardent proponent of women running for office. Bess Reed, too, advocated for women's political involvement. In a speech to the Helena Soroptimists, she decried the fact that women did not exercise the right to vote, saying, "It is a sacrilege that this privilege is taken so lightly." Reed also strongly supported equal rights under the law for women, including the Equal Rights Amendment, a cause that Toni Fraser Rosell would continue to push through the 1970s.

Betty Friedan's *The Feminine Mystique*, published in 1963, famously criticized the stereotype of the happy housewife and supposedly sparked a renewed push for women's rights, but the experiences of Montana's postwar politicians show that there was more continuity in women's politics than we might have suspected. These women opted for a life of wifery and public service, and they were repeatedly supported by Montana's voters. Though few in number, their activity and advocacy laid the groundwork for the gender equality movement of the 1960s and 1970s.

Theresa Walker Lamebull Kept Her Language Alive

Laura Ferguson

THERESA CHANDLER WALKER LAMEBULL was still teaching when she died in 2007 at 111 years of age. Her subject was A'aniiih, or White Clay, the language of the A'aninin (Gros Ventre) people and one of the world's most endangered languages. By the 1990s, Theresa Lamebull was one of only a dozen people to speak the language fluently. Her willingness to share her knowledge of the White Clay language became the foundation for its recovery.

Theresa Elizabeth Chandler, or Kills At Night, was born to Kills In The Brush and Al Chandler in 1896 in a tepee near Hays on the Fort Belknap Reservation. Raised by her grandmother, Sharp Nose, for the first few years of her life, young Kills At Night was fully immersed in White Clay culture. She then lived with her mother and stepfather, White Weasel, until she was twelve and the federal government mandated she go to school. Without the option of a day school, Theresa attended St. Paul's Catholic boarding school in Harlem, Montana. She long remembered the fences that surrounded the mission school to keep children from running away and returning to their families.

As institutions of assimilation, Indian boarding schools forbade indigenous children from speaking their mother tongue. Thousands of Native people who attended such schools between the 1880s and early 1930s came to associate their first languages with shame and punishment. As adults, many of them refused to teach their languages to their own children, hoping to protect them from incurring shame at being "Indian." This situation created a language gap of two or even three generations in many families.

Perhaps because she attended English-speaking schools for only about four years, then married a fellow tribal member, John Walker, and settled near her childhood home, Theresa Walker retained her fluency in the White Clay language. Her second husband, Andrew Lamebull, also spoke it fluently. For smaller tribes like the A'aninin, who numbered around six hundred people at the beginning of the twentieth century, only a few lifelong speakers remained at the century's end.

After her ten children grew up, Theresa Walker Lamebull often longed to talk with someone who spoke the White Clay language. She visited the senior center to speak with other elders and shared her knowledge with the reservation schools' bilingual programs in the 1970s. Inconsistent funding and the scarcity of fluent speakers, however, made it difficult to establish lasting language programs.

Then, in the late 1990s, Fort Belknap College received a grant to develop a mentorship program, Speaking White Clay, which paired elders like Theresa Walker Lamebull with new learners. Lamebull traveled seventy miles twice a week to the tribal college to teach. One of her students was educator Terry Brockie, who had begun studying A'aniiih with his traditional grandmother, Madeline Colliflower.

Born near Hays on the Fort Belknap Reservation in 1896, Theresa Chandler Walker Lamebull dedicated much of her later years to language preservation. She taught until shortly before her death in 2007. Courtesy Terry Brockie

Brockie understood that the endeavor was about more than learning words and phrases. It was about regaining what had been nearly lost for all time: their identity as White Clay people. Theresa Lamebull was essential to that process. "She is one of the few keepers of our way of life, our traditional way of life," he told the *Great Falls Tribune* in 2005.

Reflecting on his studies with Lamebull, Brockie said, "She taught me traditional values that I use today to teach my own children. She was humble, spiritual, and never had a bad word to say about anyone. Over time I learned that those qualities are vested in our language, so it was natural to model that way of life."

Realizing that their elderly mentors would not always be around, younger adult students in the Speaking White Clay program committed themselves to preserving the language. The tribal education department had previously collected stories from elders, but those memories were written in English. A few older audiotapes existed but without translations into English. Then Brockie discovered a new technology—the "Phraselator," a device originally developed for military use. With Brockie's help, Lamebull recorded hundreds of A'aniiih words and phrases and their English definitions into the Phraselator, teaching Brockie the more complex aspects of the White Clay language while sharing tales of the old way of life and the tribe's history. The more he learned, the more Brockie realized the responsibility members of his own generation had to teach their culture to future generations.

Although reservation-based Head Start preschools had tried to incorporate Native languages, funding for bilingual programs waxed and waned over the years, making it impossible to teach children the language. In 2003, Brockie's classmate from the Speaking White Clay program, Lynette Chandler, developed a K–8 White Clay immersion school. Funded by private grants, the immersion school's first class of graduates not only speak their ancestral language, but have excelled in other academic subjects as well, including English. With over one hundred digital audio recordings of elders like Lamebull, Chandler and her husband, Sean, are now creating a new digital curriculum for young speakers, including White Clay language apps for iPhones and iPods. Brockie is helping to develop a user-friendly A'aniiih dictionary.

As the number of White Clay speakers grows, so has the appreciation for all Lamebull and her peers did to enable younger A'aninin to regain their language and heritage. In 2005, members of the tribe renamed the Hays Education Resource Center the Kills At Night Center in her honor. At the dedication, Terry Brockie sang an honor song for Theresa Walker Lamebull, and he sang it in A'aniiih.

Merle Egan Anderson: Montana's "Hello Girl"

Annie Hanshew

THE STORY OF women's military service during World War II is relatively well known; less familiar is the story of the women who served during World War I, sometimes on or near the front lines. During World War I, over twenty-five thousand women worked for American forces or support organizations in Europe. These women performed integral work and helped chip away at gender stereotypes, paving the way for the more famous WACs and WAVEs of World War II.

Among those serving during World War I was Merle Egan of Helena, a telephone switchboard operator for the U.S. Army Signal Corps. A vitally important technology to U.S. military operations, telephones allowed officers to communicate across battlefields, between dispersed units, and with other allied forces. Unfortunately, war had devastated the French telephone system, so in 1917, when the Army was building up its forces in France, General John Pershing ordered the construction of an American telephone system throughout the country.

The creation of a military telephone system opened up new opportunities for female service since civilian telephone operators were almost exclusively female. As Colonel Parker Hitt, chief signal officer of the U.S. First Army, explained, "[A]n Army telephone central would have to have American women operators to be a success. Our experience in Paris with the untrained and undisciplined English-speaking French women operators, and experience elsewhere with the willing but untrained men operators was

Initially, the U.S. Army Signal Corps only accepted women fluent in French. Merle Egan joined after the military lifted the language requirement. Pictured here are some of Egan's colleagues operating a switchboard in Chaumont, France. *Getting the Message Through: A Branch History of the U.S. Army Signal Corps* (Washington, D.C., 1996), 171

almost disastrous." Thus, in November 1917, General Pershing requested that the War Department deploy one hundred French-speaking American women with telephone operating experience. Thousands of women applied, and the first of these "Hello Girls" traveled overseas in the spring of 1918.

Merle Egan had eleven years of telephone operating experience when General Pershing put out the call for female operators. She trained in the summer of 1918 and headed to France that August. "As we sailed out of the harbor past the Statue of Liberty," she recalled in later years, "there was an emotional tension experienced, I am sure, by every Veteran who has served overseas. For some, there would be no returning, but we knew we were answering our country's call and we were proud of that mission."

Egan docked in Liverpool and then went on to Paris before arriving at her station in Tours. She expected to serve as a telephone operator, but because of her technological expertise (Montana's rural switchboards were very much like the primitive switchboards used in the field), she ended up instructing male soldiers in switchboard operation instead. The men were initially hostile: "'Where's my skirt?' was their standard greeting. . . . [After] I reminded them that any soldier could carry a gun, but the safety of a whole division might depend on the switchboard one of them was operating I had no more trouble."

Two days after the November 11, 1918, armistice, Egan was awestruck to learn that she was being reassigned to the position of chief operator for the American Peace Commission in Paris. Looking back, she recalled, "Even now, after more than fifty years, it seems incredible that a young woman from a small city in Montana could rate an assignment that would involve telephone service to not only the outstanding men of our own country, but the world. Calls from President Wilson's residence to Lloyd George of England, to Clemenceau of France, and Orlando of Italy were a daily occurrence."

Egan served in Paris until late May 1919, always assuming that on her return home she would be treated as a veteran. It was not to be. Once back in Montana, she married H. R. Anderson, also an employee of the Mountain States Telephone Company. She recalled that her new husband was "very proud of my service" and "wrote one day to the Army to obtain my victory medal. We were astounded to receive the Army's reply that I was a civilian employee. This, I believe, was my first indication that my former military status was in question. This was an even greater shock since I had just a few weeks earlier received a citation from General Pershing for Meritorious Service."

Jarred by the army's decision to label its female operators civilians, Merle Egan Anderson began a lifelong quest for formal recognition of the Hello Girls' military service and veteran status. The evidence for her case was overwhelming. She had been sworn in by the adjutant general of the Montana National Guard. She had worn a military uniform with army buttons and the Signal Corps' insignia. She had traveled to Europe on a ship that carried seven thousand male troops. She had an injured toe that was treated in an army hospital. The Hello Girls all followed military regulations, were subject to court-martial, and "were at all times under the command of male Army Signal Corps officers and constantly reminded by them that we were in the Army." Even after she returned to the United States, Anderson remembered that "when I protested a routing in my travel orders, I was told, 'Young lady you are still in the Army.'"

In spite of the seemingly obvious evidence, the fight for veteran status took six decades. According to historian Lettie Gavin (who credits Anderson for "leading the charge"), "More than fifty bills granting veteran status to the Hello Girls were introduced in Congress over the years, but none was passed." Finally, with help from veterans' groups and the National Organization for Women, the Hello Girls received veteran status in 1977. By the time their veterans' benefits had been processed in 1979, only 18 of the 223 women who had served in the Signal Corps were still alive. Fortunately, Merle Anderson was one. She died in 1986, an acknowledged veteran of the U.S. Army.

"A Man in the Mountains Cannot Keep His Wife": Divorce in Montana in the Late Nineteenth Century

Annie Hanshew

IN THE LATE nineteenth and early twentieth centuries, a series of economic and social changes culminated in a nationwide increase both in divorce rates and in the liberalization of divorce laws. This pattern played out in Montana on an even larger scale. Based on her extensive study of Montana divorces in the late nineteenth century, historian Paula Petrik found that frontier conditions in mining cities like Helena and Butte created a climate in which divorces were common. Petrik also argues that, over the course of the late nineteenth century, women seeking to divorce ushered in changes to Montana law that made divorces easier to obtain and on terms more favorable to women. In doing so, they confirmed the ideal of "companionate marriage"—or marriage based on mutual affection and reciprocal duties. This ideal would come to define the institution in the early twentieth century.

For Montanans facing the frontier conditions of social upheaval, an unbalanced ratio of men to women, and rising and falling fortunes, divorces were common. Indeed, in 1868, Helenan Elizabeth Chester Fisk remarked, "Divorces are common here, and it is a common comment that a man in the mountains cannot keep his wife." Fisk's observation was based in fact, as Lewis and Clark County had an unusually high divorce rate in that era. In 1867, the number of divorces actually exceeded the number of marriages.

Montana's sex imbalance was one important factor. Due to the surplus of men, women could use divorce to better their economic position. During her divorce proceedings, for example, Silver Bow County resident Lucinda Forrest freely admitted that she left her husband for Abraham Lory because "she could get more money out of Lory."

There were also darker reasons for divorce. Women most frequently charged their husbands with desertion, adultery, cruelty, or drunkenness.

Women seeking divorce had to make their case before male judges or, in contested cases, all-male juries, despite the constitutional guarantee of a "jury of one's peers." Most practicing lawyers—with the exception of women such as Ella Knowles Haskell—were also men. The men on the Montana Supreme Court, like those pictured here ca. 1903, ultimately decided what level of violence constituted "extreme cruelty." MHS Photo Archives 957-455

Montana law also allowed for divorce on the grounds of impotency, bigamy, or conviction of a felony. Montana's relatively liberal divorce laws (and correspondingly high number of divorces) was in line with other western states and territories. However, unlike many western states, Montana did not list neglect as a "reasonable and acceptable cause for divorce." Husbands could not abandon their wives or cheat on them, but they did not have a legal obligation to provide for them financially.

Of the causes for divorce, the issue of cruelty was most complicated. The courts required evidence of extreme cruelty, or "physical, life-threatening violence over a period of time." A husband beating his wife once was not enough. A woman seeking divorce had to establish that there had been multiple episodes of violence. Lizette Davis of Helena, for example, detailed how her husband locked her out of the house in winter, threw boiling water on her, and beat her head against a nail. During one incident, she fell and suffered a miscarriage. Asked why she endured her husband's abuse, Davis responded, "The men had been talking about putting him in jail for mistreating me, and he was crying. I knew he was my man. I got ashamed for him and thought it was best to make it up."

Although not embedded in statute, many judges used a "three beating rule" to determine whether extreme cruelty applied. Even after 1885, when the Montana Supreme Court ruled, in *Albert v. Albert*, that one beating was sufficient to establish cruelty, judges in the working-class town of Butte continued to use a conservative standard of multiple incidents, suggesting that grounds for divorce differed depending on a woman's social status.

Even as Butte judges excused abusive husbands—particularly, according to one judge, if the wife provided provocation—the middle- and upper-class women of Helena were arguing for a new definition of cruelty that did not hinge on physical violence. Instead, these women sought divorce on the grounds of mental cruelty, which could encompass anything from tyrannical behavior to verbal abuse and violent behavior. Mary Monroe even alleged mental abuse on the basis of the humiliation she endured when her husband publicly escorted known prostitutes around Helena.

In suing for divorce on the grounds of mental cruelty, these women inadvertently furthered a version of marriage based on mutual respect and obligation. The courts responded, and the Montana legislature codified mental cruelty as grounds for divorce in 1907. Ironically, in the same bill they also required that cruelty—physical or mental—had to exist for a year before a suit could be filed, effectively offering a one-year grace period for domestic violence.

While Montanans did not seem overwhelmingly concerned with the state's high divorce rate, which in some places was on par with modern levels, turn-of-the-century easterners were gripped in what historian William O'Neill has termed a "national crisis" in divorce. Concerned about the growing number of divorces, conservative clergy and some Progressives tried to reform divorce laws to prevent what they perceived to be an attack on the family, and by extension, civilization.

For a time, public opinion was on their side, but ultimately this crusade would fail. Sociologists, feminists, and even some liberal theologians increasingly emphasized mutual affection, female sexual pleasure, and women's freedom as vital elements of a marriage. Without those elements, they argued, a married couple should be able to part.

Montana, then, was ahead of its time. As an early adopter of companionate marriage in law, the divorcées, jurists, and lawmakers anticipated new gender ideals and pioneered greater freedoms for married women in the state.

Drawing on Motherhood: The Cartoons and Illustrations of Fanny Cory Cooney

Kirby Lambert

FOR THIRTY YEARS—from 1926 to 1956—newspaper readers across the country shared their morning coffee or evening pipe with "Sonny," a rambunctious toddler always willing to share his unique take on the world. In all likelihood, few of those readers realized that the mischievous namesake of the internationally syndicated cartoon *Sonnysayings* was the creation of an unassuming ranch wife working from her rural Montana home located "27 miles from Helena . . . and '3 miles from anything.'" Drawing under the pen name F. Y. Cory, Fanny Cory Cooney crafted not only *Sonnysayings*, her longest-running and most popular effort, but two additional cartoons—*Other People's Children* and *Little Miss Muffett*—which also relied upon the humorous antics of impish youngsters.

While Cooney's comics meshed thematically with a number of other cartoons popular during the 1920s and 1930s, the artist herself did not fit the mold of women cartoonists, who were themselves a rarity in a male-dominated profession. Author Trina Robbins begins her book *Pretty in Ink: North American Women Cartoonists, 1896–2013* by identifying three notable twentieth-century women cartoonists who started their careers in the late

The caption to this classic *Sonnysayings*, reads "I'm letting Baby spoil my block house—But if Christmas wasn't most here, I'd knock the stuffin' out ob her." Fanny Cory Cooney, 1926, MHS Museum 2001.45.15

1890s as illustrators working in New York City. Of the three, Cooney was the only one whose lifestyle Robbins does not describe as "bohemian."

Fanny Cory was born in Illinois in 1877. Following her mother's death, her father moved the family to Helena, where young Fanny—who "could not remember any time in her youth when she was not interested in drawing"—studied with the highly regarded, European-trained artist and educator Mary C. Wheeler. With Wheeler's encouragement, after graduating from high school, Fanny followed her cartoonist brother, Jack Cory, east to New York. Years later, she remembered, "She [Wheeler] and I thought I was quite wonderful, but in New York they didn't think so." Fanny, however, was not easily deterred from pursuing her dream of becoming an illustrator.

Her ailing sister Agnes accompanied her on her move east. With Jack's help, Fanny enrolled at the Metropolitan School of Fine Arts in New York City and joined the prestigious Art Students' League. When Agnes's health deteriorated, however, Fanny left school, determined to find work that would enable her to take care of her sister. She pounded the streets of New York, portfolio in hand, until *St. Nicholas Magazine* bought a drawing from her. "I was taken aback," she later recalled, describing the editor's offer of twelve dollars for the illustration. I "hesitated to tell him I thought it too much," she continued, so "he kindly reduced it to ten dollars." By 1897, Fanny was selling her illustrations regularly to *St. Nicholas Magazine* as well as other national periodicals, including *Harper's Bazaar, Scribner's, Youth's*

Companion, *McClure's,* and *Saturday Evening Post.* In addition, she received commissions to illustrate a number of books, including two works by Frank Baum—*The Master Key* and *The Enchanted Island of Yew*—as well as a 1902 edition of Lewis Carroll's *Alice's Adventures in Wonderland.* Almost all of her illustrations were either for or depicted children, and critics praised her original style and her wry humor.

When Agnes died in 1902, a bereft Fanny returned to Montana. Two years later, she married Fred Cooney, who owned a ranch on the Missouri River near the community of Canyon Ferry. Finding the story of the rancher and the illustrator newsworthy, the *Minneapolis Tribune* covered their union in a lengthy article titled "Romantic Marriage of the Girl Who Draws Cute Babies: Won Like the Heroine in a Melodrama." Initially, Cooney attempted to pursue her career as an illustrator, but, following the births of her three children—Sayre, Robert, and Ted—the demands of motherhood took precedence, and, according to author Douglas Green, she "illustrated only those books which had a special appeal to her." This changed in the mid-1920s when, spurred by the need for money to send Sayre to art school and the boys to college, Cooney decided to return to work. At Jack's suggestion, instead of focusing on illustration, she turned her attention to creating a newspaper cartoon, and *Sonnysayings* was born.

In a 1930 newspaper interview, Cooney related that her hardest task with the character of Sonny was "to keep him from growing up." The interview continued:

> Close association with children and a study of childhood antics which filled notebooks during early years on the ranch have made it possible to continue the cartoon. Not only our own family but the neighbors as well feel a personal interest in "Sonny." They call up instantly if one of their children makes a bright remark. Strangers and readers also send occasional childish remarks which have been sent throughout the newspaper world via "Sonningsayings." One lady assured me that she had been almost standing over her two little girls with pencil and notebook in hand, waiting for bright or precocious remarks, but that "[T]he dumb little things never said a word worth writing down."

Fred Cooney died in 1946. Seven years later, the backwaters of Canyon Ferry Dam flooded most of the Cooneys' cherished ranch. But Fanny continued producing *Sonnysayings* and *Little Miss Muffett* until arthritis and failing eyesight led to her retirement in 1956. She moved to the Puget Sound area to be near her daughter Sayre and died there in 1972, just shy of her ninety-fifth birthday.

Montana's "Rosies": Female Smelter Workers during World War II

Annie Hanshew

World War II represented a turning point for women's employment in the United States. While women, especially unmarried women, had increasingly taken jobs outside the home since the turn of the century, most worked in service and clerical positions. In the early 1940s, however, wartime production combined with labor shortages to open new opportunities for women in high-paying industrial jobs.

Many of these jobs required moving to the Pacific Coast, but Montana did have its own version of "Rosie the Riveter" laboring in the smelters of Anaconda and Great Falls. Working in production and industrial maintenance positions for the first time, these Montana Rosies broke economic and social barriers. Their gains, however, were short-lived. Considered a temporary expedient rather than a permanent workforce, women were quickly pushed out of industry after the war, and their experiences foreshadowed the conservative gender expectations that women encountered in the 1950s.

Demand for Montana's minerals skyrocketed during the war, largely because copper, zinc, manganese, and other Montana-mined minerals were key ingredients in munitions and machinery. As men joined the service, the Anaconda Copper Mining Company struggled to find workers, and as labor shortages became more acute, the federal government pressured the company to employ nontraditional workers, including women.

The move met with resistance. Union officials and copper workers argued that women could not work in mines or smelters because they lacked the physical strength and stamina to do the job. Additionally, some men feared the loss of masculine power if women entered the industrial workforce. A 1942 *Anaconda Standard* editorial titled "The Amazons among Our Women" mourned shifting gender roles: "[W]e used to think, with an air of fancied superiority, that woman's place was in the home while the man was the self-reliant and sturdy breadwinner of the family. . . . If the present trends keep up, men some day may be the nursemaids, tending the babies

Despite some initial resistance, the Anaconda Company celebrated women's war work in its magazine *Copper Commando*, July 16, 1943.

while the women run the world. . . . May it all be merely a fanciful dream."

Despite these fears, in 1943 Anaconda did begin hiring women in smelter positions, a move that many women, enticed by the high wages, welcomed. Ursula Jurcich remembered, "Everybody was talking about it, 'Oh, the women are working on the Hill.' That was a big 'baloo' around here . . . so I thought I might as well go and see if I can get on. . . . The money was big. That was important. They were paying $7.75 a day." Katie Dewing, working as a waitress at the time, also applied because the smelter paid "good money."

Women worked in a variety of positions throughout the smelter, from picking up debris to bending wire to oiling machinery. Many of the women expressed pride that they could hold their own doing "men's work." Ursula Jurcich recalled that smelter work "wasn't any more strenuous than housework." Dorothy Anderson also joked that work in the smelter compared favorably to other women's work. She left a position wrapping donuts at Sweetheart Bakery—work that gave her carpal tunnel syndrome—for a job moving anodes at the Black Eagle smelter near Great Falls. "I used to think that it would be a hard job out there," Anderson recalled. "These men that go out and work all day, they have to be coddled and everything else at night 'cause they're so tired 'cause they worked all day. Heck, I wasn't tired when I came home from doing that job."

Many men at the smelter came to appreciate the women's stamina. Tom Dickson recalled the story of one "girl" who was helping stack sixty-pound zinc slabs. "A guy came by and saw her handling these slabs," Dickson recounted, "and he said, 'You know you girls aren't supposed to lift anything over fifty pounds.' She said . . . 'OK then, to hell with it.' And she wouldn't do it anymore! But they performed very well, I thought."

Although women proved their mettle, most men and women considered smelter work a temporary wartime expedient. After the war, women were expected to relinquish their positions and return to the traditional female roles of wife and mother. According to historian Matthew Basso, women's temporary foray into masculine labor paradoxically "did more to reveal the sustainability of Black Eagle's entrenched patriarchal value system . . . than to catalyze change."

Some women accepted that war work was temporary. Dorothy Anderson worked at Black Eagle during the war but felt that women did not belong at the smelter during peacetime. "[Women's] bodies are not made for that heavy kind of work," Anderson argued. "I had a home to go to, and I felt that is where I belonged."

For other women, wartime industrial work sparked small—but important—changes: many continued to wear pants instead of skirts, and even stopped by a bar from time to time. Erma Bennett suggested that women took what they learned from working in the smelter and "kind of passed it on" to their daughters. Most remembered their work with pride. When asked whether she had a college education, Julia Francisca said, "Oh yes, I finished high school and went on to college—'The Copper College.' It was the only place I knew of where you could get an all-around education and get damn good pay along with it."

Martha Edgerton Rolfe Plassmann: A Montana Renaissance Woman

Ken Robison

MARTHA EDGERTON came to Bannack as a teenager in 1863. As a teacher, musician, wife, mother of seven, clubwoman, and leader in the women's suffrage movement, she successfully balanced traditional gender roles with an active public life. Widowed young, she entered the workforce, becoming the first woman editor of a Montana daily newspaper, a local and state leader in the Montana Socialist Party, and a prolific writer. Hers was a long life of striking achievements.

Edgerton was thirteen when she arrived in Bannack in 1863 after her father was appointed governor of Idaho Territory. Two years later, the family returned to Ohio, and she subsequently enrolled at Oberlin College to study music. Later, while teaching at the Ohio Institute for the Blind in Columbus, she met and married Herbert P. Rolfe. In 1876, the couple moved to Helena, where Herbert became the superintendent of public schools. Herbert and Martha Rolfe were kindred spirits: passionate advocates for equality of African Americans, women's suffrage, and the rights of the workingman.

Their activism eventually took them to Great Falls, where, in 1884, the Rolfes took out a homestead right outside the city, which had been newly surveyed and platted by Herbert himself. Four years later, Herbert—long a Republican Party activist—established *The Leader,* a newspaper designed to counter the influence of Great Falls founder Paris Gibson's Democratic *Tribune.* Though occupied with home-schooling the couple's seven children, Martha also wrote for *The Leader* and stayed closely involved in her husband's political crusades.

The Panic of 1893 erased much of the couple's wealth. Nevertheless, the paper survived, and the Rolfes remained active in politics, including the women's suffrage movement. Early in 1895, together with other Great Falls women, including Ella Vaughn, Josephine Trigg, and Josephine Desilets, Martha formed the Political Equality Club. The club gathered over a thousand signatures—about half of those from men—supporting women's suffrage. Later that same year, a suffrage bill passed by over two-thirds in the Montana House, only to be tabled in the Senate.

Within weeks of the bill's defeat, Herbert died suddenly of typhoid, leaving Martha a widow with seven children to support. At the urging of her cousin Wilbur Fisk Sanders, she undertook the challenge of editing *The*

Martha Edgerton arrived in Bannack in 1863. In later years, she supported herself by writing articles about life in Montana Territory, some of which were based on her own memories. E.C. Ely, photographer, MHS Photo Archives 942-065

Leader herself, thereby becoming the first woman to edit a daily newspaper in the state. As she remembered, "I agreed to try running a daily political paper, although absolutely ignorant of what this entailed and never having corrected a line of proof. Thanks to the help received from printers and those on the staff of the paper, I did not entirely fail, although some Republicans felt outraged to think that a mere woman was editing their party organ."

Martha Rolfe operated the newspaper for the next fourteen months, and, according to the *Anaconda Standard*, she did it well: "Since the death of the late H. P. Rolfe, Mrs. Rolfe has had absolute control of the *Leader* and to the surprise of many has improved that paper in many ways. She has developed real newspaper ability."

In October 1895, Martha married *The Leader's* business manager, Theodore Plassmann, who convinced her to sell the paper. When Plassmann died a few months later, Martha was left with little means of support. She described the next few years as "a nightmare I do not like to recall." With help from Herbert's lodge associates, she survived by undertaking a series of business ventures, including selling life insurance, writing poetry, and running a cattle ranch, though none were very successful financially.

To save expenses, Plassmann moved her family from Great Falls to a small ranch near Monarch in the Little Belt Mountains. She wrote verses and sold them to *Good Housekeeping* magazine. When her ranch house burned to the ground, she suffered thousands of dollars in property loss, but with the help of neighbors, she rebuilt a large log home.

One day at the Monarch railway station, the agent, James M. Rector, asked Plassmann to read some political literature he kept near the ticket window. Thus began her conversion to socialism, which she believed "offered the best solution for many of our social ills." She shocked Rector when she asked to join the Monarch Socialist Party, which she did, becoming its first woman member.

Later, with two of her daughters and son Edgerton, Plassmann moved to Missoula so the children could attend the university. There, she became a leader in the local and state socialist movement. She wrote a weekly column, "Socialist Notes," for the *Missoulian* and supported the radical Industrial Workers of the World during the 1909 Missoula free-speech fight. In 1911, she even traveled to Butte to operate Louis Duncan's office during his Socialist successful mayoral bid. Through it all, she remained a tireless advocate for women's suffrage and rejoiced when Montana's equal suffrage amendment passed in 1914. Two years later, on November 7, 1916, she wrote her daughter Helen: "This is a red letter day for me—I went to the polls in an auto and cast my first vote for President of the United States."

Plassmann moved frequently during the following years, living with each of her seven children in turn. By 1920, she was settled down once again in Great Falls, where she began writing historical articles for the *Great Falls Tribune* and the Montana News Association, basing many of those pieces on her own experiences or on interviews with other Montana pioneers. Despite her advancing age, she continued writing until her death on September 25, 1936, at the age of eighty-six.

Fighting for Female Athletes: Title IX in Montana

Annie Hanshew & Marcella Sherfy Walter

"Some say basketball is a metaphor for life," mused NBA Hall of Fame coach Phil Jackson during an interview about Montana's Class C girls' basketball tradition, "but it's bigger than that. It's . . . joy."

For the first half of the twentieth century, Montana's young female basketball players knew that joy—sprinting full court in front of enthusiastic crowds. In 1904, ten girls from the Fort Shaw Indian boarding school drew enormous Great Falls crowds and beat all rivals at the St. Louis World's Fair. Phil Jackson's mother captained her 1927 Wolf Point girls' basketball team. Patricia Morrison's 1944–1945 Fairfield High girls' team beat the boys, playing boys' rules.

But by 1950, mainstream sensibilities and school funding limits had corralled Montana's exuberant female athletes. Their opportunities became limited to tamer intramural activities—often characterized by cast-off equipment, unskilled coaching, and poor facilities. It took congressional action and a court fight to bring equal opportunity in all sports to Montana's young women athletes.

The question, of course, was never about girls' physical prowess or fearlessness. Instead, the issue was equal access to resources. In response, Congress enacted the Education Amendments of 1972. These regulations covered many educational issues, but the best-known section reads, "No person in the United States shall, on the basis of sex, be excluded from participation in, be denied the benefits of, or be subjected to discrimination under any educational program or activity receiving Federal financial assistance." Though it prohibited gender discrimination in all areas of education, Title IX's most far-reaching impact occurred in women's sports.

While Montanans clearly enjoyed women's sports, many opposed Title IX as unwelcome governmental interference. An op-ed piece in the *Billings Gazette* called Title IX "federal blackmail." Educators and school administrators agreed, claiming that the issue "would have worked itself out in a few years."

Not so. Ten years after Title IX became law, there were still significant disparities between boys' and girls' sports. Montana high school girls had fewer sports options than did boys. Boys' athletics received more money; greater publicity; and better practice times, uniforms, locker rooms, coaches, and transportation. So, in May 1982, a group of female athletes and their parents sued the Montana High School Association (MHSA), alleging

Long before the passage of Title IX in 1972, Montana's female students—like the members of Butte's Sacred Heart 1936 field ball championship team—were active in a variety of sports. Title IX, however, sought to ensure that girls would benefit from the same opportunities traditionally awarded to boys in athletics. MHS Photo Archives PAc 96-8.10

that such discrepancies violated Title IX and the equal protection clause of the Fourteenth Amendment.

Karyn Ridgeway, the named plaintiff in *Ridgeway v. Montana High School Ass'n*, was an all-state basketball player at Missoula's Hellgate High School. "I defined myself in basketball terms and my self-worth depended on it. . . . I loved the pressure. But it was hard not to notice that the boys' teams were frequently given the better equipment, facilities and schedules," she said. With her mother, Karyn attended town hall meetings on the issue. When a moderator asked for volunteers for a test case challenging athletic inequities, Ridgeway stepped up.

The *Ridgeway* parties arrived at a settlement for the 1985–1986 year. The MHSA agreed that districts should offer the same number of sports for girls and boys; all coaches should be equally qualified and compensated; and practice times, uniforms, equipment, publicity, and recognition should be comparable. The agreement also established procedures for filing grievances with the MHSA and the Office of Public Instruction—a crucial element since federal agencies did not have the resources to investigate Title IX claims, especially in Montana's smaller school districts.

But the *Ridgeway* parties could not agree on seasons for girls' basketball and volleyball. Going against national norms, Montana held girls' basketball in the fall and girls' volleyball in winter. The plaintiffs argued that switching seasons would allow athletes to compete in national tournaments and attract college recruiters. But schools resisted the change because splitting boys' and girls' basketball seasons allowed them to use the same coaches and facilities. The real issue, a facilitator studying the problem concluded, was "sexually biased attitudes of some of the coaches, athletic directors, administrators and others." The facilitator concluded that changing seasons wouldn't fix the fundamental problem.

Proponents for conventional seasons—the final piece of Title IX's implications—refused to give up. And in 2000, the Montana Human Rights Bureau finally ordered MHSA to make the switch.

A century after young Montana women burst onto the world scene as basketball stars at the St. Louis World's Fair, Title IX continues to pay big dividends. A track star herself in the 1960s, Bonnie Sheriff, now a coach at University of Montana–Western in Dillon, sees firsthand the benefits of Title IX: "It just kind of strengthened the whole student body, really, by recognizing [girls] as equals."

Karyn Ridgeway carried the lessons and values of sports with her well into adulthood. After several years of teaching and coaching, she enrolled in medical school. Today, she specializes in emergency medicine. "The ER is fast-paced and stressful—high stakes every day," she says. "So I need to be in the zone, and my concentration must be complete. Basketball prepared me for this. It's like being at the free-throw line, needing to make a shot in a crucial game. . . . I'll be ready when a critical case bursts through the door."

There's No Place like Home: The Role of the Montana State Orphanage

Jodie Foley

AT FIRST no one noticed the children as they sat quietly in the Silver Bow County Courthouse. The six Freedman children, ages eight to fifteen, had filed in with their mother early that morning in 1938. Recently divorced from her husband and earning little in her job as a research editor, Alice

Freedman was overwhelmed. Before leaving the children, she told them to wait for her return. As the day wore on, county workers noticed the children. At noon, they bought them lunch and contacted the juvenile court. That evening, the Freedman children were taken to a local receiving home. Within two weeks, they were committed to the state orphanage and on their way to the facility in Twin Bridges.

Similar scenarios played out for the thousands of other residents of the Montana State Orphanage. Most, like the Freedman children, were not true orphans but rather "orphans of the living," from homes shattered by devastating poverty, turbulent parental relationships, substance abuse, poor parenting skills, or physical and emotional abuse. In the absence of local, state, or federal social welfare programs, the state orphanage was one of the few options available to these children and the destitute families who could no longer care for them.

Between 1894, when the facility opened, and 1975, when legislative cuts forced its closure, the Montana State Orphanage housed over five thousand children. Established to provide "a haven for innocent children whose poverty and need might lead to lives of crime," the orphanage was designed along nineteenth-century lines to prepare children for productive adult lives by segregating them and providing them with food, education, vocational training, and a rigid structure.

However, even as the orphanage's first building, a sprawling Victorian structure known as "The Castle," was being completed, attitudes toward needy children were changing. By the early 1900s, Progressive Era reformers began arguing that orphanages were dehumanizing and rife with abuse. Children, they claimed, needed a healthy home life, with their parents, if possible, or, if not, with a worthy foster family. To achieve this goal, they advocated for the creation and expansion of government agencies to address the needs of abandoned, abused, or widowed women and their children.

Emma Ingalls and Maggie Smith Hathaway, the first women elected to the state legislature in 1916, worked to advance these goals in Montana. Hathaway championed creation of the Montana Mother's Pension, which provided direct financial support to abandoned or widowed women, allowing some of them to keep their children at home. Ingalls advocated for creation of the Montana State Bureau of Child and Animal Protection to provide oversight for children adopted or placed in foster care. With the creation of the bureau and the Mother's Pension, the state orphanage began its transformation from a predominantly long-term care institution to a way station for children until foster homes could be found.

The trend away from institutionalizing children continued in the 1930s, when the Depression brought the expansion of government social welfare programs. Aid to Dependent Children (ADC), established in 1935, provided direct relief to poor single mothers. With the expansion of this and other social welfare programs, as well as a growing emphasis on foster care and a postwar prosperity that left fewer families destitute, increasingly fewer children ended up in the orphanage. In the 1930s, the average population of the Twin Bridges institution was 282. By 1959, when the facility was more appropriately renamed the Children's Home, the average number of residents had declined to 156. By 1975, when the facility closed, only 50 children were in residence, awaiting placement in foster care.

One hundred years after the Montana State Orphanage opened its doors, the issue of how government should respond to poor women and their children reignited during the debate over welfare reform. In fact, Congressman Newt Gingrich, the author of the Republican Party's

Children pose in front of "The Castle" in 1896, three years after the Montana State Orphanage was built. Many of them were not true orphans but from destitute families whose parents could not care for them. MHS Photo Archives 951-328

"Contract with America," specifically espoused reopening orphanages as a cost-cutting measure.

At a reunion held in 1995, former residents of the orphanage—who had lived there between 1914 and 1969—discussed the debate over reopening orphanages and their varied experiences in the facility. Some felt that with reforms—more affection for individual children, more oversight of staff, and more allowances for siblings to be together—orphanages could provide proper care.

Most agreed, however, that the orphanage system, as they experienced it, had failed them. Harold Freedman, one of Alice Freedman's oldest children, stated, "It was in some ways a rather shocking move . . . to be put in an orphanage, but . . . I felt a lot of pressure lifted off me because I had worried so much about our situation." Fred Wentz found orphanage life particularly hard because he had siblings who had remained at home. "The problem was that I knew I had brothers and sisters somewhere. . . . I just didn't know why I was in the orphanage and not with them. That hurt me. I've carried that throughout my life." For Donna Engebretson, the orphanage provided an important safety net. Even so, she said, "I had a lot of difficulty in my later years . . . understanding how the outside world worked, how a family functions, and understanding relationships."

Alice Freedman, and other women like her, did not want their children growing up in the orphanage; it was simply their only option. In the years following her children's placement, Freedman worked to have the four oldest children released to her. The youngest, a set of twins, left the home in 1945.

Expansion of social welfare programs led to the orphanage's closure. While these programs did not guarantee healthy homes for destitute women and families like the Freedmans, they clearly expanded the possibility of achieving such homes.

Elouise Pepion Cobell: Banker-Warrior

Laura Ferguson

TELLING A YOUNG Blackfeet woman that she was "not capable" of understanding basic accounting may have been the most ridiculous thing the Bureau of Indian Affairs (BIA) ever did. The woman was Elouise Pepion Cobell, treasurer for the Blackfeet tribe and founder of the first American Indian–owned national bank. She became the lead plaintiff in *Cobell v.*

Salazar, successfully suing the Department of the Interior (DOI) and the BIA on behalf of nearly half a million American Indians for mismanagement of trust funds.

Elouise Pepion Cobell grew up in the 1950s in a home without electricity or indoor plumbing. Across the Blackfeet Reservation, many families lived in similar circumstances despite the existence of income-producing enterprises such as oil and gas extraction and ranching on land belonging to tribal members. Cobell wondered how such profitable development on the Indians' lands could fail to provide them with a significant income.

The problem had a long history. In 1887, Congress passed the General Allotment Act, which mandated that Indian reservations be divided into parcels (allotments) for individual, rather than collective, ownership. Government representatives then deemed that many allottees were "incompetent" to manage their own lands and financial affairs. The DOI held these Indians' lands in trust, often leasing the allotments for grazing or mineral extraction. Revenues from the leases and royalties were supposed to be put into Individual Indian Money accounts (IIMs) managed by the BIA and paid in regular installments to the individual landowners, thus providing them with a steady income.

As Cobell began to investigate the concerns of tribal members who received only paltry incomes—sometimes pennies a month—from the lease of their allotments, it became apparent that the system was broken. Although it leased millions of acres of productive, Indian-owned land, the DOI failed to keep adequate records of how much money was generated through those leases, to document where that money actually went, or to ensure that the landowners were paid. When tribal members made inquiries about their IIM accounts, the BIA and DOI flatly refused to provide documentation. "We were treated like nobodies, even though it was our own money," Cobell told the *Great Falls Tribune*.

After several attempts to meet with the federal government, Cobell finally decided to take the matter to court. Washington, D.C, banking attorney Dennis Gingold agreed to take the difficult case, and in 1996, Cobell and four other plaintiffs filed a class action suit, originally *Cobell v. Babbitt,* on behalf of half a million Indians against the BIA and DOI. The suit demanded a full accounting of all IIM accounts, the creation of a new accounting system for individual and tribal money held by the DOI, and the payment to individual Indians of the money—perhaps as much as $127 billion dollars—that was rightfully theirs.

The Justice Department, representing the BIA and Interior Department, fought back. They hired teams of lawyers from thirty-five of the most prestigious American law firms and spent over $30 million trying to hide their misdeeds. It quickly became apparent that the DOI had not kept accurate or sufficient records. In 1999, U.S. District Court judge Royce Lamberth ruled in Cobell's favor and ordered a full accounting dating back to 1887. The Interior and Treasury departments failed to provide it, instead destroying hundreds of boxes containing tens of thousands of IIM account documents. Lamberth held Interior Secretary Bruce Babbitt—and then his successors, Gale Norton and Dirk Kempthorne—in contempt of court. In retaliation, the DOI had Lamberth removed from the case and froze all IIM accounts, blaming the Cobell lawsuit.

Cobell persisted, knowing she wasn't fighting just for the return of the Indians' money, but also to reform the system and to prevent such abuses from happening again. In all, the case went through nine appeals; in each instance, Cobell's side won. During the process, her team discovered that Interior had funneled IIM funds into other government activities, such as

In 1996, banker Elouise Cobell became the lead plaintiff in a class-action suit demanding back payment and better accounting on Individual Indian Money accounts managed by the BIA. Thirteen years later, the federal government settled for $3.4 billion, the largest settlement in U.S. history. Robin Loznak, photographer, *Great Falls Tribune*, 2005

bailouts during the savings and loan scandal and payments on the national debt. When the MacArthur Foundation granted Cobell a $310,000 "genius award" for exposing government corruption, she donated the money toward lawsuit expenses.

In 2009, thirteen years after Cobell had first filed suit, Secretary of the Interior Ken Salazar agreed to settle the case. A year later, President Barack Obama signed the Claims Resolution Act. The $3.4 billion settlement is the largest in U.S. history but far less than the hundreds of billions of dollars actually owed to Indian landowners. Yet Cobell and her team accepted the settlement, knowing that a full reckoning would only extend the case for years.

Cobell's courage and tenacity galvanized American Indians who suffered without recourse against governmental corruption. To them, "Elouise will always be remembered . . . as a woman who fought the battle many of us didn't know how to fight." *Cobell v. Salazar* set the precedent for tribal trust cases that are still ongoing.

Closer to home, the Blackfeet tribe formally honored Cobell with warrior status in 2002. Cobell passed away in 2011, but her legacy to her people is evidenced in a statement made by a Blackfeet student, who wrote in a letter to Cobell, "I think you did a miraculous thing. Who would've known it would be a Native American woman from the Blackfeet Reservation to do something most people wouldn't dare to do. . . . One day I desire to be like you. . . . I want to become a Native American Rights Activist to stand up for my people."

Afterword

IN A QUEST for strong female role models, early twentieth-century suffragists embraced Sacagawea as a paradigm of fortitude and exemplar of women's contributions to American history. Embellishing her life story, they wrote articles about her contributions to the Lewis and Clark Expedition and erected monuments to her in Portland and Astoria, Oregon; Kansas City, Missouri; Wind River, Wyoming; Mobridge, South Dakota; and on Lemhi Pass and in Three Forks, Montana. In so doing, they catapulted her to mythic status. Sacagawea remains, without a doubt, the most famous woman associated with Montana history.

The trend of celebrating exceptional individual women has continued ever since. When I was growing up, my feminist parents fed me biographies of physicist Marie Curie, suffragist Susan B. Anthony, labor organizer Mother Jones, and civil rights activist Rosa Parks. These are certainly lives worth honoring—as are the lives of such Montana icons as Jeannette Rankin and lesser known but frequently celebrated Montana women such as lawyer Ella Knowles Haskell, rodeo star Fanny Sperry Steele, and Blackfeet banker and activist Elouise Cobell, all of whom are featured in this collection. The problem comes when we turn them into idols.

Longtime Montana legislator and feminist activist Diane Sands, who served on the advisory committee for the Montana Historical Society's Women's History Matters project, the genesis of this book, first articulated this problem in a discussion we had about Jeannette Rankin some fifteen years ago. Focusing on "the greats" like Jeannette Rankin, she said, "is disempowering. Traditional history paints her as the single reason we have woman's suffrage in Montana when it was really a mass movement. Putting her on a pedestal makes people feel as if only a woman like Jeannette can make things happen. People don't see themselves in her. But I say, 'we are all Jeannette Rankin.'"

"We are all Jeannette Rankin" is a hard sell. That's one reason *Beyond Schoolmarms and Madams* includes women we can more easily choose to emulate—the extraordinary ordinary women who joined together to create libraries and support churches; worked to preserve their indigenous languages; nursed their neighbors through epidemics; fed their families during hard times; organized for political change; and embellished their worlds with beadwork, quilts, gardens, and poetry.

This book, however, does more than celebrate women's contributions and provide role models to emulate. Women's equality will never be achieved until women are recognized fully as human beings—selfish and self-sacrificing; self-deceptive and wise—real people, in other words, who mostly did the best they could in the circumstances they found themselves.

We hope that the kaleidoscope of stories included in this volume expands readers' understandings of women's history and women's roles. That they encourage contemplation: about how gender has affected Montanans' experiences and about how ordinary people can influence the lives around them. That they expand an understanding of what was possible for women then, and, therefore, what is possible now. That they break down stereotypes. That they inspire action to improve our common future.

MARTHA KOHL

Bibliography

Abbreviations used include Montana Historical Society Research Center, Helena, Montana (MHS); Merrill G. Burlingame Archives and Special Collections, Montana State University Libraries, Bozeman; *Montana The Magazine of Western History* (*MMWH*); K. Ross Toole Archives and Special Collections, Mike and Maureen Mansfield Library, University of Montana, Missoula (UM). Unless otherwise noted, all papers were published in Montana.

Nineteenth-Century Indigenous Women Warriors
Barry, Neilson J. "Ko-Come-Ne Pe-Ca, The Letter Carrier." *Washington Historical Quarterly* 20, no. 3 (July 1929): 201–3; Beckwourth, James. *The Life and Adventures of James P. Beckwourth.* New York: Harper and Brothers, 1856; Brown, Mark H. *The Plainsmen of the Yellowstone: A History of the Yellowstone Basin.* 1961. Reprint, Lincoln: University of Nebraska Press, 1969; "Confederated Salish and Kootenai Tribes." New World Encyclopedia. www.newworldencyclopedia.org/entry/Confederated_Salish_and_Kootenai_Tribes_of_the_Flathead_Nation; Denig, Edward Thompson. *Five Indian Tribes of the Upper Missouri: Sioux, Arickaras, Assiniboines, Crees, Crows.* Edited by John C. Ewers. Norman: University of Oklahoma Press, 1961; "Gone-To-The-Spirits, A Kootenai Berdache." Native American Netroots. http://nativeamericannetroots.net/diary/316; Koster, John. "The Other Magpie and the Woman Chief Were Crow Warriors of the 'Weaker Sex': Cheyenne and Lakota Women Also Took Up Arms." *Wild West*, June 2013, 24–26; Roscoe, Will. *Changing Ones: Third and Fourth Genders in Native North America.* New York: St. Martin's Press, 1998; Schaeffer, Claude E. "The Kutenai Female Berdache: Courier, Guide, Prophetess, and Warrior." *American Society for Ethnohistory* 12, no. 3 (Summer 1965): 193–236; Sperlin, O. B. "Two Kootenay Women Masquerading as Men? Or Were They One?" *Washington Historical Quarterly* 21, no. 2 (Apr. 1930): 120–30; Women Leaders from the Buffalo Days. Little Big Horn College Library. http://lib.lbhc.edu/index.php?q=node/67.

"Becoming Better Citizens of Our Adopted Country"
Lebanese Family Stories (booklet), 2014. Butte-Silver Bow Public Archives, Butte, Mont.; "Celebrating 100: Daughters of Norway Solheim Lodge #20 Celebrates 100th Anniversary in Butte, Montana." *Norwegian American Weekly*, Apr. 5, 2013; Finnegan, Alice, ed. *Goosetown in Their Own Words, 1900–1945: An Oral History of Anaconda's Ethnic, Working-Class Neighborhood.* Helena, Mont.: Farcountry Press, 2012; Ghenie, Kerrie. "The Butte *Kolo*: Circle of Serbian Sisters." In *Motherlode: Legacies of Women's Lives and Labors in Butte, Montana*, edited by Janet L. Finn and Ellen Crain. Livingston, Mont.: Clark City Press, 2006; Herein, Rakel Oline "Lena." Diary, 1899–1943. SC 2547. MHS; Mallas, Georgia. Interview by Diane Sands, 1987. OH 1014. MHS; Mercier, Laurie. "'We Are Women Irish': Gender, Class, Religious, and Ethnic Identity in Anaconda, Montana." *MMWH* 44, no. 1 (Winter 1994): 28–41; Murphy, Mary. *Mining Cultures:*

Men, Women, and Leisure in Butte, 1914–41. Urbana: University of Illinois Press, 1997; Ostberg, J. H. *Sketches of Old Butte.* Butte, Mont.: 1972; Regan, Ellen. "The Scandinavians of Butte: A Short History." 2002. Butte-Silver Bow Public Archives, Butte, Mont.; Tubbs, Stephanie Ambrose. "Montana Women's Clubs at the Turn of the Century." *MMWH* 38, no. 1 (Winter 1988): 26–35.

The Métis Girlhood of Cecilia LaRance

Grande, Irene Ford. Interview by Melinda Livezey, Oct. 28, 1994. OH 1895. MHS; Wiseman, Alfred. Interview by Melinda Livezey, Feb. 10, 1994. OH 1659. MHS; Wiseman, Cecilia. Interview by Melinda Livezey and Al Wiseman, Feb. 18, 1994. OH 1656. MHS; Wiseman, Cecilia. Interview by Melinda Livezey and Al Wiseman, Mar. 1, 1994. OH 1661. MHS.

Montana's Whiskey Women

Baumler, Ellen. "Birdie Brown." *Montana Moments* blog. Oct. 16, 2013; Baumler, Ellen. "Josephine Doody." *Montana Moments* blog. Mar. 11, 2013; Carter, Sarah, ed. *Montana Women Homesteaders: A Field of One's Own.* Helena, Mont.: Farcountry Press, 2009; *Kalispell Daily Inter Lake*, Apr. 24, 2009; Malone, Michael P. "Montana Politics at the Crossroads, 1932–1933." *Pacific Northwest Quarterly* 69, no. 1 (Jan. 1978): 20–29; *Missoula Missoulian*, July 22, 2012; Moriarity, Bill. "'Gibraltar' against Prohibition," Apr. 18, 2003. Prohibition Vertical File. MHS; Murphy, Mary. "Bootlegging Mothers and Drinking Daughters: Gender and Prohibition in Butte, Montana." *American Quarterly* 46, no. 2 (June 1994): 174–94; Murphy, Mary. *Mining Cultures: Men, Women, and Leisure in Butte, 1914–41.* Urbana: University of Illinois Press, 1997.

Faith Inspired Early Health Care

Baumler, Ellen. "Methodist Deaconesses." *Montana Moments* blog. Mar. 4, 2013; Baumler, Ellen, and Sister Dolores Brinkel. "What Can a Woman Do?: The Sisters of Charity and Their Pioneer Missions." *Montana Woman*, Nov. 2012, 83–85; Sisters of Charity of Leavenworth Vertical File. MHS; Stephens, Myka Kennedy. "Called to Serve: A Brief History of the Methodist Deaconess Movement." *The Flyer*, June 2011. http://theflyer.gcsrw.org/theflyer/page6.aspx.

The Lifelong Quest of Frieda Fligelman and Belle Fligelman Winestine

Brown, Bob. "Suffragists Fought to Win Montana Women's Rights 100 Years Ago." *Helena Independent Record*, Jan. 24, 2014; Butler, Amy. "Belle Winestine (1891–1985)." Jewish Women's Archive. http://jwa/org/encyclopedia/article/winestine-belle; Fligelman, Frieda. Interview by Kathryn Kress, 1976. OH 615. MHS; Fligelman, Frieda, Papers, 1927–1984. MSS 184. UM; Fligelman, Frieda. *Notes for a Novel: The Selected Poems of Frieda Fligelman.* Edited by Rick Newby and Alexandra Swaney. Helena, Mont.: Drumlummon Institute, 2008; Giles, Ken. "Behind the Doors of 'Academe' Is Freedom at Work." *Helena Independent Record*, Jan. 16, 1977, 31; Olds, Virginia. "Jeannette Rankin Recalls Fight for Woman Suffrage in State." *Helena Independent Record*, Aug. 9, 1964, 1, 3; "She Is No Longer 'Transparent.'" *Billings Gazette*, May 1, 1975, 18; Winestine, Belle Fligelman. "Mother Was Shocked." *MMWH* 24, no. 3 (Summer 1974): 70–79; Winestine, Belle Fligelman. Interview by George Cole, 1976. OH 87. MHS; Winestine, Norman and Belle Fligelman. Collection, 1882–1986. MC 190. MHS; "Women Plan MSU Symposium." *Billings Gazette*, Mar. 29, 1973, 28; Wynn, Lee. "Frieda Fligelman: A Garland for Her Crown." *Helena Independent Record*, June 30, 1968, 30; Wynn, Lee. "Looking In on the Arts." *Helena Independent Record*, Apr. 21, 1968, 16.

Rose Gordon

Gordon, Emmanuel Taylor, Papers, 1881–1980. MC 150. MHS; "Ruth Gordon" (obituary). *White Sulphur Springs Meagher County News,* Nov. 21, 28, 1968.

The Women's Protective Union

Ross, Marilyn Maney, and Janet L. Finn. "Sisterhood Is Powerful: The Labors of the Butte Women's Protective Union." In *Motherlode: Legacies of Women's Lives and Labors in Butte, Montana,* edited by Janet L. Finn and Ellen Crain. Livingston, Mont.: Clark City Press, 2006; Weatherly, Laura Ryan, and Margaret Harrington. "Bucket Girl, Yard Girl, the Women Who Worked in Butte." *Catering Industry Employee,* Oct. 1975, 22–23; Webster, Valentine C. Interview by Mary Murphy, Feb. 24, 1980. OH 0098-047. UM; Women's Protective Union, No. 457. (Butte) Montana. Records, 1901–1974. MC 174. MHS.

"You Have to Take What They Send You Now Days"

Cooke, Juanita. Interview by John Terrea, Helena, Mont., Mar. 27, 1991. OH 1252. MHS; Cooke, Juanita. Interview by John Terrea, Helena, Mont., May 8, 1991. OH 1473. MHS; Hopwood, Mary Jo. Interview by Diane Sands, Darby, Mont., Sept. 4, 1987. OH 1035. MHS; Johnson, Peter. "Heart Butte Rancher Was First Native American Female in the U.S. Marines." Montanacana. www.greatfallstribune.com/multimedia/Stories/spottedwolf.html; "Memo to Pocahontas." *San Antonio Express,* Dec. 21, 1943; Meyer, Leisa D. *Creating GI Jane: Sexuality and Power in the Women's Army Corps during World War II.* New York: Columbia University Press, 1996; Miller, Grace Porter. *Call of Duty: A Montana Girl in World War II.* Baton Rouge: Louisiana State University Press, 1999; "Minnie, Pride of the Marines, Is Bronc-Busting Indian Queen." *Charleston Gazette,* Aug. 3, 1943; White, Cody. "Minnie Spotted Wolf and the Marine Corps." *Prologue: Pieces of History* (blog). http://blogs.archives.gov/prologue/?p=12708.

Ella Knowles

Baumler, Ellen. *Montana Moments: History on the Go.* Helena: Montana Historical Society Press, 2010; Montana Historical Society. "Ella Knowles Haskell (1860–1911): The Portia of the People." Montana Historical Society Gallery of Outstanding Montanans online; Roeder, Richard B. "Crossing the Gender Line: Ella L. Knowles, Montana's First Woman Lawyer." *MMWH* 32, no. 3 (Summer 1982): 64–75; Tardiff, Oliver. "Ella Louise Haskell: Pioneer Woman Attorney." Seacoast Women. http://seacoastnh.com/women/haskell.html.

Discrimination

Calavita, Kitty. "Collisions at the Intersection of Gender, Race, and Class: Enforcing the Chinese Exclusion Laws." *Law and Society Review* 40, no. 2 (June 2006): 249–81; Calavita, Kitty. "The Paradoxes of Race, Class, Identity, and 'Passing': Enforcing the Chinese Exclusion Acts, 1882–1910." *Law and Social Inquiry* 25, no. 1 (Winter 2000): 1–40; Cole, Richard P., and Gabriel J. Chin. "Emerging from the Margins of Historical Consciousness: Chinese Immigrants and the History of American Law." *Law and History Review* 17, no. 2 (Summer 1999): 325–64; Everett, George. *The Butte Chinese: A Brief History of Chinese Immigrants in Southwest Montana.* Butte, Mont.: Mai Wah Society, 1995; Holmes, Krys. *Montana: Stories of the Land.* Helena: Montana Historical Society Press, 2008; Lee, Rose Hum. "Occupational Invasion, Succession, and Accommodation of the Chinese of Butte, Montana." *American Journal of Sociology* 55, no. 1 (July 1949): 50–58; Peffer, George Anthony. "Forbidden Families: Emigration Experiences of Chinese

Women under the Page Law, 1875–1882." *Journal of American Ethnic History* 6, no. 1 (Fall 1986): 28–46; Stevens, Todd. "Tender Ties: Husbands' Rights and Racial Exclusion in Chinese Marriage Cases, 1882–1924." *Law and Social Inquiry* 27, no. 2 (Spring 2002): 271–305; Swartout, Robert, Jr. "From Kwangtung to the Big Sky: The Chinese Experience in Frontier Montana." In *Montana Legacy: Essays on History, People, and Place*, edited by Harry W. Fritz, Mary Murphy, and Robert R. Swartout Jr. Helena: Montana Historical Society Press, 2002.

Work Fit for "Two Fisted" Rangers

Fisher, Carla Renee. "You're Not Getting Rid of Me: Cultivating Space for Women in the U.S. Forest Service, 1950–1990." PhD diss., Purdue University, 2010; Lewis, James G. *The Forest Service and the Greatest Good: A Centennial History*. Durham, N.C.: Forest History Society, 2005; Mayell, Hillary. "Women Smokejumpers: Fighting Fires, Stereotypes." *National Geographic News*, Aug. 8, 2003; Maynard, Kim. Interview by Susan Green, Oct. 31, 1984. OH 133-70. UM; "Now the Girls Are on the Fire Line." *New York Times*, July 6, 1971, 38; Rothwell, Tara. "Women Celebrate 20 Years of Smokejumping." *Smokejumper Magazine*, Apr. 2002; Williams, Gerald W. Women in the Forest Service: Early History. www.fs.fed.us/aboutus/history/women.shtml; "Women's History and the Forest Service." www.fs.fed.us/news/2012/releases/03/womens-history.shtml.

Pretty Shield's Success

"Alma Hogan Snell." *Billings Gazette*, May 6, 2008; Linderman, Frank Bird. *Pretty Shield, Medicine Woman of the Crows*. 1932. Reprint, Lincoln: University of Nebraska Press, 2000; Pretty Shield Foundation. http://prettyshieldfoundation.org/; Snell, Alma. *Grandmother's Grandchild: My Crow Indian Life*. Edited by Becky Matthews. Lincoln: University of Nebraska Press, 2000; Snell, Alma Hogan, and Lisa Castle. *A Taste of Heritage: Crow Indian Recipes and Herbal Medicines*. Lincoln: University of Nebraska Press, 2006.

More Than Just a Happy Housewife

Creswell, Mary E. "The Home Demonstration Work." *Annals of the American Academy of Political and Social Science* 67 (Sept. 1916): 241–49; McKinney, Amy. "From Canning to Contraceptives: Cooperative Extension Service Home Demonstration Clubs and Rural Montana Women in the Post–World War II Era." *MMWH* 61, no. 3 (Autumn 2011): 57–70; McKinney, Amy. "'How I Cook, Keep House, Help Farm, Too': Rural Women in Post–World War II Montana." PhD diss., University of Calgary, 2011; Mercier, Laurie K. "Montanans at Work: Businesswomen in Agricultural Communities." *MMWH* 40, no. 3 (Summer 1990): 77–83; Mercier, Laurie K. "Women's Role in Montana Agriculture: 'You Had to Make Every Minute Count.'" *MMWH* 38, no. 4 (Autumn 1988): 50–61.

Nannie Alderson

Alderson, Nannie T., and Helena Huntington Smith. *A Bride Goes West*. New York: Farrar and Rinehart, 1942; Bevis, William. "Nannie Alderson's Frontiers: And Ours," *MMWH* 39, no. 2 (Spring 1989): 29–33; Dusenberry, Verne. "The Northern Cheyenne: All They Have Asked Is to Live in Montana." *MMWH* 5, no. 1 (Winter 1955): 23–40; Malone, Michael P., Richard B. Roeder, and William L. Lang. *Montana: A History of Two Centuries*. Rev. ed. Seattle: University of Washington Press, 1991; Northern Cheyenne Curriculum Committee. *Bringing the Story of the Cheyenne People to the Children of Today: Northern Cheyenne Social Studies Units*. Helena, Mont.: Montana Office of Public Instruction, 2006; Svingen, Orlan J. "Reservation Self-Sufficiency: Stock Raising vs.

Farming on the Northern Cheyenne Indian Reservation, 1900–1914." *MMWH* 5, no. 1 (Winter 1955): 23–40.

Feminism Personified

Cohen, Betsy. "Women's Rights, Peace Activist Judy Smith Remembered for Her Legacy." *Missoula Missoulian,* Nov. 11, 2013; Embree, Alice. "Alice Embree and Phil Prim: Remembering Judy Smith" *Rag Blog.* Jan. 15, 2014. www.theragblog.com/alice-embree-and-phil-primm-remembering-judy-smith/; Judy Smith obituary. *Missoula Missoulian,* Nov. 10, 2013; Kendrick, Terry. Interview by Anya Jabour, Jan. 2, 2014; Sands, Diane. Interview by Anya Jabour, Dec. 12, 2013; Smith, Judy. Interview by Dawn Walsh, Apr. 23, 2001. OH 378-48. UM; Smith, Judy. Interview by Erin Cunniff, Mar. 7, 2002. OH 378-3. UM; Smith, Judy. Interview by Jack Rowan, Apr. 30, 2006. OH 400-3. UM; Smith, Linda. Interview by Erin Cunniff and Darla Torres, Mar. 19, 2002. OH 378-4. UM; "Think BIG & ACT: Missoula Feminists Judy Smith and Honorable Jim Wheelis." *Blue Mountain Clinic History Project*; Interview by Lynsey Bourke, Jan. 28, 2013. www.youtube.com/watch?v=L3aEK4U0_nc; Weddington, Sarah. *A Question of Choice: Roe v. Wade 40th Anniversary Edition.* New York: Feminist Press, 2013.

Julia Ereaux Schultz, Health Advocate and Cultural Champion

Costello, Gladys. "Oldest News Staff Member Observes 90th Birthday." *Malta Phillips County News,* Sept. 9, 1962, 1, 12; "Helena's Women's Club Will Hear Talk by Mrs. Julia Schultz." *Helena Independent Record,* Oct. 11, 1951, 10; "Julia Schulz [*sic*] Had Long and Interesting Life." *Malta Phillips County News,* Sept. 15, 1972; "150 Will Attend Tuberculosis Meetings Today." *Helena Independent Record.* Apr. 19, 1941, 1–2; Schultz, Julia E. "The Gros Ventres Tribe of the Blackfoot Nation." In *Prize Essays on the Traditional Background of the Indians,* compiled by Mrs. Joseph Lindon Smith, 5–14. [Washington, D.C.].: General Federation of Women's Clubs, Department of Public Welfare, 1932; Stallcop, Emmett A. "Julia Schulz Biography." Emmett A. Stallcop, Writings 1993. SC 727. MHS.

Elizabeth Clare Prophet, the Church Universal and Triumphant, and the Creation of Utopia in Montana's Paradise Valley

Church Universal and Triumphant Vertical File. MHS; *Butte Montana Standard,* Nov. 17, 2008, and Nov. 7, 2009; Prophet, Erin. *Prophet's Daughter: My Life with Elizabeth Clare Prophet inside the Church Universal and Triumphant.* Guilford, Conn.: Lyons Press, 2009; Starrs, Paul F., and John B. Wright. "Utopia, Dystopia, and Sublime Apocalypse in Montana's Church Universal and Triumphant." *Geographical Review* 95, no. 1 (Jan. 2005): 97–121; Whistsel, Bradley. *The Church Universal and Triumphant: Elizabeth Clare Prophet's Apocalyptic Movement.* Syracuse, N.Y.: Syracuse University Press, 2003; Wright, John B. "The Church Lady in Paradise." In *Montana Ghost Dance: Essays on Land and Life,* edited by John B Wright, 157–77. Austin: University of Texas Press, 2008.

"Be Creative and Be Resourceful"

Anderson, Faye. Interview by Mary Melcher, Jan. 5, 1982. OH 229. MHS; Connor, Mary Frances Benton, Papers (1921). SC 2575. MHS; Jarussi, Loretta, and Lillian Jarussi. Interview by Laurie Mercier, Sept. 24, 1982. OH 363. MHS; McManus, Blanche. Interview by Rex C. Myers, Sept. 14, 1982. OH 352. MHS; Swift, Amanda O., Writings. SC 821. MHS.

The Watchers

McFarland, Rose Naglich. "Rose's Story." In *Senior Reflections: Montana's Unclaimed Treasure.* Helena, Mont.: Sweetgrass Books, 2002; Nickel, Dawn Dorothy. "Dying in the

West: Health Care Policies and Caregiving Practices in Montana and Alberta, 1880–1950." PhD diss., University of Alberta, 2005. Nickel, Dawn. "Dying in the West," Pts. 1 and 2. *MMWH* 59, no. 3 (Autumn 2009): 25–45; 59, no. 4 (Winter 2009): 3–23.

Cultivating Female Reform

Harvie, Robert A., and Larry V. Bishop. "Police Reform in Montana, 1890–1918." *MMWH* 33, no. 2 (Spring 1983): 46–59; Marilley, Suzanne M. "Frances Willard and the Feminism of Fear." *Feminist Studies* 19, no. 1 (Spring 1993): 123–46; Montana Woman's Christian Temperance Union Records, 1883–1976. MC 160. MHS; Petrik, Paula. *No Step Backward: Women and Family on the Rocky Mountain Mining Frontier, Helena, Montana, 1865–1900.* Helena: Montana Historical Society Press, 1987; Tubbs, Stephenie Ambrose. "Montana Women's Clubs at the Turn of the Century." *MMWH* 36, no. 1 (Winter 1986): 26–35; Tyrrell, Ian. "Temperance, Feminism, and the WCTU: New Interpretations and New Directions." *Australasian Journal of American Studies* 5, no. 2 (Dec. 1986): 27–36.

World-Class Champions

Baumler, Ellen. "The Ladies Busted Broncs." *Distinctly Montana,* Summer 2007; Blake, Tona, and Liz Stiffler. "Fannie Sperry-Steele: Montana's Champion Bronc Rider." *MMWH* 32, no. 2 (Spring 1982): 44–57; Flood, Elizabeth Clair, and William Manns. *Cowgirls: Women of the Wild West.* Santa Fe, N.M.: Zon International Publishing, 2000; Marge and Alice Greenough Vertical File. MHS; National Cowgirl Museum and Hall of Fame. "Marie Gibson." www.cowgirl.net/portfolios/marie-gibson/.

Speaking for Those Who Could Not Speak for Themselves

Billings, Harry. "*The People's Voice*: The Dream and the Reality." *Montana Journalism Review* 20 (1977): 2–4; Billings, Leon. Interview by Don Nicholl, Nov. 29, 2001, Portland, Maine. MOH 321. Bates College, Lewiston, Maine; "Gretchen Billings, Longtime Journalist, Dies." *Helena Independent Record,* Feb. 24, 1999; Malone, Michael P., and Dianne G. Dougherty. "Montana's Political Culture: A Century of Evolution." *MMWH* 31, no. 1 (Winter 1981): 44–58; *100 Montanans: Our Pick of the Most Influential Figures of the 20th Century.* Missoula, Mont.: The Missoulian, 1999; Pettinger, Anne Elizabeth. "Harry and Gretchen Billings and *The People's Voice*." Master's thesis, University of Montana, 2006; Pratt, William C. "The Montana Farmers Union and the Cold War, 1945–1954," *Pacific Northwest Quarterly* 83, no. 2 (Apr. 1992): 63–69; Swibold, Dennis L. *Copper Chorus: Mining, Politics, and the Montana Press, 1889–1959.* Helena: Montana Historical Society Press, 2006.

Behind Every Man

Bottomly O'looney, Jennifer, and Kirby Lambert. *Montana's Charlie Russell: Art in the Collection of the Montana Historical Society.* Helena: Montana Historical Society Press, 2014; Dippie, Brian. "Charles M. Russell: The Artist in His Prime." In *The Artist in His Heyday,* 13–22. Santa Fe, N.M.: Gerald Peters Gallery, 1995; Coates, Grace Stone. Letter to James R. Rankin, Dec. 16, 1936. James Brownlee Rankin Research Collection. MC 162. MHS; Russell, Austin. *C.M.R.: Charles M. Russell, Cowboy Artist, A Biography.* New York: Twayne Publishers, 1957; Russell, Nancy. "Biographical Note." In *Good Medicine: The Illustrated Letters of Charles M. Russell,* by Charles M. Russell, 15–23. Garden City, N.Y.: Doubleday, Doran & Company, 1930; Stauffer, Joan. *Behind Every Man: The Story of Nancy Cooper Russell.* Norman: University of Oklahoma Press, 2011; Taliaferro, John. *Charles M. Russell: The Life and Legend of America's Cowboy Artist.* Norman: University of Oklahoma Press, 2003.

"Lifting as We Climb"

Arnold, Angie Mills, ed. "Montana Federation of Negro Women's Clubs." 1922. Montana Federation of Women's Clubs Records, 1921–1978, MC 281. MHS; Behan, Barbara Carol. "Forgotten Heritage: African Americans in the Montana Territory, 1864–1889." *Journal of African American History* 91, no. 1 (Winter 2006): 23–40; "Equal Rights Act before Senate Committee." *Helena People's Voice*, Feb. 11, 1955; "Intolerance Issue Starts Bitter Debate in House." *Great Falls Leader*, Feb. 11, 1953; Lang, William. "The Nearly Forgotten Blacks on Last Chance Gulch, 1900–1912." *Pacific Northwest Quarterly* 70, no. 2 (Apr. 1979): 50–57; Riley, Glenda. "American Daughters: Black Women in the West." *MMWH* 38, no. 2 (Spring 1988): 14–27; "Senate Hits Faster Pace." *Kalispell Daily Inter Lake*, Mar. 3, 1955, 5; "Unity and Perseverance . . . Our Motto." *Pre-Vue: Billings Weekly Entertainment Guide*, Aug. 1–7, 1971, 4–5.

Empowering Women

Baumler, Ellen. "Helena YWCA Independent: A Brief History." Helena As She Was: An Open History Resource for Montana's Capital City. www.helenahistory.org/ywca.htm; Helena YWCA. www.ywcahelena.org/; Lincoln, Marga. "It Takes a Community." *Helena Independent Record*, Dec. 7, 2008; YWCA Vertical File. MHS; Young Women's Christian Association (Helena, Mont.) Records, 1911–1998. MC 346. MHS.

From Poultry to Poetry

"Bozeman Woman Throws Party after She Died." *Helena Independent Record*, Aug. 19, 1978, 6; Burlingame, Merrill G. *The Montana Cooperative Extension Service, 1893–1974.* Bozeman: Montana State University, 1984; Cushman, Harriette. "4-H Poultry Manual." *Bulletin of the Montana Extension Service in Agriculture and Home Economics* 233 (Sept. 1945); Harriette Cushman Extension Service Records, 1898–1975. Acc. 75040. MSU; Cushman, Harriette Eliza, Papers, 1893–1978. Coll. 1253. MSU; Harriette Eliza Cushman Vertical File. MHS.

Family Planning and Companionate Marriage in Early Twentieth-Century Montana

Bailey, Martha J. "'Momma's Got the Pill': How Anthony Comstock and *Griswold v. Connecticut* Shaped U.S. Childbearing." *American Economic Review* 100, no. 1 (Mar. 2010): 98–129; Dykeman, Wilma. *Too Many People, Too Little Love; Edna Rankin McKinnon: Pioneer for Birth Control.* New York: Holt, Rinehart and Winston, 1974; Evans, Sara M. "Flappers, Freudians, and All That Jazz." In *Born for Liberty: A History of Women in America,* 175–96. New York: Free Press, 1989; Hill, Jennifer J. "Midwives in Montana: Historically Informed Political Activism." PhD diss., Montana State University, 2013; Melcher, Mary. "'Women's Matters': Birth Control, Prenatal Care, and Childbirth in Rural Montana, 1910–1940." *MMWH* 41, no. 2 (Spring 1991): 47–56; Murphy, Mary. *Mining Cultures: Men, Women, and Leisure in Butte, 1914–41.* Urbana: University of Illinois Press, 1997; Sanger, Margaret. *Happiness in Marriage.* New York: Brentanos, [1926]; "Some Legislative Aspects of the Birth-Control Problem." *Harvard Law Review* 45, no. 4 (Feb. 1932): 723–29; Tubbs, Stephenie Ambrose. "Montana Women's Clubs at the Turn of the Century." *MMWH* 36, no. 1 (Winter 1986): 26–35.

The Life and Legend of Mary Fields

Behan, Barbara Carol. "Forgotten Heritage: African Americans in the Montana Territory, 1864–1889." *Journal of African American History* 91, no. 1 (Winter 2006): 23–40; Cooper, Gary, as told to Marc Crawford. "Stagecoach Mary: A Gun-Toting Black

Woman Delivered the U.S. Mail in Montana." *Ebony*, Oct. 1959. Reprinted in *Ebony*, Oct. 1977; Garceau-Hagen, Dee. "Finding Mary Fields: Race, Gender, and the Construction of Memory." In *Portraits of Women in the American West,* edited by Dee Garceau-Hagen, 185–242. New York: Routledge, 2005; Graham, Art. Review of James A. Franks, *Mary Fields: The Story of Black Mary. MMWH* 53, no. 1 (Spring 2003): 74–75; Harris, Mark. "The Legend of Black Mary." *Negro Digest*, Aug. 1950, 84–87; Lang, William. "The Nearly Forgotten Blacks on Last Chance Gulch, 1900–1912." *Pacific Northwest Quarterly* 70, no. 2 (Apr. 1979): 50–57; *Life of the Rev. Mother Amadeus of the Heart of Jesus.* New York: Paulist Press, 1923; Mary Fields Vertical File. MHS; Nash, Sunny. "Mother Amadeus and Stagecoach Mary." *True West,* Mar. 1996; "Old Timer Passes Away," *Cascade Courier,* Dec. 14, 1914; Shirley, Gayle C. "Mary Fields: The White Crow." In *More than Petticoats: Remarkable Montana Women,* 1–5. Guilford, Conn.: Globe Pequot, 2011; Sister Genevieve. "Mary Fields." In *Mountains and Meadows: A Pioneer History of Cascade, Chestnut Valley, Hardy, St. Peter's Mission, and Castner Falls, 1805 to 1925,* compiled by Mrs. Clarence J. Rowe. N.p . [1970].

The Long Campaign

Alderson, Mary Long, Papers, 1894–1936. SC 122. MHS; Cole, Judith K. "A Wide Field for Usefulness: Women's Civil Status and the Evolution of Women's Suffrage on the Montana Frontier, 1864–1914." *American Journal of Legal History* 34, no. 3 (July 1990): 262–92; *Harlem Enterprise,* Nov. 19, 1914; Larson, T. A. "Montana Women and the Battle for the Ballot." *MMWH* 23, no. 1 (Winter 1973): 24–41; Petrik, Paula. *No Step Backward: Women and Family on the Rocky Mining Frontier, Helena, Montana, 1865–1900.* Helena: Montana Historical Society Press, 1987; Schaffer, Ronald. "The Montana Woman Suffrage Campaign: 1911–14." *Pacific Northwest Quarterly* 55, no. 1 (Jan. 1964): 9–15; Smith, Norma. *Jeannette Rankin, America's Conscience.* Helena: Montana Historical Society Press, 2002; *Helena and Butte Suffrage Daily News,* Sept. 24–26, Nov. 2, 1914; Ward, Doris Buck. "The Winning of Woman Suffrage in Montana." Master's thesis, Montana State University, 1974; Wheeler, Leslie A. "Woman Suffrage's Gray-Bearded Champion Comes to Montana, 1889." *MMWH* 31, no. 3 (Summer 1981): 2–13; Winestine, Belle Fligelman. "Mother Was Shocked." *MMWH* 24, no. 3 (Summer 1974): 70–79.

After Suffrage

Chase, Candace. "Emma Ingalls: Trailblazing Journalist, Legislator." *Kalispell Daily Inter Lake,* Apr. 12, 2009; "Maggie Smith Hathaway." 125 Montana Newsmakers. www.greatfallstribune.com/multimedia/125newsmakers2/hathaway.html; "Women Wielding Power: Pioneer Female State Legislators." National Women's History Museum. www.nwhm.org/online-exhibits/legislators/Montana.html; "Akers, Dolly Smith Cusker." Northwest Digital Archives online finding aid.

Freda Augusta Beazley and the Rise of American Indian Political Power

"Affiliated Tribes Take Stand against Bill." *Kalispell Daily Inter Lake,* Jan. 26, 1967, 11; "Anti-Poverty Plan Aimed at Indians." *Billings Gazette,* Jan. 22, 1966, 6; Arsenian, Victoriah. "Remembering the Affiliated Tribes of Northwest Indians." Affiliated Tribes of Northwest Indians. www.atniedc.com/atni-edc%20history.htm; Beazley, Freda Augusta, Papers, 1960–1975. MC 187. MHS; Bohn, Dorothy. "Liberating the Indian: Euphemism for a Land Grab." *Nation,* Feb. 20, 1954, 150–51; Clarkin, Thomas. *Federal Indian Policy in the Kennedy and Johnson Administrations, 1961–1969.* Albuquerque: University of New Mexico Press, 2001; "Freda Beasley Named to High Tribal Post." *Helena Independent Record,* Oct. 3, 1965, 25; "Metcalf, Murray Criticize Treatment of Indians by GOP

Administration." *Great Falls Tribune,* Dec. 4, 1958; "Mission and History." National Congress of American Indians. www.ncai.org/about-ncai/mission-history; "Office of Economic Opportunity." *Wikipedia* online encyclopedia; Scott, Patricia. "Senate Action on Knowles under Attack." *Kalispell Daily Inter Lake,* July 13, 1963, 1, 2.

Champions
McNeel, Jack. "Before Schimmel: The Indian Women Who Became Basketball Champions." Indian Country Today Media Network. http://indiancountrytodaymedianetwork.com; Peavy, Linda, and Ursula Smith. *Full-Court Quest: The Girls from Fort Shaw Indian School, Basketball Champions of the World.* Norman: University of Oklahoma Press, 2008; Peavy, Linda, and Ursula Smith. "Unlikely Champion: Emma Rose Sansaver, 1884–1925." In *Portraits of Women in the American West,* edited by Dee Garceau-Hagen, 179–208. New York: Routledge, 2005; Peavy, Linda, and Ursula Smith. "World Champions: The 1904 Girls' Basketball Team from Fort Shaw Indian Boarding School." *MMWH* 51, no. 4 (Winter 2001): 2–25; *Playing for the World* (DVD). Montana PBS. 2009.

Early Social Service Was Women's Work
Baumler, Ellen. "Into the Heartlife of Children." www.intermountain.org/cen/index.php; Baumler, Ellen. "The Making of a Good Woman: Montana and the National Florence Crittenton Mission." *MMWH* 53, no. 4 (Winter 2003): 50–63; Baumler, Ellen. "Montana Deaconess School to Intermountain." *MMWH* 59, no. 1 (Spring 2009): 23–41; Baumler, Ellen. "Methodist Deaconesses." *Montana Moments* blog. Mar. 4, 2013; Baumler, Ellen and Sister Dolores Brinkel. 'What Can a Woman Do?' The Sisters of Charity of Leavenworth and Their Pioneer Montana Missions." *Montana Woman,* Nov. 2012; Billings Catholic Schools. www.billingscatholicschools.org/about-us/history/; Intermountain Healthcare. www.intermountain.org/about-us/history/; "Montana." *New Advent Catholic Encyclopedia.* www.newadvent.org/cathen/10516b.htm; Shodair Children's Hospital. www.shodair.org/.

Saving Girls
Baumler, Ellen. "Mountain View School for Girls." *Montana Moments* blog. May 20, 2013; Holmes, J. D. "Girls' Vocational School Now in Its 40th Year." *Helena Independent Record,* Sept. 29, 1960; Office of the Legislative Auditor. "Juvenile Justice in Montana: Department of Family Services, Montana Youth Courts, Montana Board of Crime Control." Performance audit, 1993. https://archive.org/details/juvenilejusticei1993mont; Kidston, Martin. "Scrawlings in Solitary." *Helena Independent Record,* Sept. 19, 2004; Montana State School for Girls Vertical File. MHS; Westenberg, John. "State Vocational School for Girls." National Register of Historic Places Nomination, 1980. On file at State Historic Preservation Office, Helena, Mont.

"She Really Believed in Families"
Dunbar, Anna. Interview by Diane Sands, June 16, 1981. OH 164–01. UM; Gudmunson, Pat. "Counts Babies, Not Birthdays." *Billings Gazette,* Apr. 19, 1964, 6; Hill, Jennifer J. "Midwives in Montana: Historically Informed Political Activism." PhD diss., Montana State University, 2013; Jones, Helen Carey, comp. *Custer County Area History, As We Recall: A Centennial History of Custer County, Montana, 1889–1989.* Dallas: Curtis Media Corporation, 1990; LaBoe, Barbara. "A Mother's Day Story: Roadmap to Her Roots." *Butte Montana Standard,* May 10, 2003; Melcher, Mary. "'Women's Matters': Birth Control, Prenatal Care, and Childbirth in Rural Montana, 1910–1940." *MMWH* 41, no. 2 (Spring 1991): 47–56; "Sadie Lindeberg, Pioneer Doctor, Dies at Age 84." *Billings Gazette,* Feb. 9,

1969, 8; Sands, Diane. "Using OH to Chart the Course of Illegal Abortions in Montana." *Frontiers: A Journal of Women Studies* 7, no. 1 (1983): 32–37; Savitt, Todd, "Abortion in the Old West: The Trials of Dr. Edwin S. Kellogg of Helena, Montana." *MMWH* 57, no. 3 (Summer 2007): 3–20; Stout, Tom, ed. *Montana, Its Story and Biography: A History of Aboriginal and Territorial Montana and Three Decades of Statehood.* Vol. 3. Chicago: American Historical Society, 1921; Winter, Malcolm D., Jr., Malcolm D. Winter Sr., and Friends. *Miles City Medical History, 1876–2005.* Miles City, Mont.: Judson H. Flower Jr. Library, 2007.

Childbirth and Maternal Health in Early Twentieth-Century Montana

Apple, Rima D. *Perfecting Motherhood: Science and Childrearing in America.* New Brunswick, N.J.: Rutgers University Press, 2006; Baumler, Ellen. "'The Making of a Good Woman': Montana and the National Florence Crittenton Mission." *MMWH* 53, no. 4 (Winter 2003): 50–63; Hill, Jennifer J. "Midwives in Montana: Historically Informed Political Activism." PhD diss., Montana State University, 2013; Ladd-Taylor, Molly. *Mother-Work: Women, Child Welfare, and the State, 1890–1930.* Champaign: University of Illinois Press, 1995; Melcher, Mary. "'Women's Matters': Birth Control, Prenatal Care, and Childbirth in Rural Montana, 1910–1940." *MMWH* 41, no. 2 (Spring 1991): 47–56; Nickel, Dawn. "Dying in the West, Part I: Hospitals, Health Care in Montana and Alberta, 1880–1950." *MMWH*, 59 no. 3 (Autumn 2009): 25–45; Paradise, Viola. *Maternity Care and the Welfare of Young Children in a Homesteading County in Montana.* U.S. Children's Bureau Publication no. 34. Washington, D.C.: U.S. Government Printing Press, 1919; Radosh, Polly. "Midwives in the United States: Past and Present." *Population Research and Policy Review* 5, no. 2 (1986): 129–46.

Mary Ann Pierre Topsseh Coombs and the Bitterroot Salish

Adams, Louis. "Salish Removal from the Bitterroot Valley." Transcript of video. Lewis and Clark Trail—Tribal Legacy Project. http://lc-triballegacy.org/ftp/transcripts/LAdSa4D-bitterroot.txt.; "Ancestors Remembered during Bitterroot Valley Treks." *Pablo Char-Koosta News,* Sept. 22, 2000, 1; Azure, B. L. "Bitterroot Culture Camp to Expose Non-Indian Youth to the History and Culture of the Bitterroot Salish." *Pablo Char-Koosta News,* June 9, 2011, 12; Confederated Salish and Kootenai Tribes. *Fire on the Land* (DVD). Lincoln: University of Nebraska Press. 2006; Hill, Lonny. "Treaty History." *Pablo Char-Koosta News,* July 30, 1999, 7; Matt, Don. "Mary Ann Topsseh Coombs." *Pablo Char-Koosta* News, Nov. 15, 1975, 7–8; "New Interpretive Signs Touch on Salish History." *Pablo Char-Koosta News,* Sept. 3, 1993, 4; Montana Fish, Wildlife and Parks. Council Grove: Site of the Hellgate Treaty of 1855. www.opi.mt.gov/pdf/indianed/resources/fwp/CouncilGrove.pdf; "Fire and the Forced Removal of the Salish People from the Bitterroot Valley." Native Peoples and Fire. www.cskt.org/fire_history.swf; Salish-Pend d'Oreille Culture Committee. *The Salish People and the Lewis and Clark Expedition.* Lincoln: University of Nebraska Press; Salish Kootenai College. *Challenge to Survive: History of the Salish Tribes of the Flathead Indian Reservation.* Helena, Mont.: Montana State Library, 2008; Sessions, Patti. "Tribal Monument Dedicated Monday." *Pablo Char-Koosta News,* Oct. 18, 1991, 1; Confederated Salish and Kootenai Tribes. "Treaty of Hellgate, July 16, 1855." www.cskt.org/documents/gov/hellgatetreaty.pdf.

A "Witty, Gritty Little Bobcat of a Woman"

"An Editorial Forethought." *MMWH* 24, no. 3 (Summer 1974): 80; "Dorothy Johnson." *125 Montana Newsmakers.* www.greatfallstribune.com/multimedia/125newsmakers3/johnson.html; "Dorothy Johnson, Author of 'Liberty Valance,' Is Dead." *New York*

Times, Nov. 13, 1984; Hart, Sue. "Dorothy M. Johnson: A Woman's Voice on the Western Frontier." *English Journal* 74, no. 3 (Mar. 1985): 60–61; Hintze, Lynnette. "Influential Whitefish Author Dorothy Johnson Inducted into Gallery of Outstanding Montanans." *Kalispell Daily Inter Lake,* Mar. 13, 2005; Johnson, Dorothy M. "Carefree Youth and Dudes in Glacier." *MMWH* 25, no. 3 (Winter 1975): 48–59; Johnson, Dorothy M. "The Foreigners." *MMWH* 26, no. 3 (Winter 1976): 62–67; Johnson, Dorothy M. Letter to the Editor. *MMWH* 23, no. 3 (Summer 1973): 61; Johnson, Dorothy M. "The Safe and Easy Way to Adventure." *MMWH* 24, no. 3 (Summer 1974): 80–87; Johnson, Dorothy M. "A Short Moral Essay for Boys and Girls: Or How to Get Rich in a Frontier Town." *MMWH* 24, no. 1 (Winter 1974): 26–35; Mathews, Sue, and James W. Healey. "Winning of the Western Fiction Market: An Interview with Dorothy M. Johnson." *Prairie Schooner* 52, no. 2 (Summer 1978): 158–67; Library of Congress. "National Film Registry 2007." *Information Bulletin* (online) 67, nos. 1–2, Jan.-Feb. 2008. www.loc.gov/loc/lcib/08012/registry.html.

Progressive Reform and Women's Advocacy for Public Libraries in Montana

Barger, J. Wheeler. "The County Library in Montana." Bulletin no. 219, University of Montana Agricultural Experiment Station, Bozeman, Montana, Jan. 1929. Public Libraries Vertical File. MHS; Hamilton Woman's Club Records, 1913–1989. MC 212. MHS; Martin, Marilyn. "From Altruism to Activism: The Contributions of Literary Clubs to Arkansas Public Libraries." *Arkansas Historical Quarterly* 55, no. 1 (Spring 1996): 64–94; Richards, Susan. "Carnegie Library Architecture for South Dakota and Montana: A Comparative Study." *Journal of the West* 30 (July 1991): 69–78; Ring, Daniel. "Carnegie Libraries as Symbols for an Age: Montana as a Test Case." *Libraries and Culture* 27, no. 1 (Winter 1992): 1–19; Scott, Anne Firor. "On Seeing and Not Seeing: A Case of Historical Invisibility." *Journal of American History* 71, no. 1 (June 1984): 7–21; Scott, Anne Firor. "Women and Libraries." *Journal of Library History* 21, no. 2 (Spring 1986): 400–405; Smith, Clare M. "Miles City Carnegie Library." *Montana Woman,* Apr. 1968, 9.

Queens of the Clouds

Billings Gazette, Mar. 10, 1928; *Butte Montana Standard,* Nov. 24, 1928; "Esther Vance." *125 Montana Newsmakers.* www.greatfallstribune.com/multimedia/125newsmakers1/vance.html; "Frequently Asked Questions." International Society of Women Airline Pilots. www.iswap.org/content.aspx?page_id=275&club_id=658242&item_id=1506&ad=yes; *Great Falls Leader,* June 6, 1928; *Helena Independent Record,* Mar. 12, 1928; *Missoula Daily Missoulian,* Sept. 21, 1913; Oakes, Claudia M. "United States Women in Aviation: 1930–1939." Washington, D.C.: Smithsonian Institution Press, 1985. www.sil.si.edu/smithsoniancontributions/AirSpace/pdf_lo/SSAS-0006.pdf; Pawlowski, A. "Why Aren't More Women Airline Pilots?" *CNN Travel.* Mar. 18, 2011. www.cnn.com/2011/TRAVEL/03/18/female.airline.pilots/; Vance, Esther Combes, Papers, 1904–1977. MC 153. MHS; Wiley, Frank W. *Montana and the Sky: The Beginning of Aviation in the Land of Shining Mountains.* Helena, Mont.: Montana Aeronautics Commission, 1966.

"Men Were My Friends, but Women Were My Cause"

"Attorney Remembered for Wit and Devotion to Causes." *Billings Gazette,* Sept. 29, 1991; "Banquet to Honor Former Official." *Helena Independent Record,* Jan. 26, 1992; Barz, Diane G. "Francis [*sic*] C. Elge: 'A Chic and Wise Magistrate.'" *Montana Lawyer,* Dec. 1991, 10; Clawson, Roger. "For Fifty Years She's Fought for Women." *Billings Gazette,* Nov. 3, 1980; "Elder Lawyer Lore." *Montana Lawyer,* Jan. 1983, 3; "Elge, Frances C. (Miss)" and "Interview: Fran Elge–Ms. Montana." Frances C. Elge Papers, 1921–1991. UPMC

77. MHS; Frances C. Elge Vertical File. MHS; "Frances C. Elge, 1906–1991," *Montana Law Review* 53, no. 1 (1992); "'His Honor' Is a Woman." *Billings Gazette,* July 23, 1974, 17; "House Kills Montana ERA Nullification." *Helena Independent Record,* Mar. 11, 1979, 12; McCammon, Holly J. "Explaining Frame Variation: More Moderate and Radical Demands for Women's Citizenship in the U.S. Women's Jury Movements." *Social Problems* 59, no. 1 (Feb. 2012): 43–69; "Miss Elge Woman of the Year." *Billings Gazette,* June 6, 1971.

Oshanee Cullooyah Kenmille

Devlin, Vince. "Elder Takes Her Final Journey: Agnes Oshanee Kenmille." *Missoula Missoulian,* Feb. 13, 2009; National Endowment for the Arts. "Agnes Oshanee Kenmille." NEA National Heritage Fellowships, 2003, online; Plummer, Maggie. *Passing It On: Voices from the Flathead Indian Reservation.* Pablo, Mont.: Salish Kootenai College Press, 2008; Salish Kootenai College. *Honoring Native Women's Voices: A Collection of Stories.* Pablo, Mont.: Salish Kootenai College Press, 2006; "Tribes Honor the Passing of Oshanee." *Pablo Char-Kootsa News,* Feb. 19, 2009.

Sister Providencia

Billings, Gretchen. "American Indian Being Pushed Further into Never-Never Land." *Helena People's Voice,* Aug. 17, 1956; Bishop, Joan. "From Hill 57 to Capitol Hill: 'Making the Sparks Fly,' Sister Providencia Tolan's Drive on Behalf of Montana's Off-Reservation Indians, 1950–1970." *MMWH* 43, no. 3 (Summer 1993): 16–29; Community Council of Cascade County Vertical File. MHS; Deligdish, Andrea. *Our Indian Neighbors: A Report to the Great Falls Citizens' Committee on Indian Affairs.* Great Falls, Mont.: College of Great Falls, 1964; Lamere, Eunice, and Gertrude Lindgren. "Hill 57 Goes to Washington." Indian Project Report to Great Falls Business and Professional Women, 1957. Community Council of Cascade County Records, 1948–1968. SC 1989. MHS; "Landless Indian Hearing Reveals Need for Action by Congress." *Great Falls Tribune,* Sept. 10, 1955; Landless Indians of Montana Vertical File. MHS; "Lions Members Informed . . . Hill 57 Exemplifies Stage of Indian Pride Dying Out." *Great Falls Tribune,* Dec. 1956; "Montana Legislative Memorials Stress Indian Neglect." *Great Falls Tribune,* Mar. 8, 1957; Sister Providencia (Tolan) Vertical File. MHS; Tolan, Sister Providencia. "Indian Bureau at Fault. Hardships on Reservations Are 'Cause and Consequence.'" Letter to Frank Murray, Montana Secretary of State. Reprinted in *Helena People's Voice,* Apr. 11, 1958.

Number, Please

Arguimbau, Ellen. "From Party Lines and Barbed Wire: A History of Telephones in Montana." *MMWH* 63, no. 3 (Autumn 2013): 34–45.

"You Had to Pretend It Never Happened"

Dunbar, Anna. Interview by Diane Sands. OH 164-001. UM; Melcher, Mary. "'Women's Matters': Birth Control, Prenatal Care, and Childbirth in Rural Montana, 1910–1940." *MMWH* 41, no. 2 (Spring 1991): 47–56; Sands, Diane. "Using OH to Chart the Course of Illegal Abortions in Montana." *Frontiers: A Journal of Women Studies* 7, no. 1 (1983): 32–37; Savitt, Todd. "Abortion in the Old West: The Trials of Dr. Edwin S. Kellogg of Helena, Montana." *MMWH* 57, no. 3 (Autumn 2007): 3–20.

Expanding Their Sphere

Bradley, Frances Sage. *Biennial Report of the Child Welfare Division, Montana State Board of Health, for 1923–1924.* Helena, Mont.: State Board of Health, 1924; "Child Health

Council Formed Here Yesterday." *Helena Independent,* Feb. 19, 1929, 10; "Community Schedule for State Health Nurse." *Kalispell Daily Inter Lake,* Dec. 15, 1924, 1; Gannon, John. *First Annual Report of the Superintendent of Public Instruction of the State of Montana, for the Year Ending Aug. 31, 1890.* Helena, Mont.: Journal Publishing, 1891; Helton, Dorothy. "Henrietta Crockett Wing Will Be Dedicated at Ceremony Wednesday Morning." *Helena Independent Record,* Aug. 14, 1952, 24; Kenyon, Virginia. Interview by Therese Sullivan, Nov. 5, 1984. OH 1834. UM; McKinnon, L. C. "Dedicate Henrietta Crockett Indian Wing." *Milwaukee Road Magazine,* Dec. 1952, 15; Montana Legislative Services Division et al. *Celebrating Women Elected to Serve the State of Montana.* Helena, Mont.: Capitol Complex Advisory Council, 2009; Montana Nurses' Association Records, 1912–1987. MC 170. MHS; Paradise, Viola. *Maternity Care and the Welfare of Young Children in a Homesteading County in Montana.* Rural and Child Welfare Services no. 3, U.S. Department of Labor. Washington, D.C.: Government Printing Office, 1919; "Public Health Nurse Holds School Clinics." *Havre News Promoter,* Oct. 7, 1926, 3.

Laura Howey, the Montana Historical Society, and Sex Discrimination in Early Twentieth-Century Montana

"Death Claims Popular Woman." *Helena Independent,* Sept. 22, 1911, 9; Ferguson, Mary C. "Laura Howey." In *Contributions to the Historical Society of Montana with Its Transactions, Officers, and Members,* Vol. 6, 24A–28A. Helena, Mont.: Independent Publishing Company, 1907; Laura Howey Vertical File. MHS; *Joliet (Ill.) Journal,* Apr. 12, 1907; "Mrs. Laura Howey Dies." *Anaconda Standard,* Sept. 22, 1911, 1; Petrik, Paula. "Strange Bedfellows: Prostitution, Politicians, and Moral Reform in Helena, 1885–1887." *MMWH* 35, no. 3 (Summer 1985): 2–13; *Sheridan (Wyo.) Enterprise,* Apr. 5, 1907; Shovers, Brian. "Saving Montana's Past: The Creation and Evolution of the Montana Historical Society and *Montana The Magazine of Western History.*" *MMWH,* 52, no. 1 (Spring 2002): 48–59.

Susie Walking Bear Yellowtail

"Big Heart." American Society of Registered Nurses. www.asrn.org/journal-chronicle-nursing/205-big-heart.html. Jackson, Connie Yellowtail. "Susie Walking Bear Yellowtail." Dave Walter, "Susie Yellowtail (1903–1981)." and Joe Medicine Crow. "Susie Yellowtail, 1903–1981." All in Yellowtail, Susie, Vertical File. MHS; Scozzari, Trish Erbe. "The Journey of America's First Native Nurse." *Yellowstone Valley Woman,* 2009.

Minnie Two Shoes

Hendricks, Steve. *The Unquiet Grave: The FBI and the Struggle for the Soul of Indian Country.* New York: Thunder's Mouth Press, 2006; Locke, Deborah. "Remembering Minnie." *Minneapolis (Minn.) Twin Cities Daily Planet,* May 2, 2010; McKosato, Harlan, with Paul DeMain and Minnie Two Shoes. Interviews with Robert Pictrou-Branscombe, Russell Means, Vernon Belcourt, and Richard Little Elk. Transcript of "Native American Calling" broadcast, Nov. 3, 4, 1999, and "Denver Press Conference." www.indiancountrynews.info/nativecalling1.cfm.htm, www.indiancountrynews.info/denverpress.cfm.htm; "Minnie Two Shoes, NAJA Founding Member, Dies at 60." Apr. 10, 2010. Maynard Institute. http://mije.org/richardprince/david-mills-service-set-monday-md#Two%20Shoes; "Minnie Two Shoes." *Wikipedia* online encyclopedia; "Native American Journalists Association Celebrates 25 Years." *Dawn of Nations Today* 4, no. 1 (May 2009); *Rezinate* (blog). Nov. 14, 2013. http://rezinate.wordpress.com/tag/minnie-two-shoes/; Oh Gee Pro, comp. "Gun in Her Mouth." Posted on YouTube by LakotaLance, Feb. 12, 2011. www.youtube.com/watch?v=0pm1Ic9A4aU; "Remembering Minnie Two Shoes–Assiniboine Sioux." News from Indian Country.

http://indiancountrynews.net/index.php/walking-on-sections-menu-57/8858-remembering-minnie-two-shoes-assiniboine-sioux; "Remembering Minnie Two Shoes (3/24/1950–4/9/2010)." Posted on YouTube by Skabewis, Apr. 9, 2010. www.youtube.com/watch?v=FWtKMQb7a-Q; *Poplar Wotanin Wowapi.* Feb. 12, 1992, and Mar. 16, 1995; Snell, Lisa. "Minnie Two Shoes: Mar. 24, 1950–Apr. 9, 2010." *Native American Times,* Apr. 11, 2010; Washines, Ronnie. "Remarks about Minnie Two Shoes." *Native American Times,* Apr. 14, 2010.

A Department of One's Own
Sands, Diane. Interview by Erin Cunniff and G. G. Weix, Dec. 15, 2000. OH 378-02. UM; University of Montana Department of Women's Studies Records. RG 087. UM; "About." University of Montana Women's, Gender, and Sexuality Studies. www.cas.uMont.edu/wsprog/about/default.php; Wheeler, Carolyn. Interview by Diane Sands, Mar. 10, 2001. OH 378-30. UM; "Women's Studies Explores Issues Ignored by Academics, History." *Missoula Montana Kaimin,* Jan. 29, 1992; "Women's Studies Makes Its Mark." *Missoula Montana Kaimin,* Mar. 14, 1996.

Legalized Midwifery
Browder, Dolly. Interview with Darla Torres, Missoula, Mont., Mar. 4, 2002. OH 378-1. UM; Hill, Jennifer J. "Midwives in Montana: Historically Informed Political Activism." PhD diss., Montana State University, 2013; Jamison, Mona. Interview by Jennifer Hill, Helena, Mont., Oct. 29, 2012; U.S. Department of Health and Human Services. "Births: Final Data for 2009." *National Vital Statistics Reports* 60, no. 1 (Nov. 3, 2011).

Work Done by Muscle Power or Grit
Dahl, Anna Boe, Scrapbook, 1940–1986. SC 909. MHS; Carmody, John M. "Rural Electrification of the United States." *Annals of the American Academy of Political and Social Science* 201 (Jan. 1939): 82–88; Holmes, Krys. *Montana: Stories of the Land.* Helena: Montana Historical Society Press, 2008; Kline, Ronald. "Ideology and Social Surveys: Reinterpreting the Effects of 'Laborsaving' Technology on American Farm Women." *Technology and Culture* 38, no. 2 (Apr. 1997): 355–85; Long, David. "'We're Not Isolated Now!' Anna Boe Dahl and the REA." *MMWH* 39, no. 2 (Spring 1989): 18–23; Mercier, Laurie. "Women's Role in Montana Agriculture: 'You Had to Make Every Minute Count,'" *MMWH* 38, no. 4 (Autumn 1988): 50–61.

"Women . . . on the Level with Their White Sisters"
Lee, Rose Hum. *The Growth and Decline of Chinese Communities in the Rocky Mountain Region.* New York: Arno Press, 1978; Lee, Rose Hum. "Occupational Invasion, Succession, and Accommodation of the Chinese of Butte, Montana." *American Journal of Sociology* 55, no. 1 (July 1949): 50–58; Merriam, H. G. "Ethnic Settlement of Montana." *Pacific Historical Review* 12, no. 2 (June 1943): 157–68; O'Malley, M. G. "Echoes from the Distant Past." *Butte Montana Standard,* Feb. 15, 1942; Wunder, John R. "The Chinese and the Courts in the Pacific Northwest: Justice Denied?" *Pacific Historical Review* 53, no. 2 (May 1983): 191–211; Yu, Henry. "Rose Hum Lee." In *Thinking Orientals: A History of Knowledge Created about and by Asian Americans.* New York: Oxford University Press, 2000.

A Farm of Her Own
"Bangs Farm, Centennial Farm and Ranch Program." *Montana Historical Society Montana History Wiki* online; Baumler, Ellen. *Beyond Spirit Tailings: Montana's Mysteries, Ghosts and Haunted Places.* Helena: Montana Historical Society Press, 2005;

Carter, Sarah. *Montana Women Homesteaders: A Field of One's Own.* Helena, Mont.: Farcountry Press, 2009; Cederburg, Leon, and Nellie Cederburg. "Anna Scherlie Homestead Shack." National Register of Historic Places Nomination. On file at Montana State Historic Preservation Office, Helena, Mont.

Womanhood on Trial

Basso, Matthew L. *Meet Joe Copper: Masculinity and Race on Montana's World War II Home Front.* Chicago: University of Chicago Press, 2013; Del Mar, David Peterson. *What Trouble I Have Seen: A History of Violence against Wives.* Cambridge, Mass.: Harvard University Press, 1996; Finn, Janet L. *Mining Childhood: Growing up in Butte, Montana, 1900–1960.* Helena: Montana Historical Society Press, 2012; Finn, Janet L., and Ellen Crain, eds. *Motherlode: Legacies of Women's Lives and Labors in Butte, Montana.* Livingston, Mont.: Clark City Press, 2006; Gordon, Linda. *Heroes of Their Own Lives: The Politics and History of Family Violence, Boston, 1880–1960.* New York: Viking, 1988; Hartog, Hendrik. *Man and Wife in America: A History.* Cambridge, Mass.: Harvard University Press, 2000; May, Elaine Tyler. *Homeward Bound: American Families in the Cold War Era.* Rev. ed. New York: Basic Books, 2008; Murphy, Mary. *Mining Cultures: Men, Women, and Leisure in Butte, 1914–41.* Urbana: University of Illinois Press, 1997; Pleck, Elizabeth. *Domestic Tyranny: The Making of American Social Policy against Family Violence from Colonial Times to the Present.* New York: Oxford University Press, 1987; Tuttle, William M. *Daddy's Gone to War: The Second World War in the Lives of America's Children.* New York: Oxford University Press, 1993.

Alma Smith Jacobs

"Alma S. Jacobs (1916–1997)." *Online Encyclopedia: African American History in the West.* http://www.blackpast.org; Hanshew, Annie. "Emma Riley Smith." In *Border to Border: Historic Quilts and Quiltmakers of Montana,* edited by Annie Hanshew and Mary Murphy, 116–17. Helena: Montana Historical Society Press, 2009; Meredith, Scott. "Identifying African American Resources Project." *MMWH* 57, no. 1 (Spring 2007): 61–66, 96; Robison, Ken. "Breaking Racial Barriers: 'Everyone's Welcome' at the Ozark Club, Great Falls, Montana's African American Nightclub." *MMWH* 62, no. 2 (Summer 2012): 44–58; Robison, Ken. "'She is Gentle, Good, and Virtuous': Exceptional Librarian and Community Leader Alma Smith Jacobs." *Best of Great Falls,* Winter 2012, 20–23; Robison, Ken. "Alma Jacobs Memorial Plaza." *Historical Black Americans in Northern Montana* (blog). http://blackamericansMont.blogspot.com/2009/05/alma-jacobs-memorial-plaza.html; Taylor, Quintard, and Shirley Ann Wilson Moore, eds. *African American Women Confront the West, 1600–2000.* Norman: University of Oklahoma Press, 2003. Taylor, Quintard, "The Emergence of Black Communities in the Pacific Northwest: 1865–1910." *Journal of Negro History* 64, no. 4 (Autumn 1979): 342–54; "More Interested in Goals Than Achievements." *Great Falls Tribune,* Oct. 29, 1967, 2–3; Alma Jacobs obituary. *Great Falls Tribune,* June 21, 2009.

The Power of Strong, Able Women

Anderson, Jean. *League of Women Voters of Montana Bozeman MT.* Mar. 1972 newsletter; Grace Bates Vertical File. MHS; Chambers, Gus, and Paul Zalis, producers. "For This and Future Generations: Montana's 1972 Constitutional Convention." Missoula: KUFM-TV/Montana PBS, 2004; Cook, Kathleen. "Facts on the Line; Payment on Progress." *Butte Montana Standard,* Oct. 7, 1975; Eck, Dorothy. Interview by Jodie Foley, May 27, 1997. OH 1771. MHS; Eck, Dorothy, Papers. UPMC 87. MHS; Dorothy Eck Vertical File. MHS; Kirk, Kelly. "State of Change: Gender and the 1972 Montana Constitutional Convention."

Master's thesis, Montana State University, 2011; League of Women Voters of Montana. *A Constitutional Convention for Montana*. Bozeman: Artcraft Printers, 1971. PAM 2917. MHS; League of Women Voters of Montana Records, 1921–1989. MC 180. MHS; League of Women Voters of Montana. http://lwvMont.org/; "Nine League Members Go to Con-Con." *Montana Voter*, Dec. 1971; Arlyne Reichert Vertical File. MHS; Schontzler, Gail. "Dorothy Eck: Champion for Women, Open Government." *Bozeman Chronicle*, Sept. 4, 2011; "Should Men Be Members?" *Montana Voter*, Mar. 1974.

Working to Give Women "Individual Dignity"

Constitution of the State of Montana; "Democrats Control State Legislature," *Kalispell Daily Inter Lake*, Nov. 7, 1974, 8; Elison, Larry M., and Fritz Snyder. *The Montana State Constitution: A Reference Guide*. Westport, Conn.: Greenwood Press, 2001; Fritz, Harry. "The 1972 Montana Constitution in Contemporary Context." *Montana Law Review* 51, no. 2 (Summer 1990): 270–74; Griffing, Betsy. "The Rise and Fall of the New Judicial Federalism under the Montana Constitution." *Montana Law Review* 71, no. 2 (Summer 2010): 383–93; Hutchinson, Arthur. "Skimpy Funds Don't Help Human Rights Panel." *Helena Independent Record*, Nov. 19, 1974; Koester, Jeanne M. "Equal Rights." *Montana Law Review* 39, no. 2 (Summer 1978): 238–48; Malone, Michael P., and Dianne G. Dougherty. "Montana's Political Culture: A Century of Evolution." *MMWH* 31, no. 1 (Winter 1981): 44–58; Montana Women's Political Caucus Records, 1974–1982. SC 2036. MHS; Nelson, Inga Katrin. "'Each Generation of a Free Society': The Relationship between Montana's Constitutional Convention, Individual Rights Protections, and State Constitutionalism." Master's thesis, Portland State University, 2011; "New Dawn in State Politics," *Kalispell Daily Inter Lake*, Nov. 7, 1974; Robbin, Tia Rikel. "Untouched Protection from Discrimination: Private Action in Montana's Individual Dignity Clause." *Montana Law Review* 51, no. 2 (Summer 1990): 553–70; Treadwell, Lujuana Wolfe, and Nancy Wallace Page. "Equal Rights Provisions: The Experience under State Constitutions." *California Law Review*, 65, no. 5 (Sept. 1977): 1086–1112; "Virginia Blend Testimony Regarding Providing Equal Rights." Montana Constitutional Convention Records, 1971–1972. RS 22. MHS; Women's Political Caucus Vertical File. MHS.

Defining Gender Equality

Bradley, Dorothy. "Equal Rights–Where from Here," and Montana Equal Rights Council, "Montana and the Equal Rights Amendment" [n.d., after 1978]. Frances C. Elge Papers, 1921–1991. UPMC 77. MHS; Clark, Phyllis. "Equal Rights Amendment Is Not 'Women's Lib.'" *Kalispell Daily Inter Lake*, Jan. 23, 1974, 4; Clawson, Roger. "Friends, Foes Debate ERA." *Billings Gazette*, Jan. 25, 1974, 12; Constitution of the State of Montana. courts.Mont.gov/content/library/docs/72constit.pdf; Cook, Kathleen. "Equal Rights Proponent Says: 'Sometimes Majority Is Wrong.'" *Butte Montana Standard*, Sept. 15, 1974, 26; Cook, Kathleen. "Why Fight Equal Rights?" *Butte Montana Standard*, Sept. 8, 1974, 18; Elkin, Larry. "ERA and Constitution in a Timely Fight." *Helena Independent Record*, Feb. 8, 1979; "ERA Outcome Is Praised." *Helena Independent Record*, Mar. 13, 1979, 9; Frances C. Elge Vertical File. MHS; Jepsen, Gary. "ERA Stand Is Explained." *Helena Independent Record*, Feb. 19, 1979; Kessler-Harris, Alice. *In Pursuit of Equity: Women, Men, and the Quest for Economic Citizenship in 20th Century America*. New York: Oxford University Press, 2001; Moes, Garry. "House Kills Montana ERA Nullification." *Helena Independent Record*, Mar. 11, 1979; "The National Countdown on ERA." *Helena Independent Record*, Mar. 11, 1979, 12; Quinn, Michael D. "The LDS Church's Campaign against the Equal Rights Amendment." *Journal of Mormon History* 20, no. 2 (Fall 1994): 85–155; Rosenfeld, Steven P. "ERA May Go to the People." *Billings Gazette*, Jan. 11, 1974, 1; Rygg, Brian. "Making a Mockery of Equality." *Great Falls Tribune*, Mar. 12, 1979;

"Senate Faces ERA, Gambling Bills." *Kalispell Daily Inter Lake,* Jan. 14, 1974, 2; Sherrill, Patrick. "Defends Stance on ERA." *Helena Independent Record,* Mar. 12, 1979, 4; Soule, Sarah, and Brayden G. King. "The Stages of the Policy Process and the Equal Rights Amendment, 1972–1982." *American Journal of Sociology* 111, no. 6 (May 2006): 1871–1909.

Writing a Rough-and-Tumble World

Clayton, John. *The Cowboy Girl: The Life of Caroline Lockhart.* Lincoln: University of Nebraska Press, 2007; Culpin, Mary Shivers. "Caroline Lockhart Ranch: Bighorn Canyon National Recreation Area." National Park Service, Rocky Mountain Regional Office, 1981. www.nps.gov/parkhistory/online_books/bica/caroline_lockhard_ranch. pdf; Davison, Stanley. "Chip of the Flying-U: The Author Was a Lady." *MMWH* 23, no. 2 (Spring 1973): 2–15; Furman, Necah Stewart. "Western Author Caroline Lockhart and Her Perspectives on Wyoming." *MMWH* 36, no. 1 (Winter 1986): 50–59; "B. M. Bower." *125 Montana Newsmakers.* www.greatfallstribune.com/multimedia/125newsmakers1/ bower.html; National Park Service. "Caroline Lockhart Ranch." www.nps.gov/bica/ historyculture/caroline-lockhart-ranch.htm; Tompkins, Jane P. *West of Everything: The Inner Life of Westerns.* New York: Oxford University Press, 1992.

Biased Justice

Baumler, Ellen. "Justice as an Afterthought: Women and the Montana Prison System." *MMWH* 58, no. 2 (Summer 2008): 41–59, 97–99; Baumler, Ellen., and J. M. Cooper. *Dark Spaces: Montana's Historic Penitentiary at Deer Lodge.* Albuquerque: University of New Mexico Press, 2008; Butler, Anne. *Gendered Justice in the American West: Women Prisoners in Men's Penitentiaries.* Urbana: University of Illinois Press, 1997; Byorth, Susan. "History of Women Inmates: A Report for the Criminal Justice and Corrections Advisory Council," 1989. www.cor.mt.gov/content/About/HistoryofWomenInmates; Montana State Prison Records, 1871–1981. SMF 36. MHS.

Helen Piotopowaka Clarke and the Persistence of Prejudice

"Brief News Column Includes Clarke's Charges against Agent Monteath. *Sacred Heart Review* 30, no. 17 (Oct. 24, 1903): 3; *Marshall (Mich.) Marshall Expounder,* Friday, Oct. 30, 1903: 2; Chapman, Berlin B. *The Otoes and Missourias: A Study of Indian Removal and the Legal Aftermath.* Oklahoma City: Times Journal Publishing Company, 1965; Clarke, Helen P. Letter to Mr. Edwin Royle. Feb. 15, 1911. Helen P. Clarke Papers. SC 1153. MHS; Graybill, Andrew R. "Helen P. Clarke in 'the Age of Tribes': Montana's Changing Racial Landscape, 1870–1920." *MMWH* 61, no. 1 (Spring 2011): 3–19; "Lost Everything through Indians." *Sausalito (Calif.) News,* Dec. 28, 1901; "Maligned by a Newspaper." *Helena Montana Daily Record,* Sept. 26, 1903.

A Glamorous Façade

Baumler, Ellen. "Devil's Perch: Prostitution from Suite to Cellar in Butte, Montana." *MMWH* 48, no. 3 (Autumn 1998), 4–21; Baumler, Ellen. "The End of the Line: Butte, Anaconda and the Landscape of Prostitution." *Drumlummon Views,* Spring 2009, 283–301; *Butte Miner,* Jan. 19, 1902; Fry, Monroe. "The Three Most Wide-Open Towns." *Esquire,* June 1953, 49; *Great Falls Tribune,* Oct. 13–18, 1968; Murphy, Mary. *Mining Cultures: Men, Women, and Leisure in Butte, 1914–41.* Urbana: University of Illinois Press, 1997.

Doris Brander and the Fight to Honor Women's Military Service

Brander, Doris. Interview. OH 1276. MHS; Brander, Doris, Papers, A3:3-4, MHS; "Highlighting the Doris Brander Papers and Montana Women in Military Service for America (WIMSA)." *Montana Historical Society Montana History Wiki* online;

Women in Military Service for American Memorial Foundation (WIMSA). http://www.womensmemorial.org/H&C/h&cwelcome.html. Women in Military Service for American Memorial Foundation. MC 343, MHS.

"I Am a Very Necessary Evil"

Cantarine, Liz. "She's Dolly Akers, 69-Year-Old Dynamo." *Billings Gazette*, July 18, 1971; Dolly Smith Cusker Akers, Papers, 1927–1985. A9:1-5. MHS; Dolly Akers Vertical File, MHS; "Fort Peck Tribal Board Orders General Election." *Great Falls Tribune*, Feb. 5, 1959: 5; Fourstar, Odessa Jones. Letter to the editor, March 5, 1976. *Wotanin Wowapi*, March 11, 1976, 3; Freda Augusta Beazley, Papers, 1960–1975. MC 187. MHS; "Indian Relief Setup Organized for Peck." *Helena Daily Independent*, Dec. 21, 1934; Miller, David, Dennis Smith, Joseph McGeshick, James Shanley, and Caleb Shields. *The History of the Assiniboine and Sioux Tribes of the Fort Peck Indian Reservation, 1800–2000*. Poplar and Helena, Mont.: Fort Peck Community College and Montana Historical Society Press, 2008; Palmer, Tom. "My People, My Life: Indian Elder Still Serving Her Tribe." *Helena Independent Record*, Mar. 3, 1985; White Wolf, Shawn. "Montana's 1st Indian Lawmaker Fought Her Entire Life to Keep Intact Her People and Their Way of Life." *Helena Independent Record*, Jan. 26, 2003; "Woman Indian Leader Finds Liberation Movement 'Old Hat.'" *Farmington (N.M.) Daily Times*, July 14, 1971.

A Young Mother at the Rosebud and Little Bighorn Battles

Healy, Donna. "American Indian Images: Northern Cheyenne History Told in Photos, Interviews." *Billings Gazette*, Aug. 6, 2006; Hoxie, Frederick E., ed. *Encyclopedia of North American Indians*. New York: Houghton Mifflin, 1996; Little Bear, Richard, ed. *We, The Northern Cheyenne People: Our Land, Our History, Our Culture*. Lame Deer, Mont.: Chief Dull Knife College, 2008; Marquis, Thomas. *Custer on the Little Big Horn*. Lodi, Calif.: End-Kian Publishing Company, 1967; Michno, Gregory F. *Lakota Noon: The Indian Narrative of Custer's Defeat*. Missoula, Mont.: Mountain Press, 1997; Weist, Tom. *A History of the Cheyenne People*. Rev. ed. Billings, Mont.: Montana Council for Indian Education, 1984.

"Things to Be Done Which Money and Men Will Never Provide"

AAUW Montana Division. *Montana Treasure Stater* 63, no. 4 (Spring 2012); AAUW Montana. http://www.aauwmontana.org. AAUW Vertical File. MHS; American Association of University Women (AAUW) Montana Division Records. MC 202, MHS; Davies, Doris. *A History of the Montana AAUW, 1926–1994*. Billings, Mont.: American Association of University Women, 1994; *Governor's Commission on Status of Women. Montana Women. . . .* Helena: Governor's Commission on Status of Women, 1967; Gronfein, Norma. Interview by Mary Murphy, Oct. 9, 1987. OH 1038. MHS; Harriett Meloy Vertical File, MHS; Johnson, Maxine. Interview by Diane Sands, Sept. 17, 2001. OH 378-45. UM; MacDonnell, Katherine. Interview by Diane Sands, June 9, 1987. OH 1012, MHS; Meloy, Harriett. Interview by Laurie Mercier, Sept. 15, 1987. OH 1036. MHS; Schaffer, Deborah. *Feats and Faces: Chronicles of 26 Billings Women, with Photographs*. Billings, Mont.: American Association of University Women, 1994.

"We Are No Longer Criminals"

Constitution of the State of Montana; "Gay-sex Decision." *Independent Record*, Mar. 15, 1996; "Gay-sex Law Struck Down." *Independent Record*, July 3, 1997. *Gryczan v. State of Montana*, Montana Supreme Court decision, July 2, 1997; Grygiel, Chris. "Suit Would Overturn Homosexual Law." *Independent Record*, Dec. 7, 1993; "High Court

Strikes Ban on Gay Sex," *Independent Record*, June 27, 2003; "Law That Made Gay Sex in Montana a Crime Repealed." *Missoulian*, Apr. 19, 2013; Legal Voice (previously the Northwest Women's Law Center). Linda Gryczan personal collection; "Montana's Gay Sex Ban Overturned." *Great Falls Tribune*, July 3, 1997; "Plaintiff Says Ruling Is Just the Beginning." *Independent Record*, July 6, 1997; Selden, Ron. "Out in Montana: After a Winter of Fear and Defeat, Advocates Renew Their Fight for Same-sex Rights." *Missoula Independent,* May 31–June 7, 2001.

Gifts of Love and Gratitude

Highwalking, Belle. "Belle Highwalking: The Narrative of a Northern Cheyenne Woman." Edited by Katherine M. Weist. Translated by Helen Hiwalker. Billings, Mont.: Montana Council for Indian Education, 1979.

"The Men Would Never Have Survived"

Aulette, Judy, and Trudy Mills. "Something Old, Something New: Auxiliary Work in the 1983–1986 Copper Strike." *Feminist Studies* 14, no. 2 (Summer 1988), 251–68; Basso, Matthew L. *Meet Joe Copper: Masculinity and Race on Montana's World War II Home Front.* Chicago: University of Chicago Press, 2013; Finn, Janet L. "A Penny for Your Thoughts: Women, Strikes, and Community Survival." In *Motherlode: Legacies of Women's Lives and Labors in Butte, Montana.* Edited by Janet L. Finn and Ellen Crain. Livingston, Mont.: Clark City Press, 2006, 61–75; Mercier, Laurie. *Anaconda: Labor, Community, and Culture in Montana's Smelter City.* Urbana: University of Illinois Press, 2001; Mercier, Laurie. "Reworking Race, Class, and Gender in the Pacific Northwest." *Frontiers: A Journal of Women Studies* 22, no. 3 (2001), 61–74; Murphy, Mary. *Mining Cultures: Men, Women, and Leisure in Butte, 1914–41.* Urbana: University of Illinois Press, 1997.

The Work Was Never Done

Armitage, Susan. "Western Women: Beginning to Come into Focus," *MMWH* 32, no. 3 (Summer 1982); Kinsey-Cartwright, Suzan. "Jesse and Ruth Lane," Montana Law Enforcement Officers Memorial, Garfield County Page, 1999, http://www.rootsweb.ancestry.com; Mercier, Laurie K. "Women's Role in Montana Agriculture." In *Montana Heritage: An Anthology of Historical Essays.* Edited by Robert R. Swartout Jr. and Harry W. Fritz. Helena: Montana Historical Society Press, 1992. "Schillreff, Fern, and Jessie M. Shawver." *Montana Historical Society Montana History Wiki* online; Work, Clemens P. *Darkest before Dawn: Sedition and Free Speech in the American West.* Santa Fe: University of New Mexico Press, 2006.

A "Compassionate Heart" and "Keen Mind"

Baumler, Ellen. "Caroline McGill." *Montana Moments* blog, Sept. 26, 2012; Caroline McGill Papers. SC 2445. MHS; Chaney, Rob. "A True Pioneer: Caroline McGill." *Bozeman Chronicle*, Mar. 11, 1997; Lindsay, Mary Redfield. "'Woman of Distinction' Describes Dr. Caroline McGill." *Great Falls Tribune*, Dec. 28, 1958; McGill, Caroline, Vertical File, MHS; "Dr. Caroline M. McGill (1879–1959)." Montana Historical Society Gallery of Outstanding Montanans online; Pendland, Brenda. "Letters from the World's End: A Young Couple's Portrait of Butte, 1936–1941." *MMWH* 53, no. 4 (Winter 2003): 36–49; Staudohar, Connie. "The 320 Ranch." *MMWH* 55, no. 2 (Summer 2002): 75–77.

The Education of Josephine Pease Russell

Medicine Crow, Joe. Interview by Bill LaForge. Jan. 30, 1989. OH 1226. MHS; Russell, Josephine Pease. Interview by Bill LaForge. Feb. 24–25, 1989. OH 1227. MHS.

Mamie and Octavia Bridgewater and Montana's African American Community

Baumler, Ellen. "Octavia Bridgewater." *Montana Moments* blog, Feb. 25, 2013; Octavia Bridgewater Vertical File, MHS; U.S. Army Medical Department, Office of Medical History. "African American Nurse Corps Officers." http://history.amedd.army.mil/ANCWebsite/articles/blackhistory.html.

"You Design It and You Make It"

"Clay Artists–Frances Senska." Craft in America. http://www.craftinamerica.org/artists_clay/story_222.php?PHPSESSID=30f5f8a73b89f6b2fffd175383713bbb; "Frances Maude Senska (1914-2009)." *Bozeman Daily Chronicle*, Dec. 28, 2009; "Frances Senska: Art All the Time." *Montana: Second Century*, Montana PBS. 1997; "Frances Senska Suitcase." http://my.umwestern.edu/Academics/library%5Clibinstruct%5Csuitcase%5CSENSKA.HTM; "Humble Grace: A Tribute to Frances Senska." Exhibit at the Yellowstone Art Museum, Billings, Mar. 19, 2010-June 27, 2010; McMillan, Scott. "Artists in the West: Frances Senska." *Big Sky Journal*, Summer 2003, 34–39; Rod, Luann. "Tea with Frances Celebrates Life of Art." *Bozeman Daily Chronicle*, Jan. 29, 2010; Senska, Frances. Interview by Chere Juisto and Rick Newby, June 9, 1998. OH 1805. MHS; Senska, Frances. Interview by Donna Forbes, Apr. 16, 2001. Transcript. http://www.aaa.si.edu/collections/interviews/oral-history-interview-frances-senska-13078; Senska, Frances, and Jesse Wilber. Interview by Martin Holt, 1979. OH 1441. MHS; Smith, Marjorie. "I Make Pots." *Montana State University Newsletter*, Oct. 1, 2010.

Lucille Otter

Knox, Margaret L. "The New Indian Wars: A Growing National Movement Is Gunning for Tribal Treaties, Reservations and Rights." *Los Angeles Times*, Nov. 7, 1993; Laskowski, Jeannine, Jackie Drews, and Cynthia Kingston. "Women Making It Happen: Lucille Otter." *InterMountain Woman*, Oct./Nov. 1996, 40–43; Otter, Lucille T. Interview. June 24, 1995. SC 1623, MHS; "Lucille Otter Laid to Rest." *Pablo Char-Koosta News*, June 20, 1997; "Lucille Otter Rounding Up Tribal Votes." *Pablo Char-Koosta News*, Oct. 1, 1974; Montana Human Rights Network. *Drumming Up Resentment: The Anti-Indian Movement in Montana*. N.p., Jan. 2000, 4. Otter, Lucille. "Circle June 6th on Your Calendar." *Pablo Char-Koosta News*, June 1, 1978.

Montana Women of the Ku Klux Klan

Blee, Kathleen M. *Women of the Klan: Racism and Gender in the 1920s*. Berkeley: University of California Press, 1991; Erickson, Christine K. "'Kluxer Blues': The Klan Confronts Catholics in Butte, Montana, 1923–1929." *MMWH* 53, no. 1 (2003), 44–57; Johnston, H. W. "Historical Note." Guide to the Knights of the Ku Klux Klan, Butte, Montana, Records Finding Aid. 1995. Northwest Digital Archives; KKK advertisement, *Billings Gazette*, Sept. 30, 1923; Ku Klux Klan Vertical File, MHS; Sturdevant, Anne. "White Hoods under the Big Sky: Montanans Embrace the Ku Klux Klan." In *Speaking Ill of the Dead: Jerks in Montana History*, edited by Dave Walter. Guilford, Conn.: Globe Pequot Press, 2011; "Women of the Ku Klux Klan. Constitution and Laws of the Women of the Ku Klux Klan. First Imperial Klonvocation at St. Louis, Missouri, Jan. 6, 1927." http://brbldl.library.yale.edu/pdfgen/exportPDF.php?bibid=2107186&solrid=3577023.

"Must a Woman . . . Give It All Up When She Marries?"

Cooke, Dennis H., W. G. Knox, and R. H. Libby. "Local Residents and Married Women as Teachers." *Review of Educational Research* 13, no. 3 (June, 1943), 252–61; Kohl, Martha.

I Do: A Cultural History of Montana Weddings. Helena: Montana Historical Society Press, 2011; Kohl, Seena. "'Well I Have Lived in Montana Almost a Week and Like It Fine': Letters from the Davis Homestead, 1910–1926."*MMWH* 51, no. 3 (Autumn 2001): 32–45; Rankin, Charles E. "Teaching: Opportunity and Limitation for Wyoming Women." *Western Historical Quarterly* 21, no. 2 (May 1990): 147–70. Women in Education, Discrimination Vertical File. MHS.

Writing Our Lives

Andre-Beatty, Pandora. "Disrupted Conventions: Gender Roles in Mildred Walker's *The Curlew's Cry* and *Winter Wheat.*" Master's thesis, University of Montana, Missoula, 2007; Blew, Mary Clearman. *Bone Deep in Landscape: Writing, Reading, and Place.* Norman: University of Oklahoma Press, 1999; Blew, Mary Clearman. Introduction to *The Curlew's Cry*, by Mildred Walker. Lincoln: University of Nebraska Press, 1994, 1–7; Hugo, Ripley. *Writing for Her Life: The Novelist Mildred Walker.* Lincoln: University of Nebraska Press, 2003. McNamer, Deirdre. Introduction to *Unless the Wind Turns,* by Mildred Walker. Lincoln: University of Nebraska Press, 1996, vii–xiii; Welch, James. Introduction to *If A Lion Could Talk*, by Mildred Walker. Lincoln: University of Nebraska Press, 1995, vi–xiii; Welch, James. Introduction to *Winter Wheat*, by Mildred Walker. Lincoln: University of Nebraska Press, 1992, ix–xiii.

Sarah Gammon Bickford

Baumler, Ellen. "Celebrating Sarah Bickford." *406 Woman* 6, no. 2 (2008): 72–73; "Building Freedom in the American West: The Sarah Bickford Project." http://buildingfreedom. wordpress.com/; Madison County History Association. *Pioneer Trails and Trials: 1863–1920.* Virginia City, Mont.: Madison County History Association [1976?]; Peterson, Bill, and Orlan Svingen. "Finding Sarah Bickford." Ford Foundation and the National Trust for Historic Preservation. http://sarahbickford.org/index.html; "Sarah Bickford" (obituary). *Virginia City Madisonian,* July 14, 1931.

Bonnie HeavyRunner

Craig, Bonnie. "Native Americans and Cancer." http://www.natamcancer.org/interact/bc2-palliative.html; "Craig Loses Fight With Cancer, Dies at 46." *Pablo Char-Koosta News,* Nov. 28, 1997; Desmond, Brenda. "Bonnie Heavy Runner Craig." *Montana Law Review* 59 (1998); Florio, Gwen. "Bonnie's Building." *Missoula Magazine,* Summer/Fall 2010, 31–33; "Founder of UM Native American Studies Dies." http://www2.umt.edu/montanan/w98/oval.htm; Jahrig, Gary. "Bonnie Heavy Runner Craig." *The Missoulian* online; Miller, Kay. "Bridging the Cultural Divide." *Star-Tribune,* July 12, 1993; "Native American Studies Leader Lauded for Contributions to UM." *Pablo Char-Koosta News,* Mar. 7, 1997.

Me, Me, Me, Me

Halvorsen, Cathryn Luanne. "Autobiography, Genius, and the American West: The Story of Mary MacLane and Opal Whiteley." PhD diss., University of Michigan, 1997; MacLane, Mary. *I, Mary MacLane.* New York: F. A. Stokes, 1917; MacLane, Mary. *The Story of Mary MacLane.* Chicago: Herbert S. Stone, 1902; Mattern, Carolyn J. "Mary MacLane: A Feminist Opinion." *MMWH* 27, no. 4 (Autumn 1977): 54–63; Murphy, Mary. *Mining Cultures: Men, Women and Leisure in Butte, 1914–41.* Urbana: University of Illinois Press, 1997; Tovo, Kathryne Beth. "'The Unparalleled Individuality of Me': The Story of Mary MacLane." PhD diss, University of Texas at Austin, 2000; Wheeler, Leslie. "Montana's Shocking 'Lit'ry Lady.'" *MMWH* 27, no. 3 (Summer 1977): 20–33.

"I Was a Strong Woman"

"Atliyi 'Adeline' Paul Abraham Mathias" (obituary), *Pablo Char-Koosta News*, Feb. 15, 2007; Plummer, Maggie. "Adeline Mathias: Going Strong at 95." *Pablo Char-Koosta News*, Oct. 20, 2005, 5; Plummer, Maggie. *Passing It On: Voices from the Flathead Indian Reservation*. Pablo, Mont.: Salish Kootenai College Press, 2008; Rave, Jodi. "Kootenai Matriarch, 95, Tribe's Key Link to History, Customs." *Missoula Missoulian*, Oct. 22, 2005; Salish Kootenai College. *Honoring Native Women's Voices: A Collection of Stories*. Pablo, Mont.: Salish Kootenai College Press, 2006; Shelby, Velda. "Adeline Paul Abraham Mathias Kuki Palki." *Pablo Char-Koosta News*, Oct. 2, 2010; Stromnes, John. "Many Fear That the Kootenai Language Will Die with Its Elders." *Missoula Missoulian*, Aug. 26, 2000.

Head, Heart, Hands, and Health

"Augusta Dillman Evans: First Montana State 4-H Leader" and "Geraldine G. Fenn—Montana State 4-H Staff." National 4-H Hall of Fame 2008, Montana. www.4-h-hof.com/mt2008.pdf; Burlingame, Merrill G. *The Montana Cooperative Extension Service, 1893–1974*. Bozeman: Montana State University, 1984; Carter, Betty. Betty Wilson Vimont Carter and Harvey Carter interview, Mar. 20, 1983. Interviewed by Laurie Mercier. OH 503. MHS; Cushman, Harriette E., Vertical File. MHS; Kappel, Tana. "Latvia and Montana Exchange 4-H Ideas." Montana State University online. http://www.montana.edu/cpa/news/wwwpb-archives/yuth/latvia.html; MacDonald, Marie. "Country Kids in Chicago: Montana's First Delegation to the National 4-H Club Congress, 1925." *MMWH* 32, no. 4 (Autumn 1982), 74–77; McCoy, Betty, ed. *Past, Present, Possibilities: Exploring 100 Years of Montana 4-H*. Bozeman: Montana State University, 2012; McManus, Irene. Interview by Laurie Mercier. Mar. 20, 1984. OH 776. MHS; United States Bureau of Indian Affairs. "Sioux Girl from Fort Peck Wins Trip to Washington as 4-H Delegate." *Indians at Work*, July 1940, 7, 11.

"She Spoke the Truth"

Basso, Matthew L. *Meet Joe Copper: Masculinity and Race on Montana's World War II Home Front*. Chicago: University of Chicago Press, 2013; Finn, Janet. *Mining Childhood: Growing Up in Butte, Montana, 1900–1960*. Helena: Montana Historical Society Press, 2012. Martinez, Lula. Interview by Laurie Mercier. Sept. 1987. Portland, Ore. OH 1017, MHS; Martinez, Lula. Interview by Teresa Jordan, Butte, Mont., Apr. 2, 1986. Butte-Silver Bow Public Archives, Butte Mont.; Mercier, Laurie. "'We're All Familia': The Work and Activism of Lula Martinez," 268–77. In *Motherlode: Legacies of Women's Lives and Labors in Butte, Montana*, edited by Janet L. Finn and Ellen Crain. Livingston, Mont.: Clark City Press, 2005; Mercier, Laurie. "Creating a New Community in the North: Mexican Americans of the Yellowstone Valley." In *Montana Legacy: Essays on History, People, and Place*, edited by Harry W. Fritz, Mary Murphy, and Robert R. Swartout Jr. Helena: Montana Historical Society Press, 2002.

Jeannette Rankin

Giles, Kevin S. *Flight of the Dove: The Story of Jeannette Rankin*. Beaverton, Ore.: Lochsa Experience Publishers, 1980; Hardaway, Roger D. "Jeannette Rankin: The Early Years." *North Dakota Quarterly* 48, no. 1 (Winter 1980): 62–68; Harris, Ted C. "Jeannette Rankin in Georgia." *Georgia Historical Quarterly* 58, no. 1 (Mar. 1974): 55–78; Jeannette Rankin Papers, 1916–1919. MHS; Josephson, Hannah. *Jeannette Rankin, First Lady in Congress: A Biography*. Indianapolis: Bobbs-Merrill, 1974; La Guardia, Fiorello H. *The Making of an Insurgent*. New York: Lippincott, 1948; Lopach, James J., and Jean A. Luckowski,

Jeannette Rankin: A Political Woman. Boulder: University Press of Colorado, 2005; Shirley, Gayle C. *More than Petticoats: Remarkable Montana Women.* Helena: Falcon Press, 1995; Wilson, Joan Hoff. "'Peace is a Woman's Job . . . ': Jeannette Rankin and American Foreign Policy, The Origins of Her Pacifism." *MMWH* 30, no. 1 (Jan. 1980): 28–41.

The Right to Procreate

Montana State Board of Eugenics. "Annual Report of the Board of Eugenics." Helena, Mont., n.p., 1972; Chamberlain, Chelsea. "Montana State Training School Historic District National Register Nomination Form." 2014. On file at Montana State Historic Preservation Office, Helena; Dillingham, Brint. "Sterilization of Native Americans." *American Indian Journal* 3, no. 7 (July 1977), 16–19; Johansen, Bruce E. "Sterilization of Native American Women." In *Encyclopedia of the American Indian Movement,* edited by Bruce Johansen. Santa Barbara, Calif.: Greenwood, 2013; Josefeson, Deborah. "Oregon's Governor Apologises for Forced Sterilisations." *British Medical Journal* (Dec. 14, 2002): 1380; Kaelber, Lutz. "Eugenics: Compulsory Sterilization in 50 American States. Montana." 2011. University of Vermont, Sociology Department. http://www.uvm.edu/~lkaelber/eugenics/MT/MT.html; Kluchin, Rebecca M. *Fit to Be Tied: Sterilization and Reproductive Rights in America, 1950–1980.* New Brunswick, N.J.: Rutgers University Press, 2009; Larson, Karmet. "And Then There Were None." *Christian Century,* Jan. 26, 1977, 61; O'Sullivan, Meg Devlin. "'We Worry about Survival": American Indian Women, Sovereignty, and the Right to Bear and Raise Children in the 1970s." PhD diss., University of North Carolina–Chapel Hill, 2007; "Patients Mistreated and Mutilated by Illegal Operations at Insane Asylum While Relatives Are Forced to Pay Exorbitant Charges to Superintendent." *Helena Independent,* Oct. 5, 1924; Paul, Julius. "Three Generations of Imbeciles Are Enough . . . ," 404–7. In *State Eugenic Sterilizations Laws in American Thought and Practice.* Washington, D.C.: Walter Reed Army Institute of Research, 1965; "People and Events: Eugenics and Birth Control." PBS Web, http://www.pbs.org/wgbh/amex/pill/peopleevents/e_eugenics.html; Rubin, Nilmini Gunaratne. "A Crime against Motherhood: Involuntary Sterlization Was a Horrifying Exercise in Genetic Engineering." *Los Angeles Times,* May 13, 2012; Schultz, Louisa Frank. "Sterilization for Those Involved in Mental Retardation History, Issues and Options for Montana?" Montana Developmental Disabilities Planning and Advisory Council, 1986. https://archive.org/stream/sterilizationfor1986schu#page/no/mode/2up; Schultz, Louisa Frank, and Anne Moylan. "Further Consideration of the Question: Should Montana Have a Public Policy on Sterilization of Those Involved in Mental Retardation and If So, What Should It Be?" Montana Developmental Disabilities Planning and Advisory Council, 1987. https://archive.org/details/furtherconsidera1987schu; "16 Helpless Human Beings Are Said to Have Been Unsexed at Hospital." *Helena Independent,* Apr. 24, 1924; *Missoula Daily Missoulian,* Mar. 30, Feb. 14, 1914.

Montana's Postwar Women Politicians

"Antoinette 'Toni' Fraser Rosell." *Billings Gazette,* Apr. 28, 2011; "Bertha Streeter of Lake County Becomes Third Woman Senator in Montana." *Helena Independent Record,* Nov. 8, 1956; Bridenstine, Ellenore M. "My Years as Montana's First Woman State Senator." *MMWH* 39, no. 1 (Winter 1989): 54–58; Coontz, Stephanie. *The Way We Never Were: American Families and the Nostalgia Trap.* New York: Basic Books, 1992; Meyerowitz, Joanne. "Beyond the Feminine Mystique: A Reassessment of Postwar Mass Culture, 1946–1958." *Journal of American History* 79, no. 4 (Mar. 1993): 1455–82; Minard, Louise. "Rep. Bess Reed Has No. 1 Desk." *Butte Montana Standard,* Jan. 16, 1953; "Montana

Legislature Hard Working Group of Citizens." *Helena Independent Record*, Feb. 22, 1953; Muncy, Robyn. *Creating a Female Dominion in American Reform, 1890–1935*. New York: Oxford University Press, 1991; "Mrs. Bess R. Reed Speaker at Soroptimist Club." *Helena Independent Record*, Jan. 12, 1951; "Nutter Criticized on Two Issues." *Kalispell Daily Inter Lake*, July 17, 1961; Rosell, Antoinette Fraser. Interview by Bob Brown, July 6, 2005. OH 396-29, UM; "State Legislator Rep. Bess R. Reed." *Butte Montana Standard*, Jan. 22, 1951; "Women Seek State Offices," *Billings Gazette*, July 6, 1956; "Women Elected Officials." *Montana Historical Society Montana History Wiki* online.

Theresa Walker Lamebull Kept Her Language Alive

Boswell, Evelyn. "MSU Grads Preserve a Native Language, Keep Tribal Philosophies Alive." MSU News Service, Dec. 4, 2008; Brockie, Terry. Correspondence with Laura Ferguson, Feb. 18, 2014; Capriccioso, Rob. "The Phraselator II." *The American: The Online Magazine of the American Enterprise Institute*. http://www.american.com; Ivanova, Karen. "Revitalizing Native Tongues." *Great Falls Tribune*, Apr. 14, 2002; Ogden, Karen. "Gros Ventre Woman, 110, A Living Bridge to the 'Buffalo Days.'" *Great Falls Tribune*, Sept. 19, 2006; "Theresa Lamebull—Gros Ventre (A'aninin)." *Wikipedia* online encyclopedia; Thompson, Ellen. "Elders Honored for Helping Keep Native Language, Traditions Alive." *Havre Daily News*. Feb. 4, 2005; Umbhau, Kurt. "Firing up White Clay." *Tribal College Journal*. Winter 2009; Wipf, Briana. "State's Native Languages Diverse." *Great Falls Tribune*, June 30, 2013.

Merle Egan Anderson

Affidavit of Merle Egan Anderson, State of Washington, County of King. Mar. 29, 1976. Copy courtesy Mark Hough; "An All-Telephone Wedding." *Mountain States Monitor*, n.d., 21. Copy courtesy Mark Hough; Anderson, Merle. "The Army's Forgotten Women." Copy courtesy Mark Hough; Anderson, Merle. "Battling the Pentagon." Copy courtesy Mark Hough; Evans, Martin Marix. *American Voices of World War I: Primary Source Documents, 1917–1920*. London: Fitzroy Dearborn Publishers, 2001; Frahm, Jill. "The Hello Girls: Women Telephone Operators with the American Expeditionary Forces during World War I." *Journal of the Gilded Age and Progressive Era* 3, no. 3 (July 2004): 271–93; Gavin, Lettie. *American Women in World War I: They Also Served*. Niwot: University Press of Colorado, 1997; Zeiger, Susan. *In Uncle Sam's Service: Women Workers with the American Expeditionary Forces, 1917–1919*. Philadelphia: University of Pennsylvania Press, 2004.

"A Man in the Mountains Cannot Keep His Wife"

May, Elaine Tyler. *Great Expectations: Marriage and Divorce in Post-Victorian America*. Chicago: University of Chicago Press, 1980; O'Neill, William. "Divorce in the Progressive Era." *American Quarterly* 17, no. 2, part 1 (Summer 1965): 203–17; Petrik, Paula. "If She Be Content: The Development of Montana Divorce Law, 1865–1907." *Western Historical Quarterly* 18, no. 3 (July 1987): 261–91; Petrik, Paula. *No Step Backward: Women and Family on the Rocky Mountain Mining Frontier, Helena, Montana, 1865–1900*. Helena: Montana Historical Society Press, 1987; Petrik, Paula. "Not a Love Story: *Bordeaux v. Bordeaux*." *MMWH*, 41, no. 2 (Spring 1991): 32–46.

Drawing on Motherhood

Cooney, Bob, and Sayre Cooney Dodgson. "Fanny Cory Cooney: Montana Mother and Artist." *MMWH* 30, no. 3 (Summer 1980): 2–17; Cory, F. Y. *A Fairy Alphabet*. Helena, Mont.: Riverbend Publishing, 2011; "Fanny Cory Cooney." Museum "Artist's File." MHS;

F. Y. Cory Publishers, Inc., http://fycory.com/; King, Judy. "Fanny Cory Cooney Visiting Son and Family in Helena." *Helena Independent Record,* July 23, 1961; Robbins, Trina. *Pretty in Ink: North American Women Cartoonists, 1896–2013.* Seattle: Fantagraphics Books, 2013; "Romantic Marriage of the Girl Who Draws Cute Babies: Won Like the Heroine in a Melodrama." *Minneapolis Tribune,* May 1, 1904; Walter, Dave. "Fanny's World: The Life and Art of Fanny Cory Cooney." *Montana Magazine,* May-June 1988, 4–12.

Montana's "Rosies"

Basso, Matthew L. *Meet Joe Copper: Masculinity and Race on Montana's World War II Home Front.* Chicago: University of Chicago Press, 2013; Furdell, William J. "The Great Falls Home Front during World War II." *MMWH* 48, no. 4 (Winter 1998), 63–75; Goldin, Claudia. "The Role of World War II in the Rise of Women's Employment." *American Economic Review* 81, no. 4 (Sept. 1991): 741–56; Kossoudji, Sherrie A., and Laura J. Dresser. "Working Class Rosies: Women Industrial Workers during World War II." *Journal of Economic History* 52, no. 2 (June 1992): 431–46; Mercier, Laurie. *Anaconda: Labor, Community, and Culture in Montana's Smelter City.* Chicago: University of Illinois Press, 2001; Mercier, Laurie. "'The Stacks Dominated Our Lives': Metals Manufacturing in Four Montana Communities." *MMWH* 38, no. 2 (Spring 1988): 40–57.

Martha Edgerton Rolfe Plassmann

Bodkins, Sharon Lenington, comp. *A Light at the End of the Canyon 1889–1989.* N.p., 1989; Calvert, Jerry W. *The Gibraltar Socialism and Labor in Butte, Montana 1895–1920.* Helena: Montana Historical Society Press, 1988; "Editorial." *Daily Missoulian,* Jan. 4, 1914; "Mrs. Martha Edgerton Rolfe Plassmann." *Great Falls Daily Leader,* Oct. 23, 1895; Plassmann, Martha. Letter to Mrs. Helen Yule, Nov. 7, 1916. Author's Collection; Plassmann, Martha. "Memories of a Long Life." Copy in Great Falls Public Library, Great Falls, Mont.; Robison, Ken. "'A Red Letter Day': Woman's Suffrage in Montana." *Best of Great Falls,* Winter 2015; "Socialist Notes." *Daily Missoulian,* Nov. 3, 1912; "Splendid Meeting Is Held; Equal Suffrage Club Joins with Socialist Local in Observing Day." *Daily Missoulian,* Mar. 31, 1913; "The Struggle for Political Equality in Montana in 1895." *Great Falls River Edge,* Feb. 2005; "Why Socialists Favor Woman's Suffrage." *Montana Socialist,* Oct. 19, 1913.

Fighting for Female Athletes

Bittle, Edgar H., and Larry D. Bartlett. "Recent Developments in Public Education: Committee on Public Education." *Urban Lawyer* 129, no. 4 (Fall 1987): 987–1020; Cole, Robert. "Title IX: A Long Dazed Journey into Rights." *Phi Delta Kappan* 57, no. 9 (May 1976): 575–55, 586; Kuehn, Amber. "Advocates Say Title IX Has Been Boon for Girls." *Helena Independent Record,* May 2, 2012; Kuehn, Amber. "Forty Years of Title IX: Locals Reflect on Landmark Law." *Helena Independent Record,* May 2, 2012; Lintemuth, Elisa. "What Makes a Sports Season Disadvantageous? An Argument That Same-Season Sports Compliance Plans Run Afoul of Title IX." Michigan State University College of Law, 2010; Lubke, Jason, and Shasta Grenier. "Class C: The Only Game in Town." Bozeman: Class C Productions, 2008; McCallum, Carl W. "Federal Blackmail." *Billings Gazette,* Jan. 25, 1976, 3-E; "Faces of Title IX: Karyn Ridgeway." National Women's Law Center. http://www.nwlc.org/title-ix/karyn-ridgeway; *Ridgeway v. Montana High School Ass'n,* 858 F.2d 579, 582 (9th Cir. 1988); Schafer, Courtney E. "Following the Law, Not the Crowd: The Constitutionality of Nontraditional High School Athletic Seasons." *Duke Law Journal,* Oct. 2003, 223–56; Skidmore, Bill. "Title IX: Changing Quiet Stereotypes?" *Helena Independent Record,* Dec. 5, 1976; U.S. Commission on Civil Rights. *More Hurdles to Clear* (1980). Reprinted in *Yellow Springs Exempted Village Sch. Dist. Bd. of Educ. v. Ohio High Sch. Athletic Ass'n, 647 F.2d 651 (6th Cir. 1981).*

There's No Place like Home

Baumler, Ellen. "After Suffrage: Women Politicians at the Montana Capitol." *Women's History Matters* (blog); Engebretson, Donna. Interview by Jodie Foley, July 22, 1995. OH 1632 MHS; Freedman, Harold. Interview by Jodie Foley, July 21, 1995. OH 1634. MHS; Freedman, Noel. Interview by Jodie Foley, July 21, 1995. OH 1633. MHS; "Memories of the Orphanage." *Seattle Times,* July 21, 1995. Montana Children's Center Records. Box 5 and 7. RS 95, MHS; "The Rise and Demise of the American Orphanage." *Johns Hopkins Magazine,* Apr. 1996; Wentz, Fred. Interview by Jodie Foley, July 22, 1995. OH 1635. MHS; "White House Conferences on Children." *Encyclopedia of Children and Childhood in History.* http://www.faqs.org/childhood/Wh-Z-and-other-topics/White-House-Conferences-on-Children.html.

Elouise Pepion Cobell

Berger, Bethany R. "Elouise Cobell: Bringing the United States to Account." In *Our Cause Will Ultimately Triumph: The Men and Women Who Preserved and Revitalized American Indian Sovereignty,* edited by Tim Alan Garrison. Durham, N.C.: Carolina Academic Press, 2013; Cates, Kristen. "Cobell's Impact Felt Far and Wide." *Great Falls Tribune,* Oct. 18, 2011; Coleman, Travis. "Blackfeet Woman's Battle for Trust Settlement Long, Pitched." *Great Falls Tribune,* Jan. 3, 2010; DesRosier, Ed. "Elouise Cobell Found and Won More Than One Battle for Natives." *Great Falls Tribune,* Nov. 10, 2011; "Elouise P. Cobell." *Wikipedia* online encyclopedia; "Elouise Remembered" and "President Barack Obama Remembers Elouise Cobell." Nov. 27, 2011; "Indian Leader Cobell, 65, Dies." *Helena Independent Record,* Oct. 18, 2011; Johnson, Peter. "Blackfeet Activist Cobell Wins $310,000 'Genius Grant.'" *Great Falls Tribune,* June 17, 1997. Maas, Peter. "The Broken Promise." *Parade Magazine.* Sept. 9, 2001, 4–6; Mauk, Sally. Interview with Keith Harper. Apr. 16, 2013. http://mtprnews.wordpress.com/tag/cobell-v-kempthorne/; Puckett, Karl. "Indians Extol Hard-Fought Trust Victory." *Great Falls Tribune,* Jan. 16, 2011; Szpaller, Keila. "Cobell Speech Inspires, Shames." *Great Falls Tribune,* July 4, 2005; Whitty, Julia. "Elouise Cobell's Accounting Coup." *Mother Jones,* Sept. 1, 2005.

Key to Institution Abbreviations in Credits

BSBA—Butte Silver Bow Public Archives, Butte, Montana

MHS—Montana Historical Society, Helena

MSU—Archives and Special Collections, Montana State University Libraries, Bozeman

UM—Archives and Special Collections, Mansfield Library, University of Montana—Missoula

WHC—Western Heritage Center, Billings, Montana

Index

after leaving the *People's Voice*, 65; photograph of, **64**; physical and mental stress endured by, 64–65; style of, 64
Billings, Harry, 63–65
Billings, Leon, 63
Binks, Grace, 149, **150**
birth control: Belle Fligelman Winestine as a supporter of, 77, 78; forces and attitudes affecting access to, 76; idea of companionate marriage and, 77–78; national and state legislation affecting, 77, 78; opposition to, 77, 78; as the personal mission of Edna Rankin McKinnon, 77; reasons for seeking, 76; sources of information on and devices for, 76. *See also* abortion; sterilization, forced
Black Coyote, 182, 183, 184
Black Eagle smelter, 256
Blackfeet Reservation, 87–88
Blackman, Kayla, 138–41, 188–90, 210–13, 237–40
"Black Mary," 78
Blackwell, Henry, 82
Blair, John, 219
Blend, Virginia, 163
Blue Mountain Women's Clinic, 44–45
Boas, Franz, 17–18
Bonnie HeavyRunner Gathering Place, 223
bootlegging: as an economic opportunity for women, 11, 12, 13; Bert (Birdie) Brown and, 12; bootlegger's still, **12**; in Butte, 11–12; demise of, 13; Great Northern Railway workers as patrons of, 13; Helen McGonagle Moriarty and, 12; ideal conditions in Montana for, 11; Josephine Doody and, 12–13; Lavinia Gilman and, 12; Nora Gallagher and, 12; passage of statewide referendum prohibiting alcohol and, 11
Bower, B. M.: advantage gained by using "B.M.," 167–68; birth of, 168; marriage of, 168; photograph of, **167**; portrayal of ranch life in novels, 168
Bowman, Charlotte, **159**
Bowman, Mrs. E. K., **159**
Bradley, Dorothy, 162–63, 165
Bradley, Margaret, 40
Braided Locks, 191

Brander, Doris: birth of, 177; campaign to ensure recognition of women's military service, 178; commitment to promoting women's military service, 178; joins Women Accepted for Voluntary Emergency Service, 177; photograph of, **161**, **177**; postwar career of, 178; reasons for enlisting, 177; records gathered by, 178–79; on sexism in the military, 176–77
Brander, Margaret, 61
Brander, Violet, 61
Branson, Caroline, 225
Bray, Archie, 207
Brice, Joseph, **15**
Bride Goes West, A, 41, **42**, 43
Bridenstine, Ellenore, 86, 240, **240**, 241, 242
Bridgewater, Herbert, **203**
Bridgewater, Leon, **203**
Bridgewater, Mamie Anderson: birth of, 202; as a leader of Helena's black Baptist congregation and the Pleasant Hour Club, 203; legacy of, 205; marriage to Samuel Bridgewater, 202–3; photograph of, **203**; strength of, 203; works as a domestic, 203
Bridgewater, Octavia: accepted into U.S. Army Nurse Corps, 204; as an advocate for overturning army and navy ban on black nurses, 204; education of, 204; legacy of, 205; as a nurse at St. Peter's Hospital, 204–5; photograph of, **203**
Bridgewater, Samuel, 202–3
Brockie, Terry, 243–45
bronc-busters, women. *See* rodeo bronc-busters, women as
Brooke, Vivian, 188
Browder, Dolly, 141
Brown, Bert "Birdie", 12
Brown, Eva, 219–20
Brown, John, 219–20
Buck v. Bell, 239
Buffalo Calf Road Woman: death of, 184; is captured and taken to Fort Keogh, 184; participates in Battle of the Little Bighorn, 183–84; rescues brother in Rosebud Battle, 182, **183**
Buffalo Woman, 108

formation of Sheridan County Electric Cooperative, 145; as a champion of rural electrification, 145–46; on farm/ranch life, 197–98; photograph of, **145**
Daly, Margaret, 109
Damn! The Story of Willie Complain, 225
Dana, Fra, 216
Dana, Ina, 149
Daszkiewicz, Rosemary, 188
Daughters of Erin, 7
Daughters of Norway, 7, 8
Daughters of Penelope, 8
Daughters of Scotia, 7
Daughters of St. George, **6**, 7
Davies, Doris, 186
Davis, Dennis, 214
Davis, Lizette, 250
Davis, Maggie Gorman, 214
Deaconess Movement: establishment of Deaconess Hospital under Augusta Ariss, 15, 16; establishment of nursing school affiliated with Montana State College, 16; opening of hospitals in Butte, Sidney, Havre, Billings, Glasgow, and Bozeman, 16; purposes of, 15–16; role in establishment of health care and evolution of nursing, 13, 16. *See also* Sisters of Charity of Leavenworth, Kansas
Dean, Maria, 71–72, 97
Dean, Ruth Marie Hladik Nelson, 113
Deer Lodge prison, 168, 169, 170
Denison, Mrs. James Floyd, 213–14
Desilets, Josephine, 257
De Smet, Father Pierre-Jean, 4
Deveau, Rubie, 111
deviate sexual misconduct. *See* sexual misconduct law, Montana's deviate
Devil's Letters to Mary MacLane, The, 225
Devil's Pocket, 195
Dewing, Katie, 255
Dickson, Tom, 256
Dippie, Brian, 66
divorce, in the late nineteenth century: companionate marriage and, 248–49, 251; cruelty as the most complicated reason for, 250; crusade against high rate of, 251; Montana as part of a pattern of nationwide change, 248–49; Montana's unbalanced ratio of men

to women and, 249; most common reasons for, 249–50; "three beating rule," 250
domestic violence: activism against, 154; contemporary data on, 154; murder of Hazel Kauf as a case study in, 151–54; victim-blaming in, 152–54; World War II emancipation of women and, 152
Doody, Dan, 13
Doody, Josephine, 12–13
Dorr, Hazel, 104
Dougherty, Dianne G., 63
Drouillard, Mary Angeline, 168–69
Duggan, Jack, 212
Dull Knife, 184
Dumas Hotel, 174–75, 176
Dunbar, Anna, 100–101, 125
Duncan, Louis, 259
Dunne, Edmund, 79
Dykeman, Wilma, 77

E

Eagle Cap, **159**
Eagle Forum, 189
Eck, Dorothy, 157, 158, 160
education administration and public health: accomplishments of women in, 129–30; challenges faced by women in, 128–29; election of women as county school superintendents, 127; intersecting goals of, 128; legacy of women in, 130; rise of women as public health nurses, 127–28; as socially acceptable career paths for women, 127, 128
electrification, rural. *See* rural electrification
Elge, Frances: birth, childhood, and education of, 114; as a champion of women's rights, 115–16; death of, 116; efforts in support of the Equal Rights Amendment, 115–16; election as Lewis and Clark County Attorney, 115; establishes private practice in Helena, 114; federal-level positions of, 115; legacy of, 114, 116; photograph of, **115**; political style of, 116; as a proponent of jury service for women, 115
Elison, Larry, 163
Ellis, Mrs. J. B., **81**
Emmons, Glenn, 121

of, 16; establishment of Institute for
Social Logic, 18; as first secretary of
the Helena YWCA, 72; as a graduate
student, 17–18; legacy of, 19; photo-
graph of, **17**; as a poet, 18; recognition
of academic accomplishments, 18–19;
as a University of Wisconsin student
and activist, 17
Florence Crittenton Home, 94, 95
Flying U ranch, 168
Foley, Jodie, 20–22, 176–79, 262–65
Foley, Mrs., 213
Fong, Lin, 147
Foote, Mrs. R. F., **81**
Ford, John, 107
Forister, Doyle, 188
Forrest, Lucinda, 249
Fort Belknap Clothing Club, 230
Fort Belknap Reservation, 47, 48
Fort Laramie Treaty (1868), 182
Fort Peck Friendly Homemakers Club,
39
Fort Shaw Government Industrial
Indian Boarding School basketball
team: accomplishments of, 91, 92;
benefits of, 91–92; enthusiastic support
for, 90, 91–92; life experiences held in
common by, 90; members of, 90, **91**,
92; photograph of, **91**; purposes and
demands of, 90; as world champions,
89–90; at the 1904 World's Fair, 92
4-H Clubs, Montana: commitment to
community well-being expanded to
global level, 231; diversification of
membership and activities, 229–30;
early efforts to apply industrial
approach to farming, 229; extension
to Indian reservations, 230; growth
of, 228; increased involvement of girls
in agricultural production, 230; as a
means of helping youth gain proficiency in emerging technologies,
230; participation of today's girls in,
231; role of Harriette Cushman in
expansion of, 230; travel opportunities
provided by, 230–31
Fraley, John, 13
Francisca, Julia, 256
Freedman, Alice, 262–63, 265
Freedman, Harold, 265

"From Party Lines and Barbed Wire: A
History of Telephones in Montana," 122
Fry, Monroe, 173–74
Frye, "Big Eva," 169
"Furnishing of a Model Indian Home,"
229

G

Galen, Albert, 131–32
Gallagher, Nora, 12
Galt, Jack, 162
Gammon, Nancy, 219
Garceau-Hagen, Dee, 80
Garfield, James, 102–3
Garfield, Ruth, 197
Garrett, Ruby, 176
Gavin, Lettie, 248
gay sex. *See* sexual misconduct law,
Montana's deviate
Gehr, Anne, 188, 189
General Allotment Act, 172, 266
General Federation of Women's Clubs,
70
Gibson, Marie, 61, 62
Gibson, Tom, 61
Gilman, Lavinia, 12
Gingrich, Newt, 264–65
giveaway custom, 190–92
Gleim, Mary, 169
Goebel, Doris, 40
Gone Are the Days, 20–21
Good Government Club, 97
Good Medicine, 67
Gordon, John, 20
Gordon, Mary, 20
Gordon, Rose: attempts to publish her
memoir, 20–21; attempts to receive
higher education, 20; birth and early
childhood of, 20; as a businessperson,
20; as a caregiver, 21, 55; as a commu-
nity historian, 21–22; death of, 22; as a
follower of Booker T. Washington, 20;
as high school valedictorian, 20; loses
mayoral race, 22; photograph of, **21**;
statements on race relations, 22
Gordon, Taylor, 20, **21**
Grainger, Ruth, 230
*Grandmother's Grandchild: My Crow
Indian Life,* 37
Grant, U. S., 102

150; from Canada, 150–51; Grace Binks, 149, **150**; Gwenllian Evans, 149; impact of Homestead Act and Enlarged Homestead Act on, 149; Ina Dana, 149; Laura Etta Smalley, 150–51; Margaret Majors, 149, **150**; as a percentage of total Montana homesteaders, 149. *See also* farm/ranch wives and mothers

HomeWORD, 46

Hop, Mrs. Wo: papers verifying legal status, **32**; precarious position as a female Chinese immigrant, 31–32

Hopwood, Mary Jo: serves in Women Accepted for Volunteer Emergency Services (WAVES), 25–26; on women's need for protection in the armed forces, 26–27

Horst, Betty, 225

Hotel and Restaurant Employees International Union, 23

Houchin, Betty Jo, 194

Howard, Joseph Kinsey, 216

Howey, Laura Spencer: as an ardent progressive, 130; appointed head librarian of the Historical and Miscellaneous Department of the Montana State Library, 130–31; birth, childhood, and education of, 130; death of, 132; dismissed as head librarian because she could not vote, 131; editorial reaction to dismissal as head librarian, 132; legacy of, 130

Howey, Robert E., 130

Human Rights Bureau, 164

I

I, Mary MacLane, 223, 225

I Await the Devil's Coming, 224

idols, extraordinary ordinary women as, 269–70

If a Lion Could Talk, 218

Indian Arts and Crafts Act, 49

Indian Citizenship Act, xi, 81, 179

Indian Civil Rights Act, 181

Indian Health Service (IHS), 134, 239

Indian warriors. *See* Native American warriors

Indian Welfare Committee of the Montana Federation of Woman's

Clubs, 47–48

"individual dignity" clause, 163, 165

Individual Indian Money accounts (IIMs), 266–68

Industrial Workers of the World (IWW), 23

Ingace Onton, 4

Ingalls, Emma: as an advocate for creation of the Bureau of Child and Animal Protection, 263; as an advocate for separate boys and girls reform facilities, 97; as co-founder of the *Kalispell Inter Lake,* 84; legacy of, 86; legislative accomplishments of, 84; as one of the first two women to serve in the Montana House of Representatives, 81, 84, 85; as a proponent of women's suffrage, 84

Inter-club Committee on the Status of Women, 185

Intermountain, 95

International Farm Youth Exchange (IFYE), 231

International Union of Mine, Mill and Smelter Workers, Local 117 (Mine-Mill): women's auxiliary, 193–95

Ironside, Ella, **167**

J

Jabour, Anya, 43–46

Jackson, Phil, 260

Jacobs, Alma Smith: birth, childhood, and education of, 155; death of, 157; as Great Falls Public Library head librarian and Montana State Librarian, 154–55; honors awarded to, 157; marriage to Marcus Jacobs, 155; photograph of, **156**, **186**; as a proponent of civil rights and racial justice, 155–56; racial identity of, 155; stature of, 156–57

Jamison, Mona, 141, 143

Jarussi, Lillian, 54

Jarussi, Loretta, 52, 54

Jeannette Rankin Brigade, 236

Jessie Wilber Gallery, 207

Johnson, Belle, 90, **91**, 92

Johnson, Charles S., 65

Johnson, Dorothy M.: birth and childhood of, 106, 107, 108; on B. M. Bower, 168; death of, 107; education, early career, and return to Montana, 107; female characters created by, 108; Indian characters of, 108; literary accomplishments of, 106–7; male characters created by, 108; photograph of, **107**; on social stratification she experienced, 108; stories that became movies, 107; as telephone operator, 124; on women as authors of Western novels, 108–9, 167, 168

Johnson, Maxine, 187

Johnson, Robert, 113

Judge, Thomas, **164**

Jurcich, Ursula, 255, 256

jury service for women: Belle Fligelman Winestine as a proponent of, 115; Frances Elge as a proponent of, 115; redefinition of "jury" and, 86, 169

K

Kamm, Wendy, 34

Kauf, Hazel: divorce, 152; guilty verdict against husband, 154; impact of World War II on, 152; marriage to Howard Kauf, 152; murder of, 151–52; photograph of, **153**; as a recipient of victim-blaming, 152–54

Kauf, Howard, 151–54, **153**

Kaúxuma Núpika, 3–4

Kellogg, Edwin, **126**

Kempthorne, Dirk, 267

Kendrick, Terry, 45, 46

Kenmille, Camille, 117

Kenmille, Oshanee Cullooyah: birth and childhood of, 116–17; develops tanning and beadwork talents, 117; honors awarded to, 118; marriages to Edward Stasso, Joe Mathias, and Camille Kenmille, 117; photograph of, **118**; positive example set by, 118, 119; self-reliance of, 117; as an instructor at Pablo tribal college, 117

Kenyon, Virginia, 128, 129–30

Kicking Horse Jobs Corps, 209

Kills At Night, 243

Kills At Night Center, 245

Kills In The Brush, 243

Kills In The Night, 36

Kimbell, Abigail, 35

King, Rev. Martin Luther, Jr., 22

Kinsley, Joseph W., 29

Kline, Robert, 146

Knowles, Ella: as an advocate of women's rights, 30; birth of, 28; death of, 30; induction into Gallery of Outstanding Montanans, 30; marriage to Henri Haskell, 30; as Montana's first female national political convention delegate, 30; moves to Montana and resumes legal studies under Joseph W. Kinsley, 29; passes bar exam after statutory change, 28; photograph of, **29**; schooling and early career as an educator, 28–29; secures first client, 29; as a successful Butte attorney, 30; unsuccessful campaign for Montana attorney general, 30

Koester, Jeanne M., 165

Kohl, Martha, 81–83, 213–16, 269–70

Kolo, 8

Kootenai, 102, 116, 226–28

Koutnik, Laurie, 189

Ku Klux Klan (KKK), women's auxiliary of. *See* Women of the Ku Klux Klan (WKKK)

Kwilqs (Kuilix), 4

L

Lacey, Marie, 70

Lady Doc, The, 166

La Guardia, Fiorello, 235–36

Lakota, 181–84

Lambert, Kirby, 65–67, 251–54

Lamberth, Royce, 267

Lamebull, Andrew, 243

Lamebull, Theresa Chandler Walker: attends St. Paul's Catholic boarding school, 243; birth and childhood of, 243; death of, 242; honors awarded to, 245; impact on Terry Brockie, 244; marriages to John Walker and Andrew Lamebull, 243; as one of very few individuals fluent in White Clay, 242–43; participates in Fort Belknap College Speaking White Clay program, 243; photograph of, **244**

Langley, Josephine, 90

LaRance, Cecilia: birth of, 8; childhood of, 9–10, 11; education, 10–11; marriage, 11; Métis heritage, 8–9; photograph of,

includes programs addressing Indian needs, 122; forms alliances with local groups to advocate for change, 120–21; invites Robert McCormick to produce documentary on governmental neglect, 121–22; photograph of, **121**

public health. *See* education administration and public health

public libraries: differing motives of men versus women in helping create, 110–11; Hamilton Woman's Club as an example of women's role in establishing, 109; importance of Carnegie funds to, 110; role of women and women's groups in establishing, 109–10, **110**, 111

Puutio, Aino Hamalainen, 106

R

ranch wives and mothers. *See* farm/ranch wives and mothers

Randall, Eunice, 55–56

Randash, Arlette, 189

Rankin, Jeannette: as an advocate for separate boys and girls reform facilities, 97; birth and education of, 234; as a congressional proponent of progressive reform, 236; as the first woman elected to the U.S. House of Representatives, 81, 84, 234; loses Senate bid, 236; as Montana's most famous suffragist, 82; as a peace advocate in semiretirement, 236; photograph of, **235**; politics of, 236; as the single reason for achieving suffrage versus being part of a mass movement, 269; U.S. Capitol Statuary Hall statue of, 237; votes to oppose U.S. entry into both world wars, 235, 236; wins second election to U.S. House of Representatives, 236

Rankin, John, 234

Rankin, Olive Pickering, 234

Rankin, Wellington, 77, 114

Rector, James M., 259

Red Cloud, 182

"Red Road Home," 137

Reed, Bess, 242

reform schools: creation of Montana State Vocational School for Girls, **96**, 97–98; establishment of Pine Hills Boys and Girls Industrial School, 96–97; Mountain View School, 98; need for, 95–96; separating delinquent boys and girls in, 95–97

Regan, Ellen, 8

Relocation, 119

Reynolds, Hanna Lindeberg, 100

Rialto Theater (Butte), **24**

Ridgeway, Karyn, 261

Ridgeway v. Montana High School Ass'n, 260–62

Riel, Louis, 47

Ring, Daniel, 110

Robbins, Trina, 251

Robert E. Lee, 79

Roberts, Ben, 66

Roberts, Jessie, 230

Roberts, Lela, 66

Robinson, Mae Nan, 159, 187

Robison, Ken, 257–59

Rodeo Association of America (RAA), 61

rodeo bronc-busters, women as: Fannie Sperry Steele, **60**, 60–61, 62; Marge and Alice Greenough, 61–62, **62**; Marie Gibson, 61, 62; Montana as a source of famous women riders, 59–60; in the National Cowboy Hall of Fame, 62; in today's rodeos, 62–63; transition of rodeo into a profession, 61

Roe v. Wade, 44

Rolfe, Herbert P., 257

Roullier, Phillip, 209

Roullier, Renee, 209

Ronan, Peter, 103

Roosevelt, Eleanor, **121**

Roosevelt, Theodore, 41

"Rose Gordon's Reflections," 22

Rosell, Antoinette (Toni) Fraser, 241, 242

Rowe, Adelaide, 213

rural electrification: Anna Dahl as a champion of, 145–46; as an outgrowth of other collective efforts, 144; challenges of farm work without electricity, 144; creation of Rural Electrification Administration, 145; and the transformation of rural women's work, 146

Rural Electrification Administration (REA), 145

Russell, Austin, 66

Russell, Charlie, 65–67, **67**, 237
Russell, Jack Cooper, 67
Russell, Josephine Pease: birth and childhood of, 200; as Head Start director,
  202; legacy of, 202; as one of the first
  Crow to graduate from college, 200,
  201; teaches at Soap Creek and Crow
  Agency School and in Teacher Corps,
  202
Russell, Nancy Cooper: birth and
  childhood of, 65–66; as Charlie's
  business manager, 66–67; death of, 67;
  impact on husband's career, 65; marries
  Charlie Russell and moves to Great
  Falls, 66; personal challenges of, 66–67;
  photograph of, **67**

S

Sacagawea, 269
Sacred Heart 1936 field ball champion-
  ship team (Butte), **261**
Salazar, Ken, 268
Salholm, Mrs. H., **81**
Salish, 101–4, 116, 226–28
Sanchez, Felicita, 168, 169
Sanchez, Marie, 239
Sanders, Wilbur Fisk, 171, 257
Sands, Dianne, 44, 140, 190, 269
Sanger, Margaret, 77–78
Sansaver, Emma, 90, **91**, 92
Scheidler, Natalie F., 151–54
Schemm, Christopher, 216
Schemm, Ferdinand, 216
Schemm, George, 216
Schemm, Mildred Walker. *See* Walker,
  Mildred
Schemm, Ripley, 216, 218
Scherlie, Anna, 150
Scherlie family, 149–50
Schlafly, Phyllis, 161
school teachers, ban on married women
  as: arguments against, 213–14; attempts
  to circumvent, 213; effect of World War
  II on, 215; efforts to end ban in Billings,
  214, 215; exceptions for women with
  husbands unable to provide a living,
  214–15; impact of federal Civil Rights
  Act on, 215–16; rationale for, 213; ruling
  of Montana attorney general on, 215
school teachers, rural: autonomy of, 54;

Blanche McManus, 52, 53, 54; certification of, 52, 54; challenging conditions
  for, 52–53, **53**; duties in addition to
  teaching, 53; gender-specific standards
  for, 54; living conditions of, 54; Loretta
  Jarussi, 52, 54; versus teachers in urban
  areas, 54
Schultz, Julia Ereaux: birth and childhood of, 46–47; combats spread
  of tuberculosis on Fort Belknap
  Reservation, 47; death of, 49; education of, 47; forms Indian women's club
  at Fort Belknap, 47; helps American
  Indian families survive Great
  Depression, 48–49; leads Works
  Progress Administration program to
  revive traditional arts and crafts, 49;
  marriage to Al Schultz, 47; photograph
  of, **48**; as a reporter for *Phillips County
  News,* 49; serves on Indian Welfare
  Committee of Montana Federation of
  Woman's Clubs, 47–48
Scott, Anne Firor, 111
Senska, Frances: birth and childhood
  of, 206; designs house and studio with
  Jessie Wilber, 207; disapproval of large
  university ceramics departments, 206–
  7; discovers love for clay, 206; helps
  build Archie Bray Foundation, 207;
  hired to teach ceramics at Montana
  State College, 205; humility of, 207–8;
  low-tech approach to ceramics, 206;
  meets life partner Jessie Wilber, 205;
  photograph of, **205**; as a supporter of
  the arts in Montana, 207
Senska Studio, 207
Serbian Circle, 8
Serbian Orthodox Church, 8
Serbian Sisters, 8
Seth, Helen, **159**
sexual misconduct law, Montana's
  deviate: bills introduced to repeal,
  188, 190; definition of deviate sexual
  relations, 188; lawsuit to seek invali-
  dation of, 188, 189; Montana Supreme
  Court ruling on, 189–90; pin supporting repeal of, **189**; public reactions to
  debate over, 189, 190; repeal of, 190;
  support for constitutional amendment
  defining marriage, 190

Winestine, Norman, 19
Winter Wheat, 217
Wirth, Lizzie, 92
Wirth, Nettie, 90, **91**, 92
Wiseman, Cecilia LaRance. *See* LaRance, Cecilia
Wister, Owen, 165
Wold, Irene, **ii**, iv
Wolk, Jewell Peterson, 196
Woman Chief, 4–5, **5**
Women Accepted for Volunteer Emergency Service (WAVES), 25–26, 177
Women in Military Service for American Memorial Foundation (WIMSA), 178
Women of the Ku Klux Klan (WKKK): attraction of, 211–12; dwindling influence and membership of, 213; Montana Realm of, 211, **211**; xenophobic and racist policies of, 211–12
Women's Air Force Service Pilots (WASPS), 26
Women's Army Corps, 25
Women's Auxiliary Army Corps, 25
Women's Bureau, 164
Women's Christian Temperance Union (WCTU): as an advocate of social reform, 57–58; founding of Montana chapter, 57; idea of women's natural moral superiority and, 58–59; inclusion of suffrage in the political agenda of, 59; and prohibition in Montana, 11, **58**, 59; as a proponent of women's suffrage, 83
Women's History Matters project, 269
Women's Jury Service Act, 115
Women in Military Service for America Memorial, 178
Women's Opportunity and Resource Development (WORD), 46
Women's Place, 45
Women's Protective Union (WPU): affiliation with western United States labor movements, 23; as an equivalent to men's unions, 23; formation of, 22–23; merger into Culinary and Miscellaneous Workers Union, 25; relationship of women's work to men's work, 23; successes of, 24, 25; support

from male unions, 25; wide agenda of, 24–25; workers encompassed by, 23
Women's Resource Center (WRC), 44, 45, 45–46
Women's Studies Program, University of Montana: courses and programs offered by, 139; culture of activism, 140, 141; as a formal university program, 140; inside versus outside of class activities, 139–40; opposition to discriminatory university policies, 140; relationship to other activist movements, 139–40; transition to Women and Gender Studies Program and Women's, Gender, and Sexuality Studies, 140
women's suffrage: Belle Fligelman Winestine as a proponent of, 82; hard-fought victories in, 81–82; Jeannette Rankin as Montana's most famous suffragist, 82; lengthy campaign for, 82–83; Maggie Smith Hathaway as a proponent of, 82–83; Missoula Teachers' Suffrage Committee, Montana Equal Suffrage Association, and Women's Christian Temperance Union campaigns for, 59, 83
Word, Samuel, 219
World War I, women's service in: creation of military telephone system as an opportunity for, 246–47; fight to achieve veteran status for telephone operators, 247–48; versus World War II, 245
World War II, women's service in: conservative postwar gender expectations, 28; creation of Women's Auxiliary Army Corps as a step toward recognition of, 25; Doris Brander on, 176–77; Grace Porter Miller, 28; Juanita Cooke, 26; Mary Jo Hopwood, 25–26; Minnie Spotted Wolf, 26, **27**; negative attitudes of servicemen toward, 26, 176–77
World War II industrial workers, women as: in Anaconda and Great Falls smelters, 254–56; high wages received, 255; male resistance to, 254–55, 256; as portrayed in *Copper Commando*, 255;

World War II as a turning point for women's employment, 254, 256
Wotanin Wowapi, 137
Wright, John, 51

Y

Yellowtail, Connie, 134
Yellowtail, Susie Walking Bear: as an advocate for Indian education and health care, 134, 135; birth and childhood of, 133; education of, 133–34; honors awarded to, 135; marriage to Thomas Yellowtail, 134; photograph of, 133
Yellowtail, Thomas, 134, 135

Young Women's Christian Association (YWCA), Helena: as an independent chapter, 72–73; builds forty-three room facility, 71, 72; continued service of, 73; functions of, 72; hiring of Frieda Fligelman as first secretary, 72; Maria Dean as the driving force behind the organization of, 71; national origins of, 70; organization and incorporation of, 71–72; as a reaction to Victorian era social rules, 70–71; YWCA chapters in other Montana cities, 71

Z

Zonta, 185

Contributors

ELLEN ARGUIMBAU retired in 2012 from the Montana Historical Society after thirty-five years as an archivist. She received her bachelor's degree from Swarthmore College and master's degrees in history and library science from the University of Colorado and the University of Washington.

ELLEN BAUMLER is the interpretive historian at the Montana Historical Society. She received her PhD from the University of Kansas and has worked at the Montana Historical Society since 1992. She has authored dozens of articles and several books, among them *Beyond Spirit Tailings*, honored with an Award of Merit from the American Association for State and Local History. She is also the editor of *Girl from the Gulches: The Story of Mary Ronan*, a 2004 Finalist Award winner of the Willa Literary Awards. You can find more of her work online on her blog, *Montana Moments*.

KAYLA BLACKMAN received a master's degree in history and a certificate in Women's and Gender Studies from the University of Montana, Missoula. She began working with the Montana Historical Society on the Women's History Matters project in the summer of 2013.

LAURA FERGUSON is a freelance writer from Helena, Montana, and works as an independent Indian education consultant and curriculum developer. She holds a master's degree in Native American Studies from Montana State University.

JODIE FOLEY is the state archivist/manager of the Archives Program at the Montana Historical Society. Born and raised in Missoula, she did her graduate and undergraduate work at the University of Montana in the history program. She has written several "From the Society" articles for *Montana*

The Magazine of Western History and is a contributing author to the first volume of *Speaking Ill of the Dead: Jerks in Montana History* and a coeditor of the sequel.

Kate Hampton is the community preservation coordinator at the Montana Historical Society's State Historic Preservation Office, where she works with local communities to document and preserve their cultural resources. Among many other projects, she directed "Identifying African-American Heritage Resources in Montana," which identified and documented Montana Historical Society collections associated with African Americans in Montana.

Annie Hanshew is a native of Helena, Montana, and has degrees from Carroll College and the University of Utah. Her book, *Border to Border: Historic Quilts and Quiltmakers of Montana*, was published by the Montana Historical Society Press in 2009.

Jennifer J. Hill has a PhD in American Studies from Montana State University, and focuses her research on reproductive history, women in the American West, and museology.

Anya Jabour is a professor in the History Department and a past co-director of the Women's and Gender Studies Program at the University of Montana. She has authored three books: *Marriage in the Early Republic: Elizabeth and William Wirt and the Companionate Ideal, Scarlett's Sisters: Young Women in the Old South*, and *Topsy-Turvy: How the Civil War Turned the World Upside Down for Southern Children*. In 2013, Professor Jabour was named the University of Montana's Distinguished Scholar.

Martha Kohl is a historical specialist at the Montana Historical Society. She received both her BA and MA in history from Washington University in St. Louis. She served as project manager and lead historian for *Montana: Stories of the Land*, the Society's award-winning middle-school history textbook. Her book, *I Do: A Cultural History of Montana Weddings*, was published in 2011.

Kirby Lambert manages the Outreach and Interpretation Program for the Montana Historical Society. He has served as museum registrar, curator of collections, and curator of art before assuming his current position as program manager in October 2007. He is coauthor of *Montana's Charlie Russell*, published by the Montana Historical Society Press in 2014.

Mary Murphy is the Letters and Science Distinguished Professor at Montana State University. She has published ten books and book chapters, including *Hope in Hard Times: New Deal Photographs of Montana, 1936–1942*, which won the Montana Book Award in 2003. Her *Mining Cultures: Men, Women, and Leisure in Butte, 1914–41*, received the 1998 Barbara Sudler Award from the Colorado Historical Society and was a Choice Outstanding Academic Book in 1997. Murphy received the Governor's Humanities Award in 2013.

Ken Robison, a native Montanan, is historian at the Overholser Historical Research Center in Fort Benton and author of five books including *Confederates in Montana Territory* and *Montana Territory and the Civil War*. The Montana Historical Society named him "Montana Heritage Keeper" in 2010. He retired as a Navy captain after a career in naval intelligence. You can find more of his work online on his blogs, fortbenton.blogspot.com and blackamericansmt.blogspot.com.

Natalie F. Scheidler is a PhD candidate in U.S. History at Montana State University. Her research interests include race, gender, and sexuality in American history. Her dissertation, "And They All Fell Silent: Violence against Women in Butte, Montana, 1910–1950," provides a legal, cultural, and statistical analysis of rape and wife assault.

Marcella Sherfy Walter began her career in public history at Gettysburg National Military Park. Before moving to Montana, she worked in National Park Service preservation programs in Washington, D.C. Between 1980 and 2006, she served as Montana's state historic preservation officer, education officer, and chief of heritage operations for the Montana Historical Society.